ENGLISH
idioms
a complete study course

compiled by

Ronald Lister

Hugo's Language Books Limited

ISBN: 0 85285 206 1

Written by
Ronald Lister

Illustrations by
Michael Turner

Set in 11/12 Plantin by
Keyset Composition, Colchester, Essex
Printed and bound by
Page Brothers, Norwich, Norfolk

Introduction

In our own countries at one time or another, most of us will have encountered the situation where a foreigner, speaking our language with an acceptable degree of proficiency, has requested some information from one of our fellow countrymen and received a colloquial or idiomatic reply which has baffled him or her. The person addressed has automatically and erroneously assumed that any foreigner who has mastered the formal form of the language must be familiar with colloquialisms – a form of speech long (and unjustly) considered inferior.

The reasons for the relative shortage of serious works and courses dealing with colloquialisms lie not only in this attitude which has prevailed hitherto, but in the inherent difficulty of the subject. Colloquialisms contain some of the most difficult forms of speech for foreigners – idioms, phrasal verbs, compound nouns and adjectives. This difficulty is made harder by the fact that colloquialisms have a habit of occurring in groups of two or three. For example, 'You can bank on Uncle Sam to screw you.' (i.e. you can rely on the Americans to cheat you.).

Nowadays, the importance of colloquialisms is universally recognized. There is almost no sphere of human activity where they are not prevalent, whether it be in industry, the office or the home. With regard to English, the advent of mass tourism and improved communications have made a knowledge of English idiom and colloquialisms indispensable to all those who are dealing with an English-speaking public on a professional or cultural level.

'*English Idioms: a complete study course*' has been written to meet this need and consists of 30 work modules containing some 3700 colloquialisms. The 30 work modules are designed to coincide with the 30+ weeks of the college or university year, with around three hours per week allocated to each module, but the book is equally suitable for self-study. Each of the work modules contains a comprehensive selection of the most common English colloquialisms organized into categories of similar generic meaning, and an exercise section. Some of the categories overlap to a certain degree, and a subjective choice has been made when assigning phrases which may relate to more than one category. The definition given for a particular colloquialism does not necessarily indicate that it can be used in this way in other contexts – i.e. 64/8 **healthy** = large . . . but you would not say "He has a healthy car". Similarly, 22/29 **hand over fist** = very rapidly or with great progress . . . but to say "Travelling by Concorde ensures you get to New York hand over fist" would be a wrong use of this idiom. Within each category, similar or synonymous colloquialisms have been grouped as closely together as possible and the exercises are accordingly planned to encourage the student to garner a collection of these synonyms or phrases of similar meaning. The underlying intention of this thematic, non-alphabetical approach is to facilitate 'memory by association' by removing the necessity for the student to perform this mental grouping him- or herself. The student may note that the colloquialisms are not always cited in typically colloquial contexts (i.e. as spoken in a casual fashion); often nowadays these expressions can be – or are – used in more formal written or conversational contexts such as news reports and so on.

Common vulgarisms have also been included, since the aim of the work is to give an honest practical reflection of linguistic reality, bearing in mind that the reader will be in the 16+ age range – i.e. a mature student with a reasonable working knowledge of English, who has a right to understand and avoid any risqué expressions in a possibly embarrassing situation. However, all vulgarisms have been clearly marked and no attempt has been made to dwell on them unduly.

The book has been written for universal use and is also suitable for teaching in a non-English environment where the majority of students may never have visited an English-speaking country. English is a lingua franca, and although the modules emphasize UK colloquialisms, a selection of the most common American variations has been included. In addition, many examples have been internationally biased with regard to subject matter, family names and terms. Words such as 'organize', 'emphasize', 'civilize' and others which you will see written either -ize or -ise are in this text generally spelt -ize (the form favoured not only in America but also by British authorities such as the Oxford University Press and others).

This book is not exhaustive, but certainly comprehensive, and the student who has worked conscientiously through the modules and exercises will have a good command of English colloquialisms.

Contents

Categories

Grammatical Notes

Since colloquialisms are, by their very nature, more often spoken than written, linguistic authorities sometimes differ as to the correct spelling or use.

Comparative sentences. In comparative colloquial sentences such as 'he is as bald as a coot' or 'she is as thick as two short planks', the first 'as' is commonly omitted – i.e. 'he is bald as a coot', 'she is thick as two short planks'.

Christian names. Many Christian names which occur in common colloquialisms such as 'smart alec', 'silly billy' or 'not on your nelly' may be written with or without a capital letter. Others such as 'Tom, Dick and Harry' or 'before you could say "Jack Robinson"', where there is more emphasis on the naming element of the phrase, still retain the capital.

The endings ie/y. Many words such as 'cutie', 'softie' or 'chippie' may also take an ending with 'y' – i.e. 'cuty', 'softy' and 'chippy'.

Someone + possessive pronoun. When 'someone' or 'somebody' is the subject of a sentence, some grammatical purists prefer to place the possessive pronoun in the masculine singular – i.e. 'his', unless it is evident from the context that 'her' would be more appropriate.

e.g. Someone has parked *his* jalopy in my drive.

In the interests of sexual equality, it is becoming more and more acceptable to use 'their' in preference to 'his'.

e.g. Someone has parked *their* jalopy in my drive.

Students should be aware of this distinction and make their own choice.

Key to symbols and abbreviations

#	warning sign.	(#US)	American term or phrase that may
(#?)	term or phrase may cause offence.		possibly not be understood by a
(#??)	term or phrase is decidedly vulgar		speaker of UK English.
	and should be avoided.	pr.	pronounced.
(US)	American term or phrase that is	so.	someone.
	widely understood.	sth.	something.

viii

Work [A]

1: WORK/PERFORMANCE

1/1 **Kick off:** Begin work or an activity. The phrase is derived from the kick-off or start of a football match. □ Some Japanese factories kick off in the morning with a session of aerobics.

1/2 **Knock off:** Stop working. *(See Index for other meanings)* □ Our office knocks off at five o'clock.

1/3 **Call it a day:** Stop working for the day. □ Let's call it a day at four o'clock!

1/4 **Land a job:** To obtain work, orders or contracts. □ In two years, he hasn't landed a single job. □ Our firm has landed a large contract.

1/5 **Hold down a job:** Keep a job for a reasonable period. □ Owing to frequent bouts of heavy drinking, the draughtsman became incapable of holding down a job.

1/6 **Fill/stand in** for someone: Replace someone temporarily; act as a substitute. The person doing this is a 'stand-in'. □ Last week I had to fill (stand) in for a secretary who had fallen ill.

1/7 **Rope in** someone: Persuade someone to take part in an activity. □ When Mr Singh's business began to expand, he roped in several of his relatives to help out.

1/8 **Muck in:** Share tasks or help with menial work. □ All children at the summer camp are expected to muck in with the washing up and cleaning.

1/9 **Pull one's weight:** Do one's fair share of work. □ Every worker in this firm is expected to pull his weight.

1/10 **Do a stint:** Perform an allotted task for a fixed period. □ All trainee sales persons must do a two-month stint in the Advertising department.

1/11 **Put/get in** work: Spend time working. □ As a result of rainy weather the house-painters put (got) in only twenty hours this week.

1/12 **Dash off** something: Write hastily. □ The secretary was dashing off invoices on a word processor.

1/13 **Polish off** a task: Complete speedily. *(See also 16/7, 150/6 and 163/2)* □ The maintenance crew polished off the gas-main repair in two hours.

1/14 **Knock up** something: Construct or arrange hastily. *(See also 188/21)* □ The gardener knocked up a shed out of old planks. □ Diplomats spent the night knocking up a peace plan.

1/15 **Do things by halves:** Do things superficially or only partly. □ Your car will soon be in running order again; Heinz is a good mechanic and he doesn't do things by halves.

1/16 Make a (good) job of something: Perform a task thoroughly or successfully. *(For 'make a bit of a job of' see 4/30)* □ Your nephew has made a (good) job of wall-papering the kitchen.

1/17 Deliver the goods: Carry out or perform what one promises. □ For years the country has promised to release all political prisoners with no intention of delivering the goods.

1/18 All in a day's work: Part of one's normal duties. □ Administering mouth-to-mouth resuscitation is all in a day's work for firemen.

1/19 Come with the job: Be a necessary part or responsibility of the job. □ As a manager, I sometimes have the unpleasant task of dismissing staff, it comes with the job.

1/20 Pull in money: Earn an amount of money. *(See also 36/7)* □ Welders working on oil-rigs can pull in a normal month's salary in one week.

1/21 Bring home the bacon: Earn a living for oneself or one's family. □ I don't enjoy my job, but I have to bring home the bacon somehow.

1/22 Someone's **bread and butter:**   The main source of someone's income or livelihood. □ As solicitors we also deal with criminal cases, but house purchases are our bread and butter.

1/23 Quarrel with one's bread and butter: Seek problems with the source of one's livelihood. □ Don't argue with customers, you're only quarrelling with our bread and butter!

1/24 A dead-end job: A job without any prospect of advancement.

1/25 The daily grind: Monotonous routine or work. *(See also 2/6 below)* □ Pierre saw the adventurous life in the paratroops as a way of escaping the daily grind of a nine-to-five job in Paris. □ The holidays are over and tomorrow it's back to the daily grind.

1/26 A plum job: A very desirable or top job. □ Executive posts with the European Commission are often regarded as plum jobs.

1/27 A **cushy number**: A pleasant and easy job. □ Contrary to popular opinion, a job in the Civil Service is not always a cushy number.

1/28 A **one-off job**: A single task with no prospect of being repeated. □ The giant excavator contract for Syria is a one-off job with unique technical specifications.

1/29 **Moonlight**: Work on a second job in the evenings, especially illegally or illicitly. The verb has a secondary meaning of leaving or disappearing overnight, usually owing rent or other debts. □ As a result of massive inflation, many Polish workers were forced to moonlight in order to supplement their day-time wages. □ The debtor had moonlighted before his creditors arrived.

1/30 **The business end**: The working end of a tool which is not the handle. □ The bank cashier suddenly realized that she was looking down the business end of a gun. □ The business end of this machine is dangerous and should have a safety-guard.

2: WORK HARD

2/1 **Work like a dog/horse/Trojan**: Work hard. The use with 'Trojan' is generally heard in a commendatory context. □ They make you work like a horse (dog) in that factory. □ My engineers worked like Trojans all night, and by morning they'd restored power to the factory.

2/2 **Sweat one's guts out**: Work hard. □ Groups of sugar-cane cutters were sweating their guts out to bring in the crop.

2/3 **Work one's fingers to the bone** *or* **work one's butt off** (*US*): Work hard. □ Luigi worked his fingers to the bone (worked his butt off) to support his large family.

2/4 **Slog/beaver away**: Work hard. □ The city was one vast building-site where thousands of workers could be seen beavering (slogging) away like ants.

2/5 **Graft**: Work hard. 'Graft' is also a noun meaning hard work, and a 'grafter' is a hard worker. (*See also 34/15*) □ Give him a seat, he's been grafting all day!

2/6 A **(hard) slog/grind**: A task involving much hard work. □ For many students, achieving their final diploma is a hard slog (grind).

2/7 **Donkey work**: The boring part of a job, especially the physical or menial tasks. □ On many ships, much of the donkey work is done by seamen from countries in the developing world.

2/8 **Spade work**: The hard preparatory work. □ The spade work of searching out information for the technical manual was done during the summer, when the university library was almost empty of students.

2/9 **Burn the midnight oil**: Work late into the night. □ Newspaper editors often have to burn the midnight oil to meet the morning deadline.

2/10 A **workaholic**: A person addicted to work. The term is a play on the word 'alcoholic'.

2/11 **Chivvy** someone: Urge someone to hurry or work harder. □ The cargo was delayed at the docks, and the firm was constantly chivvying the customs authorities to clear the goods for export.

2/12 **Keep** someone **on his toes**:   Keep someone alert or attentive; spur on to be more efficient. □ The foreman regularly patrolled the quarry to keep the navvies on their toes.

3: BUSY/INACTIVE

3/1 **Have enough on one's plate**:   Be extremely busy; have a large amount of work to deal with. □ Sorry I can't help you, I've enough on my plate at the moment.

3/2 **A plateful**:   A large amount of work. □ The translation of this tractor prospectus into Polish is a plateful.

3/3 **Up to one's ears/eyes** in work: Have more than enough work. (*See also* 57/9) □ Business was slack last year, but this year we're up to our eyes (ears) in work.

3/4 **Snowed under** with work: Overwhelmed with work or tasks to be processed. □ We placed an advert in the 'Situations Vacant' column of the local newspaper and we were snowed under with job applications.

3/5 **Rushed off one's feet**:   Have so much pressing work that one is forced to hurry. □ At Xmas, staff in the store are rushed off their feet.

3/6 **It's all systems go**:   Everything is in running order and working; everyone is busy. The expression derives from aeronautics and signifies that the rocket or plane systems are functioning and that the launch or take-off can proceed. □ Order books are full and it's all systems go at the factory. □ In one month it will be all systems go for the grape harvest.

3/7 **Hard at it**:   Extremely busy. □ Students are hard at it now, preparing for the exams.

3/8 **At full stretch** *or* **fully stretched**:   Working to the limit of one's powers or capacity. □ In the aftermath of the gales, roofing contractors were fully stretched (at full stretch) repairing the damage.

3/9 **Tied up**:   Unavailable owing to work or commitments. □ The director can't see you now, he's tied up in a meeting.

3/10 **Put business** someone's **way**:   Place orders with, or create business for someone. □ If your factory can deliver the printed-circuit boards at the right price, we can put a lot of business your way.

3/11 **Have nothing on**:   Have no work or commitments; have free time. □ I have nothing on this afternoon, so I can take the car for a service check.

3/12 **At a loose end**:   Be without a definite task *or* unable to occupy oneself. □ Retirement doesn't suit my husband, he always seems to be at a loose end.

3/13 **Twiddle one's thumbs**:   Have nothing to do. □ When a sub-contractor failed to deliver motors on time, car production came to a halt and workers stood around twiddling their thumbs.

3/14 **Not do a stroke/scrap** of work: Do nothing at all. □ Those plasterers haven't done a stroke (scrap) all afternoon.

4: EFFORT/ENERGY

4/1 **Buckle to** *or* **buckle down to** work: Make a vigorous start on work. □ Your son must buckle to (buckle down to study), or his classmates will leave him behind.

4/2 **Knuckle down** *or* **knuckle down to** a task: Begin to work earnestly on a task. □ You must knuckle down or fail. □ The government has knuckled down to reducing inflation.

4/3 **Get stuck into** *or* **get one's teeth into** work: Concentrate one's efforts or energy on a task. *(See also 150/3)* □ This term I'll get stuck (my teeth) into advanced maths and calculus.

4/4 **Tackle** a task: Attempt to master a problem or task. *(See also 150/4)* □ I've only just started learning to drive and I'm not ready to tackle motorway traffic yet.

4/5 **Grapple with** something: Struggle with a problem; expend a lot of energy on a task. □ Gudrun has been grappling with Japanese for two years now.

4/6 **Turn one's hand to** something: Apply oneself to a task. *(Do not confuse with 'try one's hand' 77/4)* □ Leo is an all-round carpenter and can turn his hand to most woodworking jobs.

4/7 **Go all-out** to do something: Make every possible effort. □ Our firm is going all-out to win the contract.

4/8 **Pull out all the stops**:   Make a tremendous effort. □ Various charities pulled out all the stops to raise cash for orphanages in Romania.

4/9 **Lean/bend over backwards**:   Do one's utmost to please someone. □ Host families leant (bent) over backwards to make the foreign students feel at home.

4/10 **Do one's level best** *or* **do one's damnedest**:   Do one's utmost. □ I'll do my level best (my damnedest) to beat the track record.

4/11 **Leave no stone unturned**:   Spare no effort; try every possible means. The expression refers to a battle in 477 BC when the Greek victors searched under every stone for the hidden treasure of the defeated Persians. □ The police will leave no stone unturned to catch the criminal who carried out this horrific murder.

4/12 **Explore every avenue**:   Exhaust every means; explore every possibility. □ The UN Security Council explored every avenue in its attempt to mediate in the border dispute.

4/13 **By hook or by crook**:   By any possible means, lawful or unlawful. A feudal right granted to peasants in the Middle Ages was that of collecting

5

firewood from trees using a hook or a crook (a stick with a crooked handle). □ The Bolshevik emigrés vowed to seize power in Russia by hook or by crook.

4/14 **Go to great lengths**: Do one's utmost; be extremely thorough. □ The burglar had gone to great lengths to remove any trace of fingerprints.

4/15 **Go out of one's way**: Put oneself to some trouble; exert oneself. □ We were continually modifying the design of our new house and the architects went out of their way to accommodate our wishes.

4/16 **Go hammer and tongs at** something: Undertake a task with great energy or vigour. *(See also 32/3)* □ Building the escape tunnel was a daunting task, but the prisoners-of-war went at it hammer and tongs. □ Rescue squads went hammer and tongs at getting survivors out of the rubble.

4/17 **Get/pull one's finger out**: Get on with the job; make an effort. □ The first phase of the new motorway was behind schedule and the contractors were told to get (pull) their finger out.

4/18 **Pull one's socks up**: Make a greater effort; improve one's performance or conduct. □ The manager is not satisfied with your work, so if you don't pull your socks up we'll be saying goodbye to you.

4/19 **Put more beef (*or* elbow grease) into** a task: Apply more energy or muscle strength to a task. □ It's no use polishing the car half-heartedly, you must put more beef (elbow grease) into it for a good shine!

4/20 **Put one's back into** a task: Make the maximum physical effort. □ We'll never push the car to the nearest garage if you don't put your back into it!

4/21 **Punch/go/zing/pep/vim/oomph**: Energy or vigour. □ Tinneke hasn't got enough zing (vim/pep etc.) for the job. □ Salesmen should show more pep (zing/go etc.) when selling our products!

4/22 **Full of beans**: Bursting with energy; in high spirits. □ George is usually fairly slow and lethargic but today he's full of beans.

4/23 **For all one is worth**: With the utmost speed or energy. □ Enemy soldiers were deserting the battlefield for all they were worth. □ As the intruder crawled through the window, Myra hit him for all she was worth with a vase.

4/24 **Like anything** *or* **like nobody's business**: With great intensity, speed or vigour. □ Mustafa studied like nobody's business (like anything) to get his degree. □ She loves him like anything (like nobody's business). □ The fire engine was going like anything (like nobody's business) through the streets.

4/25 **Fight tooth and nail**: Fight very fiercely. □ The villagers fought tooth and nail against the closure of their school.

4/26 **Put up a good fight/show**: Make a good effort; be a worthy opponent. □ Bayern Munich won the match, but FC Hamburg put up a good show (fight).

4/27 **Give** someone **a run for his/her money**: Make a good but unsuccessful effort against an opponent. □ After lengthy litigation, the property developers were able to cut down the old oak trees, but conservation groups had certainly given them a run for their money.

4/28 **Not lift a finger** (to help):   Make no effort or attempt to help. □ Two warehousemen struggled to unload the crate from the lorry, while the driver looked on without lifting a finger.

4/29 **Don't bust yourself**:   Ironic manner of urging someone to make a greater effort, or a sarcastic comment on someone's performance. □ Is this all the work you've done this morning? Don't bust yourself, will you!

4/30 **Make a bit of a job of** something: Turn a fairly simple task into a harder one, or make out that it is more difficult than in reality. *(See also 1/16)* □ Your nephew's made a bit of a job of that wallpapering – he could have done it in half the time!

5: LAZY

5/1 **Laid back**:   Relaxed or lazy. □ You are very laid back about your work.

5/2 **Bone idle**:   Very lazy. □ Marco is just bone idle.

5/3 **Scrimshank/shirk/skive**:   Dodge or avoid work; malinger or feign illness in order to avoid working. The person is a 'shirker', a 'scrimshanker' or a 'skiver'. □ Juan's back complaint is only an excuse for skiving (scrimshanking/shirking). □ As soon as there is talk of work, Olaf disappears; he's a proper shirker (skiver/scrimshanker).

5/4 **Slack**:   To be lazy about work. The person is a 'slacker'. □ The weather may be hot, but there must be no slacking in the workshop; we must complete the order on time.

5/5 **A lazybones**:   A lazy person. □ Get out of bed, lazybones!

5/6 **A layabout**:   A lazy person who avoids working for a living.

5/7 **A dole-wallah**:   A lazy person who lives from unemployment benefit (dole) from the state. *(For 'wallah', see also 170/2)* □ In our region many firms are seeking staff, so clearly a large proportion of those unemployed is made up of dole-wallahs.

5/8 **Loaf/bum/arse** (#?) **/fart** (#?) **around**:   Spend time idly; saunter around lazily. □ Instead of seeking work, Carlo loafs (bums/arses/farts) around in bars.

5/9 **Cannot be bothered**:   Be too lazy; not wish to trouble oneself. □ It's a nice morning and I can't be bothered to clean the house.

6: DISMISSAL

6/1 **Axe** someone: To dismiss someone or reduce the number of jobs. □ Short-term working is preferable to axing jobs. □ Freda and two other girls have been axed.

6/2 **Lay off** someone: Dismiss. □ All around, firms are laying off men.

6/3 **Fire/sack** someone: Dismiss someone from employment. □ Two hundred workers were sacked (fired). □ You are fired (sacked)!

6/4 **The sack/boot/chop/push:** Dismissal from employment. □ I can't count how many times I've had the sack (push/chop/boot) in my career. □ In that firm, as soon as you turn forty, they give you the chop (sack/push/boot).

6/5 **One's marching orders** *or* **one's cards:** One's dismissal. □ That's the third employee this year who has had his cards (marching orders) for smoking in a restricted area.

6/6 **Be through:** Be dismissed. *(See also 19/15)* □ My employer told me that I was through and that I should empty my locker.

6/7 **A shake-out:** A reorganization involving dismissals. □ The new management of the supermarket had a shake-out, and ten employees were dismissed.

6/8 **On the dole:** Unemployed and receiving financial support from the state. □ If the factory closes, two hundred workers will be on the dole.

EXERCISES 1: WORK (A)

A) From the module, choose a colloquial alternative to the underlined word or phrase, paying attention to the tense of the verb. For example:

"The meeting begins at seven this evening." (= *kicks off*)

1) Mrs Hamzah is very busy and can't see you now.
2) They made a great effort to complete the work on time.
3) The porter made no effort to help with the suitcases.
4) Your father is very lazy.
5) The young engineer got a good position in the motor industry.
6) I have so much work that I'll have to work late into the night.
7) Today we stopped working at midday.
8) The preparatory work for the project was completed last year.
9) Ahmed is always avoiding work.
10) The staff have all received their dismissal notices.
11) My secretary is addicted to work.
12) His father has given him a well-paid, easy job.
13) Women had to fight fiercely to gain the vote.

→

8

B) Insert an item of food, an animal or a tool to complete the sentence. For example: "He is a hard worker, he works like a (ANIMAL)." (= *horse* or *dog*)

1) Professional boxing is a hard way to bring home the (FOOD).
2) Marie is always lively and full of (FOOD).
3) There are many applicants for those (FOOD) jobs.
4) Don't (FOOD) around the house, go and repair the fence!
5) They are rich and have servants to do their (ANIMAL) work.
6) The ancient Egyptians (ANIMAL)ed away for years to build the pyramids.
7) He was eager and went at it (TOOL) and (TOOL).
8) I am determined to get rich by (TOOL) or by (TOOL).

C) The following sentences are incorrect. Insert the correct form of the colloquialism. For example: "There is no one to fall in for her if she is absent." (= *fill in* or *stand in*)

1) She polished up her work quickly and went home.
2) Put more elbow work into it!
3) The boys ran away like anybody's business.
4) Mother has gone to great distances to prepare this meal.
5) You are falling behind in your work, you'd better pull your pants up!
6) We have explored every street for a solution to the problem.

D) The following sentences are ambiguous when taken out of context. Explain their possible literal and colloquial meanings.

1) They have really gone out of their way.
2) When I phoned her, she said she had nothing on.
3) I have been given a plateful.
4) He cannot deliver the goods.
5) Everyone is tied up.

E) Insert the correct adverb to complete the following phrasal verbs and colloquialisms. For example: "He hasn't the ability to hold . . . a job." (= *down*)

1) She pulls . . . a good salary.
2) We slogged . . . all that time for nothing.
3) I am snowed . . . in/with work.
4) You must knuckle . . . to your studies!
5) Many workers were laid . . . when the factory closed.
6) Life . . . the dole is not easy.

Work [B]

7: SKILL/ABILITY/EXPERIENCE

7/1 **The hang/knack**:   The ability to do something skilfully. (*For 'knack' see also 80/18*) □ It took me several years to get the knack (hang) of playing the piano. □ Eberhardt still hasn't got the hang (knack) of opening a can properly.

7/2 **The ropes**:   The routine or methods of working. □ Commercial trainees spend a month in each of the firm's departments to learn the ropes.

7/3 **The drill**:   The procedure to be followed. □ What's the drill for getting a shower on this campsite?

7/4 **The tricks of the trade**:   Techniques or methods of working which come with experience. □ Young engineers just out of college may be well-qualified, but they still don't know the tricks of the trade.

7/5 An **old-timer**:   Someone with many years' experience and some status in his trade. □ An old-timer in the baking industry showed me a former method of making dough.

7/6 An **old hand**:   A person with long experience and considerable ability in doing something. □ That fisherman is an old hand at mending nets.

7/7 A **past master**:   An expert. □ Some diplomats are past masters at giving non-committal replies.

7/8 A **dab hand**:   Someone skilled in something of a practical nature. □ You're a dab hand with a drill, so put up these shelves for me!

7/9 A **smooth operator**:   Someone who achieves his goals with a minimum of fuss or effort. (*Distinguish from 'smoothie' 116/14*) □ Those electricians were smooth operators; they rewired our house and we hardly noticed it.

7/10 **Hot at/in**:   Skilled in; good at. □ Yoko is hot in (at) maths. □ I'm not so hot at tennis.

7/11 **Hot stuff**:   A person of great skill; something high-powered. (*See also 187/11*) □ That computer programmer is hot stuff. □ If the car can reach that speed, it really is hot stuff.

7/12 **Have what it takes**:   Have the necessary skill or ability. □ Many university graduates don't have what it takes to be a teacher.

7/13 **Cut out** for a task: Having the qualities or abilities needed for a task or profession. □ After two years on the job, I realized that I wasn't cut out to be an accountant. □ I doubt whether this applicant is cut out for the job.

7/14 **On the ball** *or* **with it**:   Alert or competent. □ Air-traffic controllers must be on the ball (with it) at all times. □ The technology of communications is developing so quickly that our staff are given regular refresher courses to stay on the ball (with it).

7/15 **Shift for oneself**: Cope or manage. □ As regards washing and cooking, my husband will have to shift for himself while I'm in hospital.

7/16 **Take** something **in one's stride**: Cope or manage without particular difficulty or effort. □ Unlike Europeans, the Bedouins take extreme heat and lack of water in their stride.

7/17 **Under one's belt**: (Of qualifications or experience) Already achieved or obtained. □ That architect has three major shopping complexes under his belt. □ Candidates for the position should have at least ten years' experience under their belt.

7/18 **Keep one's hand in**: Maintain one's skill or ability. □ I'm retired now, but I still do a little carpentry, just to keep my hand in.

7/19 **Put through his/its paces**: Test the capabilities of someone or something. □ The training period of the new recruits is now over and tomorrow they'll be put through their paces in the factory itself. □ These long uphill stretches really put the rally cars through their paces.

7/20 A **dry/dummy run**: A trial run or practice to gain experience for the real thing. □ Before putting the new magazine into circulation, we did dummy runs (dry runs) of two editions.

8: INABILITY/INEXPERIENCE

8/1 **Lick** someone: Defeat or be too much for someone. (*See also 16/1*) □ That pump repair has licked him; he doesn't have the experience. □ After years of seeking a solution to the inter-ethnic disturbances, the Interior Minister had to admit that he was licked.

8/2 **Beyond** someone: Too difficult for someone to do or understand. □ Algebra is beyond me.

8/3 **Out of one's depth**: Attempting to do something that is too difficult for one's abilities. □ Sven is a qualified electrician, but he's out of his depth in electronics.

8/4 **Stymie** someone: Block or thwart someone's actions or plans. A 'stymie' is a situation in golf where one player's ball blocks the path to the hole of an opponent's ball. □ Financial set-backs have stymied the firm's expansion plans.

8/5 **Snooker** someone: Thwart or defeat. Similar in meaning to 'stymie'. A 'snooker' is a situation in the game of snooker where one player so positions the cue-ball that his opponent is denied a direct line to the next ball to be struck. □ He had hoped to sell his goods in China but was snookered when the Chinese wouldn't grant him an import licence.

8/6 **Stump** someone: Be too difficult for someone; baffle. The term is derived from a method of dismissing a batsman in the game of cricket. □ I can't solve the crossword – I'm stumped.

11

8/7 **Floor** someone: Baffle or overwhelm someone. □ The sudden influx of refugees into the country has floored the authorities.

8/8 **Stick on** something: Encounter an insoluble problem or a difficulty which halts progress. □ A lot of students stuck on the third question of the exam paper.

8/9 **Bite off more than one can chew**:   Attempt more than one can manage. □ To their cost, several European companies have bitten off more than they can chew by competing with US computer giants in the American market.

8/10 **For the life of me**:   Expressing an inability to do something 'even if my life depended on it'. □ For the life of me, I don't know where he is.

8/11 **Not do** something **for nuts/toffee**:   Be totally unable to do something. □ That group can't sing for nuts (toffee). □ Ingrid can't swim for toffee (nuts).

8/12 **Not be able to organize a piss-up in a brewery** *(#?)*:   Be totally incompetent. *(For 'piss-up' see 155/20)* □ We shouldn't appoint Mr Patel as club treasurer – he couldn't organize a piss-up in a brewery.

8/13 **Wobbly**:   Weak or lacking ability in some subject or area. □ Nina is wobbly in Biology and Physics.

8/14 **Rusty/dusty**:   Lacking experience or practice; inefficient through lack of use. □ I haven't been to Spain for years, so my Spanish is a little rusty (dusty).

8/15 **Still wet behind ears**:   Still inexperienced or a novice. The expression alludes to children who neglect to dry behind their ears after washing. □ The enemy has battle-hardened soldiers and all we've got are recruits who are still wet behind the ears.

8/16 **A greenhorn**:   A naïve and inexperienced person. The adjective describing such a person is 'green'. □ Isobel was only sixteen and still green (still a greenhorn) when she arrived in San Francisco.

8/17 **A rookie**:   A novice or new recruit. □ The chief of police doesn't allow rookie cops on murder inquiries.

9: CLUMSINESS/BUNGLE

9/1 **All fingers and thumbs**:   Clumsy in handling or doing something, as if each finger were a thumb. □ As soon as Erik has to do any practical task, he's all thumbs.

9/2 **Ham-fisted** *or* **ham-handed**:   Clumsy with one's hands. □ The sink unit was installed by some ham-handed (ham-fisted) fitter and came loose from the wall after a week.

9/3 **A butter-fingers**:   Someone who continually drops things, as if his fingers were slippery with butter. □ That's the third plate this butter-fingers has dropped.

9/4 Like a bull in a china-shop: Clumsy and destructive; tactless. □ When cutting out door panels, don't go at it like a bull in a china shop, you'll only waste wood. □ A nurse should employ tact when discussing patients' complaints with them, and not be like a bull in a china shop.

9/5 Cowboys: Unscrupulous and careless workmen who pretend to be professional tradesmen. The corresponding adjective is 'cowboy'. □ Beware of cowboy building-firms! □ Your roof was obviously repaired by cowboys.

9/6 Tinker with something: Work in a casual, clumsy, meddlesome or desultory manner with something. □ Don't tinker with the TV; leave the repair to a qualified technician! □ I'm no good at d-i-y [do-it-yourself] – if something goes wrong with the car I might tinker with it, but end up calling the garage.

9/7 Monkey with something: Interfere or tamper with something in a clumsy, damaging manner. □ Some electrical appliances have special locks to stop children monkeying with them.

9/8 Botch/fluff something: Spoil through clumsiness or lack of skill. Something spoiled in this way is a 'botch' or a 'fluff'. □ You've botched (fluffed) our chances of winning the competition! □ Don't put Yuri on that job, he'll just fluff (botch) it!

9/9 Muck/louse/screw/foul up something: To bungle or spoil through clumsiness. Something spoiled in this way is a 'screw-up' or a 'foul-up'. □ Victor screws up (fouls up/louses up/mucks up) every job he gets.

9/10 A cock-up (#?): A bungle or clumsy failure. □ Bad organization made the athletics meeting a total cock-up.

9/11 Make a hash/balls (#?)/**bollocks** (#?) **of** something: Bungle or make a mess of something. □ Government control has made a balls (bollocks/ hash) of the Russian economy.

13

10: ORGANIZATION

10/1   A **set-up**: The structure of an organization. *(See also 37/5)* □ Our company has an international set-up.

10/2   An **outfit**: An organization or firm. □ That company is a multi-million dollar outfit.

10/3   **Lay on** something: Arrange, provide or organize. □ Accommodation for the seasonal workers has been laid on. □ The farmhouse is too far from the nearest cable, which makes it too expensive to lay on electricity.

10/4   **Fix up** someone with something: Organize, arrange or provide for. □ How are you fixed up for the night? □ The stores department can fix you up with a boilersuit and work boots.

10/5   **Get/put one's act together**: Get oneself organized. □ During the 'Great Leap Forward' in the '70s, Chinese economic planners started getting their act together.

10/6   **Do**: Organize or provide. *(See Index for other meanings)* □ That restaurant does only Indian meals. □ This travel agency does safari holidays to Kenya.

10/7   **Red tape**: Excessive or unnecessary bureaucracy. In the 18th and 19th centuries, there existed a practice of tying up official documents with a reddish tape. □ Red tape is responsible for a lot of the delay in importing wild animals for zoos.

11: TRADES/PROFESSIONS

11/1   The **troops**: Staff or workers. □ It is questionable whether the troops in the factory will accept a three-shift system. □ Every morning the manager greeted his staff with "Morning troops!".

11/2   A **spark/sparky**: An electrician.

11/3   A **chippy**: A carpenter or joiner. *(See also 149/16)*

11/4   A **bricky**: A bricklayer.

11/5   A **jack tar**: A sailor.

11/6   A **squaddy**: A private (the lowest rank) in the (British) army.

11/7   A **char**/a **Mrs Mop**: A charlady or charwoman (someone hired to do household cleaning). □ In the evenings Olga worked as a Mrs Mop.

11/8   A **lollipop man/lady**: A children's escort at a pedestrian crossing. The 'lollipop' refers to the portable stop-sign resembling a giant lollipop.

11/9   A **bookie**: A bookmaker; someone who accepts bets professionally.

11/10 A **shrink** *or* a **head-shrinker**: A psychiatrist. □ Many Hollywood actors find it fashionable to consult a shrink (head-shrinker).

11/11 A **pen-pusher**: An office clerk or bureaucrat.

11/12 A **Girl Friday**: A girl or secretary performing general office duties. The term is a variation of 'Man Friday', the faithful native servant of Robinson Crusoe in Daniel Defoe's book of the same name.

11/13 A **sandwich man**: A man who walks the streets carrying advertisement boards strapped to his front and back.

11/14 A **busker**: A street musician living by begging.

11/15 A **boffin**: A scientist engaged in technical research.

11/16 **Backroom boys**: Scientists or technicians working anonymously behind the scenes, out of the public gaze. □ It's the backroom boys who deserve the credit for this new development.

11/17 A **Jack of all trades**: Someone with a knowledge of many skills; someone who masters many skills only superficially. Derived from the phrase 'a Jack of all trades and master of none'.

11/18 An **odd-job man**: A handyman performing a variety of minor repairs and maintenance tasks.

11/19 A **dogsbody**: Someone who performs routine or menial tasks.

11/20 A **gaffer**: A boss or supervisor. Don't confuse with 'gaffer' meaning an old (and usually rustic) man, as in "This old gaffer in the pub told us . . .". □ My gaffer at work gave me time off when my wife was ill.

11/21 A **temp**: A temporary employee. □ I worked for a while as an office temp.

11/22 A **ref**: A referee in sports.

11/23 A **rep**: A business representative or travelling salesman.

11/24 A **doc**: A medical or academic doctor.

11/25 A **GP** (*pr. 'gee-pee'*): A general practitioner or family doctor. (Do not confuse with 'JP' below.)

11/26 A **JP** (*pr. 'jay-pee'*): A Justice of the Peace (a type of magistrate).

12: ADVERTISING/MARKETING

12/1 A **logo**: A printed symbol used by a corporation or business as an emblem.

12/2 A **jingle**: A catchy tune or rhyme advertising some product or service.

12/3 A **commercial**: A commercial break; a TV or radio advertisement spot. □ Many TV and radio stations are financed by commercials.

12/4 A **gimmick**: A trick or device attracting attention or publicity. □ Petrol companies are fond of such gimmicks as gift-vouchers and free mugs to boost sales.

12/5 A **freebie**: A free gift. □ Doctors get inundated with freebies from pharmaceutical companies. □ I saw the advertisement in a freebie newspaper.

12/6 **Plug** a product: To recommend a product or service by mentioning it indirectly. Such a mention is called a 'plug'. □ Radio stations are often offered bribes to plug certain records. □ The TV chat show allowed the author to get in several plugs for his new book.

12/7 A **blurb**: An article on a book jacket or in a newspaper praising an artistic work. □ The blurb was a lot better than the book.

12/8 **Hype**: Extravagant or misleading publicity. □ The film was accompanied by a lot of media hype.

12/9 **Razzle-dazzle**: Excitement or bustle; showy advertising. □ The razzle-dazzle of Las Vegas attracts many gamblers.

12/10 **Razz(a)matazz**: Showy, noisy publicity or display. □ The opening of the new shopping mall had all the usual razz(a)matazz: a release of balloons, speeches and free snacks.

12/11 **Junk mail**: Unsolicited advertising literature or circulars which are often thrown away unread. □ Half of my morning post is junk mail.

12/12 **Up-market**: Towards the more expensive end of the market. □ Harrod's in London is an up-market store. □ The firm has gone up-market with more sophisticated advertising and packaging.

12/13 **Down-market**: Towards the cheaper end of the market. □ We stock not only luxury items, but also more down-market products.

12/14 **Corner the market**: Gain a monopoly or total control of the market. □ A number of European countries are afraid that the Japanese will corner the market for many electrical appliances.

EXERCISES 2: WORK (B)

A) Replace the underlined text with colloquialisms from the module, rephrasing where necessary. For example: "He is alert and working well today." (= *on the ball* or *with it*)

1) She has worked here for a long time and knows the method of working.
2) I haven't got the necessary ability for the job.
3) When I became a student, I left home and had to manage on my own.
4) The launch of the new car involved much showy advertising.
5) You must learn to cope with small misfortunes.
6) The problem has defeated many people.
7) She shouldn't accept more commitments than she can manage.
8) One has to go through a lot of unnecessary bureaucracy to build one's own home. →

16

9) After so many years' absence, my knowledge of Helsinki is a little <u>weak</u>.
10) This is your last chance to prove yourself, don't <u>bungle it</u>!
11) Can you <u>organize a car for me</u>?

B) Give a colloquial term for the following occupations.

1) sailor. 2) carpenter. 3) electrician. 4) psychiatrist. 5) an unscrupulous and careless workman. 6) someone with many skills. 7) a cleaning lady. 8) a general office girl. 9) a novice or new recruit. 10) a supervisor.

C) The following sentences are incorrect. Insert the correct form of the colloquialism used. For example: "He is inexperienced and still green behind the ears." (= *wet behind the ears*)

1) This difficult problem is above me.
2) She has several qualifications under her hat.
3) That shop sells expensive down-market goods.
4) We receive a lot of rubbish mail.
5) She is not made out for the job.
6) For the sake of me, I am unable to do it.
7) We must put the new apprentice through his strides.
8) That is a technical problem for the backroom men.

D) Insert a body part or an animal to complete the following sentences.

1) She is a dab . . . at gardening.
2) That clumsy fellow is like a . . . in a china shop.
3) She is always dropping things, the butter- . . . that she is.
4) Someone has . . . ed with the lock and it won't open.
5) If you wish to retain your skill, you should practise to keep your . . . in.
6) He ruins everything with his ham- . . . ed approach.
7) He is an old- . . . in this business.

E) Replace the underlined phrase with a less vulgar colloquialism from the module, rephrasing where necessary.

1) They have made a <u>bollocks</u> of their work.
2) She couldn't <u>organize a piss-up in a brewery</u>.
3) Bad organization has <u>made a cock-up of</u> our delivery schedule.

Progress/Success

13: PERSEVERANCE

13/1   **Plug away at** something: Work diligently and persistently at a task. □ It is only by plugging away at a language that one can master it.

13/2   **Soldier/bash on**: Persevere doggedly or stubbornly. □ Breaking into the male-dominated profession of train driver was a difficult task, but Ingrid bashed (soldiered) on with job applications.

13/3   **Stick to one's guns**: Stubbornly defend one's opinion or position in the face of criticism or attack. □ City councillors were criticized for proposing to spend so much money on a new theatre, but they stuck to their guns and the building programme went ahead.

13/4   **Stick/hang out for** something: Persist in one's demands for something. □ Despite military defeats and internal divisions, the Afghan rebels stuck (hung) out for a Muslim-clerical state.

13/5   **Stick with** someone/something: Remain faithful to someone or something; stay with someone. □ At the elections, many voters stuck with the ruling party. □ Mrs Chang stuck with her husband, even after his affairs with other women.

13/6   **Stick at it**: Continue with one's efforts. □ Jasmin's school reports started to improve and her father promised her a computer if she stuck at it.

13/7   **Stick it out**: Endure or remain to the end, in spite of difficult circumstances. □ The outbreak of war brought food-rationing and stricter controls on aliens, but many foreign journalists decided to stick it out for the sake of a news story.

13/8   **Hang on like grim death**: Persevere unrelentingly under difficult circumstances. □ The situation at work became more and more unpleasant but he hung on to his job like grim death.

13/9   **Go the distance**: Persevere until the end; remain for the allotted period. □ Our firm has a six-month contract in the Sahara, and we need technicians that can go the distance.

13/10   **Muddle through**: Succeed after a persistent but inefficient effort. □ I had never fitted a mortise lock in my life, but I somehow managed to muddle through.

13/11   **Muddle along/on**: Continue working in a disorganized and ineffective manner. □ Prior to the country's independence in 1947, Britain had a long history of muddling along (muddling on) in India as a colonial power.

13/12   **Flog a dead horse**: Continually repeat the same outdated and ineffective arguments. □ Any fresh appeal by local residents against the planned airport runway would be flogging a dead horse, since the plan has already been approved by a tribunal.

13/13 **Keep the ball rolling**: Keep something going. □ The children's hospital was due to close for lack of funds, when a sudden large donation kept the ball rolling.

14: PROGRESS/IMPROVEMENT

14/1 **Get/put a foot in the door**: Gain access to a business, occupation or to an opportunity to progress further. □ Many school leavers are willing to accept a low starting wage, just to get a foot in the door with a large firm.

14/2 **Get off to a flying start**: Begin extremely well; make a very promising start. □ Mr Nordlund's horticulture business got off to a flying start with a large order from the Stockholm parks authority.

14/3 **Pick up**: Improve or make progress. *(See also 182/1)* □ Business is picking up after a slow start at the beginning of the year.

14/4 **Well away**: Have started and be making good progress. □ The yacht race is well away on a favourable breeze. □ Construction work is well away and should be completed soon.

14/5 **On the up and up**: Steadily improving. □ Sales figures are on the up and up. □ The patient is on the up and up.

14/6 **Go great guns**: Act with energy and efficiency; make fast progress. □ The tunnel builders are going great guns and are almost half-way under the river already.

14/7 **Get there**: Achieve one's goal; make reasonable progress. □ The railway authorities have a long way to go to improve their service, but they're getting there.

14/8 **On the right track**: Following the right path or procedure to success. □ Management consultants can put badly-organized firms on the right track. □ Our shipyard is on the right track, concentrating on commercial rather than military vessels.

14/9 **Winning**: Progressing. □ Factory technicians have been trying to solve the breakdown problem for a week now, and they're still not winning. □ The foreman went off to another job for a few hours, and when he returned, he asked the workmen if they were winning.

14/10 **Make out**: Fare or progress. *(Do not confuse with 85/12)* □ How are you making out with decorating your house? □ Mrs Van der Veldt travelled to Johannesburg to see how her daughter was making out.

14/11 **Do a/the world of good**: Be extremely beneficial or make a huge improvement. □ A short holiday will do you the (a) world of good. □ That new valve did a (the) world of good to the motor's performance.

14/12 Work wonders/magic: Produce an astonishing improvement. □ The investment programme has worked wonders (magic) for the economy.

14/13 Bog down: Make much slower progress; come to a halt. □ Our organization is getting bogged down in paperwork.

14/14 Get nowhere fast: Make no progress at all. □ The detectives on the investigation were getting nowhere fast until they changed their line of inquiry.

15: SUCCESS

15/1 Go like a bomb: Be very successful. *(But not in US, where 'to bomb' means 'to fail' – see 18/14)* □ Mr Sakamura's career went like a bomb. □ The firm's export-drive went like a bomb.

15/2 Go over big *(US)*: Become very successful or popular. □ Breakfast TV went over big in the United Kingdom.

15/3 Go down well with: Be well received or successful with someone. □ The première of the film went down well with the newspaper critics. □ The new tax scheme has gone down well with those on a low income.

15/4 A smash hit: An extremely successful thing. □ The play was a smash hit. □ The new training-shoes were a smash hit with joggers.

15/5 In the big time: At the top level in a field or activity; be enjoying success. □ Our company would like a modern new office block in the city centre, but we're not in the big time yet.

15/6 Hit the jackpot: Have sudden great success or good fortune. A 'jackpot' is the money staked in certain games, which increases until won. □ The firm hit the jackpot when they won a massive export contract.

15/7 Score a bull's-eye: Achieve one's aim or have great success. A bull's eye is the high-scoring centre of a darts board. □ Tests of the new drug proved positive on animals and the pharmacologists knew that they had scored a bull's-eye.

15/8 Chalk/notch up a success: Score points or goals; achieve success or a victory. □ We have chalked (notched) up several major US companies as our clients. □ One week into the Gulf War, Allied airmen had chalked (notched) up hundreds of Iraqi aircraft.

15/9 Make it: Be successful. *(See also 188/11)* □ The Wong brothers have made it in the textile trade.

15/10 Make good: Become successful or prosperous; also, to reform one's bad ways. □ Mr and Mrs Khan were illiterate, but they were determined to see their son have a good education and make good. □ On his release from prison for the second time, Oscar promised that he would make good.

15/11 Go places: Become successful. □ Our business is starting to go places. □ It helps to have influential connections if you want to go places.

15/12 **Never look back:** Continue to be successful or prosperous. □ Since we opened up our retail outlets in Germany, we've never looked back.

15/13 **Have it made:** Be sure of success. □ Michael knew that if he graduated from the world-famous Harvard Law School, he had it made.

15/14 **A yuppie:** An ambitious young social climber employed usually in financial services or other professional capacities. The word is an acronym formed from the expression 'young upwardly-mobile professional person'. □ London's redeveloped docklands area was favoured by yuppies seeking homes close to their places of work.

15/15 **A whiz-kid:** An exceptionally bright or successful young person. □ This boy will go far – he's a whiz-kid on computers.

15/16 **Make a go of** something: Make a success of something. □ Mr Petersen is looking for a partner to help make a go of his salmon-farming business.

15/17 **Bring/pull** something **off:** Achieve success in something; succeed in doing something. □ Tomorrow, Ogorodnikov will make an attempt at the high-jump record, and if anyone can pull (bring) it off, he can. □ We will do our best to bring (pull) off this deal.

15/18 **Pull/produce the rabbit out of the hat:** Succeed against the odds, as if by magic. □ Just when we thought the firm would collapse, Herman pulled (produced) the rabbit out of the hat by securing a large bank loan.

15/19 **Get away with** something: Be successful in spite of adverse circumstances or danger. *(For 'get away with murder' see 48/6)* □ The oil-well inferno was very difficult to put out, but Red Adair got away with it. □ Some people get away with illegal parking, but I never do.

15/20 **Buck** something: Be successful against great adversity. □ Most retailers have had reduced turnovers, but 'Supermac' stores have bucked the trend with increased profits. □ One motorist refused to pay a parking fine and was warned by the judge not to try to buck the system.

15/21 **Wangle** something: Achieve something through craftiness or persuasion. □ Everyone else has to work overtime, yet Karl is able to go on holiday for that period; I'd like to know how he wangled it. □ The match is a sell-out but I can wangle some tickets.

15/22 **Come off:** End successfully. *(See also 80/14)* □ Your little trick didn't come off. □ The attempt to climb Mount Everest didn't come off.

15/23 **Pay off:** Yield good results or produce success. □ Staff training pays off in the long run.

15/24 **The proof of the pudding (is in the eating):** The real test for the success of something is its practical application or use. Also: suggests you don't know how good or bad something is until you've tried it for yourself. □ Design engineers say that the new train will out-perform all others, but the proof of the pudding will be when it has been in service during poor weather conditions. □ I may not like this new job, but I'll have a go at it; the proof of the pudding is in the eating.

15/25 **Come out in the wash:** (Of mistakes or problems) Be successfully solved or remedied with time, as if washed away. □ Programmers should concentrate on getting the computer system running, small subroutine faults will come out in the wash.

15/26 **Sort itself out:** Be successfully resolved or come to a successful conclusion without external interference. □ The Müllers are just having a domestic dispute, it will sort itself out without calling in the police.

15/27 **Bob's your uncle!:** Success has been achieved. □ Putting up a greenhouse is simple; you just use the proper tools, follow the assembly instructions and Bob's your uncle!

15/28 **Bingo!** *or* **hey presto!:** An exclamation at a sudden success or occurrence. □ Our car had just broken down when bingo! (hey presto!), along came a breakdown truck. □ The mayor pressed a button and hey presto! (bingo!), the whole sea-front promenade was illuminated.

16: WIN/DEFEAT

16/1 **Lick** someone: To defeat. *(See also 8/1)* □ That problem has licked me. □ We licked the other team.

16/2 **Knock the spots off** *or* **slaughter** someone: Defeat someone utterly. □ The Democratic party knocked the spots off (slaughtered) its opponents in the national election.

16/3 **Beat hollow:** Defeat totally. □ The chess grandmaster was beaten hollow by his challenger.

16/4 **Make mincemeat of** someone: Defeat someone utterly; totally destroy an argument. □ The enemy guns made mincemeat of our troops. □ The state prosecutor made mincemeat of the defence lawyer's case.

16/5 **Run rings around** someone: Totally outmatch or be far better than someone. □ The Italian prince was rich and handsome, and could run rings around other suitors for the hand of the princess.

16/6 **See off** an opponent: Chase away or defeat. □ The beaver saw off a rival that wanted to take over his lodge.

16/7 **Polish off** someone: Defeat easily. *(See also 1/13, 150/6 and 163/2)* □ Napoleon polished off one European country's army after another.

16/8 **Sew up** (*occasionally* **stitch up**) something: Totally to defeat; gain control of, or master an objective. *(For 'stitch up' see also 59/7)* □ With the score at 5–0 and only three minutes to full-time, Juventus knew they had the game all sewn up. □ Don't worry, I'll soon have the job stitched up.

16/9 **Romp home** *or* **romp away with** something: Be an easy winner. □ The Romanian gymnasts romped away with all the medals. □ The favourite racehorse romped home.

16/10 **Win hands down**:   Win easily or completely. □ At Cruft's dog show, an Afghan hound won hands down.

16/11 A **walk-over**:   An easy victory or achievement. □ Our team had a walk-over when their opposition failed to turn up for the match.

16/12 A **landslide**:   An easy victory. □ It looks as if there'll be a landslide victory for the Democrats in the US Presidential election.

16/13 **Pip at the post**:   Defeat someone at the last moment. □ Just before the deadline for tunnel contract offers, a French firm pipped the other contractors at the post with a lower tender.

16/14 **. . . and whose army?**:   Sarcastic comment that someone will never win on their own without help. □ "Celtic will win the match tonight." "Celtic and whose army?"

EXERCISES 3: PROGRESS/SUCCESS

A) Replace the underlined text with colloquialisms from the module, rephrasing where necessary.

1) That drug has <u>been amazingly beneficial</u> for the patient.
2) Many holidaymakers returned home early because of the bad weather, but we <u>remained till the end</u>.
3) Christians in ancient Rome refused to renounce their religion and <u>remained true to their faith</u>.
4) Scientists are <u>following the right methods</u> to prevent cancer.
5) She <u>started extremely well</u>, but <u>made slower progress</u> towards the end.
6) <u>The real test</u> for our products is whether the customers buy them.
7) He <u>used craftiness to get</u> me a parking permit.

→

8) The film <u>was a resounding success</u>.
9) Since those early days, I've <u>always been successful</u>.
10) Honesty doesn't always <u>have its rewards</u>.
11) Our team <u>was an easy winner</u>.
12) The Kenyan runner led most of the race, but he <u>was defeated at the last minute</u>.

B) Insert a person or animal from colloquialisms in the module to complete the following sentences.

1) I won't give up, I'll ... on.
2) Now, just put it in the oven, and Bob's your ... .
3) The rich young banker lived in a housing development for ... on the riverside.
4) At Yale, he was a whiz- ... and excelled in everything.
5) Don't continually repeat that outdated argument, you're just flogging a dead ... .
6) When all seemed lost, he pulled the ... out of the hat.
7) I've scored a ... 's eye with my driving test.

C) The following sentences are incorrect. Give the correct form of the colloquialism.

1) Our organization needs volunteers to keep the ball going.
2) We'll sell the goods to the company at a low price, to get our leg in the door.
3) We're not getting anywhere quickly.
4) The strike has lasted a month now, and the workers are still hanging on for grim life.
5) How did you make with your job application?
6) Everything will sort itself together.
7) I managed to do it eventually by muddling up.

D) From the module, choose a colloquial expression to complete the following sentences, paying attention to the tense of the verb. For example: "Her health is improving. It is ...". (*on the up and up* or *picking up*)

1) The company has won an extremely large order. It has ... .
2) The problems will be solved later automatically. They will ... .
3) We are making very good progress. We are ... .
4) We have marked up a success. We have ... a success.
5) They have been successful in spite of the trend. They have ... the trend.
6) The attempt to beat the record didn't succeed. It didn't ... .
7) He reformed his bad ways. He ... .
8) We inflicted a crushing defeat on our opponents. We ... them.

Failure

17: MISTAKE

17/1   **A boob/booboo:**   A silly mistake. To 'boob' is to make such a mistake. (*See also 189/9*) □ I made a boob (booboo); I gave him the wrong number.

17/2   **A howler/bloomer:**   A foolish or ridiculous mistake; a blunder. □ The guest speaker was unprepared and made a few bloomers (howlers).

17/3   **A goof:**   A serious mistake or blunder.

17/4   **Goof it:**   Cause an undertaking to fail by committing a serious mistake or blunder. □ We missed the plane to Palma because father goofed it – he got the departure times mixed up.

17/5   **Drop a brick/clanger** *or* **put one's foot in it:**   Say something tactless or indiscreet. □ Branka dropped a brick (put her foot in it) at work with her criticism of Americans; she didn't know that the boss's wife is American.

17/6   **Gone and done it:**   To have made a serious mistake or blunder. □ Now you've gone and done it! You'll be in big trouble now!

17/7   **Slip/slip up** *or* **trip up:**   Make an accidental or casual mistake. The mistake is a 'slip' or a 'slip-up'. □ One of the check-out girls in the supermarket had been slipping (slipping up/tripping up) and allowing groceries through uncharged.

17/8   **Bark up the wrong tree:**   Direct one's efforts or complaints in the wrong direction; be mistakenly pursuing the wrong solution to a problem. □ Several US banks believed that the Treasury would rescue them from financial collapse, but they were barking up the wrong tree.

17/9   **An off-day:**   A day when one is making mistakes or not performing well. □ Everyone has an off-day now and then.

17/10 **Trip** someone **up:**   Cause someone to make an error, thus revealing his faults or inconsistencies. □ In court, the public prosecutor tripped up several witnesses for the defence.

17/11 **Catch** someone **out:**   Detect someone in a mistake; reveal someone as unprepared. □ I hadn't revised French history and I was caught out by several exam questions on Napoleon.

18: FAILURE

18/1   **Go downhill:**   Deteriorate or be failing. □ The economy of the country is going downhill fast. □ Felipe's health is going downhill; he'll have to go to hospital.

18/2 **Fight a losing battle:**   Struggle with no chance of success; make an effort that is doomed to failure. □ The cosmonauts fought a losing battle to repair the damaged solar panel and finally decided to jettison it into space.

18/3 **Run out of steam:**   Lose energy or vigour; be slowing down or failing. □ 'Greenpeace' will not let the campaign to save the whales run out of steam.

18/4 **Fizzle/peter out:**   End feebly or unsuccessfully; diminish gradually and cease to exist. □ Many peace movements in Ulster have petered (fizzled) out. □ All interest in forming a neighbourhood-watch committee to combat crime has petered (fizzled) out.

18/5 **Come a cropper:**   Fail badly or fall. *(See also 146/15)* □ The former East German regime came a cropper because it didn't trust its own people.

18/6 **Fall through:**   (Of a plan) Fail or come to nothing. □ The plan to set up a new factory fell through because of lack of cash.

18/7 **Fall flat on one's face:**   Fail miserably. □ Anneke fell flat on her face in her attempt to start up her business.

18/8 **Come unstuck/undone:**   Suffer failure or disaster. □ The experiment came unstuck (undone) when the radio transmitter on the satellite failed to operate.

18/9 **Go to pot** *or* **go to the dogs:**   Deteriorate or fail. □ My grandmother is always complaining that the morals of young people today have gone to pot (gone to the dogs).

18/10 **Down the drain/tube/Swanee:**   Lost, wasted or failed. □ My catering firm is going down the tube (drain/Swanee) because of competition.

18/11 **Go under** *or* **fold/fold up** *or* **go to the wall:**   Suffer failure, collapse or ruin. □ If we get another poor year for tourism, many travel agents will go under (fold/fold up/go to the wall).

18/12 **Go bust:**   Become bankrupt. □ The firm has gone bust and can't pay its staff.

18/13 **Collapse around one's ears:**   Fail or collapse quickly, in spite of someone's efforts. □ The country's economy was collapsing around the government's ears.

18/14 **A flop/a turkey** *(#US)* **a bomb** *(#US)*:   A failure. *(For 'turkey' see also 82/26; for 'bomb' see also 15/1)* To 'flop' is to fail. □ The airline flopped after six months in operation.

18/15 **Sunk** *or* **cooked:**   Doomed to failure or disaster. □ If you entrust your affairs to a disreputable lawyer like him, you're cooked (sunk).

18/16 **On one's/its last legs:**   About to fail or collapse. *(See also 162/1)* □ My old TV set is on its last legs. □ The leading marathon runner appears to be on his last legs. □ The company has large debts and is on its last legs.

18/17 **Have had it** *or* **be a goner:**   Be doomed to failure or destruction. *(See also 162/4 and 162/5)* □ My washing machine has broken down; this time I think it has had it (it's a goner). □ If ivory poaching continues on this scale, then the African elephant is a goner (has had it) as a species.

18/18 Curtains for someone/something: The end; failure or death. *(See also 162/7)* □ Withdrawal of subsidies from the Ministry of Sport will mean curtains for many swimming-pools.

18/19 That's torn/done it!:   That has spoilt or ruined everything. □ That's torn (done) it! We can't get through customs because you've left our passports at home.

18/20 A dead duck: Something useless or unsuccessful; a useless plan. □ Marxism has become a dead duck in the modern age. □ The funds can't be raised, so the project is a dead duck.

18/21 A dead loss: A useless person or thing. □ That method of giving up smoking is a dead loss. □ I'm a dead loss at cooking.

18/22 A dead-beat: A useless person or failure. *(Do not confuse with 'dead beat' meaning 'exhausted' – see 180/1)* □ Johann is fast becoming an alcoholic dead-beat.

18/23 An also-ran: A person who fails to win distinction in his activities. The term is derived from a horse or dog which does not occupy the first three winning places of a race. □ Most of his class at school went on to university or good jobs, but Phillipe was an also-ran.

18/24 A has-been: A person or thing no longer enjoying former fame or success. □ His last hit record was five years ago – he's just a has-been now.

18/25 Washed up: Useless or unwanted; ruined. □ Kowalski was once a brilliant scientist, but now he's all washed up. □ My business is washed up after two bad years.

18/26 A wash-out: A complete failure. *(See also 141/12)* □ Their marriage was a wash-out.

18/27 Back to square one *or* **back to the drawing board**:   As the result of a failure or misfortune, going back to the very beginning of an enterprise with no progress made. □ Tanya was pleased to get an interview after all her unsuccessful applications but when she was turned down for the job, it was back to square one (back to the drawing board).

18/28 Swings and roundabouts: Failure and success; a situation where the advantages and disadvantages are evenly balanced. From the expression 'what you lose on the swings, you gain on the roundabouts'. □ Working part-time enabled Greta to spend more time with her children, but her reduced income made the job a matter of swings and roundabouts.

18/29 Snakes and ladders: Failure and success. Alludes to a children's board game where the snakes signify a loss of points, and the ladders a gain. □ Our firm was not awarded the building contract, but tendering is like snakes and ladders: some you win, some you lose.

18/30 Take the rough with the smooth: Accept luck and misfortune or success and failure. □ As a vegetable gardener, you must take the rough with the smooth and not be disheartened by a year of drought or pests.

18/31 A wild goose chase: A profitless journey; a fruitless search. □ It's no use sending the rescue helicopter out on a wild goose chase in this storm, as any survivors from the shipwreck couldn't have survived long in the icy water.

18/32 **Pull the plug on** something/someone: Cause an undertaking to fail by withdrawing support or revealing a secret. □ His business collapsed when bankers pulled the plug on the company by refusing further credit. □ An unknown convict pulled the plug on the prison escape to gain a reduced sentence.

18/33 **Pull the rug from under** someone's **feet:** Cause to fail by suddenly withdrawing support. □ The organizers of the Moscow Olympics had the rug pulled from under their feet by a number of countries which refused to compete in protest at Soviet intervention in Afghanistan.

18/34 **Cop out:** Fail in one's duty; fail to do what one has promised. Such a failure to act is a 'cop-out'. □ Until Syrian intervention, the Lebanese army was weak and it copped out when confronting the war-lords and their militias.

19: STOP/ABANDON

19/1 **Lay off** something: Stop doing something, especially causing annoyance, injury or trouble. □ You should lay off the drink! □ Manuel kept pestering me for money, and I told him to lay off.

19/2 **Knock it off** or **cut it (out)** or **pack it in:** Stop or cease doing something. □ Knock it off (Cut it/Cut it out/Pack it in)! I can't hear the phone for your shouting. □ It is prohibited to play football here, so cut it out (cut it/knock it off/pack it in)!

19/3 **Give it a rest** or **give over** or **drop it:** Stop doing or saying something. □ Give it a rest (Give over/Drop it), I'm sick of hearing that I made a mistake.

19/4 **Give it a miss:** Stop doing something; avoid something. □ As for going abroad on holiday, we'll give it a miss this year. □ I can't stand your continual complaints; give it a miss!

19/5 **Leave off** or **leave be:** Stop doing something; cease to interfere; stop being a nuisance. □ Nina told her brother to leave off (leave be) when he started to tease her.

19/6 **Kick** a habit: Give up a habit. □ I want to give up smoking, but it's hard to kick the habit. □ Addicts come to our organization when they decide to kick drugs.

19/7 **Wrap up** something: Finish; cease talking. □ We can all go home when this job's wrapped up. □ My speech has dragged on, so I'll wrap up now.

19/8 **Shut up shop:** Stop working; abandon one's business. □ If agricultural subsidies are reduced, many farmers might as well shut up shop.

19/9 **Skip/scrub it!:** Leave that subject. □ I don't want to talk about my family, so skip it (scrub it)!

19/10 Scrub/scrap something: (Of plans) Cancel or abandon. □ The organizers have scrubbed (scrapped) the planned concert. □ After the accident, he had to scrap (scrub) all hopes of ever playing professional football again.

19/11 Put the lid on *or* **put paid to** something: Put an end to hopes, prospects or activities. □ Stormy weather has put the lid on (put paid to) our yachting trip. □ Nikolai's defeat in the 2000 metres has put paid to (put the lid on) his chances of getting into the Olympic team.

19/12 Chuck/jack in something: Give up or abandon. □ Marina chucked (jacked) in her studies at college to care for her invalid mother.

19/13 Ditch something: Abandon; (of a plane) make an emergency landing in the sea. □ When Fernandes became famous, he ditched his old friends. □ Engine failure forced the pilot to ditch (ditch his plane) into the sea.

19/14 Drop something/someone **like a hot potato**: Suddenly abandon something problematic or embarrassing. *(See also 27/7)* □ When certain leaders of puppet East European regimes became an embarrassment to the Soviet Union, they were dropped like hot potatoes.

19/15 Through with someone/something: Finished with. *(See also 6/6)* □ I'm not yet through with writing this letter. □ Chandra is through with her boyfriend.

19/16 Leave in the lurch: Abandon someone in an awkward or difficult situation. □ The country was in dire need of financial aid and appealed to the World Bank not to be left in the lurch for political reasons. □ Yang emigrated to Taiwan and left his wife and children in the lurch on mainland China.

19/17 Vote with one's feet: Abandon one's country through dissatisfaction; go over to the other side. □ Before the demolition of the Berlin Wall, thousands of East Germans voted with their feet and escaped to the West.

19/18 Get rid/shot of something: Succeed in selling; give away. *(For 'get shot of' see also 163/4)* □ As soon as my car began to break down regularly, I got shot (rid) of it quickly.

19/19 Good riddance!: Expression of relief that one has freed oneself of a burden by disposing of it. □ I put the old bookcase on a bonfire and good riddance too – it was always in the way!

EXERCISES 4: FAILURE

A) From the colloquialisms in the module, insert a part of the body or an animal to complete the following sentences.

1) What a blunder, you've put your . . . in it again!
2) The organizers fell flat on their . . . with the concert.
3) My business is collapsing around my . . . .

→

4) The pop-group's tour was a . . . and attracted few fans.
5) The expedition to find the Loch Ness monster is a wild . . . chase.
6) Skilled workers are voting with their . . . and emigrating.
7) The slide-rule is a dead . . . in the age of the electronic calculator.
8) As one country after another left, the Warsaw Pact was on its last . . . .
9) Several firms have cancelled their sponsorship and pulled the rug from under the . . . of the football club.
10) After years of war, the country's economy has gone to the . . . .

B) From the unit, choose a colloquial alternative to the underlined text, rephrasing where necessary.

1) You have made a <u>silly mistake</u>.
2) The firm has <u>gone bankrupt</u>.
3) That has <u>spoilt everything</u>!
4) Our team lost the match, but in sport you must <u>accept both success and failure</u>.
5) Politics is a question of daily <u>success and failure</u> and the fortunes of parties can change very quickly.
6) You shouldn't touch the exhibits, so <u>stop doing it</u>!
7) These tablets will help you <u>give up</u> smoking.
8) He no longer lives here, and <u>I am glad of that</u>!
9) The agricultural show was a <u>failure owing to rain</u>.
10) The deserter left the other soldiers <u>in a difficult position</u>.
11) I <u>no longer want anything to do with her</u>.
12) He <u>gave up</u> a well-paid job to help the poor in the slums.

C) The colloquialisms in the following sentences have been used incorrectly. From the module, give the correct form of the colloquialism, paying attention to the tense of the verb.

1) We must start again, it's back to the first square.
2) During the scandal, the firm dropped its managing director like a hot brick.
3) I didn't steal your money, you're looking up the wrong tree.
4) What a silly mistake – the announcer has dropped a hot potato!
5) My health has gone to the pot.
6) He is no use as a dentist any more, he is washed out.

D) Give colloquialisms for the following definitions.

1) a useless person.
2) a person of mediocre performance.
3) a person who was once much more successful than he or she is now.
4) a day when things go wrong for one.
5) a failure to act or do one's duty.
6) an accidental or casual mistake.

Time

20: LENGTH OF TIME/FREQUENCY

20/1 **Donkey's years**: A very long time. □ I haven't seen a trolley-bus like that for donkey's years.

20/2 **Yonks/ages**: A long time. □ I've been waiting here for ages (yonks). □ The train took yonks (ages) to arrive.

20/3 **A month of Sundays**: A very long time. □ The cooker is very heavy and you won't get it down the stairs on your own in a month of Sundays. □ It's a dreadful place – I'd never go there in a month of Sundays.

20/4 **The year dot**: A very long time ago. □ We don't need police in the village – we haven't had a crime here since the year dot. □ The last time Luciano was at the dentist was in the year dot.

20/5 **Until the cows come home**: For ever *or* a very long time. □ You can wait there until the cows come home, but she won't come. □ Aad would laze around until the cows come home, if you let him.

20/6 **Make** a day **of it**: Devote a period of time, such as a day or morning etc., to some activity. □ We intended to visit them for only an hour, but when we got there, we decided to make an evening of it.

20/7 **Spin out** something: Cause to last a long time. □ It was a trivial story, but the newspaper reporter spun it out to a whole page.

20/8 **A nine days' wonder**: Something that attracts much attention at first, but is soon forgotten. □ Some successful films generate a great demand for certain products, which often prove to be nine days' wonders.

20/9 **A flash in the pan**: Something that makes a sensational start, then fails after a short time. □ After Boris Becker won the Wimbledon tennis tournament for the first time, he set out to prove that his success was not just a flash in the pan.

20/10 **A jiffy/mo/tick**: A moment or similarly short space of time. □ Half a mo (jiffy/tick), that's not what I said! □ It will only take a mo (tick/jiffy).

20/11 **In a trice** *or* **in (less than) no time**: In an instant. □ The punctured tyre was changed in a trice (in less than no time).

20/12 **Before you can say 'Jack Robinson'/'knife'**: Very quickly or suddenly. □ Before you could say 'Jack Robinson' ('knife') he had changed from his working-clothes into a suit.

20/13 **On the trot** *or* **on end**: In succession; consecutively. □ Apple growers have had record crops for three years on the trot (on end).

20/14 **At a stretch**: Without interruption. □ Some shepherds can shear fifty sheep at a stretch. □ Jiro can stay underwater without air for three minutes at a stretch.

31

20/15 **All along the line**: Continually; at every stage. □ I warned my daughter all along the line not to marry him, but she would have her way.

20/16 **Right from the word 'go'**: From the very beginning or outset. □ I never wanted anything to do with his plan, right from the word 'go'.

20/17 **Once in a blue moon**: Very rarely. □ Since we sold our car, we only get out into the countryside once in a blue moon. □ Fatima lives a long way away and I see her only once in a blue moon.

20/18 **Half the time**: Very often; frequently. □ Ivan is a good worker when he's sober, but he's drunk half the time. □ Where we live, it rains half the time.

20/19 **More times than** someone **has had hot dinners**: Very often; countless times. □ The pilot has flown this plane more times than you've had hot dinners.

21: TIMING/POINT OF TIME

21/1 **Up front**: In advance. □ Some landlords want two months' rent up front.

21/2 **For starters**: To begin with. □ For starters, we don't need a new lawn mower; secondly, we've no money for one.

21/3 **First thing**: Before anything else. □ I'll do it first thing tomorrow.

21/4 **First come, first served**: Advantages or profits accrue to those who act early, before anyone else. □ You should get your name on the housing list soon as possible; for flats, it's first come, first served.

21/5 **Start from scratch**: Begin at the very beginning with no advantage or preparation. □ When they got to Canada, the refugees had to start their lives from scratch.

21/6 **Bright and early**: Early in the morning. □ On the farm, we get up bright and early to milk the cows.

21/7 An **ungodly hour**: A very inconvenient time, especially a time when most people are asleep. □ Two o'clock in the morning is an ungodly hour to phone anyone.

21/8 **Cut it fine/close**: Leave hardly enough time to do something or for unforeseen circumstances. □ You should get to the station a lot earlier – five minutes before the train is due to leave is cutting it too fine (close).

21/9 **On the stroke of**: At an exact time of the clock. □ They arrived on the stroke of six.

21/10 **On the dot**: Exactly on time. □ The ten o'clock flight took off on the dot. □ My lodgers all pay their rent at the beginning of the month, on the dot.

21/11 **Sharp**: Punctually. □ Be there at three o'clock sharp!

21/12 **Slap bang**: Exactly. *(See also 66/24 and 146/11)* □ Computer magazines need to be slap bang up to date. □ French high-speed trains are usually slap bang on time.

21/13 Split-second: Accurate to a fraction of a second; extremely rapid. □ Some video games require split-second timing. □ The pilot had to make a split-second decision to avoid a mid-air collision.

21/14 In the nick of time: Only just in time; at the last possible moment. Originally game scores were recorded by notches or 'nicks' on sticks, and a last-minute victory was thus recorded by a nick just within the game time. □ In cowboy films, the cavalry always arrives in the nick of time to rescue people from the Indians.

21/15 In one's tracks: Instantly; at the very place one is standing at a particular moment. □ As the soldier got out of the trench, a bullet stopped him in his tracks. □ Blinded by the car's headlights, the hedgehog froze in its tracks.

21/16 On the spur of the moment: On an impulse; without planning or previous intent. □ On the spur of the moment, Simone jumped on the train to join him. □ The thief stole the car on the spur of the moment.

21/17 Off the cuff: Without rehearsal or preparation. □ The minister made some off-the-cuff remarks to journalists, which he regretted later. □ I haven't seen the financial accounts, but off the cuff I would say that the company is healthy.

21/18 Off the top of one's head: Without preparation, careful thought or accurate information. □ Speaking off the top of his head, the policeman estimated the number of cars involved in the motorway pile-up as thirty.

21/19 Straight *or* right: Immediately, especially in the expressions 'right/straight there' and 'straight/right away'. □ Go on ahead, I'll be right (straight) there. □ You must leave right (straight) away. □ The doctor will be right with you. (*For 'be straight with someone' see 100/4*)

21/20 High time: A time for long-overdue action. □ It's high time you got out of bed. □ The house repairs are being carried out, and high time too!

21/21 Have one's last fling: Enjoy oneself or make one's influence felt for the last time. □ In his last fling before retirement, the veteran footballer scored a hat-trick (three goals). □ It was spring in the valley but in the hills, winter was having its last fling.

21/22 Chucking-out time: Closing time in restaurants and bars. □ "Drink up, gents – it's chucking-out time!"

21/23 The home stretch/straight: The final stage. Alludes to the final stage of a race-track or racecourse between the last bend and the finishing-post. □ The Finance Bill is on the home stretch (home straight) in Parliament and should become law by autumn.

21/24 Late in the day: At a late stage in an activity or process. □ These two pensioners prove that it's never too late in the day to get married. □ It's a bit late in the day to tell us we can't have the flat; after all, we're already making preparations to move in.

21/25 Squeeze someone/an appointment **in**:   Fit someone or an appointment into a busy schedule; manage to find time for something. □ The dentist can't see you today, but he can squeeze you in for tomorrow. □ He's a very busy man, but he always squeezes in time for golf.

22: SPEED

22/1 **Get one's skates on** *or* **get cracking** *or* **get weaving**: Hurry up; make a hasty start on work. □ If you don't get your skates on (get cracking/get weaving), you'll be late for school. □ The coffee break is over and it's time those decorators got weaving (got cracking/got their skates on).

22/2 **Shake a leg**: Hurry up. □ Shake a leg, the bus is coming.

22/3 **Jump to it**: Make a hasty start on work. □ Fire had broken out in the engine room, and all sailors were told to jump to it with the extinguishers.

22/4 **Get a move on**: Hurry up. □ If she doesn't get a move on with dressing, we'll be late for the concert.

22/5 **Look sharp**: Make haste. □ It was only a bomb hoax, but all staff were told to look sharp and leave the building.

22/6 **Make it snappy**: Be quick about it. □ Waiter, three pizzas please, and make it snappy!

22/7 **Put one's best foot forward**: Hurry or walk faster. □ We'll have to put our best foot forward to reach the hut by nightfall.

22/8 **Step on it**: Hurry. □ Drive me to the hospital and step on it! □ I'll have to step on it to get the washing indoors before it rains.

22/9 **Chop chop!**: Hurry up! From pidgin English used in the Far East. □ Come on, chop chop! Otherwise we'll miss the bus.

22/10 **Pronto**: Immediately; without delay. An Italian word adopted into English. □ He ordered his children off to bed pronto. □ Bring me some bandages pronto!

22/11 **At the double**: Very quickly; as fast as one can. □ As soon as the earth tremors started again, the whole population left their houses at the double.

22/12 **Like a house on fire**: Very quickly. *(See also 164/12)* □ She went through her exam questions like a house on fire.

22/13 **Like billy-o/blazes**: Vigorously; quickly. □ Snow-plough teams worked like billy-o (blazes) to get the road clear.

22/14 **Get/go through** a task **like a dose of salts**: Finish a task very quickly. A dose of (Epsom-) salts is a fast-acting laxative. □ With the help of a calculator, pupils can get (go) through the maths questions like a dose of salts.

22/15 **Hell for leather** *or* **like hell**: At a recklessly fast speed. □ The hunters galloped hell for leather (like hell) after the fox. □ When the shooting started, we ran like hell (hell for leather) for cover.

22/16 **Like mad/crazy**: At a great speed; vigorously. □ I drove like mad (like crazy) down the motorway. □ Elena loves him like mad.

22/17 **At a cracking/spanking/rattling pace**: At a brisk or speedy pace. □ The work is going at a cracking (rattling/spanking) pace. □ The skiers descended the slope at a rattling (cracking/spanking) pace.

22/18 **Like a shot:** Without hesitation; at once. □ At the approach of danger, the squirrel disappeared like a shot up a tree. □ If I was offered that job, I would take it like a shot.

22/19 **Like greased lightning:** Extremely fast; with very great speed. □ The ramblers ran like greased lightning from the bull.

22/20 **Like the clappers:** Very fast. □ I drove there like the clappers. □ We worked like the clappers all day.

22/21 **Flat out:** At top speed; at the limit of one's strength or resources. □ Order books are full and the factory is working flat out. □ The Porsche was going flat out along the Autobahn.

22/22 **Shift/travel:** Move quickly; travel at high speed. □ Those greyhounds can really shift (travel). □ It was only after leaving the built-up area that the express train began to travel (shift).

22/23 **Scoot:** Dart; move or leave at high speed. □ The hare scooted away over the field.

22/24 **Belt/pelt:** Hurry; run or move fast. □ As soon as I heard the good news, I belted (pelted) over to congratulate them.

22/25 **Bowl along:** Move reasonably fast in a vehicle, and for a good distance. □ We were bowling along without any cares in the world, when the back tyre suddenly blew out.

22/26 **Scorch:** Drive or ride at very high speed. □ During the Grand Prix, racing cars can be seen scorching through the streets of Monte Carlo.

22/27 **Clock up** speed/distance/overtime: Achieve a certain speed, register a distance covered or extra hours worked. □ Bobsleighs can clock up tremendous speeds. □ The hovercraft expedition up the Amazon clocked up more than 5000 kilometres.

22/28 **Spread like wildfire:** Spread with great speed. □ The cholera epidemic spread like wildfire. □ Rumours that the bank would soon collapse spread like wildfire in financial circles.

22/29 **Hand over fist:** Very rapidly; with great progress. □ Speculators are making money hand over fist.

22/30 **Cut corners:** Achieve speed by breaking rules or making omissions. □ Apprentices should avoid cutting corners, even though more experienced craftsmen sometimes do it.

22/31 **Rush one's fences:** Act hastily or prematurely, without proper preparation. □ When learning a foreign language, you shouldn't rush your fences, but take your time.

22/32 **Jump the gun:** Start or act before the permitted or appropriate time; be too hasty. The reference is to an athlete who begins a race before the starting-pistol is fired. □ There is a waiting-list for flats and Mr Konovalov tried to jump the gun by bribing officials. □ No examination centre may allow candidates to jump the gun and start before the permitted time.

22/33 **A quickie:** Anything done or made quickly. □ "There's time for another game of squash." "OK, but just a quickie!"

23: SLOWNESS/WAITING

23/1   **Dither**:   Hesitate indecisively. □ Stop dithering and get down to work.

23/2   **Shilly-shally**:   Hesitate; be unable to make up one's mind firmly. □ The government has shilly-shallied with the introduction of a minimum wage.

23/3   **Dilly-dally**:   Hesitate or take one's time. □ Kyoko spent half the afternoon dilly-dallying and got little work done.

23/4   **Drag one's feet**:   Be deliberately slow or reluctant to act. □ Tatiana requested a visa to emigrate to Israel, but the Soviet authorities dragged their feet for over a year.

23/5   **Faff around**:   Waste one's time idly with petty matters. A 'faff' is a petty fuss involving time-wasting. □ I've got no time to faff around here with you, I've got work to do.

23/6   **A snail's pace**:   A very slow pace or speed. □ The renovation is progressing at snail's pace and it will be months before it's finished. □ The train slowed down to a snail's pace.

23/7   **A slowcoach** *or* **a slowpoke** (#*US*):   Someone slow in actions or work.

23/8   **Let up**:   Become less intense or slow down. □ The rain is beginning to let up. □ On the second day, the air raids on the city didn't let up.

23/9   **Grind to a halt**:   Slow down to a (sometimes noisy) stop. □ Transport in the congested cities is grinding to a halt. □ The lorry ground to a halt.

23/10   **Easy does it!**:   Command or request to go gently, carefully or without rushing. □ Mind how you go about moving that piano – easy does it!

23/11   **Hold one's horses**:   Wait a moment; not act too hastily. □ Hold your horses and give the other walkers time to catch up with us! □ Tell the workmen to hold their horses; the demolition can't begin until all the tenants have left the building.

23/12   **Hold/hang on**:   Wait a moment. □ The telephonist told the caller to hang (hold) on till the line became free. □ Hold on (Hang on), that's not what I meant!

23/13   **Hold it**:   Stop; not rush ahead. □ Hold it right there! I'll take your photo now. □ Hold it! Where are you going with my bag?

23/14   **Stay put**:   Remain where one is. □ We'd better stay put in this barn until the storm is over!

23/15   **Hang/stick around**:   Wait or loiter. □ This morning we had to stick (hang) around for over an hour waiting for the bus. □ There are always pickpockets hanging (sticking) around the station.

23/16   **Cool one's heels**:   Be kept waiting (often impatiently) for a long time. □ The delegation spent two hours cooling their heels in the lobby before they could see the minister.

23/17   **Sit on** something: Delay something (often deliberately); wait before proceeding with something. □ The housing department spent six months sitting on our request to be rehoused.

23/18 Sit tight: Remain firmly where one is; take no action and not yield. □ The chairman decided to sit tight, and ignored every call for his resignation. □ All residents were told to leave the area, but a few sat tight.

24: FUTURE EVENT

24/1 Pie in the sky *or* a pipe-dream: A deceptive illusion or promise of future happiness; unrealistic hopes and dreams. □ After the young pianist's hands were injured in an accident, her hopes of fame became pie in the sky (a pipe-dream). □ Lorna's pipe-dream was to win the pools and live in the south of France.

24/2 Not cross one's bridges before one comes to them: Worry about future problems only when they actually occur or arise. □ Of course the trade unions may object to the modernization plans for the factory, but let's not cross our bridges before we come to them (but we'll cross that bridge when we come to it).

24/3 Not count one's chickens (before they're hatched): Not rely on, or anticipate future events and benefits before they actually occur or accrue to one. □ Don't count your chickens . . . we may now own the land, but we still don't have planning permission for the house!

24/4 Take a rain check (*#US*): Defer one's acceptance of an offer until a future time. A 'rain check' is a ticket for a venue which allows a refund or later admission in the event of rain. □ Thanks for offering me a beer; I'll take a rain check, since I must telephone first.

24/5 In the pipeline: On the way; in the process of preparation. □ The novelist has another paperback in the pipeline. □ There are sweeping reforms in the pipeline.

24/6 **In store**: Destined to happen; ahead in the future. □ The war was over but the country still had many difficult years of reconstruction in store. □ If you continue like that, there's trouble in store for you!

24/7 **Brew**: Develop; be in preparation. □ There are problems brewing for the economy. □ One of our customers is complaining; you'd better go over there and see what's brewing.

24/8 **Budding**: Beginning to develop. □ The 'Best Young Inventor' competition aims to encourage budding scientists.

24/9 **Up-and-coming**: Enterprising and destined to achieve one's goals. □ Golf has become a fashionable sport with up-and-coming executives in Japan.

24/10 **Roll on . . .!**: Wish that a future date or event might soon occur. □ Roll on Tuesday when the holidays begin.

24/11 **That'll be the day!**: Ironic way of saying that a desirable event will never occur. □ Armando is arrogant, and when he apologizes to anyone, that'll be the day!

24/12 **Pigs might fly (if they had wings)**: Said of something impossible or unlikely ever to occur. □ "Do you think he will agree to our proposal?" "Yes, and pigs might fly!"

24/13 **Not have a crystal ball**: Be unable to predict the future. The reference is to the crystal ball used by fortune-tellers. □ A spokesman said that his country's policy depended on events in the Middle East and that he didn't have a crystal ball.

EXERCISES 5: TIME

A) From the module, give another colloquialism meaning the same as or improving upon the one underlined. For example: "The exam will start <u>at nine sharp</u>." (= *at the stroke of nine/at nine on the dot*)

1) I'll be back <u>in a trice</u>.
2) He was a member of that organization <u>right from the word 'go'</u>.
3) It rained for six days <u>at a stretch</u>.
4) I can't tell you his address <u>off the cuff</u>.
5) We worked <u>like hell</u> to meet the deadline.
6) The revolution spread <u>hand over fist</u> throughout the land.
7) The lift descended at a <u>cracking</u> pace.
8) We haven't time to <u>dilly-dally</u>.
9) You say he might help me – <u>that'll be the day</u>!
10) The bell for assembly has rung, get over there <u>at the double</u>!
11) There is a tornado <u>brewing</u>.
12) Before you could say <u>'knife'</u>, the thief had broken into the car and driven off.

→

B) Give colloquialisms for the following definitions.

1) a person who is slow.
2) a person or thing that is successful for only a very short time.
3) anything done quickly.
4) a very long time.
5) the final stage of something.
6) unrealistic promises or hopes.
7) a time long ago.

C) Insert an animal (or animals) to complete the following sentences.

1) The palace took . . . 's years to complete.
2) You can search until the . . . come home, it's not in the house.
3) Around 1900, cars went at a . . .'s pace.
4) Hold your . . . – we're not ready yet!
5) As for my wife passing her driving test, . . . might fly!
6) Don't count your . . . – there's a strong possibility we won't get any money.

D) Give colloquialisms containing the word 'time' or 'times' to fit the following definitions.

1) very quickly. 2) on countless occasions. 3) frequently or often. 4) at the last possible moment. 5) the closing hour of a bar.

E) Insert a period of time to complete the following sentences.

1) He will never climb that fence in a . . . of Sundays.
2) One a.m. is an ungodly . . . to be working.
3) The goalkeeper made a split- . . . decision to dive to his left.
4) The decision to sell the house was made on the spur of the . . . .
5) I haven't been swimming for . . . .
6) Since the suit is already being made, it's a bit late in the . . . to change your mind about the colour.
7) Wait a . . . ! You've given me the wrong letter.

Easiness/Difficulty

25: PLEASANT SITUATION

25/1 **Beer and skittles:** An enjoyable situation or time, without much hard labour. This expression is frequently used in a negative sense, as the example shows. □ When Karl left college and went out to work for the first time, he realized that life is not all beer and skittles.

25/2 **Everything in the garden is lovely:** Everything is splendid; there are no difficulties. □ The ambassador didn't claim that everything in the garden was lovely, but that the situation in his country wasn't as bad as it was painted in the press.

25/3 **A bed of roses:** A pleasant or enjoyable situation, with no problems. □ Being the mayor of a small town is a bed of roses compared with being mayor of New York.

25/4 **Not all roses** *or* **not all peaches and cream:** Pleasant or easy, but with some problems or disadvantages. □ A professional musician's life is not all peaches and cream (not all roses); there are many rehearsals and long periods away from home.

25/5 **Hunky-dory:** Favourable; without difficulties. □ The coming of 'glasnost' revealed that life in the Soviet Union was not as hunky-dory as Russian politicians had been claiming.

25/6 **In apple pie order:** In perfect order; without problems. □ The affairs of the company are now in apple pie order.

25/7 **Sitting pretty:** In a favourable or advantageous position. □ When oil prices rise, countries with large natural energy reserves are sitting pretty.

25/8 **Have a good thing going:** Have created a favourable situation or be in favourable circumstances. □ I used to complain about our National Health Service until I travelled in Africa; now I realize what a good thing we've got going.

25/9 **The party is over:** The pleasant or easy period has passed, and the difficulties are about to begin. □ The USA supported President Noriega of Panama, but when he became involved in drug smuggling, the White House decided that the party was over.

25/10 **The honeymoon is over:** The initial, easing-in period is over. □ Three months after becoming Prime Minister he realized from media criticism that the honeymoon was over.

26: EASY TASK

26/1 **Kid's stuff** *or* **child's play**: A very simple task. □ That crossword puzzle is child's play (kid's stuff).

26/2 **A doddle**: An easy task. □ The exam was a doddle.

26/3 **A cinch** *or* **a snip** *or* **a breeze** (*#US*): An easy task. (*For 'snip' see also 54/6*) □ Mending a puncture is not always a cinch (snip/breeze). □ I had no difficulty in doing it; it was a cinch (snip/breeze).

26/4 **A piece of cake**: A pleasant or easy task. □ Running a marathon is a piece of cake for an athlete of his calibre.

26/5 **Money for old rope** *or* **money for jam**: Easy money; money earned with little effort or trouble. □ That post of leisure adviser to the city is money for old rope (money for jam). □ Selling hamburgers from a prime position on the beach is money for old rope (money for jam).

26/6 **A push-over**: An easy task. (*See also 121/4*) □ Making the desert fertile is no push-over.

26/7 **Plain sailing**: A course of action or a task that is free from difficulties. □ The reform of local government wasn't plain sailing. □ Getting the bridge supports into position proved to be plain sailing.

26/8 **A picnic**: An easy task or something pleasant. □ The sea is rough and the salvage operation will be no picnic.

26/9 **Easy meat/game**: Something easily and quickly accomplished; someone easily conquered or beaten. □ Some garages leave tow-trucks near busy roundabouts to catch the easy meat (game) of cars that break down. □ Old people are easy game (meat) for fraudsters.

26/10 **A sitting duck**: A person or thing that is helpless and wide open to attack; an easy victim or target. □ Small but rich Kuwait was a sitting duck for the Iraqi army.

26/11 **Dead easy** *or* **easy-peasy**: Very easy. (*For 'dead' in the sense 'very', see 66/23*) □ Word processing is easy-peasy (dead easy).

26/12 **Easy as pie** *or* **easy as ABC** *or* **easy as falling off a log**: Very easy. □ Learning to swim is easy as falling off a log (easy as pie). □ The exam was as easy as pie (easy as ABC).

26/13 **Be able to do** something **standing on one's head** *or* **. . . with one hand tied behind one's back**: Be able to do something very easily. □ I've repaired so many water taps, I could do it with one hand tied behind my back (standing on my head).

26/14 **Open-and-shut**: Perfectly straightforward; presenting no difficulties or easily solved. □ The death was accidental, so the inquest will be an open-and-shut case.

26/15 **Walk it**: Encounter no difficulties; complete a task with ease. □ The exam was so easy – I walked it!

26/16 **No sweat!**: Said of an easy task which does not require much effort. □ Don't worry, he'll get your cat down from the tree, no sweat! □ She did it, no sweat!

26/17 **Hand** something **to** someone **on a plate**:   Make something available to someone without that person having to make much effort; make a task very easy for someone. □ The teacher said he would give his pupils a few hints about the coming exam, without handing it to them on a plate.

27: PROBLEM

27/1 **Be no object**:   Present no difficulty; not be an important or limiting factor. □ Mr Takakura is very rich and if he wants anything, money is no object.

27/2 **A hiccup**:   A minor difficulty or stoppage. □ We've had a few hiccups with the car, but nothing serious.

27/3 **A rub** *or* **a hitch**:   A temporary stoppage or difficulty. □ The road-works encountered a few hitches (rubs) due to buried cables and flooding.

27/4 **Hit a snag**:   Encounter an unexpected difficulty. □ Production hit a snag when a strike broke out in the factory. □ My application for a permit has hit a few administrative snags.

27/5 **Teething troubles**:   Initial difficulties; problems that arise in the early stages of an undertaking. □ Many newly-installed burglar alarm systems have their teething troubles, but subsequent adjustment usually solves the problem.

27/6 **Half the battle**:   Half of the problem solved; a great help towards success. □ Convincing the local authorities of the need for a new school was half the battle; there still remained the problem of raising the cash.

27/7 **A hot potato**:   A troublesome situation; a controversial issue or problem. *(See also 19/14)* □ The 'troubles' in Ulster are a hot potato for the British government.

27/8 **Strings attached**:   Several necessary conditions to be fulfilled. □ When the World Bank makes loans to developing countries there are often strings attached, such as political or economic reforms. □ You can purchase the washing-machine on interest-free credit and there are no strings attached.

27/9 **A liability**:   A handicap or disadvantage. □ Increased maintenance costs have made the property a liability and we should sell it.

27/10 **Saddled/lumbered/stuck** with a problem: Burdened with a problem or task. □ The country is saddled (lumbered/stuck) with massive foreign debts. □ They are a nice couple, but they are lumbered (stuck/saddled) with a rude and badly-behaved son.

27/11 **Wish** something **(up)on** someone: Burden someone with a problem. □ Every Friday evening they wished their awful child upon us while they went out. □ Cancer is a disease I wouldn't wish on my worst enemy.

27/12 **Play up**:   Cause problems; be mischievous or unruly. □ Grandfather's heart is playing up again. □ The children are playing up because they can't go out to play.

27/13 **Give** someone **a rough ride**:   Create a lot of difficulties for someone.
□ The government managed to get the bill through Congress, but the
opposition party gave them a rough ride.

27/14 **Give** someone **the run-around**:   Create problems for someone;
inconvenience. □ Customers with faulty goods are usually given the
run-around; the firm sends them from one department to another.

27/15 **Mess/jerk** (*#US*)/**muck** someone **around**:   Inconvenience someone
unnecessarily or without reason. □ Don't let anyone mess (muck/jerk)
you around!

27/16 **Iron out** a problem: Solve a problem. □ In previous summers, the
airport authority was able to iron out the problem of flight delays; this
year is different.

28: DIFFICULT TASK

28/1 **A tough nut (to crack)**:   A difficult task or problem to be solved. □ A
web of fictitious companies and complicated accounts made the case a
tough nut to crack for the Fraud Squad.

28/2 **A handful**:   A troublesome person or task. □ She's a tomboy and a
handful for any parents. □ Drop your other work and concentrate on the
fire-insurance claim; it's a handful on its own!

28/3 **A stinker**:   A very difficult task or question. □ The task of reviving the
economy is a stinker for any minister.

28/4 **A teaser**:   A tantalizingly difficult problem. □ Locating the strange noise
in my car proved to be a teaser for many months.

28/5 **Fight City Hall** (*US*):   Oppose an organization or body that is much
greater or more powerful than oneself. □ Victims of the Bhopal disaster
realized that they were fighting City Hall with their claims for
compensation from the multi-national chemical company.

28/6 **Up against it**:   Confronted with a difficult task or problem. □ The
Kurdish people are up against it in their struggle for an independent
state in the Middle East.

28/7 **Have one's work cut out**:   Be faced with a difficult task. □ Japanese and
Russian negotiators will have their work cut out to solve the border
dispute over the Kuril islands.

28/8 **Have a job to**:   Have difficulty in doing something. □ You'll have a job
to get to the lighthouse in this storm.

28/9 **Take a bit of doing**:   Be a difficult task. □ Convincing the judge that
she is innocent will take a bit of doing.

28/10 **Hard pushed/put/pressed**:   In great difficulty; under great pressure.
□ The shipyard will be hard put (pressed/pushed) to complete the tanker
before the planned launch date. □ Construction is behind schedule and
the firm is hard pressed (pushed/put) for both time and money.

28/11 **Break the back of:** Overcome the most difficult part of a task. □ It has taken months to introduce a computerized system in the accounts department, but we still haven't broken the back of the organizational problems.

28/12 **No joy-ride:** Not an easy or pleasant task. □ Building an airstrip in the malaria-infested jungle was no joy-ride.

28/13 **Fiddly:** Small and awkward to use or accomplish. □ The operation involves fiddly micro-surgery. □ I have large hands and find small tools fiddly.

28/14 **Go/jump in at the deep end:** Face the most difficult tasks at an early or unprepared stage; be prematurely confronted with advanced problems. □ Our travelling salesmen go (jump) in at the deep end; after only one day of training, they are sent out to sell to clients.

28/15 **Heavy/hard going:** Progress made with difficulty. □ 'Ulysses' by James Joyce is considered by many readers to be heavy (hard) going. □ Drilling the well-shaft through rock was heavy (hard) going.

28/16 **Make heavy weather of** a task: Have great difficulty in completing a relatively simple task. □ The double-glazing firm made heavy weather of installing the windows and had to return six times to correct their faults.

28/17 **Come hell or high water:** Whatever difficulties may occur. □ The weather was changing for the worse, but the climbers decided to make an attempt on the summit come hell or high water.

29: DIFFICULT SITUATION

29/1 **In a fix/jam/spot:** In a difficult or awkward situation. □ This family is really in a fix (spot/jam); they are to be evicted and have nowhere to live.

29/2 **In a pickle/the soup:** In great difficulties or trouble. □ Film producers were in a pickle (the soup) when the star actor died in the middle of shooting the film.

29/3 **In Queer Street:** In difficulties, trouble or debt. Queer Street is thought to be a corruption of Carey Street, the London street where bankruptcy cases were heard in court. □ If you are paying off a large mortgage, the smallest financial set-back, such as an interest-rate increase, can put you in Queer Street.

29/4 **Up a gum tree:** In great difficulties. □ Many firms, which invested heavily in expectation of an improvement in the economy, were up a gum tree when the recession continued.

29/5 **Up the spout:** In a hopeless situation; ruined. (*See also 188/23*) □ Fruit bushes are blossoming and the fruit growers will be up the spout if we get a late frost.

29/6 **Up the creek (without a paddle):** In difficulties. There are many variations of this expression, using rivers such as the Nile, Amazon etc., and other synonyms for the 'paddle', depending on the circumstances. □ If I don't get paid soon I'll be up the creek (up the creek without a paddle). □ Owing to an international trade boycott, the country's economy was up the Limpopo without navigating equipment.

29/7 **Bat on a sticky wicket:** Be in an unfavourable or difficult position. Refers to a wet cricket pitch, where conditions for the batsman are not favourable. □ Our ship-building industry has been batting on a sticky wicket for years; we just can't compete with heavily-subsidized foreign yards.

29/8 **A sticky patch:** A difficult or unfavourable period. □ Her work has deteriorated lately, but she's going through a sticky patch at home, on account of family illness.

29/9 **Drop** someone **in it** *or* **. . . in the shit** (*#?*): Place someone in a very difficult or embarrassing situation. □ Leaked information about a secret committee meeting dropped the government minister in the shit (in it).

29/10 **Go (put** someone) **through the mill:** Undergo (or make someone undergo) a difficult period of discipline or suffering. □ All police recruits go (are put) through the mill at police academy. □ I went (was put) through the mill during the exam.

29/11 **In deep water:** In difficulties. □ Business was good at the beginning of the year, but we're now in deep water because of increased competition.

29/12 **Get into hot water/a scrape:** Get into trouble or disgrace as a result of one's actions. □ In his teens, Ramiz was always getting into scrapes (hot water) with the police.

29/13 **A pretty pass:** A difficult state of affairs. □ Since Mr Schenk's partner left him, his business has come to a pretty pass.

29/14 **Sink or swim:** In a desperate situation, one must resort to desperate remedies. □ Many of the landed gentry disliked opening their estates to the public, but in view of inflated maintenance costs, it was sink or swim.

29/15 **Out on a limb:** Isolated and in a vulnerable or difficult position; separated from others and open to attack. □ Satellite states and economically-dependent countries often endorse the policies of the dominant power in the region, so as not to put themselves out on a limb.

29/16 **Have no come-back:** Have no rights or means of redressing the situation. □ You should have complained about the defective food mixer within the guarantee period; now you have no come-back.

29/17 **Tough/rough on** someone: Difficult for someone. □ It's tough (rough) on the kids now their parents have divorced.

29/18 **A Catch-22 situation:** A vicious circle; a problematic situation which appears insoluble. From Joseph Heller's novel 'Catch-22' (1961). □ Homeless people often find themselves in a Catch-22 situation: they can't afford lodgings, and employers won't hire them without a fixed abode.

29/19 **Out of the woods:** Clear of danger or difficulty. □ Romanians believed that the revolution against Ceausescu would solve all their problems, but they soon realized that they weren't out of the woods yet.

29/20 **A bad job:** An unfavourable or regrettable situation; a difficult person. □ It's a bad job when a woman can't walk the streets at night. □ I didn't learn much at school; teachers gave me up as a bad job.

EXERCISES 6: EASINESS/DIFFICULTY

A) From the module, give colloquialisms for the following underlined text, placing the verb in the correct tense, and rephrasing where necessary. For example: "<u>The easy period</u> will soon be over for them." (= *The party* (*The honeymoon*) *will soon be over for them.*)

1) They <u>caused me unnecessary inconvenience</u>.
2) She can do it <u>without the slightest difficulty</u>.
3) We <u>encountered several unexpected difficulties</u>.
4) The offer was genuine and there were no <u>conditions to be fulfilled</u>.
5) I <u>solved</u> the problems.
6) We <u>opposed an organization much greater than ourselves</u>.
7) He has <u>mastered the most difficult part</u> of the language.
8) They <u>made me undergo a very difficult period</u>.
9) They will have to <u>face the most difficult tasks at an early stage</u>.
10) With regard to her critics, she <u>had no support and is in a very vulnerable position</u> with her theory.

B) Give colloquialisms for the following definitions.

1) a minor difficulty.
2) difficulties at the beginning of an enterprise. →

3) a situation where the solution to a problem leads back to the original problem.
4) a very difficult task or question.
5) a controversial problem.
6) everything is splendid.

C) Insert articles of food or drink to complete the following sentences.

1) They are leading a life of ... and skittles.
2) My job is not all ... and ... .
3) Everything is in ... – ... order.
4) The task is a piece of ... .
5) The exam was as easy as ... .
6) We earned a lot, it was money for ... .
7) He has enough problems, he's in the ... already.
8) This jigsaw puzzle is a tough ... to crack.

D) From the module, give as many colloquialisms as possible to complete the following sentences.

1) Getting there by metro was as easy as ... .
2) The repair was easy, it was a ... .
3) He is in a difficult situation – he really is in ... .
4) We are ... with this problem and have to solve it.
5) You will be hard ... to complete the work on time.

E) In the following sentences, one word of each colloquialism has been used incorrectly. Give the correct form of the expression.

1) Building the cabin was plain going and we finished early.
2) The burglary is an open-and-closed case for the police.
3) They promised to help me, but they were just messing me up.
4) You think you are safe, but you are not out of the water yet.
5) Good preparation is half the conflict.
6) Our company is batting on a sticky patch because of crippling taxation.

Chaos/Quarrel/Responsibility

30: CHAOS/MESS

30/1   A **right old/an unholy/a fine** mess: A very great mess. *(For 'unholy' see also 32/1 and 65/5)* □ The room was in a right old (an unholy/fine) mess.

30/2   A **shambles**:   A scene or condition of great disorder. □ The government's foreign policy is a shambles.

30/3   **Shambolic**:   Chaotic or disorganized (from 'shambles'). □ Our filing system is shambolic.

30/4   **Dog's/pig's breakfast** *or* **dog's dinner**:   A mess. □ Computer viruses are making a dog's dinner (breakfast) of our print-outs.

30/5   **Pretty kettle of fish**:   A chaotic or difficult state of affairs. *(Do not confuse with 'different kettle of fish' – 72/7)* □ The one-way traffic system in the city is a pretty kettle of fish.

30/6   **A fine how-d'ye-do**:   A confused or difficult state of affairs. □ Management decided to leave the supermarket open for business during the renovation and are responsible for the fine how-d'ye-do that has resulted.

30/7   **Bedlam/a madhouse**:   Total chaos or uproar. □ Many airport departure lounges are absolute bedlam during peak holiday periods. □ The shop was like a madhouse when its winter sale began.

30/8   **Panic stations**:   Panic or chaos. Refers literally to the positions taken up during an emergency on a ship, plane etc. □ It was panic stations among the students when they heard how close the exam date was.

30/9   **At sixes and sevens**:   In disorder or chaos. □ Reorganization of the bus routes has put the timetable at sixes and sevens.

30/10   **Higgledy-piggledy** *or* **hugger-mugger** *or* **topsy-turvy**:   In utter disorder. *(For 'hugger-mugger' see also 123/2)* □ The burglar had left all Anna's belongings higgledy-piggledy (hugger-mugger/topsy-turvy) on the floor.

30/11   **All over the shop/place**:   Scattered everywhere in great disorder. *(See also 147/21)* □ I forgot to close the office window before I went to lunch, and my documents have been blown all over the place (shop).

30/12   **Murphy's law** *or* **Sod's law**:   Humorous pessimistic rule that if something is capable of going wrong, it will. □ While we were inflating the hot-air balloon for the journey, we became victims of Murphy's law (Sod's law); a gust of wind blew it into the sea.

30/13   **Go to pieces**:   Become disorganized or collapse; lose one's composure. □ Ulrich went to pieces after his divorce.

30/14 **Go off the rails**: Become disorganized or out of control; go crazy.
□ The house-building programme began well but later went off the rails.

30/15 **Throw a spanner in the works**: Ruin a scheme or someone's plans, not necessarily deliberately. □ She planned to emigrate, but her father's death threw a spanner in the works.

30/16 **Play hell/havoc with** something: Damage or disorganize something. □ Working with asbestos can play hell (havoc) with your health.

31: FUSS/TROUBLE

31/1 **Raise Cain/hell/a hell of a stink**: Create an uproar. □ We've been on the housing-list for three years: I'm sure the only way to get a flat is to raise Cain (hell/a hell of a stink) at the housing office.

31/2 **Kick up a rumpus**: Create an uproar. □ If dinner is not ready when my husband comes home from work, he always kicks up a rumpus.

31/3 **Make a song and dance/a to-do** about something: Make a great fuss or commotion. □ I forgot to buy bread but don't make a song and dance (a to-do) about it! I'll go again.

31/4 A **palaver** *or* a **faff**: A fuss (often unnecessary and elaborate). *(See 23/5)* The word 'palaver' originated from the 'palavers' or talks between European traders and primitive African tribes. □ Getting a refund for the faulty goods was a palaver – the sales clerk faffed around for ages.

31/5 A **kerfuffle/hoo-ha**: Fuss or commotion. □ There was a bit of a hoo-ha (kerfuffle) in the market when a woman claimed she had been robbed.

31/6 A **carry-on**: A fuss or loud complaint. To make such a complaint or fuss is to 'carry on'. *(See also 188/8)* □ What a carry-on she's making about her lost cat!

31/7 A **ballyhoo**: A loud noise or fuss; extravagant publicity. □ There has been a lot of ballyhoo about some new wonder drug.

31/8 **Raise a hue and cry**: Pursue wrongdoer noisily. □ When her bag was snatched, bystanders raised a hue and cry.

31/9 A **fusspot**: Someone who habitually creates a fuss.

31/10 **Stir it up**: Create trouble or a fuss. □ Elfriede is always stirring it up with her malicious gossip.

31/11 **Make things hum**: Create activity or a fuss. □ The announcement that there would be no wage rise that year made things hum among the staff.

31/12 **Ructions/blue murder/fireworks**: Loud protests or noisy argument. □ When Oscar came home late and his wife noticed that he had been drinking, there were fireworks (ructions/there was blue murder).

31/13 **All hell broke loose**: There was a state of uproar or extreme disorder. □ At the news that the Turkish janissaries were nearing Vienna, all hell broke loose in the city.

31/14 **Trouble at t'mill**: Trouble or uproar somewhere (usually at home or at work). "T'mill" is an imitation of a Lancashire accent and alludes to labour unrest in the cotton mills of the last century. □ There'll be trouble at t'mill if I'm late home again tonight!

31/15 **A hassle**: A quarrel or harassment; unnecessary inconvenience. The corresponding verb, 'to hassle' means to cause someone inconvenience. □ What with security checks and flight delays, we had a lot of hassle at the airport.

31/16 **Aggro**: Deliberate trouble-making; unnecessary aggravation. □ Before and after the football match, the police had to deal with outbreaks of aggro around the central station.

31/17 **Rent-a-mob**: A mob or gang of trouble-makers hired or brought in to create uproar or a disturbance. Alludes to the name of several hire companies e.g. 'Rent-a-Car'. □ It was claimed that the crowd outside the parliament were not genuinely anti-government protesters, but rent-a-mob brought in by the opposition.

31/18 **A storm in a teacup**: A great fuss or agitation over a trivial matter. □ The diplomatic protests about two of our planes crossing temporarily into their airspace are a storm in a teacup.

31/19 **Make a Federal case of** something (*US*): Make an exaggerated fuss about something. □ I broke the window accidentally, so don't make a Federal case of it.

31/20 **Make waves/a splash**: Create a disturbance. □ The collapse of such an established bank made waves (a splash) in financial circles.

31/21 **Come as a bombshell** *or* **drop a bomb**: Cause a sensation; come as a great surprise or shock. □ The news that the deputy minister was a foreign spy came as a bombshell. □ The deputy minister dropped a bomb by admitting that he was a foreign spy.

32: DISPUTE/QUARREL

32/1   An **almighty/unholy** row *or* a **stand-up/blazing** row: A very great row or quarrel. *(For 'almighty' see 65/4)* □ The couple were having an unholy row which could be heard by their neighbours over the road.

32/2   **Ding-dong**: With vigorous and alternating participation in a row or struggle. □ Two women were having a ding-dong quarrel. □ The race was a ding-dong battle between the two Kenyans.

32/3   **Hammer and tongs**: Arguing or quarrelling with great energy or vigour. *(See also 4/16)* □ In the Middle Ages, Lutherans and Catholics used to argue hammer and tongs with each other about the Reformation.

32/4   An **argy-bargy**: A heated argument. □ At the disco, an argy-bargy arose over a drink spilt accidentally.

32/5   A **barney**: A verbal dispute which may be amicable. □ Three men at a café table were having a barney about politics.

32/6   A **shindig/shindy**: A heated argument or brawl. □ A diplomatic shindy (shindig) broke out at the United Nations.

32/7   A **bust-up**: A quarrel. □ He's not speaking to me; we had a bust-up over money.

32/8   A **slanging-match**: A prolonged exchange of insults. □ An argument between the two motorists over who had the right of way soon deteriorated into a slanging-match.

32/9   A **tiff**: A petty quarrel. □ It's not a serious quarrel between them, just a lovers' tiff.

32/10   **Have a bone to pick with** someone: Have something specific to argue or complain about. □ I've a bone to pick with you about revealing information given to you in confidence.

32/11   **Unfinished business**: A quarrel or complaint against someone which is yet to be settled. □ The legal dispute over water rights had been settled in court, but one farmer still had private unfinished business on account of insults.

32/12   **Have words**: Argue or quarrel. □ I had words with my neighbours about the loud music they played late at night.

32/13   **At loggerheads**: Arguing to the point of impasse. □ Local people and industry are at loggerheads about a toxic-waste incinerator on the coast.

32/14   **Make something of it**: Provoke a quarrel. □ "I was here before you." "So, do you want to make something of it?"

32/15   **Split hairs**: Argue or quibble about something completely trifling or unimportant; make petty distinctions in an argument. □ Let's not split hairs! Strictly speaking a tomato may be a vegetable and not a fruit, but you know what I mean.

32/16   **Set the cat among the pigeons**: Provoke quarrelling or argument. □ The debate with the property owners about buying up their land was good-natured until the town council set the cat among the pigeons with the mention of a possible compulsory purchase.

32/17 **Tangle with** someone: Become involved in a quarrel or dispute with someone. □ The Minister for the Interior is a very powerful man, and you would be well-advised not to tangle with him.

32/18 **Patch up** a quarrel: Settle a quarrel or dispute. □ The two communities are trying to patch up their differences and live together in peace.

32/19 **Dead and buried**:   (Of a quarrel or dispute) Long forgotten or settled. □ The dispute between Germany and France over Alsace-Lorraine is dead and buried.

33: RESPONSIBILITY/BUSINESS

33/1 Someone's **baby/pigeon/look-out**:   Someone's responsibility or business. □ Locking the warehouse at night is the caretaker's pigeon (baby/look-out), not mine.

33/2 Someone's **funeral**:   Someone's unpleasant responsibility or concern. □ The tide is coming in fast and it's dangerous to cross the mud-flats; if you do, it'll be your funeral!

33/3 **A hot seat**:   A position or job with difficult responsibilities. □ A series of food-poisoning scares has made the post of Minister of Agriculture a hot seat.

33/4 **Not be in the business of** something: Have no intention of doing something; not occupy oneself with something. □ The US president claimed that his country was not in the business of being a world policeman.

33/5 **Have an axe to grind**:   Be involved in something and be anxious to protect one's personal interests; have personal or ulterior motives. □ UN peace-keeping forces in the region should be from neutral countries with no axe to grind.

33/6 **Have no business/call to** do something: Have no right or responsibility to do something. □ You've got no business (no call) to say such nasty things about her!

33/7 **Have a finger in the pie**:   Be actively involved in a project or lucrative undertaking. □ The industrialist had his finger in many pies, ranging from textiles to electronics.

33/8 **Have other fish to fry**:   Have more advantageous things to do. □ Work late if you want to but don't expect me to help – I've got other fish to fry.

33/9 **The ball is in** someone's **court**:   It is now someone's turn or responsibility to act. Alludes to the necessity of a tennis-player to return a ball that lands in his half of the court. □ Mechanics had worked for a month to get the car ready for the Grand Prix and now the ball was in the driver's court.

33/10 **Be up to someone**:   Be someone's responsibility. □ It will be up to you to check the stock levels every day.

33/11 Do one's stuff: Carry out or perform one's duty. □ Don't worry – I know my job and I'll do my stuff when the time comes.

33/12 Off one's own bat: Taking all responsibility on oneself without any assistance or prompting. □ If I do need more stock, I'll order it off my own bat rather than ask someone else for permission.

33/13 Hold the fort: Look after a place; perform the duties of others while they are absent; act as a temporary substitute for someone. □ My parents have gone away for the weekend and left me at home to hold the fort.

33/14 The buck stops here: This is where the responsibility or blame lies. The expression is assigned to President Truman, a keen poker player. The 'buck' is not a dollar, but a marker placed before the dealer in poker. □ After financial losses, and realizing that the buck stopped with him, the manager resigned.

33/15 Pass the buck: Shift responsibility or blame to someone else. □ The art of succeeding in politics is to pass the buck when one makes a mistake.

33/16 A . . . -merchant *or* **a . . . -monger:** Someone fond of a certain activity; someone responsible for a lot of something. □ That driver is a speed-merchant. □ The woman is a scandal-monger and is always causing trouble.

33/17 Poke one's nose into someone's **business:** Pry or intrude into the affairs of someone else. □ Tell Nazar not to poke his nose into my business!

33/18 A nosy parker: An inquisitive or meddlesome person; someone who pries into the personal affairs of others.

33/19 A busybody: A meddlesome person.

33/20 Snoop: Pry inquisitively. The person doing this is a 'snooper'. □ The farmer caught a gipsy snooping around the poultry yard.

33/21 Muscle into something: Force one's way into someone else's business or commercial affairs. □ In the USA, racketeers muscled into many profitable companies.

EXERCISES 7: CHAOS/QUARREL/RESPONSIBILITY

A) In the following sentences, replace the underlined word or phrase with a colloquialism containing one or more hyphens. For example: "The crowd disturbances were caused by a hired mob." (= *rent-a-mob*)

1) They were having a heated argument.
2) We had a great row.
3) The room was in great disorder.

→

4) We lost all our customer files during the fire and our documentation was a fine mess.
5) Don't make such a fuss about the faulty lock! It will be repaired.
6) It was a closely fought contest.

B) Replace the underlined phrase with one or more colloquialisms from the module, taking care to place the verb in the correct tense.

1) The two old enemies settled their long-standing quarrel.
2) You have ruined our efforts.
3) The labourers created a disturbance when they were not paid on time.
4) He let you do it without asking anyone for permission.
5) We have a complaint to discuss with you about your rudeness.
6) The two of them are in serious disagreement with each other.
7) When he makes a mistake, he shifts the blame to others.
8) You can go for lunch now, this other sales-girl will look after things while you are away.

C) Insert an animal or a person to complete the following sentences.

1) That woman gossips about everyone, she is just a slander- ... .
2) When our neighbour uses his drill, our TV picture becomes a ...'s breakfast.
3) That is not my business, it's your ... !
4) You shouldn't have told him about it – now you have set the ... among the ... s.
5) I can't stay here, I have other ... to fry.
6) Something is certain to go wrong, it's ...'s law.
7) The taxi driver wanted his fare and I couldn't find my money; it was a pretty kettle of ... .

D) Insert a colloquialism containing two nouns or two adjectives linked by the conjunction 'and'.

1) They will make a ... and ... about you being so late home.
2) He is a bad manager and his affairs are at ... and ... .
3) The two men could be heard quarrelling ... and ... in the next room.
4) The dispute between them was settled a long time ago and it is now ... and ... .

E) Give colloquialisms to fit the following definitions.

1) someone who is always making a fuss.
2) an interfering, meddlesome person.
3) unnecessary fuss or inconvenience.
4) deliberate trouble-making.
5) a great fuss about something relatively unimportant.
6) trouble or uproar at a particular place.

The Law

34: CRIME/OFFENCES

34/1 **Do a job**: Commit a crime, especially a robbery or burglary.
□ Giovanni admitted that the jewels were from a job he had done.

34/2 **Stick-up**: An armed robbery. □ Customers who were in the bank during the stick-up had to lie on the floor.

34/3 **A heist** *(US)*: A robbery. □ Up till then, the Chase Manhattan heist had been the biggest bank robbery in the country.

34/4 **An inside job**: A crime committed by someone living or working in the premises (i.e. an 'insider') where it occurred. □ The robbery was clearly an inside job, since the raiders knew the shift-patterns of the security guards as well as the alarm system.

34/5 **Roll** someone *(#US)*: Attack and rob. □ Don't go there at night! You can easily get rolled by drug addicts seeking cash.

34/6 **Knock off/whip/nick/pinch/swipe**: Steal or pilfer. □ Raiders rammed a stolen car into the shop window and knocked off (whipped/nicked/ swiped/pinched) the displayed electrical goods.

34/7 **Case a joint**: Inspect premises or a building for the purposes of a criminal offence. □ The gang cased the joint for a week before attempting the robbery.

34/8 **Rip off** something: Steal or defraud. The corresponding noun is a 'rip-off'. *(See also 58/3)* □ Pawnbrokers are often offered goods that have been ripped off.

34/9 **Lift** something: Steal or copy from another source. A 'shoplifter' is someone who steals from shops while posing as a legitimate customer.
□ You can't tell me this microwave oven hasn't been lifted!

34/10 **Fall off the back of a lorry**: Be stolen or obtained under dubious circumstances. □ He can sell you some cheap power-tools that fell off the back of a lorry.

34/11 **Hot** goods: Stolen goods. □ That consignment of cigarettes is hot!

34/12 **Launder money**: Conceal the source and nature of illegally obtained money by moving it between different financial institutions. □ Drug dealers attempt to cover up the crime by laundering their profits.

34/13 **A hit-and-run** case: A vehicle accident where the guilty driver leaves the scene without stopping to report the incident. □ The cyclist found dead in a country lane was the victim of a hit-and-run driver.

34/14 **Joy-riding**: Taking a motor vehicle without the owner's consent for the purposes of a pleasure ride. The person doing this is a 'joy-rider'. □ At night the empty car park was often used for joy-riding.

34/15 **Graft**:   Bribery or corruption. *(See also 2/5)* □ Graft in high office must be eradicated.

34/16 **Grease** someone's **palm** *or* **give** someone **a back-hander**:   Bribe someone. □ It's a country where you have to grease every official's palm (give every official a back-hander) to get anything done!

34/17 **Touting**:   The illegal soliciting of business by street-traders, prostitutes etc. The person doing this is a 'tout'. □ Football fans without tickets were approached by ticket-touts. □ The cell was full of prostitutes who had been arrested for touting.

34/18 **Kerb-crawl**:   Drive around slowly, looking to pick up prostitutes. A driver doing this is known as a 'kerb-crawler'. □ Women returning to the estate late at night are being accosted by kerb-crawlers.

34/19 **Fly-tipping**:   The illegal dumping of refuse in public places or beauty spots. □ The river has been disfigured by fly-tipping near the bridge.

34/20 **Fly-posting**:   The unauthorized displaying of advertisement bills or other notices, usually in public places. □ During elections, fly-posting of propaganda adverts increases dramatically.

34/21 **Jay-walking**:   Walking carelessly in a road, without regard for traffic or signals. This kind of reckless pedestrian is a 'jay-walker'. □ The lights at the pedestrian crossing showed red, but several jay-walkers could be seen crossing.

34/22 **Computer hacking**:   The unauthorized access of computer files via another computer. The person doing this is called a 'computer hacker'. □ An investigation revealed that computer hackers and not foreign agents had gained access to the top-secret database.

35: CRIMINALS/TOOLS

35/1 **Bent/crooked**:   Dishonest. *(For 'bent' in the sense of sexually perverted, see 187/25)* □ Bent (crooked) policemen give the force a bad name.

35/2 **A crook**:   A rogue or criminal.

35/3 **A hustler** *(#US)*:   A person living by dishonesty or theft, a swindler. To live in this manner is to 'hustle'. The American usage also encompasses gamblers in pool halls, and prostitutes.

35/4 **A mugger**:   A criminal who robs his victims violently, usually in public places. To 'mug' a person is to rob someone in this way. □ Central Park can be dangerous at night because of muggers.

35/5 **A yob/yobbo**:   A lout or hooligan. Yob is 'boy' spelt backwards, in the sense of a backward boy.

35/6 **A punk**:   A worthless person or young ruffian (as distinct from a devotee of punk-rock music).

35/7 **A lager-lout**:   A young (lager-)drunken hooligan. □ Some Spanish holiday resorts have a problem with lager-louts.

35/8   **A hoodlum**:   A hooligan, young thug or gangster.

35/9   **A hood**:   A gangster or gunman.

35/10   **The Mob**:   The Mafia. Members of the Mob are called 'mobsters'.
□ The Mob has divided up the city among themselves into 'spheres of interest'.

35/11   **A cat-burglar**:   A burglar who enters premises by climbing walls, drainpipes etc.

35/12   **A fire-bug**:   An arsonist; someone who maliciously sets fire to buildings or property. □ The forest fires were not due to natural causes, but the work of fire-bugs.

35/13   **A fence**:   A person who knowingly buys and then sells on stolen goods.
□ The paintings are famous, and it will be extremely difficult for the thieves to find a fence for them.

35/14   **A spiv**:   A black-marketeer or dishonest salesman, especially one smartly dressed. □ Visitors to several hotels in central Sofia are continually pestered by currency-spivs seeking to purchase dollars.

35/15   **A prowler**:   Someone who stalks an area, usually at night, for an illicit or criminal purpose. □ Residents were advised to draw their curtains and keep their doors locked at night because of prowlers.

35/16   **A road-hog**:   A reckless or inconsiderate driver. □ I'm surprised he hasn't crashed his car – he's a thorough road-hog.

35/17   **The straight and narrow**:   An honest law-abiding life. Here, 'straight' does not mean 'without bends', but 'honest' – in an allusion to the 'straight and narrow' principles of the Bible. □ That rogue left the straight and narrow a long time ago.

35/18   **Go straight**:   Give up a criminal way of life. □ Franco promised that he would go straight after serving his prison sentence.

35/19   **Jelly**:   Gelignite; explosives. □ The thieves cracked the safe with jelly.

35/20   **A jemmy** *or* a **jimmy** *(US)*:   A short crowbar used by burglars to gain entry. To open with this tool is to 'jemmy/jimmy open'. □ The door had been jemmied open.

35/21   **A shooter**:   A gun or pistol. □ It's easy for a criminal to buy a shooter.

36: POLICE/DETECTION

36/1   **The Law/the Bill**:   The police. □ That's a job for the Law (the Bill).

36/2   The **fuzz/cops/coppers/boys in blue**:   The police or policemen. □ The fuzz (cops/coppers) were swarming all over the scene of the robbery.

36/3   **A pig**:   An abusive term for a policeman.

36/4   **A dick**:   A detective.

36/5   **A cop-shop**:   A police station.

36/6   **A black Maria** *or* a **paddy wagon** *(#US)*:   Secure police van for the transport of prisoners.

36/7 **Pull in/run in/nick/cop/nab/pinch** someone: Arrest. □ Mrs Rodrigues is a kleptomaniac and is always being pulled in (run in/nabbed/ nicked/ copped/pinched) for shop-lifting.

36/8 **Bust/do** someone: Charge someone with an offence or fine someone. □ Sasha has been bust (done) three times already for speeding.

36/9 **Nail** someone: Arrest and convict someone. □ Although the drugs-baron was well known to police, he was not easy to nail.

36/10 **A bust**: A police raid, especially on illegal premises. □ Hong Kong police decided to carry out a bust on the opium den during daylight hours.

36/11 **A fair cop**: An indisputably fair arrest, especially when someone is arrested in the act of committing a crime. □ The burglar said to police "OK, it's a fair cop" after being cornered in the warehouse.

36/12 **Catch red-handed**: Catch in the act of a crime or offence. □ Every year, thousands of TV licence-dodgers are caught red-handed by detector vans outside their homes.

36/13 **Turn over** a place: Search thoroughly by moving everything. □ The dissident said that his flat had been regularly turned over by the KGB.

36/14 **Frisk** someone: Search someone quickly by passing one's hands over him, in search of concealed weapons or contraband. □ Every passenger was frisked before getting on to the plane.

36/15 **A minder**: A bodyguard; someone assigned to watch over another. □ Those two men in raincoats just behind the President are probably his minders.

36/16 **A private eye**: A private detective. □ Divorce cases provide a lot of work for private eyes.

36/17 **A mug-shot**: A photo of a criminal in police files. □ The victim looked through some mug-shots to see if she could recognize her attacker.

36/18 A **rap-sheet**:   A police record of someone's criminal history. □ He is an inveterate fraudster with a rap-sheet as long as your arm.

36/19 **Grass** on someone: Betray a conspiracy or turn informer. The informer is a 'grass'. *(See also 'supergrass' – 36/25)* □ Reward money induced him to grass on the gang.

36/20 **Squeal/sing/split/cough/snitch** on someone: Become an informer or inform on someone. A 'snitch' is an informer. □ The police knew of our plans to rob the warehouse because someone had squealed (snitched/sung/split/coughed) on us.

36/21 **Shop** someone: Inform on someone. □ Natasha shopped her husband after seeing TV pictures of the battered victim.

36/22 **Rat on** someone: Inform on someone; withdraw treacherously from an undertaking. □ Allied prisoners knew that one of their mates had ratted on them by informing the Japanese of the planned break-out.

36/23 A **stool-pigeon**:   Someone acting as a decoy to trap a criminal, *or* a police informer. □ Plain-clothes detectives are secretive about stool-pigeons in order to preserve their confidence. □ A policewoman acting as a stool-pigeon lured the rapist into the hands of the waiting detectives.

36/24 A **fink/copper's nark**:   A police informer. □ The murderers said that their victim had been a fink (copper's nark).

36/25 A **supergrass**:   Someone who informs or 'grasses' on a large number of persons. *(See also 36/19)* □ The Mafia supergrass was given an armed guard under the Witness Protection Scheme.

36/26 A **mole**:   Someone working within an organization in order to spy on it for another organization or foreign power. □ The top-secret radio-monitoring station in Cyprus has its own department of mole-hunters.

37: TRIAL/PRISON

37/1 **Have** someone **up**:   Bring a person before a court of justice or an interviewer. □ Miguel was had up for car theft last week.

37/2 **Pin** something **on** someone: Convict of a crime; make someone responsible for something. □ For a while I thought the police were trying to pin the theft on me.

37/3 **Make** something **stick**:   Establish a charge against someone as valid. □ It's one thing to accuse someone of libel, quite another thing to make it stick.

37/4 A **beak**:   A magistrate or judge. □ Susi appeared before a beak on the very same day of the theft.

37/5 A **frame-up/set-up**:   The arrangement of false evidence against an innocent person. *(See also 10/1)* □ Some experts claim that the trial of Lee Harvey Oswald for the murder of President Kennedy was a frame-up (set-up).

37/6 **Set** someone **up** *or* **frame** someone: Incriminate an innocent person.
▢ Luc claimed that the break-in had been committed by a neighbour,
who had subsequently set him up (framed him) with false testimony.

37/7 **Plant** evidence: Place objects of potential evidence so as to incriminate
an innocent person. Any evidence of this nature is a 'plant'. ▢ In court
the accused pleaded that the heroin had been planted in his flat.

37/8 A **kangaroo court**: An illegal court where justice is improbable. ▢ The
doctor alleged that the committee that had banned him from practice
was a kangaroo court not authorized by the Medical Commission.

37/9 A **clean slate**: A record of good conduct; no police record or criminal
history. ▢ After years of crime, Wang decided to start again with a clean
slate in another country.

37/10 **Get** someone **off**: Obtain an acquittal or not-guilty verdict. ▢ The
charges are serious and Brigitte's lawyer will find it difficult to get her
off.

37/11 **In the clear**: Free from suspicion of involvement in a crime. ▢ The
suspect is now in the clear; his alibi for the time of the crime has been
confirmed.

37/12 **The clink/jug/nick/slammer/quod/can** *(US)*: Prison. ▢ Schneider is due
to be released from the clink (jug/nick/slammer/can/quod) next week.
▢ The protesters were thrown into the clink (jug etc.).

37/13 **Clap** someone **in gaol/jail**: Throw someone into prison. The spelling
'jail' is less usual in British English, but normal elsewhere. ▢ Nowadays
debtors are not just clapped immediately into gaol (jail).

37/14 **Put** someone **away**: Put into prison or an institution for the mentally
ill. ▢ When their schizophrenic son started to become violent, they
decided to have him put away. ▢ The magistrate told the accused that if
the offence happened again, he would be put away.

37/15 **Get/be sent down**: Be or get sentenced to a term of imprisonment.
▢ The fraudster got (was) sent down for three years.

37/16 **Inside**: In gaol. ▢ Günther has been inside so long, he's forgotten what
beer tastes like. ▢ You can be put inside for that offence!

37/17 **Do time/bird/porridge**: Serve a prison sentence. ▢ He's doing bird
(time/porridge) for assault and battery.

37/18 A **stretch**: A period of imprisonment or service. ▢ I expected only a
large fine, instead the court gave me a six-month stretch.

37/19 A **screw**: A prison officer. ▢ Three screws were held hostage during the
prison riot.

37/20 A **gaolbird/jailbird**: A prisoner or ex-prisoner; someone who is
frequently in prison (gaol). ▢ Frank is an out-and-out gaol(jail)bird –
he's spent most of his life inside.

37/21 A **lifer**: A prisoner serving a life sentence. ▢ Lifers are housed in a
separate wing.

37/22 An **old lag**: An old convict *or* one that has served several prison
sentences.

EXERCISES 8: THE LAW

A) The following definitions consist of (or contain) a creature. Name them. For example: "Illegal posting of advertisements and bills." (= *fly-posting*).

1) an unknown enemy agent working within the organization on which he is spying.
2) an agile burglar that enters premises by climbing.
3) an arsonist.
4) an inconsiderate driver.
5) an abusive term for a policeman.
6) illegal dumping of rubbish.
7) a careless or inconsiderate pedestrian.
8) a court without correct proceedings or proper authority.
9) to betray someone to the police or authorities.
10) serve a prison sentence.

B) Give as many colloquial synonyms as possible to replace the underlined word, placing any verbs in the same tense as the example.

1) Those goods he sold me had been <u>stolen</u> the day before.
2) The thieves had already left when the <u>police</u> arrived.
3) The counterfeiter was <u>arrested</u> last night.
4) You risk being sent to <u>jail</u> for a year.
5) One of the robbers <u>betrayed</u> the rest of the gang.

C) The following list consists of persons on both sides of the law. Give colloquialisms for these definitions.

1) a drunken hooligan.   2) a receiver of stolen goods.   3) a bodyguard.   4) a private detective.   5) a magistrate.   6) a prison warder.   7) a convict.   8) a criminal who informs on a large number of others.   9) a violent street-robber.   10) the Mafia.

D) Give colloquialisms to fit the underlined phrases, rephrasing where necessary.

1) The cassette-recorders <u>were obtained under doubtful circumstances</u>.
2) That business <u>legitimizes illegally obtained money</u>.
3) Thieves <u>gave the security guard a bribe</u> to look the other way.
4) Before they carried out the bank raid, the robbers had <u>inspected the premises</u> thoroughly.
5) Some safe-breakers get caught <u>in the act of committing their crime</u>.
6) When he got married, he <u>gave up his life of crime</u>.
7) The prisoner claims that the police have <u>falsely incriminated him</u>.
8) He has <u>no criminal record</u> and he doesn't appear in the <u>police photo files</u>.

Importance/Violence

38: IMPORTANT

38/1 **The top brass**: High-ranking officers or officials. Originally a military term alluding to the gold braid of an officer's hat. □ All the top brass of the army and the party apparatus attended the May Day parade.

38/2 **A bigwig**: An important person. The term derives from the wigs worn by British barristers and judges: a commonly held view was that the importance of a lawyer could be assessed by the size of his wig. □ Her career went from office clerk to a bigwig in the Ministry of Education.

38/3 **A big noise/gun/shot/nob**: An important and powerful person. □ Today we're being visited by some big noises (guns/nobs etc.) from head office.

38/4 **Mr Big**: The important or leading person in an organization. □ So far the police have arrested only minor members of the gang; Mr Big remains untouchable.

38/5 **Pack clout**: Be very influential. *(See also 'pack a punch' – 41/22 below)* □ Circulation figures of that newspaper may be small, but it packs clout in leading circles.

38/6 **A toff/swell**: A distinguished or well-dressed person. □ During the hunting season the country estate used to be invaded by toffs (swells) from the city.

38/7 **An anchor-man**: A person of crucial importance in an organization or undertaking. □ Ratings for the TV chat-show dropped dramatically when its anchor-man left for another channel.

38/8 **His/her nibs**: Humorous reference to an important or self-important person. □ She's only been in the office three weeks and already we get her nibs telling more experienced staff what to do.

38/9 **Lord/Lady Muck**: Someone with an exaggerated idea of his or her own importance. □ Ever since he was elected to the Town Council, he thinks he's Lord Muck!

38/10 **Too many chiefs and not enough indians**: Too many bosses and not enough people to carry out the tasks. The phrase is sometimes incorrectly expressed as 'all cowboys and no indians'. □ In the construction firm I work for, there are almost as many administrative staff as building-workers; it's a case of too many chiefs and not enough indians.

38/11 **Have a handle to one's name**: Have a title or official rank (Reverend, Professor, Ambassador etc.). □ Judging by the guest-list, you have to have a handle to your name to get invited to the ceremony.

38/12 **A red-letter day:**   An important day; a day that is memorable because of some joyful occurrence. By custom, saints' days and public holidays used to be entered into calendars in red ink. □ The day their first baby was born was a red-letter day for the couple.

38/13 **A high spot:**   An important place or feature. □ For us, the high spot of the India trip was a visit to the Taj Mahal.

38/14 **A must:**   A thing that should not be overlooked or missed. □ If you go sailing, a life-jacket is a must.

38/15 **The be-all and end-all:**   The dominant and controlling factor or person. □ The Dalai Lama is regarded as the be-all and end-all by many religious Tibetans.

38/16 **The sixty-four-thousand-dollar question:**   The crucial question on which everything depends. □ For the wheat harvest, the $64,000 question is whether it will rain this month.

38/17 **Hinge on** something: Depend on; be decided or controlled by. □ Seed germination hinges on warmth and moisture.

38/18 **The name of the game:**   The purpose, essence or most important feature of an activity. □ In exporting, quick and cheap delivery is the name of the game.

38/19 **Set great store by** something: Value greatly; attach great importance to. □ I set great store by your support in these troubled times.

38/20 **Not to be sneezed at:**   Important enough to merit consideration; worth having. □ She didn't offer you a lot of money for your old ski-equipment; still, the offer is not to be sneezed at.

38/21 **Not the end of the world:**   Not of supreme importance or seriousness. □ Failing an exam is not the end of the world.

39: UNIMPORTANT

39/1 **Small fry:**   People of little importance; children. □ Compared to other companies, our firm is still small fry. □ The parents took their small fry off to the zoo.

39/2 **Two-bit/tin-pot:**   Cheap or worthless; unimportant. □ Our nation will not be held to ransom by a tin-pot (two-bit) dictator.

39/3 **Mickey Mouse** or **small-time:**   Trivial or unimportant. □ International companies of that size aren't interested in Mickey Mouse (small-time) contracts.

39/4 **Two a penny:**   Readily obtainable and so almost worthless; (of a profession) low-paid and overcrowded. □ My son wants to follow a career in the theatre, but I've told him that actors are two a penny.

39/5 **A part of the furniture:**   A long-serving person whose presence is taken for granted or overlooked. □ After twenty years in the firm, Julia had become a part of the furniture, and younger executives were promoted while she remained at the same job.

39/6   A **pipsqueak**:   A small, unimportant but self-assertive person. □ I won't have any pipsqueak telling me what to do!

39/7   **Ragtag and bobtail**:   Poor or common people. □ Tattooing is a sign of ragtag and bobtail for many.

39/8   **Riff-raff**:   Rabble; disreputable or worthless people. □ The mercenary armies of feudal princes consisted of the riff-raff of society.

39/9   **Low life**:   Worthless people; scum. □ During the Cold War, Bahnhof Zoo, the central station of Berlin, became a focal point for low life and other twilight figures.

39/10   **Cut no ice**:   Have no influence or importance. □ The fact that your father is a film star cuts no ice with that director; you'll have to prove your talent.

39/11   **Make no odds**:   Make no difference; be unimportant. □ For our firm, ethnic or religious background makes no odds when recruiting staff.

39/12   **What the heck/hell!**:   What does it matter! □ I really shouldn't go out today since I've housework to do, but what the heck (hell), I'll do it tomorrow!

39/13   **(No) big deal!**:   Signifying that something is no problem or worry. On its own 'big deal!' is often used ironically, as in the second example below. □ OK, I'll go and see the boss now if you really want me to – it's no big deal, I've loads of time. □ "Your neighbour's going to the police about your fierce dog." "Big deal!"

39/14   **Worse things happen at sea**:   The matter is relatively unimportant or trivial. □ The boy ran crying to his mother after being stung by a wasp, so she treated it with vinegar and told him that worse things happen at sea.

39/15   **Poo-poo/rubbish** something: Criticize severely; declare to be worthless; be dismissive of something. □ We are not trying to poo-poo (rubbish) the architect's design, it's just too expensive.

39/16 **Play down** something; Minimize the importance of something.
□ Industry tends to play down the importance of pollution-control measures, because of the immense costs involved.

40: FIGHTING

40/1 **Spoiling for** a fight: Eager for something, especially a fight or trouble. □ That drunk is just spoiling for a fight.

40/2 A **brawl**/a **set-to**: A noisy fight or quarrel, an argument (usually leading to a fight). To 'brawl' is to take part in such a fight. □ They argued for an hour, then they had a real set-to and one man's nose was broken in the brawl.

40/3 A **scrap**: A fight or quarrel. The corresponding verb is 'to scrap'. □ At school I was always having scraps (was always scrapping).

40/4 A **punch-up**: A fight with fists. □ From Tibor's black eye, you could see that he had been in a punch-up.

40/5 A **free-for-all**: A fight or quarrel in which anyone present can take part. □ On the first day of the sale, a dispute between two customers over some half-price china ended in a free-for-all.

40/6 A **rough-house**: A violent disturbance; a place where violent behaviour occurs. □ Package-holidaymakers, drunk on cheap wine, are turning the beach resort into a rough-house.

40/7 **Rough-and-tumble**: A haphazard fight or struggle; rough physical contact involving falls. □ Ice-hockey is a sport for those who can take a bit of rough-and-tumble.

40/8 A **bruiser**: A bully or fighter. □ If you don't pay your debts on time, he'll send a bruiser over to visit you!

40/9 A **heavy mob**: A group using brutal or violent methods. □ The owner of the tenement block hired a heavy mob to evict the remaining tenants.

40/10 A **bouncer**: A person employed to expel troublesome people from a gathering or building. □ The night club always had a bouncer on the door.

40/11 **Turf** someone **out**: Throw out or eject someone. □ The drunk was turfed out of the restaurant when he became abusive to other guests.

40/12 **Take** someone **on**: Engage in a fight or struggle with someone. □ Weasels and polecats will take on much larger animals in the defence of their young.

40/13 **Mix it** with someone: Fight. □ Uwe is always mixing it with other boys at school.

40/14 **Set about** someone: Attack with blows or words. □ As the accused left the court after his acquittal, a crowd set about him.

40/15 **Lay/weigh/pitch/wade/lam into** someone: Attack vigorously. □ Riot police waded (pitched/laid/weighed/lammed) into the demonstrators with fists and truncheons.

40/16 **Manhandle** someone: Move someone using rough treatment. □ Animal-rights protesters had to be manhandled out of the meeting.

40/17 **Frogmarch** someone: Force someone forward with his/her hands held fast. □ The unruly prisoner was frogmarched back to his cell by warders.

41: HIT/SHOOT

41/1 **Let fly** at someone: Aim a sudden blow at someone. □ The man let fly at me, but I ducked and avoided the blow.

41/2 **Clock** someone: Hit in the face. □ The insulted man clocked him one.

41/3 **Crown** someone: Hit on the head. □ The anglers dragged the shark on deck and the captain crowned it with a baseball bat.

41/4 **Whop** someone: Hit, thrash or soundly beat. □ Our team got whopped by the league champions. □ She whopped him with a broom.

41/5 **Clobber** someone: Hit hard and repeatedly; defeat. □ Inflation is clobbering the economy. □ "Did we win?" "I'd say we absolutely clobbered them!"

41/6 **Belt/sock** someone: Hit or punch hard. □ I got socked (belted) on the jaw.

41/7 **Wallop/whale** (*US*) someone: Hit hard; thrash. This thrashing is a 'whaling' or 'walloping'. □ I'll give him a whaling (walloping) when he gets home! □ She walloped (whaled) the youth with her handbag.

41/8 **Bash** someone or something: Strike or criticize violently. □ Trade-union bashing has become popular. □ The car bashed into the fence.

41/9 **Biff/dot/tag/slosh/clout** someone or something: Hit. □ Vadim biffed (dotted/tagged/sloshed/clouted) the hooligan on the chin.

41/10 **Fetch** someone **one** *or* **give** someone **it** *or* **let** someone **have it**:   Hit someone. □ If you say that to Michel, he is liable to fetch you one (give you it/let you have it).

41/11 **Slug** someone: Strike with a hard heavy blow. □ I witnessed a soldier slug an old man with a rifle-butt.

41/12 **Bonk** someone: Hit with an abrupt thudding sound. (*See also 188/14*) □ The ship bonked against the jetty in the heavy sea.

41/13 **Zap** someone: Hit; knock out or kill. (*See also 136/2*) □ The sniper zapped several enemy soldiers. □ In this scene, Superman zaps several villains.

41/14 **Knock** someone **into the middle of next week**:   Hit very hard; give someone a sound thrashing. □ The blow knocked him into the middle of next week.

41/15 **Hit** someone or something **for six**:   Hit very hard; deal a crushing blow. Alludes to the score of six in cricket, achieved when a batsman knocks the ball over the boundary without it bouncing. □ The fall in the price of cotton has hit the country's chances of economic recovery for six.

41/16 **Knock** someone **cold**: Knock unconscious. □ Several train passengers were knocked cold by the collision.

41/17 **Out for the count**: Unconscious. The 'count' refers to the count of ten in boxing. □ I can't say what happened then, since I was out for the count.

41/18 **Punch-drunk**: Stunned or dazed after a series of heavy blows. □ The boxer was punch-drunk and made no effort to defend himself.

41/19 **A smack in the chops**: Hit or punch in the face. The blow itself is a 'smack', which in this context is not to be confused with 'smack' meaning a blow made with the flat of one's hand. □ I smacked him in the chops (I gave him a smack in the chops).

41/20 **Clip** someone: Hit sharply. The blow itself is a 'clip'. □ The mother gave the naughty boy a clip on the ear.

41/21 **Cuff** someone: Strike with the open hand. The blow itself is a 'cuff'. □ I was often cuffed at school for misbehaviour.

41/22 **Pack a punch**: Be capable of delivering a powerful blow; strong. (*See also 38/5 above*) □ That boxer doesn't pack a knock-out punch. □ This vodka really packs a punch.

41/23 **A shiner**: A black eye. □ Someone had obviously given him a couple of shiners.

41/24 **A cauliflower ear/thick ear**: A swollen ear caused by a blow. □ Horst came out of the fight with torn clothes and a cauliflower (thick) ear.

41/25 **Put the nut on** someone: Butt someone with the head. The verb is 'to nut'. □ The referee was injured after a disgruntled player put the nut on him (nutted him).

41/26 **Not lay a finger on** someone: Not hurt or harm. □ Don't lay a finger on my child again! □ I don't know why he's complaining; I didn't lay a finger on him.

41/27 **Plug** someone: Shoot or strike. □ The berserk gunman had shot dead three passers-by before being plugged by police.

41/28 **Wing** someone: To wound in the wing or arm. □ The patrolman had his arm in a sling for three weeks after being winged by an armed robber.

41/29 **Stop** a bullet/blow: Receive a blow or bullet on the body. □ The dead man had stopped ten bullets from an automatic rifle.

42: BEAT UP

42/1 **A drubbing/hiding/lathering**: A beating or severe defeat. □ Last year's football cup champions received a drubbing (hiding/lathering) this year.

42/2 **Paste** someone: Thrash or beat. A 'pasting' is a thrashing. □ The crowd gave the pick-pocket a proper pasting.

42/3 **Tan** someone: Thrash. A 'tanning' is a beating. □ Your father will tan you when he hears that you've broken the window!

42/4 **Rough** someone **up**: Thrash or treat violently. □ The prisoner alleged that he had confessed only after being roughed up by police.

42/5 A **working-over/going-over**: A thorough beating or thrashing. □ The thieves gave the manager a working-over (going-over) when he refused to open the safe.

42/6 **Do over** *or* **fill in** *or* **duff up**: Beat up; thrash. □ When the company collapsed, angry investors threatened to do over (fill in/duff up) the chairman of the board of directors.

42/7 **Dust** someone's **jacket**: Beat up or thrash. □ Several sailors returned to their ships from shore-leave with their jackets dusted.

42/8 **Skin** someone **alive**: Punish severely or beat. □ The boss will skin him alive for crashing the lorry.

42/9 **Knock** someone's **block off**: Give someone a severe beating. (*'Block' is colloquial for 'head' – see 176/4*) □ The row over the garden fence led to threats from Laszlo's neighbour to knock his block off.

42/10 **Beat the living daylights out of** someone: Beat a person very severely. □ I'll beat the living daylights out of anyone who scratches my new car!

42/11 **Knock the stuffing/shit** *(#?)* **out of** someone: Beat severely; defeat utterly. □ Convicted child-molesters get the stuffing (shit) knocked out of them by other prisoners.

EXERCISES 9: IMPORTANCE/VIOLENCE

A) Insert an object or thing to complete the following sentences.

1) Today is a red- . . . day for her.
2) These managers are the top . . . of the organization.
3) Satellite TV dishes were once rare but now they are two a . . . .
4) She has worked for the firm so long, she has become part of the . . . .
5) Those ruffians threatened to dust my . . . if I didn't hand over my wallet.
6) His support is crucial, everything . . . s on it.
7) He is the . . . -man of our accounts department and without him we would have a lot of financial problems.
8) We don't want to send our children to that school; it's a rough- . . . .
9) The project was delayed by tin- . . . bureaucrats.
10) Her son had been fighting and came home with a . . . ear.
11) You mustn't forget to address him as 'doctor' – he has a . . . to his name.

→

68

B) Give colloquialisms for the persons described by the following definitions.

1) an important person.
2) a conceited woman who mistakenly believes herself to be important.
3) scum or rabble.
4) someone employed to eject troublesome guests or customers.
5) a well-dressed and important person.
6) a bully or someone who regularly employs violence on others.
7) the leading, most important member of an organization.

C) Replace the underlined phrases with as many colloquial synonyms as possible, paying attention to the degree and type of violence used.

1) I hit him with a very hard blow.
2) He threatened to punch me in the face.
3) The drunken youth head-butted a policeman.
4) His father beat him severely for his misbehaviour.
5) The teacher hit the boy sharply on the side of the head.
6) Two men were having a fight in the doorway.
7) A band of thieves attacked the travellers violently.
8) His wife hit him with a frying-pan.

D) The colloquialisms in the following sentences have been used incorrectly. Give their correct form.

1) Whether the missing girl is alive or dead, that is the sixty-five thousand lire question.
2) I crowned him hard in the stomach.
3) He was knocked into the beginning of last week.
4) Everyone here wants to give the orders – it's all chiefs and no cowboys.
5) I was hit for ten and lost consciousness.
6) The brothers duffed over the man who had insulted their sister.
7) In the catering industry, service is the sign of the business.
8) The intruder was goose-marched away by security guards.

Punishment

43: PRESSURE

43/1 **Put the screws on** someone: Put pressure on someone to do something. A 'thumb-screw' was a medieval instrument of torture. □ In the '50s and '60s Russia put the screws on those countries that wanted to break away from the Soviet bloc.

43/2 **Make it/things hot for** someone: Persecute or put someone under pressure. □ In addition to bad economic figures, the resignation of the foreign minister really made things (it) hot for the government.

43/3 **Turn on the heat**: Increase the pressure on someone. □ Competition from other tractor manufacturers has turned on the heat for our sales network in West Africa.

43/4 **If you can't stand the heat, get out of the kitchen**: If the pressure of a task is too great, one should not continue with it. □ As President Truman once said: 'If you can't stand the heat, get out of the kitchen'.

43/5 **Have** someone/something **on one's back**: Be burdened or pressurized by someone or something. □ In the business of toxic-waste disposal, firms have a mass of legislation on their backs.

43/6 **Breathe down** someone's **neck**: Supervise someone closely; be close behind or in pursuit of someone. □ Our company was accused of tax evasion, and now we've got auditors from the Inland Revenue breathing down our neck.

43/7 **Lean on** someone: Seek to influence someone by pressure or intimidation. □ We supply 80% of our production to that chain store and they are leaning on us to reduce our prices.

43/8 **Twist** someone's **arm**: Coerce someone; force someone to do something. This pressure is 'arm-twisting'. □ My husband says he has no time to change your car tyre, but don't worry, I'll twist his arm.

43/9 **Throw one's weight about/around**: Use one's influence aggressively; pressurize others. □ By forcing smaller competitors out of business and generally throwing its weight about, the large brewery became a monopoly supplier in the area.

43/10 **Railroad** someone **into** something: Rush or force someone into hasty action. □ Some Nato generals complained that the East–West thaw was railroading them into potentially dangerous cuts in military spending.

43/11 **Bulldoze** someone **into** something: Force or intimidate into doing something. □ The old couple refused to give up their house, claiming that unscrupulous property developers had bulldozed them into selling.

43/12 **Steamroller** someone: Crush or defeat by brute force or weighty influence. □ Many small shops have been steamrollered by the pricing policies of the hypermarkets and have been forced to close.

44: PUNISH/TREAT HARSHLY

44/1 **Give** someone **beans** *or* **sock it to** someone: Reprimand or beat someone; attack forcefully. *(See also 'sock it to someone' 87/13)* □ The other team were good and really gave us beans.

44/2 **Give** someone **the works**: Treat harshly or brutally. □ The examiners gave all candidates the works.

44/3 **Wipe/mop the floor with** someone: Punish severely or defeat utterly; humiliate. □ The Mongol Khans would wipe (mop) the floor with any city that refused to pay them a tribute.

44/4 **Give** someone **what-for**: Punish severely; reprimand. □ This is the third time she's been caught shoplifting; the judge is sure to give her what-for.

44/5 **Fix** someone *or* **sort** someone **out**: Deal with someone severely; punish. □ Only a prison sentence will fix him (sort him out).

44/6 **Take** someone **down a peg**: Humble someone; make someone feel small or less proud. □ I thought that I was the best watchmaker until I saw some Swiss craftsmen at work; that took me down a peg.

44/7 **Come down on** someone **like a ton of bricks** *or* **have** someone's **guts for garters**: Punish someone with great severity. □ If the authorities find out that you are illegally exporting art treasures, they'll come down on you like a ton of bricks (they'll have your guts for garters).

44/8 **Crack down on** someone: Take severe measures against something illegal or contrary to the rules. □ The Chinese authorities cracked down on the student demonstrations for democracy in Beijing.

44/9 **Put one's foot down**: Take severe measures to impose authority. □ Absenteeism in the factory is getting out of hand; the manager will have to put his foot down.

44/10 **Bring** someone **to book**: Punish or make someone answer for his conduct. □ Many fugitives from justice on the 'Costa del Crime' are afraid of being brought to book by the impending extradition treaty.

44/11 **Get one's own back**: Get one's revenge. □ I'll get my own back for that dirty trick he played on me.

44/12 **Pick on** someone: Single someone out as a target for harassment. □ No person should be picked on by the police for the colour of his skin.

44/13 **Take it out on** someone: Work off one's frustration or anger by attacking or criticizing someone. □ At work he was under great strain, and in the evenings he took it out on his family.

44/14 **Have it in for** *or* **be gunning for** someone: Bear a grudge against someone; seek to attack or punish. □ Orlov's colleagues in the factory have had it in for him (have been gunning for him) ever since he reported another workmate for stealing finished goods.

44/15 **Put the boot in** *or* **kick** someone **in the teeth**: Attack someone brutally when he is at a disadvantage □ Our firm was sued for faulty workmanship and suddenly other customers started putting the boot in (kicking us in the teeth) with compensation claims.

44/16 **Not pull one's punches**: Be unreserved in one's criticism or attack; be ruthless. □ The Cuban authorities don't pull their punches with AIDS patients; all cases are isolated, by force if necessary.

44/17 **Ride roughshod over** someone/something: Treat inconsiderately or harshly. □ Early European settlers in Australia rode roughshod over the native aborigines.

44/18 **The carrot and the stick**: Bribes and threats; reward and punishment □ The government should encourage firms to adopt pollution-control measures more with the carrot (e.g. tax incentives) than by the stick (e.g. fines).

45: REPRIMAND

45/1 A **wigging** *or* a **bollocking** (#?): A lengthy reprimand or scolding. □ My boss gave me a wigging (bollocking) for arriving late for work.

45/2 **Tick/tell** someone **off**: To reprimand. A 'ticking-off' or a 'telling-off' is a reprimand. □ The boy was ticked (told) off by a traffic warden for dropping litter.

45/3 A **dressing-down**: A reprimand or scolding. □ Andreas was given a dressing-down by the conductor for jumping on to a moving train.

45/4 A **slating** *or* a **talking-to** *or* a **carpeting**: A reprimand. □ After the defeat, the generals were called to the palace for a slating (carpeting/ talking-to).

45/5 **A rocket**: A reprimand. □ The editor received a rocket from the newspaper's owner for printing the story.

45/6 **An earful**: A reprimand using strong language. □ One woman who tried to jump the queue got an earful from the other waiting customers.

45/7 **Tell** someone **where to get off**: Give someone a strong reprimand or contradictory reply. □ Next time he comes asking me for money, I'll tell him where to get off.

45/8 **A piece of one's mind**: A reproach or scolding. (*Do not confuse with 'peace of mind', meaning freedom from anxiety*) □ The taxi-driver, who had braked suddenly to avoid hitting the pedestrian, leaned out of the cab and gave her a piece of his mind.

45/9 **Play war with** someone: Scold or rebuke someone severely. □ Mrs Endler played war with her elder son for leaving his baby sister at home unattended.

45/10 **Read** someone **the riot act**: Reprimand strongly. Under the Riot Act (1715), a meeting of twelve or more people had to disperse if a magistrate read this act to them. □ If the captain catches any sailor smoking on the tanker deck, he'll read him the riot act!

45/11 **Throw the book at** someone: Accuse a person of all possible charges. □ The car thief had the book thrown at him; the charges included having no driving licence or insurance.

45/12 **Haul** someone **over the coals**: Rebuke severely. Drawing or hauling a person over hot coals was originally a medieval method of torture. □ Every morning after assembly, the headmaster would haul naughty pupils over the coals.

45/13 **Tear** someone **off a strip**: Rebuke or reprimand angrily. □ A sales-assistant was torn off a strip by the manager for arguing with customers.

45/14 **Jump down** someone's **throat** *or* **bite** someone's **head off**: Reprimand severely; contradict strongly. □ The boss jumped down my throat (bit my head off) when I took a two-hour lunch-break.

46: SUFFER

46/1 **A rap**: Punishment; blame. (*See also 93/1*) □ The accused was given a two-year rap by the judge. □ The plant manager took the rap for the chemical leak and was dismissed.

46/2 **Carry the can**: Bear the blame or responsibility. □ The war had been a disaster for the country and the president (who carried the can for it all) was forced to resign.

46/3 **Face the music**: Suffer unpleasant consequences. □ Max has been caught driving under the influence of alcohol and will have to face the music in court next week.

46/4 **Be left holding the baby**: Be left with the unwelcome responsibility for something. □ That important job needed three of us on it; when my two colleagues went sick I was left holding the baby.

73

46/5 A **scapegoat** *or* a **fall guy** *(US)* *or* a **whipping boy**: An easy victim; someone who is made to bear the punishment or blame of others. □ The company director claimed that with his dismissal he had been made a scapegoat (fall guy/whipping boy) for the financial mismanagement of other members of the board.

46/6 **Cop/catch/get it** *or* **get it in the neck**: Suffer a reprimand or severe blow. □ When I borrowed my cousin's boat and damaged the hull on rocks, I knew I'd catch it (cop it/get it/get it in the neck) when I got back to harbour.

46/7 **Be on the receiving end**: Be the one that has to submit to something unpleasant. □ When the volcano erupts, the lava usually flows harmlessly away from our village, but last year we were on the receiving end.

46/8 A **glutton for punishment**: Someone who willingly accepts suffering or arduous tasks. □ Some joggers are gluttons for punishment; even if it's snowing they'll go out running.

46/9 **Be for the high jump** *or* **be in for it** *or* **have it coming**: Be liable to receive drastic punishment. □ The welder who has carelessly set the roof alight will be in for it (be for the high jump/have it coming) when his firm gets the bill.

46/10 **Heads will roll**: Someone will have to bear the blame and be dismissed from office. □ The American company we took over at great expense turned out to be bankrupt; heads will roll in our boardroom.

46/11 **Get what is coming to one** *or* **get one's comeuppance (one's just deserts)**: Receive one's deserved punishment. □ Some callous people say that AIDS is a punishment from God and that sufferers are only getting what is coming to them (getting their just deserts/getting their comeuppance).

46/12 **Serve** someone **right**: Be a just punishment for someone. □ Tania hasn't done enough studying and it will serve her right if she fails the exam.

46/13 A **dose of one's own medicine**: The same unpleasant treatment that one applies to others. □ There are so many thieves and vandals on that problem housing-estate that they regularly get a dose of their own medicine by being burgled themselves.

46/14 **Take one's medicine**: Accept one's punishment bravely. □ Lopez knew that collecting the eggs of protected birds was illegal, and he told the police that he was ready to take his medicine.

46/15 Someone's **chickens have come home to roost**: The consequences of unpleasant actions have reacted unfavourably on the doer. □ For decades the mills produced cheap steel by ignoring the environment; now their chickens have come home to roost and they will have to pay for an expensive clean-up operation.

46/16 **The joke is on** someone: Be the victim of one's own unpleasant actions. □ Many of that country's chemical plants are on our border to make use of the prevailing wind, but this summer the joke was on them when the wind changed direction.

46/17 Laugh on the other side of one's face: Change from amusement to dismay; suffer a sudden reversal of fortune. □ My wife is overjoyed with the new kitchen she ordered, but she'll laugh on the other side of her face when I tell her we can't afford it.

46/18 The devil to pay: Trouble or very unpleasant consequences to be expected. □ If we go on wasting water at the present rate, there'll be the devil to pay.

46/19 For my sins: (ironic) as a punishment. □ I'm an accountant, and for my sins I'm also secretary of the local history society.

46/20 Rub something in: Emphasize or remind a person constantly of his/her shortcomings or some other unpleasant fact. □ I've failed my driving-test three times and he never misses an opportunity to rub it in.

47: CRITICIZE/NAG

47/1 Pick holes in an argument: Find fault with; criticize an argument. □ The theory of a flat Earth wasn't watertight, and with time, astronomers began to pick holes in it.

47/2 Knock/bash someone/something: Criticize or insult. □ Nuclear power is always being knocked (bashed) as dangerous. □ Don't knock the pianist, he's doing his best!

47/3 Slam someone/something: Criticize severely. □ The proposals for a single European currency were slammed in several national assemblies.

47/4 Give someone **some stick:** Attack or criticize severely. □ In the Middle Ages, scientists such as Galileo were given some stick by the established Church.

47/5 Have a go at someone/something: Make critical remarks. □ In his book the author has a go at fox-hunting.

47/6 Have a dig at someone/something: Make an indirect criticism of something. □ The politician's speech was full of sly digs at the Monarchy.

47/7 Second-guess someone/something (*#US*): Criticize someone retrospectively; comment on a situation with the benefit of hindsight. □ Following criticism of his controversial verdict, the judge refused to resign, saying that it was not the task of politicians to second-guess the judiciary.

47/8 Call someone **everything under the sun** *or* **. . . in the book:** Abuse or criticize someone in every possible way. □ When Darwin suggested that Man was descended from the apes, he was called everything under the sun (everything in the book).

47/9 Mud-slinging *or* **muck-raking:** Malicious talk about someone, aimed at damaging his/her reputation. □ The defeated candidate in the election alleged that his private life had been used for mud-slinging.

47/10 Flak: Severe criticism. 'Flak' is literally anti-aircraft fire or shells. □ Government proposals to reduce spending came in for a lot of flak.

47/11 **Start on** someone/something: Attack physically or verbally; direct criticism towards something. □ In the second half of his speech, the president started on merchants who had been hoarding food.

47/12 **Let rip** (at someone):   Begin to speak or criticize violently; utter angry or forceful words. □ When the site manager heard what had gone wrong, he let rip at the building workers.

47/13 **Be on at** someone *or* **get at** someone: Nag or criticize. □ My wife has been on at me (been getting at me) all morning about mowing the lawn.

47/14 **Nit-picking**:   Petty fault-finding or criticism. 'Nits' are the tiny eggs of lice. □ Criticism that the London Marathon had become too commercialized was rejected by the organizers as nit-picking.

48: ESCAPE PUNISHMENT

48/1 Escape **by the skin of one's teeth** *or* **by a whisker**:   Only just escape. □ Our correspondent in Saigon escaped by the skin of his teeth (by a whisker) on one of the last US army helicopters.

48/2 **A close shave**:   A narrow escape from injury or failure. □ I had a close shave this morning when I was almost run over by a lorry.

48/3 **Off the hook**:   Freed from a difficulty or possible punishment; no longer under accusation or criticism. □ The captain was off the hook when the first mate of the other ship accepted blame for the collision.

48/4 **Give** someone **the slip**:   Avoid someone; escape from a pursuer. □ Police chased the get-away car, but the robbers succeeded in giving them the slip.

48/5 **Get off scot-free**:   Escape unharmed; avoid punishment completely. □ Owing to lack of evidence, many known criminals get off scot-free in court.

48/6 **Get away with murder**:   To do something wrong without being punished for it. *(See also 15/19)* □ Marianne has always been badly behaved; her parents let her get away with murder when she was a child.

EXERCISES 10: PUNISHMENT

A) Insert a part of the body to complete the following sentences.

1) I have the landlord on my . . . for the rent.
2) I escaped by the . . . of my . . . .
3) Now we will all suffer, but you especially will get it in the . . . .
4) He won't bite your . . . off if you go and ask his advice.
5) We were relying on them and they kicked us in the . . . .

→

6) ... s will roll for this blunder.
7) If you don't put your ... down, the children will become unruly.
8) Since he left prison, he has had the police breathing down his ... .
9) I collided with her by accident, but she gave me an ... ful.
10) If she doesn't agree, I'll twist her ... .

B) Complete the following sentences with an adverb (*under, on, at* etc.).

1) They are leaning ... me to pay.
2) She called him everything ... the sun.
3) You have angered him and now he has it ... for you.
4) She swindled me, but I will get my own ... .
5) When he is in a bad mood, he takes it ... on me.
6) They think that they have humiliated us, but the joke is ... them.
7) His sarcastic remarks are a dig ... you.
8) If he continues to misbehave, his father will sort him ... .
9) That bully should pick ... someone his own size.
10) The murder suspect's alibi was confirmed, and he was ... the hook.

C) From the module, insert a hyphenated colloquialism to complete the sentence.

1) We thought he would punish us, but we got off ... - ... .
2) Such petty criticism is just ... - ... .
3) I'll give him ... - ... if I catch him stealing.
4) It is easy to ... - ... the decisions of others after the event.
5) His conduct is unacceptable; I'll call him to my office for a ... - ... .
6) The press is trying to discredit me with a campaign of ... - ... .

D) Give colloquialisms for the following definitions.

1) reward and punishment. 2) someone who is blamed for the misconduct of others. 3) severe criticism. 4) the punishment of undergoing the same unpleasant treatment that one applies to others. 5) someone who willingly accepts hardship or suffering. 6) a narrow escape.

E) Complete the following sentences by inserting a verb of motion (e.g. carry, get out, etc.) in the correct tense, or a noun referring to motion.

1) It's a difficult job, and those who can't stand the heat should ... of the kitchen.
2) Our team ... the floor with the Dutch league champions.
3) Someone will have to ... the can for this train disaster.
4) If you are late, he will ... ... on you like a ton of bricks.
5) You will be for the high ... when the boss finds out.
6) Critics are always ... the architecture of the buildings I design.
7) The branch manager was called to head office and ... over the coals for his below-average performance.

MODULE 11

Money

49: AMOUNT OF MONEY

49/1 **The necessary** *or* **the wherewithal** *or* **the ready/readies:** Money needed for a purpose. □ I'd like to buy a new car this year but I don't have the necessary (the ready/the readies/the wherewithal).

49/2 **Bread/dosh/lolly/brass/dough:** Money. □ We've got no dosh (bread etc.). □ They earn a lot of lolly (dough etc.) there.

49/3 **A split:** A share of money. □ My partner gets a 50% split of the profits.

49/4 **Loot/swag:** Stolen money or goods. □ Train-robber Biggs used his share of the swag (loot) to start a new life in Brazil.

49/5 **Filthy lucre** (*pr. 'loo-ker'*): Humorous term for money, alluding to its more negative aspects. □ Galina will do anything for filthy lucre.

49/6 **Money talks:** Money is important in life. □ The receptionist kept telling us that the hotel was full until we gave him a bribe; money talks!

49/7 **A nicker/quid:** A pound sterling. □ He gave me ten nicker (quid).

49/8 **A smacker:** A pound sterling or a US dollar. □ That'll cost you 50 smackers.

49/9 **A buck:** A US dollar. □ Loan me a couple of bucks!

49/10 **Turn a quick buck:** Earn money quickly. □ During the summer season, ice-cream sellers on the sea-front turn a quick buck.

49/11 **A grand:** A thousand pounds sterling or US dollars. □ It cost me two grand.

49/12 **Stash away** money: Store or conceal. A 'stash' is money so concealed. □ President Marcos plundered the Philippines' treasury and stashed away huge sums in foreign banks.

49/13 Save **for a rainy day:** Save money for a time when one might need it. □ Don't waste your money; invest it for a rainy day!

49/14 **A nest-egg:** A sum of money saved for future use. □ When Jules became unemployed, he had to break into his nest-egg to keep up his family's standard of living.

49/15 **Go Dutch:** Share the expenses of an outing or meal. □ When we were poor students at college, my girlfriend and I used to go Dutch in snack-bars.

49/16 **Chip in:** Contribute money. *(See also 93/11)* □ All members of the United Nations must chip in to finance its upkeep.

49/17 **A whip-round:** An appeal for contributions from a number of people; a money collection. □ Staff had a whip-round for the secretary's retirement present.

49/18 **To the tune of** an amount: To the considerable amount of. □ The collapse of the Banco Ambrosiano stung several Italian investors to the tune of many million lire.

49/19 **A cool/tidy** sum: A sizeable amount of money. □ A villa in the Hamburg suburb of Blankenese cost him a cool (tidy) 800,000 marks.

49/20 **Peanuts** *or* **small beer** *or* **chicken feed**:   A small or relatively trivial amount of money. □ That job pays peanuts (small beer/chicken feed). □ Investments of 20,000 dollars are chicken feed (small beer/peanuts) to massive companies like IBM.

49/21 **A bundle/packet/bomb**:   A large amount of money. □ The manufacturers of the drug thalidomide paid out a bundle (packet/bomb) in compensation for malformed babies. □ The wedding of my daughter cost me a bundle (packet/bomb).

49/22 **A kitty**:   A fund or pool of money, usually spent by the contributors on one occasion. □ If we all put five quid into the kitty, we can drink here until it's gone.

50: MAKE MONEY

50/1 **Make a killing**:   Have a great financial success. □ Petroleum companies made a killing during the oil crisis.

50/2 **Rake it in**:   Make huge profits or big money. □ Building firms in Saudi Arabia are raking it in at the moment.

50/3 **A rake-off**:   A large commission or share of the profits. □ It is not always the best employment agency that takes the largest rake-off.

50/4 **Make a pile**:   Make a lot of money. □ Many Japanese industrialists made a pile selling armaments during the Korean War.

50/5 **Cash in on** something: Make a large profit from something. □ Manufacturers of water-purifiers are cashing in on worries about contaminated tap-water.

50/6 **On the make**:   Greedy for money. □ The California gold-rush attracted many who were on the make.

50/7 **Earn on the side**:   Earn extra money with a second job; earn secretly. (*See also 'moonlight' 1/29*) □ Some plumbers earn a bit on the side in the evening or at weekends with private work. That's what I'd call 'moonlighting'.

50/8 **A money-spinner**:   Something that brings in much profit. □ The 'Beetle' was a money-spinner for Volkswagen.

50/9 **A licence to print money**:   A business or undertaking that guarantees huge profits. □ Critics point out that the privatization of monopoly utilities such as power and water is giving those companies a licence to print money.

50/10 **A gravy train**:   A source of easy money. □ Previously, it was a commonly held view among US companies that military-supply contracts with the Pentagon were a gravy train.

50/11 Laughing all the way to the bank: Be the beneficiary of a profitable bargain or deal. □ We sold our house when land prices had doubled; now we're laughing all the way to the bank.

50/12 Rich pickings: Large profits from an undertaking. □ In the long term, the reconstruction of Russian industry promises rich pickings for Western companies.

50/13 A perk: A profit, allowance or privilege secondary to one's wage or salary, which is looked upon as one's right; a fringe benefit. The word is short for 'perquisite'. □ The position carries good perks: a company car, business lunches and a non-contributory pension scheme.

50/14 Top up an amount: Supplement or increase an amount. (*Do not confuse with 'tot up' meaning 'add up' – see 62/9*) □ Catering staff often work overtime to top up their low basic wage.

51: RICH

51/1 Flush/loaded/lousy with money: Well supplied with money; very rich. (*For 'lousy' see also 64/11 and 70/4*) □ If Perez owns three top racehorses, he must be flush (lousy/loaded) with money.

51/2 Rolling in it/money: Very wealthy. □ Howard Hughes was rolling in it (rolling in money).

51/3 In the money: Having plenty of money; rich. □ After they won the Eurovision Song Contest, 'Abba' were in the money.

51/4 Stinking rich: Excessively or vulgarly rich. □ He's stinking rich – just look at his flashy car, his jewellery and his Gucci shoes!

51/5 Have money to burn: Have an excessive amount of money. □ Anyone who spends 10,000 dollars on a diamond collar for a poodle must have money to burn.

51/6 Strike it rich: Become wealthy or prosperous. □ The dream of many Sicilian peasants was to strike it rich in America.

51/7 A money-bags *or* a fat cat (*US*): A rich person. □ Breitenfeld is a fat cat (money-bags) who lives in Beverly Hills.

51/8 Well-off *or* well-to-do *or* well-heeled: Fairly wealthy or affluent. □ That is a well-heeled (well-off/well-to-do) suburb of the city.

51/9 Born with a silver spoon in one's mouth: Born into a wealthy family or destined to be wealthy. □ A contributory factor of the English Civil War was the middle-class dislike for those landed gentry who had been born with a silver spoon in their mouths.

51/10 In Easy Street *or* in the lap of luxury: In great luxury or affluence. □ Before the invasion, citizens of Kuwait were living in Easy Street (in the lap of luxury).

51/11 In clover: In ease and luxury. □ On his accession to power, the new president ensured that all his relatives were in clover.

51/12 **Rags to riches:** From poverty to affluence. □ The story of post-war Japan is one of rags to riches.

52: POOR

52/1 **Not have a bean/red cent** *(US)*: Have no money at all. □ I haven't got a bean (a red cent).

52/2 **Not have a penny to one's name:** Be totally destitute. □ Kaminski arrived in the country as a refugee without a penny to his name.

52/3 **Not have two** cents **to rub together:** Be very poor. □ Ling needed a bicycle, but he didn't have two yuan to rub together.

52/4 **Flat/stony broke:** Without any money at all. □ Rik is usually flat (stony) broke about five days after pay day.

52/5 **Skint:** Having no money left. □ We may have to write off the money this client owes us; he's skint.

52/6 **Hard-up:** Short of money; poor. □ The restaurant has a special menu for hard-up students.

52/7 **Tight:** (of money) difficult to obtain; (of a person) stingy or mean. *(See also 155/10)* □ Money has become tight due to the closure of the town's only factory. □ My uncle was extremely rich but tight with his money.

52/8 **Tight-fisted** *or* **tight-arsed** *(#?)*: Miserly. □ Our boss is too tight-fisted (tight-arsed) to buy proper equipment for his workers.

52/9 **A skinflint:** A miserly person.

52/10 **Not made of money:** Not rich. □ I can't afford to keep buying new shoes for you; I'm not made of money.

52/11 **Down and out:** Completely destitute. A 'down-and-out' is a destitute person. □ The banks of the Seine in Paris used to be a favourite sleeping spot for down-and-outs.

52/12 **Skid Row:** A slum area where vagrants live. Originally it was a house for vagrants in Seattle (USA) made of greased logs of the type which lumbermen employed to 'skid' or slide other logs to the sawmill. □ If you keep on drinking like that, you'll end up on Skid Row.

52/13 **The poor man's . . .:** Jocular term to describe a cheaper version of some luxury object. □ Water is the poor man's wine. □ The Skoda car had a reputation of being the poor man's Mercedes.

53: EXPENSIVE

53/1 **Cost the earth** *or* **cost an arm and a leg:** Be exorbitantly expensive. □ A week's stay in that five-star hotel cost us an arm and a leg (the earth).

53/2 **Cost a few bob** *or* **cost a pretty penny**: Cost a considerable amount of money. □ I reckon that house has cost the owner a few bob (a pretty penny).

53/3 **A steep** price: Unreasonably high price. □ Twenty francs is a bit steep for a cup of coffee.

53/4 **Sky-high**: (of prices) very high; expensive. □ Inflation has made the cost of living sky-high. □ That restaurant charges sky-high prices.

53/5 **Pricey**: Expensive. □ Satellite TV-aerials range from the simple fixed dish to the pricey multi-satellite motorized versions.

53/6 **Ritzy**: High class or luxurious. 'Ritz' hotels founded by the Swiss businessman C. Ritz became synonymous with luxury. □ Aspen in Colorado is a ritzy ski-resort.

53/7 **Posh**: Very smart; luxurious. *(See also 173/6)* □ Cristina lives in a posh area of town.

53/8 **Pay through the nose**: Pay an unfairly high price for something. □ Salmon fishermen now have to pay through the nose for a day's sport.

53/9 **Make a hole/dent in** money: Use a large amount of one's monetary or other resources. □ That holiday in the Bahamas made a dent (hole) in our savings.

53/10 **Out of pocket**: Having lost money in a financial transaction when expenses are deducted. □ The musical failed to draw in the crowds and the organizers were over twenty thousand dollars out of pocket.

53/11 **Take a knock**: Receive a financial (or emotional) blow. □ Company shares took a knock in the wake of the Wall Street crash.

53/12 **Feel the pinch/draught**: Feel the effect of financial or other difficulties. □ If the car plant reduces output, many sub-contractors will feel the draught (pinch).

53/13 **A white elephant**: A large, useless and extremely expensive possession. Albino elephants were so rare in Siam (modern Thailand) that they automatically became property of the king who would give them to subjects he disliked. Since it was forbidden to use it for work, the elephant would sometimes bankrupt the subject. □ The new supersonic airliner was a white elephant for the airlines since fuel and running costs exceeded its revenue.

53/14 **A lame duck**: A person, company or organization that is in financial difficulties and cannot survive without help from an outside source. □ The government has already pumped enough aid into lame ducks and is unwilling to support these companies further.

54: CHEAP

54/1 **Dirt cheap**: Extremely cheap. □ In Northern Europe gardeners pay high prices for plants that are dirt cheap in their countries of origin.

54/2 **A rock-bottom** price: The lowest possible price. □ The prices of my carpets are rock-bottom and I won't haggle with customers.

54/3 **A knock-down** price: A very low or reduced price. □ Now the spring has arrived you can buy electric radiators at knock-down prices.

54/4 **Knock off** an amount: Deduct an amount from the price. □ For this month only, we've knocked 10% off our range of cameras.

54/5 **Going for a song** *or* **for coppers**: For sale at a very low price. □ In Krakov I found a shop where antiques were going for coppers (a song).

54/6 **A snip**: A bargain. (*See also 26/3*) □ The furniture is a snip at that price.

54/7 **On the cheap**: For a small amount of money. □ After the war, many blocks of flats were built on the cheap and now they are crumbling.

54/8 **On a shoe-string**: With very little available money or resources; on a low budget. □ Millions of people in the Third World have to survive on a shoe-string. □ We travelled around China on a shoe-string.

54/9 **Buckshee**: Free of charge. □ Our friends have a flat overlooking the stadium and they can watch football buckshee.

55: SPEND/WASTE

55/1 **On the nail**: (of payment) without delay. □ The wholesalers will supply the goods, but they want cash on the nail.

55/2 **Fork out** *or* **shell out** *or* **stump up** *or* **cough up**: Pay out money, especially reluctantly. □ We've done the work but the customer won't stump up (fork out/shell out/cough up). □ We had to fork out (cough up etc.) a lot of money to have the house insulated.

55/3 **Lash out** money: Spend lavishly. □ I lashed out two months' wages on a new motor bike.

55/4   **Go to town**: Spend money or do something lavishly. □ Your new luxury kitchen has everything; you've really gone to town.

55/5   **Shopping/spending spree**: An outing or period in which one shops or spends freely. □ My sister went to London on a shopping spree.

55/6   Spend money **like it was going out of fashion** *or* **like it grew on trees**: Spend money quickly in large amounts as if it were easily obtainable. *(The conjunction 'like' is regarded as an Americanism in the UK and often replaced by 'as if')* □ My wife spends money like/as if it grew on trees (as if it was going out of fashion).

55/7   **Flash money around**: Spend money ostentatiously; make a show of one's money. □ Mrs Almqvist is a very wealthy woman but she lives modestly and doesn't flash her money around.

55/8   **Splash** money: Spend freely and ostentatiously. □ Our firm can't afford to splash so much money on a fleet of new vans.

55/9   **Blow/blue** money: Spend recklessly; waste. □ I once blued (blew) a week's wages in one night of revelling.

55/10   Money **down the drain**: Money wasted. *(See also 18/10)* □ Any investment in that ailing company is money down the drain.

55/11   **A punter**: A customer. The word derives from a gambling term for someone who bets on horses. □ Our products come in various versions to suit punters in different countries.

55/12   **Foot the bill** *or* **pick up the tab** *(US)*: Be responsible for paying the bill or expenses. □ A charity picked up the tab (footed the bill) for the child's therapy at the Peto Institute in Budapest.

55/13   **Set/knock** someone **back**: Cost. □ A new freezer knocked (set) us back £300. □ How much will a new car-exhaust set (knock) me back?

55/14   The **damage**: The cost or charge. □ What's the damage?

56: SELL

56/1   **Flog** something: Sell. □ Uwe flogs second-hand cars for a living.

56/2   **Go like hot cakes**: Sell very quickly. □ In Russia many consumer goods go like hot cakes as soon as they reach the shops.

56/3   The **hard sell**: Aggressive salesmanship. □ Do not be persuaded by door-to-door salesmen employing the hard sell!

56/4   **Fetch** a price: Sell for a price. □ Most houses on this estate can fetch a six-figure sum. □ The painting fetched $10,000 at auction.

56/5   **A pig in a poke**: Something unsatisfactory purchased unseen or unchecked by the buyer. A trick practised at country fairs was to sell a cat in a 'poke' or sack, claiming it to be a piglet. □ The risk of mail order is that one can easily buy a pig in a poke.

56/6   **Sell** someone **a pup**: Cheat a person by selling him a worthless item. □ I think I've been sold a pup – this second-hand stereo doesn't seem to work properly.

57: BORROW/DEBT

57/1 **Touch/tap** someone **for** money: Persuade someone to give money as a loan or gift. □ Akio is always touching (tapping) his father for money.

57/2 **Cadge/bum** *(US)* (something): Ask for something as a gift; beg. Someone who regularly does this is a 'cadger' or a 'bum'. □ The tramp was told by the barman to stop cadging (bumming) drinks and cigarettes from guests.

57/3 **Sponge/scrounge** (something): Live off the generosity of others. The person who does this is a 'sponger' or a 'scrounger'. □ The new social security measures are aimed at reducing scrounging from the state.

57/4 **On the never-never** *or* **on the cuff** *(#US)*: Hire-purchase; purchase on credit with payment by instalments. □ Gerda got that colour TV on the never-never (on the cuff).

57/5 **Tick**: Credit. □ We bought the central heating on tick.

57/6 **A loan-shark**: An unscrupulous money-lender charging exorbitant rates of interest. To 'loan-shark' is to employ such methods. □ Many people turn to loan-sharks after being refused credit by banks.

57/7 **In the red**: In debt; having a negative financial balance. □ Our company is deep in the red.

57/8 **In hock** *(US)*: In debt. □ The city of New York is massively in hock and sometimes has difficulty paying even its own employees.

57/9 **Up to the eyes/ears in debt**: Deep in debt. *(See also 3/3)* □ We have a large mortgage and are up to the/our eyes (ears) in debt.

57/10 **Bounce**: (of a cheque) be returned by the bank as worthless. □ Luckily we haven't delivered that customer's goods yet, since his cheque (*US*: check) has bounced.

EXERCISES 11: MONEY

A) Insert a colloquial word or expression containing an animal or something edible.

1) He went to the bank to take out some . . . to pay for the shopping.
2) You should have tested the chess computer before you paid for it, now you've bought a . . . .
3) These early strawberries are in great demand and are selling like . . . .
4) The old couple had saved over the years and created a . . . .
5) I've spent all the money and I don't have a . . . left over.
6) The dealer offered me only . . . for my furniture and I decided not to sell.

→

7) This large house is a . . . and swallows all our money for its upkeep.
8) Lawyers get a lot of easy money from the legal-aid scheme, for them it's a . . . .
9) That expensive beach resort is frequented by . . . s with luxury yachts.

B) Give colloquial terms to fit the following definitions.

1) a pound sterling. 2) a US dollar. 3) a thousand dollars or pounds sterling. 4) a share of the profits or a commission. 5) the cost or charge of something. 6) a miser. 7) a bargain. 8) a customer. 9) someone who regularly begs things with no intention of returning them. 10) a time when one might need money.

C) In the sentences below, fill in a colloquial expression containing a hyphen.

1) We have a very small pension and we must survive on a . . . - . . . .
2) That man is a . . . - . . . and can afford every luxury.
3) Our prices are . . . - . . . and they cannot be reduced any further without making a loss.
4) She is . . . - . . . and grudges spending any money at all.
5) That idea could be a . . . - . . . for the company and earn the inventor a lot of money as well.
6) If you make a bulk purchase, we can give you the goods at a . . . - . . . price.
7) We are too . . . - . . . to afford a holiday.
8) Neighbours had a . . . - . . . and collected enough money to replace the furniture we lost in the fire.
9) That washing-machine is not mine yet, I'm paying for it by instalments on the . . . - . . . .
10) How do they expect ordinary people to pay such . . . - . . . prices?

D) Replace the underlined phrases relating to financial transactions with a colloquial verb in the correct tense.

1) She <u>sold</u> her jewellery to pay off her debts.
2) Thoroughbred cattle can <u>sell for</u> enormous sums.
3) We all <u>contributed something</u> towards the famine appeal.
4) The porters <u>supplement</u> their wages with tips from hotel guests.
5) My car was wheel-clamped, and I had to <u>pay</u> 500 francs to have the wretched thing taken off.
6) That holiday <u>cost me</u> a month's wages.
7) Is there no-one you can <u>persuade to give you</u> money?
8) You have <u>wasted</u> all our savings on something we don't need.

Deception

58: SWINDLE

58/1 **Con** someone: To persuade or swindle after winning a person's confidence. A 'con' is a swindle, and a 'con-man' is a swindler.
□ Hundreds of pensioners have been conned into investing their life savings in non-existent companies.

58/2 **Gyp/diddle** someone: To cheat or swindle. Nouns are a 'gyp' and a 'diddle'. □ Tourists are often gypped (diddled) by tradesmen giving worthless local currency as change.

58/3 **Rip** someone **off**: Defraud or steal. A 'rip-off' is a fraud. □ Refugees trying to enter Canada illegally were ripped-off with false stay-permits.

58/4 **Fleece/rook** someone: Defraud or rob by trickery; charge someone an extortionate price. □ Unless you have expert knowledge, you can easily get rooked (fleeced) by antique-dealers selling realistic imitations.

58/5 **Sting/screw** someone: Cheat a person by overcharging; extort money from someone. (*For 'screw someone' see also 188/14*) □ Companies which pocket regional development grants and then relocate their factories are stinging (screwing) the state for massive sums.

58/6 **Do/have** someone: Swindle or cheat. (*Do not confuse with 'have someone on' – see 60/9 below*) □ That amber you bought is worthless imitation; you've been had (done) for a lot of money!

58/7 **See** someone **coming**: See a good opportunity to defraud a gullible or unsuspecting person. □ You've paid far too much to have your car resprayed; that garage saw you coming.

58/8 **Take** someone **to the cleaners**: Rob or defraud someone out of all his/her money. □ The gambler left the casino regretting that he had been taken to the cleaners on the roulette table.

58/9 **Fob/palm** something **off on** someone: Induce someone to accept something false or inferior, or something which is not needed. □ As soon as his car began to develop engine trouble, Jorge fobbed (palmed) it off on a first-time driver.

58/10 **Daylight robbery**: Unashamed fraud or swindling. □ The prices in this tourist-trap are daylight robbery.

58/11 A **swiz(z)/swizzle**: A swindle; a considerable disappointment. 'Swiz' can be spelt with one z or two (like many other words which are more usually spoken than written down). □ Unfortunately, some so-called charity collectors are really operating a swizzle. □ What a swiz! They've just cancelled the concert I was going to tonight.

58/12 Cook the books: Fraudulently falsify the financial accounts of a business or undertaking. □ The businessman cooked his books to obtain a bank loan and so avoid bankruptcy.

58/13 Fiddle something: Cheat or swindle; falsify. A 'fiddle' is a swindle. □ The electricity board have developed new systems to stop people fiddling their meter.

58/14 On the fiddle: Living by swindle or deception. □ Several men were arrested for being on the fiddle by claiming unemployment benefit while working as taxi-drivers.

58/15 Have one's hands/fingers in the till: Steal from one's employer. □ Two cashiers at the supermarket were suspected of having their hands (fingers) in the till.

58/16 A twister: A swindler. □ He's a bit of a twister – I'd have nothing to do with him if I were you!

58/17 A sharper: A swindler, especially at cards. □ Don't play poker with him, he's a card-sharper!

58/18 A fly-by-night trader: A dishonest trader who disappears after a short time. □ Dissatisfied customers returned to the market with the faulty radios only to discover they had bought them from a fly-by-night trader.

58/19 A cheapskate: A contemptible, mean or dishonest person. □ I'm having nothing to do with a cheapskate like him!

59: DECEIVE/TRICK

59/1 Hoodwink someone: Deceive. □ We were hoodwinked into believing that our holiday hotel would be the one shown in the travel agent's brochure.

59/2 Fox someone: To confuse or deceive by acting craftily. □ In the old days smugglers into Hong Kong used to try to fox the police, now they rely mainly on high-powered speed boats.

59/3 Lead someone **up the garden path**: Mislead deliberately. □ Every year for the last ten years of bilateral talks, that country has been leading us up the garden path with promises of fishing rights in its territorial waters.

59/4 Pull the wool over someone's **eyes**: Deceive someone. □ Denials by the CIA of involvement in changes of government in certain countries are designed to pull the wool over the eyes of the US public.

59/5 Put/slip one across someone: Make someone believe something false. □ It's not his own sports car, he just borrowed it; he's trying to put (slip) one across you.

59/6 Take someone **in**: Deceive or cheat. □ When she first met Mats, he told her that he wasn't married, but she later discovered he had taken her in.

59/7 Stitch someone **up**: Fool a person into believing or doing something which will ultimately be to your advantage, not theirs. *(See also 16/8)*

□ He paid £500 for it, but the salesman stitched him up – it wasn't worth half the price.

59/8 **Take** someone **for a ride**: Deceive or swindle. □ The security firm told police that the night watchman had taken them for a ride with false references covering up his criminal past.

59/9 **Fall for** something: Be deluded or fooled by a deception or trick. *(See also 108/12)* □ The security services didn't fall for the spy's story that he was only a refugee fleeing tyranny.

59/10 **Accidentally-on-purpose**: Done purposely under the guise of an accident. □ I hear that a pupil accidentally set off the class fire-extinguisher today – accidentally-on-purpose, of course!

59/11 **A sham**: A pretence; a thing or person that is not genuine. □ The president's claims that human rights are being observed in his country is a sham.

59/12 **Put it on**: Feign an emotion. □ Anka believed that his apology was insincere and that he was just putting it on.

59/13 **Play possum** *(US)*: Avoid problems or blame by feigning illness or ignorance. From the possum's habit of feigning death when in danger. □ The wanted man was known to be violent and police inquiries as to his whereabouts proved fruitless; all his known associates were playing possum.

59/14 **Pull a fast one** on someone: Act unfairly towards someone in order to gain an advantage. □ While we were entrusting this manager with commercial secrets, he was pulling a fast one on us and revealing the information to competitors.

59/15 **String** someone **along**: Deceive someone. *(See also 143/20)* □ Don't be strung along by peasant rumours of a wild ape-man living in the mountains.

59/16 **Nobble** someone *or* **get at** someone: Influence by underhand means; bribe. □ The favourite race horse came in last after being nobbled (got at) with drugs. □ Even the police there can be nobbled (got at).

59/17 **Fix/rig** something: Fraudulently arrange something; use bribery, deception or other improper means to influence something. □ The opposition accused the ruling party of rigging (fixing) the election.

59/18 **A fix** *or* **a put-up job**: Something fraudulently arranged. □ Other firms talked of a put-up job (a fix) when the minister awarded the government contract to a company owned by his nephew.

59/19 **A scam** *(US)*: A fraudulent trick; a swindle. □ A series of scams and unauthorized share deals by a few US stockbrokers have resulted in lengthy prison sentences.

59/20 **Hanky-panky/skulduggery/funny business/monkey business/jiggery-pokery/hocus-pocus**: Trickery; dishonest dealing. □ The kilometre reading on that car's clock is far too low; I bet there's been some hanky-panky (skulduggery/monkey business etc.) at the dealer's garage.

59/21 The **game**: The trick or plan. □ Youssef has been acting strangely lately. I wonder what his game is.

59/22 **The game is up**: The deception is revealed. □ The bank clerk was called to the manager's office and told that the game was up and that she would be reported to the police for theft.

59/23 **Do the dirty** on someone: Play a mean trick on someone. □ Meteorological forecasts were good, but on the day the weather did the dirty on us and we got soaking wet.

59/24 **Welsh/welch** on someone: Break an agreement or promise; avoid paying one's debts. The Welsh were traditionally thought to be a race of thieves. □ Svetlana's fiancé welshed (welched) on his promise to marry her. □ As his financial difficulties mounted Mr Kamura decided to welsh on his debts.

59/25 **Sell** someone **down the river**: Betray or defraud. The phrase was originally used by black slaves who were sold to plantation owners further down the Mississippi river where conditions were much harsher. □ Some Czechoslovakians believe that Chamberlain sold their country down the river at the 1938 Munich conference by tolerating the German annexation of the Sudetenland.

59/26 **Two-time/double-cross** someone: Betray or deceive a person with whom one is pretending to collaborate. A deceptive person is a 'two-timer' or a 'double-crosser'. □ Her husband had been two-timing (double-crossing) her with another woman. □ Following the arrests, the underground resistance began to suspect that they had been double-crossed (two-timed) by one of their own members.

59/27 **A sly-boots**: A cunning or insincere person. When the old woman appeared to be dying, her sly-boots of a nephew was first at her bedside although they'd not spoken for years.

59/28 **A wide boy**: A man who is skilled in unscrupulous or dishonest practices. □ I'd not call him a spiv – he's too scruffy. But he's certainly a bit of a wide boy, and I wouldn't buy anything from him.

59/29 **Bogus**: Not genuine; counterfeit. □ A bogus gas-meter reader gained access to her house and robbed her. □ That painting is no masterpiece, it's bogus!

59/30 **Phoney**: Not genuine or sincere. A false object or person is a 'phoney'. □ His watch is a phoney Rolex. □ You can't trust him, he's a phoney.

59/31 **Eyewash** *or* **window-dressing**: Talk or behaviour intended to create a deceptively good impression. □ The 'green' image that the company presents in its public relations is only eyewash (window-dressing), it's one of the biggest polluters in the country.

59/32 **A red herring**: A misleading clue; something that draws attention away from a matter under consideration. A theory held by fox-hunters was that a dried salted herring (a 'red herring') dragged across a fox's trail would divert the hounds from the fox's scent. □ The burglar soon realized that the light was a red herring, and that the house was empty.

59/33 **Make out**: Pretend. □ They like to make out that they are rich.

60: LIE/TEASE

60/1   **A tall story**: An incredible story that is probably untrue. □ Cyrano de Bergerac excelled in telling tall stories.

60/2   **A cock-and-bull story**: A foolish incredible story. □ Sceptics believe that 'Nessie' the Loch Ness monster is a cock-and-bull story.

60/3   **Spin a yarn**: Tell an invented story. □ That old soldier isn't just spinning a yarn, he has in fact been decorated for bravery.

60/4   **Cook up** a story/excuse: Invent or concoct. □ I had to cook up an excuse for being late to work this morning.

60/5   **A fib**: A trivial or unimportant lie. To 'fib' is to tell trivial lies. □ Women sometimes tell fibs (fib) about their age.

60/6   **A white lie**: A harmless or pardonable lie. □ I told the old woman that her grandson was making a good recovery in hospital, but it was a white lie to stop her from worrying unnecessarily.

60/7   **A whopper/thumper**: An outrageous or blatant lie. *(See also 65/2)* □ How can you believe such a whopper/thumper?

60/8   **Lie through one's teeth**: Lie shamelessly. □ One motorist accused the other of lying through his teeth about the cause of the accident.

60/9   **Have** someone **on** *or* **pull** someone's **leg**: Hoax or tease someone. □ When you first told me I'd won the lottery, I thought you were having me on (pulling my leg)!

60/10 **Pull the other one (it's got bells on)!**: "I don't believe that at all!" The expression is a play on the idiom 'pull someone's leg' *(see above)*.

60/11 **Tell that to the Marines!**: "That is blatantly untrue!" The Marines were originally thought to be the most stupid unit of the British navy, capable of believing any obvious lie.

91

60/12 **Kid** someone: Tease; deceive someone especially for fun. □ I was only kidding when I said you were ugly.

60/13 **Take the mickey/piss** (*#?*) out of someone: Tease or ridicule someone. □ When Inga turned up at school with a punk hair-style, the other pupils took the mickey out of her.

60/14 **Josh** someone (*US*):   Tease or hoax in good-natured way. □ My elder sisters used to josh me for forgetting things.

60/15 **Debunk** someone: Show a deception to be false; attack a reputation or claim as exaggerated or untrue. □ The book sets out to debunk the myth that the Pope is infallible.

61: FAIR/HONEST/GENUINE

61/1 **Kosher**:   Genuine; correct; legitimate. From 'kosher', food which complies with Jewish dietary laws. □ I'll do any job, as long as it's kosher.

61/2 **Not cricket**:   Not fair play. □ Shooting pheasants during the close season is not cricket.

61/3 **Above board**:   Without deception or concealment; done honestly or fairly. □ Our company has already refused several contracts because we believed they were not above board.

61/4 **Fair dos!**:   (Pronounced '*dooze*'.) "Let us act fairly!" *or* "Let fairness prevail!" □ It's time you let your sister play with the Game Boy – come on, fair dos! You've had a whole hour!

61/5 **Fair and square**:   Straightforwardly or honestly. □ He beat you in tennis fair and square. □ I'll tell you fair and square the state of my finances.

61/6 **A square deal**:   An honest deal or fair treatment. □ Women often complain that they don't get a square deal at work. □ I can't complain about the transaction; we made a square deal.

61/7 **A raw deal**:   Unfair treatment. □ Many Palestinians feel that they have had a raw deal from the international community.

61/8 **Give** someone **a fair crack of the whip**:   Give someone a fair chance to share in something. □ World affluence is unevenly spread and developing countries are demanding that they be given a fair crack of the whip.

61/9 **On the level**:   Honestly; without deception. □ Some businessmen are unfortunately not on the level. □ Tell me, on the level, what has happened to the car!

61/10 **Even-handed**:   Impartial; unbiased; fair. □ The referee was very even-handed.

61/11 **Go by the book**:   Act in accordance with the correct procedure. □ The two policemen charged with assaulting a suspect during interrogation claimed they had gone by the book.

61/12 The **salt of the earth**: Someone or people of an upright nature with a positive influence on society. □ Farmers are the salt of the earth.

61/13 **Straight as a die**: Very honest; incorruptible. □ Many officers in the Moscow militia had become corrupt, but Sobchak remained straight as a die.

61/14 **Honest-to-goodness**: Real or straightforward. □ After being abroad, it's good to get back to an honest-to-goodness cup of English tea. □ I gave him an honest-to-goodness answer.

61/15 **The real McCoy**: The real thing; the genuine article. 'Kid' McCoy was the American welter-weight boxing champion of the world from 1890 to 1900. □ If you're looking for a computer expert, Mr Norimoto is the real McCoy. □ The party must have cost a lot – even the caviar was the real McCoy.

EXERCISES 12: DECEPTION

A) Insert an animal or person to complete the following sentences.

1) Scientists wasted a lot of time investigating a promising test-result that proved to be a red . . . .
2) Either they don't know anything, or they are playing . . . .
3) Tell that to the . . . s, it's a ridiculous story!
4) What a silly . . . and . . . story!
5) Behave yourself, and no . . . business!
6) They have taken me to the . . . s and disappeared with my money.
7) The thief . . . ed her into opening the door by claiming to be a postman.

B) Give colloquialisms to fit the following definitions.

1) a dishonest or despicable person.
2) a cunning person.
3) a swindler.
4) someone skilled in unscrupulous practices.
5) the real thing or genuine article.
6) a harmless or pardonable lie.
7) unfair treatment.
8) something fraudulently arranged in advance.
9) not genuine or false.
10) deceptive talk or behaviour.
11) a dishonest firm that never stays long in the same place.

→

C) Insert a verb of movement or activity, paying attention to the tense.

1) The accountant was accused of . . . the books.
2) Don't believe him, he's just . . . a yarn.
3) No-one could believe such a story, yet you . . . for it.
4) That market trader tried to . . . a fast one on me.
5) He has been . . . you up the garden path all along.

D) Give an adverb (*to/away/up* etc.) to complete the sentences.

1) I was completely taken . . . by his smooth talk.
2) They are dishonest and are always . . . the fiddle.
3) We gave him our trust, but he sold us . . . the river.
4) The game was . . . for the pickpocket after he was arrested in the station.
5) You are not really hurt, so don't put it . . .!
6) You are lying . . . your teeth!
7) The suspect cooked . . . an alibi for the time of the robbery.

E) From the module, replace the underlined colloquialism with as many synonymous expressions as possible, paying attention to the tense of any verb.

1) That roof repair was far too expensive, the contractors have <u>taken you to the cleaners</u>.
2) Some firms <u>fob off</u> their inferior-quality goods to countries in the developing world.
3) Don't trust him, he is <u>leading you up the garden path</u>!
4) One of our cashiers is up to some <u>hanky-panky</u> at the till.
5) Stop <u>pulling his leg</u>, he will learn with time!
6) What you are doing is <u>not cricket</u>.

Quantity

62: AMOUNT

62/1   **A whack**: A share of something. □ In the evening, the workmen went home having done their whack for the day. □ Government taxes account for a large whack of the price of a packet of cigarettes.

62/2   **A dollop**: A mass or quantity; a portion. □ The meal consisted of two sausages and a dollop of sauerkraut.

62/3   **A decent** amount: A quite large amount. □ Gilles earns a decent wage.

62/4   **Dish out** something: Distribute an amount or quantity of something; inflict punishment. □ The boxer dished out a lot of heavy punches to his opponent. □ Relief agencies are dishing out food and blankets in the famine region.

62/5   **Enough to be getting/going on with**: Enough to continue for the time being. □ The factory doesn't need any more packing-cases this week; they've got enough to be getting (going) on with.

62/6   **Hold out**: To last. □ The miners' strike was in its tenth week and people were worried about how long their coal stocks would hold out.

62/7   **Go round**: Be enough for everyone. □ The cleaning gang arrived to find there were not enough protective suits to go round.

62/8   **Give or take**: (in estimating a quantity) add or subtract an amount. □ The village is twenty kilometres from here, give or take a couple.

62/9   **Tot up** figures: Add up an amount or figures. (*Do not confuse with 'top up' – see 50/14*) □ The housewife totted up the prices on her grocery bill and discovered she had been overcharged.

62/10   **Jack up** *or* **hike** a price: Increase an amount or raise a price. □ Airlines are using the increase in fuel prices to hike (jack) up fares.

63: SMALL AMOUNT

63/1   **A smidgen**: A very small amount (sometimes spelt 'smidgin'). □ It can be done with a smidgen of care. □ Just a smidgin of milk in my coffee!

63/2   **A spot**: A small amount of something. □ We played a spot of tennis. □ I'm having a spot of bother with my car. □ How about a spot of lunch?

63/3   **Tiddly/piffling/trifling/measly/piddling**: Very small; meagre; worthless. (*For 'tiddly' see also 155/8*) □ The prisoners were given a measly (piffling etc.) half kilo of rice a day to survive on. □ Wages in that country are piddling (trifling etc.) compared to ours.

63/4 **Precious:** (Used ironically) considerably or very. □ We made precious little profit last year. □ Precious few attended the lecture.

63/5 A **drop in the ocean:** A tiny fraction of what is required. □ The scale of the earthquake damage is massive, and the aid we have collected is only a drop in the ocean.

63/6 **Within a whisker** *or* **. . . an ace of:** Within a small distance or amount from something; very near to success in doing something. *(See also 48/1)* □ The climber came to within an ace (a whisker) of death when his foot slipped. □ The amount raised by the charity race was within a whisker (an ace) of last year's sum.

63/7 **Better than a slap in the eye/face** *or* **better than a kick up the arse** *(#?):* Better than nothing at all. □ "Our wage increase doesn't keep up with inflation". "Yes, but it's better than a slap in the face (a kick up the arse)!" □ At least they said thank-you, it's better than a slap in the eye (slap in the face etc.).

63/8 A **fat lot:** Nothing or almost nothing. □ I was a year on that course, and a fat lot I learnt. □ A fat lot of help you are!

63/9 **Sod all** *(#?) or* **zilch** *or* **not a sausage** *or* **fuck all** *(#??) or* **bugger all** *(#??):* Nothing at all. □ We went fishing but we caught sod all (zilch/we didn't catch a sausage).

63/10 **Sweet Fanny Adams** *or* **sweet F.A.:** Nothing at all. 'Fanny Adams' is a euphemism or substitute expression for 'fuck all' i.e. nothing. □ Business is worse than slack, we've sold sweet Fanny Adams (sweet F.A.) all morning.

63/11 **Pushed/pressed/strapped** for something: Short of; in need of. □ He can't stop, he's pushed/pressed/strapped for time. □ Would you lend me some money, I'm strapped/pushed/pressed for cash?

63/12 **Thin on the ground:** Sparse; few and far between. □ Skilled technicians are thin on the ground in this area. □ That region is arid and oases are thin on the ground.

63/13 **Dribs and drabs:** Small amounts. □ Donations for the orphans' home arrived in dribs and drabs, but the total soon mounted.

63/14 **In a nutshell:** Concisely; expressed in the briefest possible way. □ This book explains basic electronics in a nutshell.

63/15 **Potted:** Abridged or shortened. □ That chemistry manual is too large for quick revision so I use the potted edition.

64: LARGE AMOUNT

64/1 **Tons/bags/loads/stacks/pots/oodles:** A large amount of something. □ There's no hurry, we still have stacks (tons/loads etc.) of time. □ The flats are infested with cockroaches; there are tons (loads etc.) of them.

64/2 **No end** of *or* **any amount** of something: Unlimited; a very large amount of something. □ He has no end (any amount) of money.

64/3 **Umpteen**: Very many. □ We've complained umpteen times about the leaking roof.

64/4 **A good few**: A fairly large number. □ It's no secret, a good few know about it already. □ I've been to Milan a good few times on business.

64/5 **A thousand and one**: Very many; a large number. □ There are a thousand and one ways of making money. □ The book contains a thousand and one tips for improving the home.

64/6 Something **galore**: In plenty. □ We have food galore on board, what we need is water. □ Marilyn Monroe had beauty galore.

64/7 A **power** of something: A large amount of something. □ Jogging has done me a power of good.

64/8 **Healthy**: Large. □ Their balance sheet shows a healthy profit.

64/9 A **sight**: A great deal or quantity of something. □ The furniture cost a sight. □ I feel a sight better after that rest.

64/10 **Lashings**: A lot. □ We ate strawberries with lashings of cream.

64/11 **Lousy** with something: Crowded or overrun with people or creatures; well provided with something. □ She is lousy with money. □ The village was lousy with tourists.

64/12 **Crawling** with: Crowded or overrun with people or crawling creatures. □ The city centre is crawling with armed police. □ The walls of the house were crawling with ants.

64/13 **Come out of the woodwork**: Overrun a place; occur in very large numbers.□ The military situation there is hopeless; the enemy soldiers are coming out of the woodwork.

64/14 **Common as muck**: Very common; very vulgar. □ Twenty years ago, video recorders were rare, now they're as common as muck. □ They pretend to be refined people, but in fact they're as common as muck.

64/15 **Common-or-garden**: Common or everyday; occurring in large numbers. □ Your necklace is not pearl, it's common-or-garden plastic. □ That's a common-or-garden sparrow, not a nightingale.

64/16 **Thick and fast**: In large and frequent amounts. □ Orders for our products are coming in thick and fast.

64/17 **Churn out** something: Produce in large numbers. □ The factory churns out fridges at the rate of two a minute. □ The physicist churned out a host of facts to support his theory.

64/18 **Lock, stock and barrel**: Including everything; completely. The lock, stock and barrel are the three main parts that make up a whole rifle. □ The bankrupt firm was sold lock, stock and barrel to a Japanese buyer.

64/19 **Everything but the kitchen sink**: Almost everything imaginable. □ When they went on holiday, it seemed their car was loaded with everything but the kitchen sink.

64/20 **Every mortal** thing: Everything without exception. □ The burglars took every mortal thing of value.

64/21 **The works:** Everything possible. □ The Spanish Inquisition used to apply all forms of torture on heretics: the rack, hot irons, thumb-screws – the works.

64/22 **The whole shoot/shooting-match/caboodle/shebang/boiling:** The whole lot; everything or everyone. □ Ivan is an astronomer all right; he has telescopes, a night camera, a spectrograph – the whole caboodle (shooting-match/shebang etc.). □ In the capital, corruption is rife: government officials, police, the judiciary – the whole boiling (caboodle/shoot etc.).

64/23 **The world and his wife:** Everybody. □ Monika's main worry about appearing in court was not the fine, but that the world and his wife might know about her offence through the press.

65: LARGE and SMALL SIZE

65/1 **Bumper:** Unusually large or plentiful. □ We had a bumper harvest this year. □ At Christmas the magazine will appear in a bumper edition.

65/2 **A whopper:** Something very large. (*See also 60/7*) □ This was not a usual alligator but a whopper.

65/3 **Whopping/thumping/thundering/whacking/walloping:** Very large or remarkable. □ The Lund family live in a whopping (thundering/whacking etc.) great house. □ That is a whopping (thumping/walloping etc.) lie! □ Ulrike is making a thundering (whopping etc.) nuisance of herself.

65/4 **Dirty great *or* almighty:** Very big or powerful. □ Suddenly there was a dirty great (an almighty) bang. □ He was a thick-set man with dirty great (almighty) hands.

65/5 **Unholy**: Very great; outrageous. *(See also 30/1 and 32/1)* □ The bomb left behind a scene of unholy devastation. □ Then I saw it was not a fish, but an unholy great shark.

65/6 **A whale of a** thing: Something exceedingly great or good. □ The children had a whale of a time in the fun park. □ We had a whale of a feast in the strawberry patch.

65/7 **A heck/hell of a** thing: Something exceedingly good or unpleasant. □ I used to admire your father; he was a heck (hell) of a man. □ In rough seas fishermen can have a heck (hell) of a time getting their nets back on board.

65/8 **The daddy/mammy of** *or* **the father/mother of** something: The greatest or largest example of something. □ The mammy (mother) of all hurricanes is approaching the coast. □ Harry Houdini is widely thought to be the daddy (father) of all escape artists.

65/9 **Teeny/wee**: Tiny. □ The factory girls were soldering teeny (wee) electronic components with great dexterity. □ She carried a teeny (wee) poodle in her arms.

65/10 **Teeny-weeny**: Very tiny. □ You should show a teeny-weeny bit of common sense! □ Teeny-weeny cracks had appeared on the wings of the plane.

65/11 **Dinky**: Attractively small and neat. □ The girl was wearing a dinky dress. □ The bar shelves were lined with dinky bottles of famous alcohol brands.

65/12 **Diddy**: Small and funny or strange. □ I was amazed that such a diddy satellite dish could give such a high-quality TV picture. □ Guillermo has a diddy three-wheeled car.

65/13 **Pint-sized**: Very small. □ They were an unlikely couple; she was tall and thin while her husband was pint-sized and fat.

66: EXTREME/LIMIT

66/1 **Overstep/overshoot the mark**: Do more than is allowed; exceed the limit. □ The salesmen were given a fixed advertising budget and asked not to overstep (overshoot) the mark. □ You overstepped (overshot) the mark with that impolite comment.

66/2 **Go over the top**: Act rashly or wildly; act excessively or in an extreme way. □ That newspaper has gone over the top with its inconsidered criticism of the Royal Family. □ I went over the top and spent all my savings on a new yacht.

66/3 **Go the whole hog**: Do something thoroughly or completely; make no compromise or reservation. A 'hog' is an obsolete slang term for a 'shilling' (itself an obsolete British coin now replaced by the fivepenny piece), and the phrase meant originally to spend this money all at once. □ In an attempt to recoup his betting losses, he went the whole hog and put all his remaining money on one horse.

66/4 **Take the biscuit/cake**: Be extreme or absurd; go too far. □ Everyone has bad luck sometimes, but what has happened to you takes the biscuit.

66/5 **The last straw**: The thing that makes something excessive; the breaking-point. From the proverb 'It is the last straw that breaks the camel's back. □ When the blackmailer began demanding a share in his business, it was the last straw and Van der Zwaan finally went to the police.

66/6 **Make a mountain out of a molehill**: Greatly exaggerate the importance of something or the seriousness of a difficulty. □ Of course we'll replace the damaged goods – there's no need to make a mountain out of a molehill by cancelling the contract!

66/7 **Steep/stiff/thick**: Beyond what is reasonable, endurable or acceptable. □ It's a bit thick (steep/stiff) to ask me to install a shower unit in an afternoon.

66/8 **A tall order**: A very difficult or excessive task. □ Predicting the weather a month from now is a tall order.

66/9 **Lay it on thick** *or* **lay it on with a trowel** *or* **pile it on**: Exaggerate; show excessive emotion; flatter excessively. □ The magazine is very pro-monarchy and in their articles about the royals, they lay it on with a trowel (pile it on/lay it on thick). □ Damage from the kitchen fire had been relatively minor, but in their insurance claim they piled it on (laid it on with a trowel etc.).

66/10 **At a pinch**: In a necessary or extreme situation. □ I can't raise all the money, but at a pinch I could get half that amount.

66/11 **When it comes to the crunch** *or* **when the chips are down**: When the situation becomes extreme or critical and a choice must be made. □ The pensioner had refused to pay his TV licence on principle, saying that when it came to the crunch (when the chips were down) he would go to prison.

66/12 **At the end of the day**: In the final count; if a choice has to be made. □ Several tribes had refused to take part in the 'Jihad', but the rebels calculated that, at the end of the day, they were Moslems and would join them in the 'holy war'.

66/13 **Scrape (the bottom of) the barrel**: As an extreme measure, be driven to using one's last and inferior resources. □ In the last days of the Third Reich, the German home guard was forced to scrape the barrel (the bottom of the barrel) and recruit even children and old men.

66/14 **Up to the hilt**: Completely. □ I'm up to the hilt in debt. □ He's a die-hard conservative up to the hilt.

66/15 **At the outside**: At most; at the top limit. □ At the outside, there are not more than 3000 spectators in the stadium.

66/16 **Ever so**: Extremely; very much. □ Thanks ever so! □ She refused, but ever so politely.

66/17 **Not half**: Extremely or violently. □ It wasn't half stuffy in that room! □ He didn't half hit the boy. □ "How about a beer?" "Not half!"

66/18 **Something terrible**: Excessively or outrageously. □ It has been raining something terrible lately. □ She typed the letter something terrible with mistakes in every line.

66/19 **Out-and-out**: Thorough; extreme. □ Khamed's conduct amounts to out-and-out dishonesty.

66/20 **As they make them *or* as they come**: (Of a quality or example) as is possible to find. □ He is as tough as they make them (as they come). □ That train is as fast as they come (as they make them).

66/21 **Dyed-in-the-wool**: Holding extreme and unalterable opinions. □ Walther Ulbricht was a dyed-in-the-wool communist.

66/22 **Well-and-truly**: Completely; totally. □ Our team was well-and-truly beaten. □ I am well-and-truly exhausted.

66/23 **Dead**: Extremely; completely; exactly. □ He came home dead drunk. □ The arrow hit the target dead in the centre. □ I was dead amused by his antics.

66/24 **Bang/slap-bang**: Exactly. (*See 21/12 and 146/11*) □ They arrived bang (slap-bang) on time. □ Our balloon came down bang (slap-bang) in the middle of a maize field.

66/25 **Spot-on/dead-on/bang-on**: Exact; precisely. □ Your guess was dead-on (spot-on/bang-on). □ The golfer's shot was spot-on (bang-on/dead-on).

66/26 **Right/regular/proper**: Total; thorough. □ Marie is a proper (regular/ right) fool. □ His room was in a right (regular etc.) mess. □ We had a regular (right/proper) row last night.

EXERCISES 13: QUANTITY

A) Replace the underlined text with colloquialisms from the module.

1) We have enough supplies <u>for the time being</u>.
2) The landlord has <u>increased</u> our rent.
3) The word 'horrid' describes our trip <u>concisely</u>.
4) Don't speak so loudly, we don't want <u>everyone</u> to know about it!
5) I've seen some large spiders, but this one is the <u>biggest</u> of them all.
6) <u>If the situation becomes critical</u>, I will mortgage my house to keep my business going.
7) This dictionary is <u>exactly</u> up-to-date.
8) Don't <u>exaggerate trivial matters</u>!
9) I didn't earn much from that job, but <u>it's better than nothing</u>.

→

B) Insert an object or a substance to complete the following sentences.

1) That fault of his was the last . . . ; I'm going to dismiss him.
2) They sold their firm . . . , . . . and . . . , before moving abroad.
3) Any attempt to convince him of the existence of God is useless, he's a dyed-in-the- . . . atheist.
4) In my youth, ballpoint pens were thin on the . . . ; now they are as common as . . . .
5) The film was not as bad as she claims – she's laying it on with a . . . .
6) Anyone who would marry a convicted murderer is scraping the bottom of the . . . .
7) The bailiffs came to the debtor's house and took everything but the . . . .
8) I've seen some brave men, but what he did takes the . . . .
9) She gave me nothing for my trouble, not a . . . .

C) Replace the underlined colloquialism with as many synonyms from the module as possible.

1) I allowed my daughter to bring a couple of class-friends to dinner, but she brought the whole shooting-match.
2) From these seeds you can grow whopping great melons.
3) This fuel-efficient engine consumes a measly 5 litres per 100 km.
4) Take some of my manure for your garden, I've got tons.
5) Your prediction was spot-on.
6) I searched the room for the keys, but I found zilch.

D) Insert a verb of movement or work in the correct tense.

1) The plantation covers about 6000 hectares, . . . or . . . a few hundred.
2) The farmers are . . . for time, and must get the harvest in before the monsoon arrives.
3) Some countries are short of doctors, yet here they are . . . out of the woodwork.
4) Our dinner break is a half hour, but yesterday we . . . the mark by twenty minutes.
5) The palace entrance was . . . with reporters waiting for the royal couple.
6) That boy is not as hurt as would seem from his crying, he is just . . . it on to gain sympathy.

Quality

67: EXCELLENT/GOOD/USEFUL

67/1   **A spanker/peach/stunner/belter/corker/smasher**: Something extremely good or excellent; an attractive person or thing. □ That girl is a corker (stunner/peach etc.). □ It's a corker (spanker/smasher etc.) of a car.

67/2   **A humdinger**: Anything very good or efficient. □ The chamber orchestra produced a humdinger of a performance.

67/3   **A knock-out**: An outstanding or irresistible person or thing. □ Our new caravan is a knock-out. □ That singer is a knock-out.

67/4   **The cat's whiskers**: An excellent example of something. *(See also 122/1)* □ Our new cordless telephone is the cat's whiskers.

67/5   **Top-notch/crack**: First-rate; excellent. □ The marines are top-notch (crack) troops. □ The figure-skating pair put in a top-notch performance.

67/6   **Super-duper**: Excellent; bigger or better than the others. □ The radio telescope is controlled by a super-duper computer. □ We had a super-duper time in Paris.

67/7   **Out of this world**: Wonderful; excellent. □ The view from the top of Niagara Falls is out of this world.

67/8   **Cracking/smashing/rattling**: Very good; excellent. *(See also 22/17)* □ Pablo has written a cracking (rattling/smashing) novel.

67/9   **Tiptop**: Excellent; very best. □ I feel in tiptop condition. □ Her memory for numbers is tiptop.

67/10   **Capital/swell/champion/brill/wizard**: Excellent; splendid. □ It's swell (wizard/brill etc.) of you to look after my cat while I'm away.

67/11   **Groovy**: Excellent; admirable. □ Some people find parachuting a scary experience, but I find it groovy. □ There are some really groovy suits on sale.

67/12   **Right-royal**: Excellent; high-class; of exceptional size. □ We had a right-royal dinner. □ They were having a right-royal row.

67/13   (As) **good as gold**: In excellent condition; very well behaved. □ The children were as good as gold during the train journey. □ My leg is good as gold after the injury.

67/14   **Brand-new**: Factory-new; in excellent condition. □ I couldn't afford a brand-new car, so I bought one second-hand.

67/15   **In mint condition**: In excellent condition, as if just out of the mint (the place where coins are minted or produced). □ To the archaeologists' delight, the clay had preserved the armour in mint condition.

67/16 **In good nick**:   In good condition. □ You've kept your scooter in good nick. □ We survived the crash in good nick.

67/17 **Glorified**:   Made to appear more splendid or excellent than something really is. □ They were living not in a house, but a glorified caravan.

67/18 **Come in handy**:   Serve a useful purpose. □ This old glass will come in handy for a garden cold-frame.

67/19 **Stand** someone **in good stead**:   Be of great service or advantage to someone. □ The skills learned here will stand you in good stead in the future. □ This sturdy old lawnmower has stood me in good stead over the years.

68: BETTER/SUPERIOR

68/1 **Nobody can touch** someone **for** something: Someone is far superior to all others in something. □ No competitor can touch us for speed of delivery. □ Nobody could touch him for impudence.

68/2 **Take a lot of beating**:   Be difficult to beat or surpass. □ For ease of use, this new video camera takes a lot of beating.

68/3 **A cut above** someone/something: Noticeably superior. □ That washing-machine is a cut above the rest in performance.

68/4 **Streets ahead of** someone/something *or* **leave** someone/something **standing**:   Far superior to someone or something; a long way in advance of. □ Our scientists are streets ahead of the rest of the world (leave the rest of the world standing) in electronics.

68/5 **Not in the same street/league** as someone/something: Inferior to someone or something. □ That Italian boxer is good, but not in the same street (league) as the American champion.

68/6 **Not a patch on** someone/something: Not nearly as good as. □ Earlier tape recorders are not a patch on modern versions.

68/7 **Cannot hold a candle to** someone: Be very inferior to. In the Middle Ages, those who could afford it would hire a menial person to light them home at night with a candle – from which it follows that if someone isn't even fit to 'hold a candle . . .' then he must be very inferior indeed. □ Sebastian is favourite to win the tournament since the other golfers can't hold a candle to him.

68/8 **Don't teach your grandmother/granny to suck eggs**:   Don't try to instruct someone who is superior or far more experienced in something. □ Don't teach your granny to suck eggs; I've been gardening for thirty years and know perfectly well how to prune a cherry tree!

68/9 **The pick of the bunch**:   The best of the lot. □ These job applicants that we've short-listed are the pick of the bunch.

68/10 Something **with knobs on**:   That and more; of a superior kind. □ When he insulted her, she returned the insult with knobs on.

68/11 **And** something **at that**: And in addition to that. □ Theo is an electrician, and a good one at that.

68/12 Something-**cum**-something: Serving or working in addition as something. □ I work as a handyman-cum-gardener. □ This hall serves as an office-cum-storeroom.

68/13 **The edge on** someone/something: An advantage over someone or something. □ This applicant has the edge on the other candidates through her long work experience. □ Advanced technology gives Nato planes the edge on any enemy aviation.

68/14 **Go one better**: Make a better effort than someone else. □ Rival firms reduced their prices, but we went one better by offering easy credit terms.

68/15 **One-upmanship**: The art of maintaining a psychological advantage over others. □ One-upmanship ensures a great demand for personalized car number-plates.

68/16 **Steal the show**: Outshine the competition; be better than others. □ At the annual Chopin festival in Warsaw, a Japanese pianist stole the show.

69: AVERAGE/MEDIOCRE

69/1 **So-so!**: Only moderately good or well. □ "How is your health these days?" "So-so!" □ "How did you do in the exams?" "So-so!"

69/2 **Middle-of-the-road**: Average; ordinary. □ Your daughter's school work is middle-of-the-road. □ What the country needs now is radical reform, not middle-of-the-road policies!

69/3 **Run-of-the-mill**: Average; not particularly good or interesting. □ I'm not an engineer, just a run-of-the-mill technician.

69/4 **Fair-to-middling**: Moderately good. □ My knowledge of Spanish is fair-to-middling.

69/5 **Nothing to write home about**: Nothing special or unusual; mediocre. □ The football match was nothing to write home about.

69/6 **Not all that** someone/something **is cracked up to be**: Overvalued; not as good or special as is claimed. □ Some foreign tourists to Copenhagen find the mermaid statue not all that it is cracked up to be.

69/7 **Not much cop** *or* **no great shakes** *or* **not up to much**: Not very good; mediocre. □ In carpentry I'm no great shakes (not much cop/not up to much). □ The film is not much cop (no great shakes etc.).

70: POOR QUALITY/UNPLEASANT

70/1 **Tatty**: Ragged; shabby and untidy. □ Edith wore a tatty dress. □ We used to live in a tatty two-roomed flat.

70/2 **Crummy** *or* **crappy** *(#?)*:   Dirty, inferior or worthless. □ He wore a crummy (crappy) suit. □ I got a crummy two dollars for the watch.

70/3 **Grotty**:   Nasty; unpleasant. *(See also 175/5)* □ They work in a grotty office.

70/4 **Lousy**:   Disgusting; very bad; ill. □ My Italian is lousy. □ I feel lousy today. □ It's a lousy job.

70/5 **Yucky**:   Disgusting; unpleasant. □ We had a yucky experience. □ My wife finds spiders yucky.

70/6 **Naff**:   Unfashionable, in poor taste; unappealing. *(See 110/30 for 'naff off')* □ Flared trousers were fashionable in the '70s; by 1980 they were naff. □ That's a naff idea – why don't we do something more exciting?

70/7 **Beastly/chronic/terrible/rotten**:   Very unpleasant. □ The weather there was chronic (beastly/rotten etc.). □ I have a beastly (terrible etc.) cold.

70/8 **Rop(e)y**:   Of mediocre or poor quality; inadequate. The spelling varies. □ The wine was rather ropy. □ In the last month he has made only two ropey efforts to find work.

70/9 **Suck** *(US)(#?)*:   Be of very low quality or unpleasant. □ The meals in this boarding-house suck. □ That city sucks.

70/10 **Wishy-washy**:   Lacking strength or positive qualities. □ Critics accused the president of indecisiveness and wishy-washy policies. □ This coffee is wishy-washy.

70/11 **A rule of thumb**:   A rough practical method of procedure. □ A rule of thumb for estimating the cost of a building is the number of bricks used.

70/12 **Rough-and-ready**:   Rough or crude but effective; (of a person) rough and unrefined. □ To get back to port, the fishermen made a rough-and-ready sail out of tarpaulin and rope.

71: DEFECTIVE/USELESS

71/1 **Bust**:   Broken; burst. *(See also 18/12)* □ The water pipe is bust in several places. □ Our washing machine is bust.

71/2 **Up the spout**:   Broken or ruined. *(See also 29/5)* □ My hair-drier is up the spout.

71/3 **Knackered/buggered** *(#??)*:   Broken or ruined; exhausted. A 'knacker' is a worn-out horse (or horse-slaughterer), hence the colloquialism – *see also 180/2*. To 'knacker' or 'bugger' something (in the colloquial sense) is to break or ruin it. □ That public phone is knackered (buggered).

71/4 **Clapped-out**:   Worn-out or defective; exhausted. To 'clap out' is to become defective through use. □ The police motorway control stopped a number of clapped-out and dangerous vehicles. □ He died after his liver clapped out.

71/5 **Duff/bum/dud**:   Worthless, useless or defective. □ This Biro is dud (duff/bum), give me another! □ Oskar is a duff (bum/dud) bricklayer, so don't employ him to build your wall. □ My alarm clock is duff.

106

71/6 **A crock**: Someone who suffers from bad health or lameness; an old or defective vehicle or ship. To 'crock up' is to become a defective. □ My car is such an old crock, I don't think I should drive it on the motorway. □ After being shot on duty, the young policeman was crocked up.

71/7 **The worse for wear**: Damaged by use; injured or exhausted. *(See also 180/3)* □ I work on the Metro repairing those ticket machines that are the worse for wear.

71/8 **Pack up/in**: Fail or break down. □ The bottling machine in bay 2 has packed up (packed in).

71/9 **Conk out**: Break down or fail; (of a person or animal) collapse with exhaustion or die. □ One of the plane's engines conked out over Lima. □ The caravan trail was littered with the bones of camels that had conked out.

71/10 **Go west**: Be destroyed, lost or killed. The expression alludes to the sun setting or disappearing in the west; it might also derive from the fact that Tyburn, a public hanging site, was situated to the west of London. □ Several of the stone sculptures in the park had gone west overnight.

71/11 **Go for a Burton**: Be lost, destroyed or killed. Burton beer was popular in the 1930s, and the term was coined by British airmen in World War 2 to describe comrades lost in action. □ We arrived at Cairo to find that our luggage had gone for a Burton somewhere on the journey. □ The mechanic told us that our car's petrol pump had gone for a Burton.

71/12 **A lemon**: A useless or disappointing person or thing. In the USA, 'the lemon laws' is a nickname given to legislation protecting consumers against faulty goods. □ When we got the food-mixer home, we found it was a lemon.

71/13 **Wonky**: Shaky; unsteady. □ One of my front teeth has become wonky. □ The sea crossing had been rough, and when we got off the ship, we were all feeling slightly wonky.

71/14 **Cock-eyed**: Slanting; not straight. □ You've hung the painting all cock-eyed. □ My uncle is eccentric and has a cock-eyed view of the world.

71/15 **Dicky**: Unsound; likely to collapse or fail. □ Watch out on the staircase, some of the steps are dicky! □ Mrs Rosso is ill with a dicky heart.

71/16 **Bunged up**: Blocked or clogged. □ The drainpipe is bunged up with leaves. □ My nose is bunged up.

71/17 **Go haywire**: Become totally disorganized; go crazy or out of control. □ As we neared the barrel of radio-active waste, the needle on the geiger-counter seemed to go haywire. □ Snow on the tracks has made the train timetable go haywire.

71/18 **On the blink**: Failing from time to time; (of a screen) producing a flashing or undefined image. □ A freak storm caused radar screens in the air-traffic control tower to go on the blink. □ Our TV is on the blink.

71/19 **A gremlin**: Technical disturbance or interference; unidentified problem in machinery. □ I reckon there's a gremlin in my word-processor – it keeps going wrong and nobody can trace the fault.

71/20 **Drive a coach and horses through** something: Make use of the serious defects or loopholes in a set of rules or an argument, thus revealing its shortcomings. □ Tax accountants drove a coach and horses through the new legislation.

71/21 **No earthly use/good:** Of no conceivable or possible use. □ With this back injury, I'm no earthly good (use) for heavy work.

71/22 **Need** something **like a hole in the head:** Have no need for something totally useless or harmful; be better without a person or thing which causes great problems or breakdowns. □ With all my debts, I need this electricity bill like I need a hole in the head.

72: DIFFERENT

72/1 **The odd-man-out:** A person or thing differing in some way from others in a group. □ These intelligence tests consist of various shapes, and children are asked to spot the odd-man-out.

72/2 (As) **different as chalk and cheese:** Be completely different; have nothing in common. □ They are twins but their characters are as different as chalk and cheese.

72/3 **Poles/worlds apart:** Vastly different. □ The policies of the two main parties are worlds (poles) apart.

72/4 **By a long chalk:** By far. □ Of the two sprinters, that one is the better by a long chalk. □ I'm no portrait painter, not by a long chalk.

72/5 **A far cry from** something: Greatly different from. □ Medical science today is a far cry from the situation a century ago.

72/6 **A whole new ball game**: A totally different situation or set of circumstances. □ The advent of nuclear weapons has made international confrontation a whole new ball game.

72/7 **A different/another kettle of fish**: A quite different matter. (*Do not confuse with 'a pretty kettle of fish' – see 30/5*) □ The police can't do anything about your aggressive neighbour; if he breaks the law, that's a different (another) kettle of fish.

72/8 **There is more than one way to skin a cat**: There are different ways of achieving one's aims or objectives. □ Don't try to remove the bolt by force; soak it in paraffin first – there's more than one way to skin a cat.

72/9 **Separate the sheep from the goats**: Separate the good from the bad. □ This harsher economic climate will separate the sheep from the goats, and only the more efficient firms will survive.

72/10 **A U-turn**: A reversal of policy or views; a totally different line of conduct or action. □ The club made a U-turn on its rule not to allow women members.

72/11 **Move the goal-posts**: Unfairly change the rules or objectives. □ Japanese businessmen often complain that European governments are always moving the goal-posts by introducing new regulations on imports.

72/12 **The boot is on the other foot**: The situation is reversed; the opposite is true. □ The German army had advanced almost unchecked to the Volga, but after Stalingrad the boot was on the other foot.

72/13 **A mixed bag**: An assortment of different things or people. □ The army conscripts were a mixed bag, ranging from cobblers to musicians.

73: SAME/SIMILAR

73/1 **Not a pin (to choose) between**: No difference whatsoever between two or more things. □ There was not a pin to choose between the top three singers in the contest. □ They are both rogues of the same calibre with not a pin (to choose) between them.

73/2 **(As) like as two peas**: Extremely similar; indistinguishable between each other. □ The two signatures were as like as two peas.

73/3 **Spitting image**: An exact likeness. □ People are always stopping him in the street because he's the spitting image of Ronald Reagan.

73/4 **A chip off the old block**: A child who is very like his parents in looks or behaviour. □ Arne is a chip off the old block; he became a professional footballer just like his father.

73/5 **Six of one and half a dozen of the other** *or* **six and two threes**: No difference at all between two alternatives. □ We can go in your car or mine, it's six and two threes (six of one and half a dozen of the other).

73/6 **It's (as) broad as it is long**: It amounts to the same thing. □ You can buy a ticket here or pay on board the ferry, it's (as) broad as it is long.

73/7 **Tit for tat**: An equivalent retaliation to an injury or abuse suffered. □ The inter-ethnic clashes were accompanied by tit-for-tat killings.

73/8 **Two can play at that game**: One can use the same measures or tactics as one's opponent. □ They have expelled our ambassador to their country as a protest; well, two can play at that game.

73/9 **By the same token**: Similarly; in the same way or for the same reason. □ I am polite to others, and by the same token, I expect them to be polite to me.

73/10 **Even Stephen(s)/even Steven(s)**: Even shares, scores or performance; in an even way. Many colloquialisms (essentially spoken expressions) that involve names which may be spelt in more than one way offer alternatives when printed, and the initial letters of these names may not always be in capitals. □ My partner and I share the profits even stephen(s). □ The football match was even Steven(s) at half time.

73/11 **Level-pegging**: Equal levels or scores of achievement, especially in a contest. □ After the launch of the Russian space probe, the Soviets were level pegging with the Americans in the space race to Mars.

73/12 **In the same boat**: Suffering the same problems; in the same difficult circumstances. □ The downturn in world trade has affected our exports, but our competitors are in the same boat.

73/13 **Join the club!**: 'The same applies here!'; in other words, you have experienced the same set of circumstances or hold the same views as the other person. □ If you think the road should be fenced off, join the club; all the neighbours think the same.

73/14 **The likes of** someone: People similar to someone. □ Polo is too expensive a sport for the likes of us.

73/15 **Of that ilk**: Of the same sort or kind. □ Mr Sokolov is an academic or someone of that ilk. □ They are rogues and I don't associate with persons of that ilk.

73/16 **Next-door to** something: Almost the same as; equivalent to. □ Filling in a false age on a job application form is next-door to dishonesty.

74: SUITABILITY

74/1 **Just the ticket/job** *or* **just what the doctor ordered**: Exactly what is needed. □ Iced drinks are just the ticket (just the job/just what the doctor ordered) in this heat.

74/2 **Up one's street/alley**: Within one's field of knowledge or interests. □ Gossip is right up her street (alley). □ Questions about physics are not up my street (alley), I'm a chemist.

74/3 **Fit/fill the bill**: Be what is required. □ Of all the job applicants, I think she fills (fits) the bill.

74/4 **Suit** someone **down to the ground**: Suit someone completely. □ If she doesn't want to come on the trip, that suits me down to the ground.

74/5 **Measure up to** a standard/requirement: Reach the required standards. □ The majority of applicants for the position didn't measure up to our requirements.

74/6 **Do** (someone): Be suitable, advisable or acceptable; be enough. Another one of the many meanings of 'do'. □ Sean told the grocer that two kilos of potatoes would do him.

74/7 **Do the trick**: Achieve what is required. □ Marco's bicycle wheel was buckled, but four new spokes did the trick.

74/8 **A square peg in a round hole**: A person who is not suited for his job. □ I am more the active outdoor type and feel like a square peg in a round hole when I'm sitting in the office.

74/9 **A misfit**: A person who is totally unsuited to his work or environment. □ Unable to play golf, not interested in sport generally, and a very poor mixer at social gatherings, Edward was a thorough misfit in the Nineteenth Hole Club.

74/10 **Up to scratch**: Up to the required standard. □ In the middle of a course on navigation, I discovered that my maths wasn't up to scratch.

74/11 **Make the grade**: Reach the desired standard. The 'grade' refers to the slope or gradient of a hill which must be overcome or climbed. □ Every year we have hundreds of young musicians wishing to join the orchestra, but only a few make the grade.

EXERCISES 14: QUALITY

A) Insert everyday objects or common foodstuffs to complete the following sentences.

1) Alice is an excellent student, the others can't hold a . . . to her.
2) If you mean the biggest firm in France and not in Europe, that's a different . . . of . . . .
3) The hospital librarian brought the patients a mixed . . . of novels and non-fiction books.
4) With regard to quality, there is not a . . . to choose between the two carpets.
5) He believed that killing animals was next . . . to murder.
6) When I first went to work for my firm in Italy, I knew no Italian and felt like a square . . . in a round hole.
7) The two countries share a common border, but their languages are as different as . . . and . . . .
8) Lasers have made surgery a whole new . . . game.

→

B) From the unit, give colloquialisms for the following definitions.

1) a useless person or thing. 2) an old ship or car. 3) technical problems or interference. 4) a complete reversal of policy or views. 5) a person or thing that is different to the rest. 6) an exact likeness. 7) a situation where the competing sides have equal scores or levels of performance.

C) In the following sentences containing phrasal verbs and colloquial phrases, insert the missing adverb.

1) His heart packed . . . and he was buried at sea.
2) We can't get any water, the pump is clapped . . . .
3) My quartz watch has gone . . . the blink.
4) I don't need those tools, but they may come . . . handy as a reserve set.
5) The film was not all that it was cracked . . . to be.
6) A bird's nest had bunged . . . the air-vent.
7) Steam locomotives are not a patch . . . diesel trains.
8) The repair was not . . . to scratch and the tyre began deflating again.
9) When the car broke down, our touring holiday was . . . the spout.

D) Give a verb of movement or work in the correct tense to complete the sentences below.

1) Every time local firms comply with pollution regulations, the Ministry of the Environment . . . the goal-posts.
2) If you want to lose weight, this diet will . . . the trick.
3) You've passed your exam as well! . . . the club!
4) No other shop can . . . his fish for freshness.
5) We don't have to send the injured man home by air, there's more than one way to . . . a cat.
6) Some of the tenants in the block of flats are . . . a coach and horses through the house rules.

E) From the module, give as many synonyms as possible to fit the underlined phrases.

1) That new motor launch is <u>an excellent model</u>.
2) He has a <u>dirty and unpleasant</u> job emptying dustbins.
3) The ticket machine was <u>completely defective</u>.
4) We can go today or tomorrow, <u>it's all the same</u>.

Chance

75: LUCK

75/1 **Jammy:** Unusually lucky. □ You're a jammy so-and-so – I never win raffle prizes! □ The footballer scored a jammy goal.

75/2 **A fluke:** A lucky accident or chance. □ Predicting three winning horses in a row is a fluke.

75/3 **The luck of the devil** *or* **the devil's own luck**: Unusually good luck. □ I had the luck of the devil (the devil's own luck) to come out of that plane crash alive.

75/4 **A break:** A piece or stroke of luck. *(See also 76/1 below)* □ What with her accident and all, she's had a few bad breaks lately.

75/5 **Thank one's lucky stars:** Be grateful for one's luck. □ You can thank your lucky stars that no one saw you, otherwise you'd be in trouble.

75/6 **Push one's luck (too far):** Take undue risks on the basis of past luck. □ Our firm has already given us a pay rise, and to ask for a shorter working week in addition would be pushing our luck (too far).

75/7 **While the going is good:** While luck or conditions are still favourable. □ In view of the impending storm, the fishermen decided to make for shore while the going was good. □ You're making him angry; you'd better leave now while the going is good.

75/8 **Keep's one's fingers crossed:** Hope for luck or success. □ When you sit the exam, I'll keep my fingers crossed for you.

75/9 **The best of British (luck):** The best of luck. □ Before the yachtsman set out on his round-the-world trip, hundreds of well-wishers came to the harbour to wish him the best of British (British luck).

75/10 **Touch wood!:** Said after mentioning one's own good luck in avoiding misfortune, in order to ward off future bad luck. It was a superstition that touching wood would avert misfortune. □ Everyone seems to have the 'flu except me, touch wood!

75/11 **Be a good job** *or* **be just as well**: Be lucky or fortunate. □ What heavy rain! It's a good job (just as well) you brought along your umbrella! □ It's just as well (a good job) you missed that train – it derailed just outside the station.

75/12 **No dice/joy:** No success or luck. *(See also 88/12)* □ We've had no joy getting tickets – the show's fully booked for weeks. □ "Did you get any tickets?" "No dice – they're sold out!"

75/13 **That's the way the cookie crumbles:** That is what fate or luck decides and it cannot be changed. The idea is that fate gives someone a larger share of the luck (in this case a sweet biscuit or cookie) than others. □ It is unjust that half the world suffers hunger and disease, but that's the way the cookie crumbles.

75/14 **Down on one's luck**: Unlucky or suffering a period of misfortune. □ It's a good thing my friends helped me when I was down on my luck and depressed.

75/15 **Tough/hard luck**: Bad luck. □ Claudia has had a lot of tough (hard) luck lately.

75/16 **Hard cheese** or **hard lines**: Worse luck than is deserved; unmerited misfortune. □ What hard cheese! One second faster and he'd have broken the national record. □ Hard lines, old chap; you don't deserve such bad luck.

75/17 **A jinx**: A person or thing that is thought to bring bad luck. To 'jinx' someone or to 'put a jinx on' someone means to bring a person bad luck. □ Some old sailors believe that a woman is a jinx on board ship (or that a woman jinxes a ship).

76: OPPORTUNITY/POSSIBILITY

76/1 **A break**: A fair chance. *(Compare 75/4 above)* □ Albert was a good actor, but no film director would give him a break in a leading role.

76/2 Have/stand a **fighting chance**: Have a reasonable chance of success provided one makes a good effort. □ Our firm has (stands) a fighting chance of winning this big order.

76/3 **A sporting chance**: A fair chance; a reasonable chance of success. □ With a fishing line of three kilo breaking-strain, any salmon has a sporting chance of escaping. □ Some jockeys carry handicap weights to give the others a sporting chance.

76/4 **A look-in**: A chance of participation or success. □ The zoo keeper scattered the meat among the lion cubs, but the smallest one didn't get a look-in.

76/5 **Two bites/another bite at the cherry**: A second chance or attempt (usually after an initial failure). □ Nobody else is allowed to sit the exam again, so why should you have another bite (have two bites) at the cherry?

76/6 **Not have one's cake and eat it**: Of two possibilities, be able to choose only one and not both. □ We can't afford a new carpet because we've spent the money on a holiday; we can't have our cake and eat it.

76.7 **Hobson's choice**: No possibility of choice. Tobias Hobson was a 17th-century coachman from Cambridge, who did not allow customers to choose the horses they hired from him. □ It's Hobson's choice today in the staff canteen – fish and chips or fish and chips!

76/8 **No two ways about it**: No other possibility or possible explanation. □ The city can't afford to keep the museum open, there are no two ways about it. □ My husband's conduct points to only one thing and there are no two ways about it; he's seeing another woman.

76/9 **Other pebbles on the beach** *or* **other (good) fish in the sea:** Other possibilities or chances; other possible lovers or marriage partners. □ Francesca's job-application was rejected politely by the firm with words to the effect that there were plenty of other pebbles on the beach. □ After his divorce, friends consoled him with the fact that there were plenty of other (good) fish in the sea.

76/10 **The sky's the limit** *or* **the world is one's oyster:** The opportunities for career, business or advancement are unlimited. □ For bright young executives in our firm, the world's their oyster (the sky's the limit).

76/11 **A big fish in a small pond:** A person or thing that has outgrown its surroundings in importance or influence, and has only limited opportunities for further development. □ The Dutch-based company had become a big fish in a small pond, so it decided to branch out on the world market.

76/12 **Jump at** a chance: Accept a chance or opportunity eagerly. □ My husband refused promotion because it would mean moving to a new city, yet hundreds of others would have jumped at the chance.

76/13 **Pass up** a chance: Refuse to accept an opportunity; allow an opportunity to slip by. □ I now regret passing up his offer of help! □ Don't pass up the opportunity to see the eclipse of the sun today.

76/14 **Miss the boat/bus:** Lose an opportunity to do something. □ It's too late in the season to sow tomatoes, so I'm afraid you've missed the boat (bus) there.

76/15 **Have had it:** Have missed an opportunity or chance. (*See also 18/17 and 162/5*) □ You've had it; the last train to York left ten minutes ago!

76/16 **Stand to . . .:** Be likely to; run the risk of something occurring. □ If Hasenfeld retires, you stand to become the next managing director. □ Politically, the Russians stand to gain most by this situation.

76/17 **On the cards:** Likely or possible. □ Given the massive needs for drinking-water and crop irrigation, it is on the cards that the rivers will shrink even further.

76/18 **What price . . .?:** What is the chance or possibility of/it is likely that. The 'price' is the odds in betting. □ What price he won't agree to the plan? □ Ask the weather man what price rain today!

76/19 **A hot favourite:** A competitor who is thought to have the best chances by far of winning. □ The French cardinal is hot favourite to be the new Pope.

76/20 **A no-hoper:** A person or thing with no chance of success or advancement at all. □ The slums are full of no-hopers. □ Apart from the top three runners, the rest are no-hopers.

76/21 **Stand a (good) chance:** Have a chance or opportunity. □ With qualifications like that, he stands a good chance of getting the job. □ We don't stand a chance of catching the train now.

115

76/22　**Not an earthly/ghostly** (chance):　No chance or opportunity at all. □ I haven't got an earthly (ghostly) of passing the exam.

76/23　**Not (stand/have) a cat in hell's chance/a snowball's chance in hell/a dog's chance**:　No chance at all. □ Without water and a compass, we wouldn't have a cat in hell's chance of crossing that desert alive. □ He hasn't a snowball's chance in hell of promotion.

76/24　A **fat chance**:　A negligible chance or no chance at all. □ After your poor performance in the last match, you've a fat chance of being selected for the team.

77: GAMBLE/RISK/TRY

77/1　A **shot/whack/crack/stab/bash**:　A turn, try or attempt. □ If you can't loosen the screw, let me have a whack (stab, shot, crack etc.). □ Have a shot (crack, stab etc.) at guessing her age!

77/2　**Have a go**:　Make an attempt; attack, fight someone. □ I decided to have a go at making a concrete garden pond. □ He got a thick ear after some hooligan had a go at him outside the pub last night.

77/3　**Give it a go/whirl**:　To attempt or try. □ Hang-gliding looks fun to me – I think I'll give it a go (whirl).

77/4　**Try one's hand** at:　Attempt something for the first time to see how well one can do. □ Now that I've retired, I've decided to try my hand at golf.

77/5　**Stick one's neck out**:　Take a risk by exposing oneself to criticism or unpleasant consequences. □ The Economics professor stuck his neck out by predicting a large rise in unemployment. □ After two prison sentences for theft, no employer would stick his neck out and employ her.

77/6　**A leap in the dark**:　A risky undertaking with unknown results. □ For our company, with no experience of the Chinese market, setting up a sales office there was a great leap in the dark.

77/7　**On spec**:　As a speculation or gamble; without being certain of success. □ Every year thousands of southern Italians travel to the industrialized cities of the north, looking for work on spec.

77/8　**On the off-chance**:　On the basis of only a slight possibility or chance of success. □ When her husband didn't return home, she went to the bar, on the off-chance of finding him there.

77/9　**Take pot luck**:　Accept whatever one gets. The phrase refers to accepting as a meal whatever happens to be in the cooking-pot. □ For many holiday makers, choosing a resort from the multitude on offer is often a question of taking pot luck.

77/10　A **toss-up**:　An even choice; a doubtful risk. □ The lawyer told his client that it was a toss-up which way the court would decide. □ We want a car, but it's a toss-up between a big old banger and a smaller new one.

77/11　A **flutter**:　A small gamble or bet. □ On the day of the Kentucky Derby, many Americans have their only flutter of the year.

78: DANGER

78/1 **Dicey:** Risky or dangerous. □ Emergency repairs on power pylons can be a dicey business in bad weather.

78/2 **Dodgy:** Risky, awkward or difficult. □ Driving a car without insurance is a dodgy business. □ The exit from the lift is blocked with building materials and it's a bit dodgy getting out.

78/3 **Take one's life in(to) one's hands:** Risk one's life. □ As a war cameraman, I often have to take my life in(to) my hands to get a good picture.

78/4 **In one piece:** Uninjured after a dangerous ordeal. □ Stuntmen take every precaution to come back in one piece.

78/5 **The coast is clear:** The danger has passed; there is no risk of being seen or caught. The expression probably originated with smugglers who kept watch on the coast for customs men. □ The villagers fled their houses from the marauding bandits, and the next day they sent back scouts to see if the coast was clear.

78/6 **Run the gauntlet:** Expose oneself to continuous danger or criticism; submit to a dangerous or punishing ordeal. □ Allied convoys to Murmansk had to run the gauntlet of U-boat packs.

78/7 **Skate on thin ice:** Unnecessarily expose oneself to risk, danger or criticism. □ That car is in a dangerous condition and you're skating on thin ice by driving around in it. □ Mr Schenk is skating on thin ice with some of his business deals, which are shady to say the least.

78/8 **Teeter on the brink:** Be in danger of falling, failing or collapsing. □ The economies of several African countries are teetering on the brink. □ The man was depressed and teetered on the brink of suicide.

78/9 **A cliff-hanger:** A situation full of suspense or danger. □ The last episode of the television series was a cliff-hanger, ending with Batman and Robin in mortal danger. □ Waiting for exam results is a cliff-hanger.

78/10 **Could/would not hurt a fly:** Be completely harmless; present no danger at all. □ Don't be afraid of my dog, he wouldn't hurt a fly.

79: CERTAINTY/SECURE

79/1 (As) **sure as eggs (is eggs):** Absolutely certain or sure. □ If Uta promised to come, then she'll keep her word, sure as eggs (as sure as eggs is eggs).

79/2 **Sure-fire** *(US)*: Certain to succeed or achieve the desired result. □ Swimming in that current is a sure-fire way of getting yourself drowned.

79/3 **A (dead) cert:** A certainty; something sure to happen or be successful. □ The resignation of the prime minister is now a dead cert. □ That horse is a dead cert for the race.

79/4 **You can bet your boots** *or* **. . . your bottom dollar:**   You can be absolutely certain of something. □ You can bet your bottom dollar (your boots) he won't agree to the deal.

79/5 **I'm telling you** *or* **take it from me:**   I am certain of it; you can believe me. □ That business man is a rogue, take it from me (I'm telling you).

79/6 **(Make) no mistake about it:**   It is certain that; don't believe otherwise. □ I won't pay the rent increase, make no mistake about it. □ That's the same man as the one who mugged me, and no mistake about it.

79/7 **I'm a Dutchman if** *or* **I'll eat my hat if:**   I am certain that something is not true or not the case. □ If he's a qualified engineer, then I'm a Dutchman. □ If she can lift that weight, then I'll eat my hat.

79/8 **Have another think coming:**   (Of someone with a plan or intention) be certain of disappointment or failure. □ If your mother thinks she can come and live with us, she's got another think coming.

79/9 **Bound to . . . :**   Certain to. □ Your friend is bound to help you. □ That postman is bound to know the street.

79/10 **As like/likely as not:**   Most probably or certainly. □ Don't worry about Lars; as likely (like) as not he's safe at his grandmother's house.

79/11 **No fear of** something: No possibility of. □ The forest path is clearly marked, so there's no fear of getting lost.

79/12 **Ten to one:**   Almost certainly. □ Ten to one he's not at school.

79/13 **Sure** (*US*):   Certainly. □ It sure is cold today.

79/14 **Bank on** something: Rely or base one's hopes on. □ The housing office has promised us a new flat within a month, but we're not banking on it.

79/15 **Safe as houses:**   Without risk; secure or safe. □ Investments in that company are safe as houses.

79/16 **Play safe**: Avoid taking risks. □ We'd better play safe and get to the airport early.

79/17 **All over bar the shouting**: Finished, or almost over, with the result or outcome certain. □ Next morning, with 90% of the election results declared, the Labour Party had an overall majority of 50 – it was all over bar the shouting.

79/18 **In the bag**: Secured or certain. □ That factory has two other large orders in the bag.

79/19 **Home and dry**: Certain of success with no possibility of failure. □ The team is seeking promotion to the premier league, and with only two matches to play they are already home and dry.

79/20 **Strike/clinch/swing** *(US)*/**wrap up/sew up** a deal: Conclude or secure a deal; make certain of a deal or bargain. □ The trade mission clinched (wrapped up/ swung/struck/sewed up) several contracts on the trip to Brazil.

79/21 **It's anybody's guess** *or* **there's no telling**: It is uncertain or unknown. □ It's anybody's guess (There's no telling) who will be the murderer's next victim.

79/22 **Keep** someone **guessing**: Keep someone uncertain of one's feelings or future activities. □ Several days before the invasion, air raids were mounted at various possible incursion points to keep the enemy guessing. □ Don't keep me guessing any longer – say how much you love me!

79/23 **Touch-and-go**: Uncertain as regards the outcome or result. □ It is touch-and-go whether the patient will recover from the operation.

79/24 **Iffy**: Uncertain; depending on unknown circumstances; not altogether acceptable. This adjective is formed from the conjunction 'if'. □ The boat trip is a bit iffy, since a storm is forecast. □ The deal's a bit iffy at present.

80: CAUSE/OCCUR/RESULT

80/1 **Trigger off** something: Be the immediate, but not necessarily fundamental, cause of an occurrence or chain of events. □ The assassination of Archduke Ferdinand in Sarajevo triggered off the First World War.

80/2 **How come . . .?**: Why? For what reason? □ How come you didn't tell me earlier?

80/3 **What's the big idea?**: What is the reason for this unusual occurrence or conduct? □ Hannelore arrived at the office to find another secretary sitting at her desk, so she asked her what the big idea was.

80/4 **What is** this **in aid of?**: What is the intention or purpose of this? What is it designed to do? □ What is this machine in aid of? □ No one would tell Felix where his mother was, so he asked his uncle what all the secrecy was in aid of.

80/5 **What makes** someone **tick**: What makes a person behave as he does; the driving force behind a person's behaviour or mentality. □ Historians are always arguing about what made Adolf Hitler tick.

80/6 **The thin edge of the wedge**: A change that will open the way for similar ones; a concession that results in even greater ones. □ The town council refused to allow her to keep a dog in her flat, saying that it was the thin edge of the wedge leading to other tenants wanting animals.

80/7 A **hotbed**: A place favourable to the growth of something. A 'hotbed' is a gardening term for a plant bed of warm fermenting manure. □ Most slums are hotbeds of crime. □ Universities are a hotbed of intellectuals.

80/8 **What with** something: On account of; as a result of. □ What with problems at work and accidents at home, I've had a bad week.

80/9 **What's cooking?**: What is happening or being planned? □ Every now and then, a minister from the capital would arrive in the province to see what was cooking there. □ What's cooking in your department?

80/10 **Anything doing?/nothing doing**: Is anything happening? Any luck? The negative 'nothing doing' means that nothing's happening – no luck. *(See also 110/3)* □ Is there anything doing down at the club tonight? □ "Nothing doing" said my bank manager when I asked for a loan.

80/11 **Where it's at**: Where the action occurs; the focal point of an activity. □ If you like gambling, Las Vegas is where it's at. □ Christopher is an active type and likes to be where it's at.

80/12 **Pan out**: (Of events or circumstances) turn out; be successful in outcome. □ The education ministry is waiting to see how the reforms pan out in a few test schools before introducing them on a large scale.

80/13 **Crop/pop up**: Occur unexpectedly or by chance. □ If nothing untoward crops (pops) up, we can finish the project by next week. □ Every day he would read the job- vacancy columns of the newspapers in the hope that something in his line would crop (pop) up.

80/14 **Come off**: Occur or take place. *(See also 15/22)* □ Owing to torrential rain, the athletics meeting didn't come off.

80/15 **A turn-up for the books**: An unexpected or surprising occurrence or event. □ Kirsten is smartly dressed today; that is a turn-up for the books. □ Seeing an eagle so near the city was a turn-up for the books, since they usually avoid heavily populated areas.

80/16 **As** (things) **go**: On the average; compared to what is usual for something. □ As gardens go, yours is well tended.

80/17 **Off-beat**: Unconventional or unusual; not usually encountered. □ His conduct is slightly off-beat. □ Some linguists would classify Welsh or Basque as off-beat languages.

80/18 A **knack**: A habit or frequent occurrence. *(See also 7/1)* □ The weather in Scotland has a knack of changing very quickly. □ My washing-machine has a knack of breaking down.

80/19 **Boil down to** something: Be basically due to; result from. □ The problems in the region all boil down to religious intolerance.

80/20 **The bottom line:**   The basic essential requirement or result. □ I could make excuses for not paying you now, but the bottom line is that I don't have the money.

80/21 **A knee-jerk reaction:**   An involuntary reaction to something; an automatic unplanned response. □ When I heard the explosion, my knee-jerk reaction was to dive for cover.

80/22 **A spin-off:**   A secondary unintended benefit or result of some action. □ Quite a lot of domestic technology is a spin-off from the space race.

EXERCISES 15: CHANCE

A) Insert the missing person or thing(s).

1) I have driven for years without any accident, touch . . . !
2) He had the luck of the . . . to win the lottery.
3) It was hard . . . that you didn't get that job.
4) She has arrived early for once, that is a turn-up for the . . . .
5) Your compensation claim is the thin end of the . . . and could lead to many more.
6) It's impossible! If that is true, then I'm a . . . .
7) We must do this correctly the first time, for we won't get two bites at the . . . .
8) Get your application form in early and don't miss the . . . !
9) You can bet your . . . that he won't come.
10) We lost the match, but that's the way the . . . crumbles!

B) Give colloquialisms to fit the following definitions.

1) a small financial bet.
2) a situation where there is no choice as to the course of action.
3) a lucky accident or chance.
4) a beneficial side-effect or secondary result of some activity.
5) a suspense-filled situation.
6) an even choice or doubtful risk.
7) someone without any prospects in life or any chance of success.
8) a person or thing that brings bad luck.
9) the basic requirement for something.
10) an involuntary or automatic reaction to something.

C) From the module, insert the missing adverbs (up/down/on/over etc.) to complete the sentences below.

1) Your exam failure boils . . . to laziness.
2) It is . . . the cards that the firm will close down.
3) This is a great opportunity, so don't pass it . . . !

→

121

4) We couldn't raise enough money, so the renovation didn't come . . . .
5) He was once successful, but now he is . . . on his luck.
6) There was almost no possibility of winning the competition, but I entered . . . the off-chance.
7) She decided to stick her neck . . . and invest all her money in the company.
8) The train may arrive on time, but don't bank . . . it!
9) Something cropped . . . and he had to leave suddenly.

D) From the module, give as many synonyms as possible for the underlined word or phrase.

1) I don't think I can repair the clock, but I'll have a try.
2) We have no chance at all of finishing the job before Wednesday.
3) The co-operative has concluded a deal to supply a German firm with bananas.
4) She won't like travelling by air one little bit, that is certain.

E) Insert a verb of motion or action in the correct tense to complete the following sentences.

1) I always . . . safe and don't pay up until I receive the goods.
2) Lending money to firms in financial difficulties is . . . on thin ice.
3) When she was offered a place in music college, she . . . at the chance.
4) My parents let me stay out late yesterday, but if I do it again tonight that would be . . . my luck.
5) There is no pedestrian crossing on that busy road, and every day hundreds of people have to . . . the gauntlet to get to the shops.
6) I'll . . . my hat if they catch any fish at all in that polluted river!

122

The Mind

81: MADNESS

81/1 **Have a screw loose** *or* **have bats in the belfry**: Be slightly mad or eccentric; be not quite sane. □ He's got a screw loose (got bats in the belfry).

81/2 **Not right in the head** *or* **soft in the head**: Slightly crazy or eccentric. □ The authorities can't be right in the head (must be soft in the head) to spend so much money on that project.

81/3 **Not all there**: Absent-minded or slightly crazy. □ I'm sorry I didn't hear what you said – I'm not all there today. □ Don't mind Fernando's strange conduct, he's not all there!

81/4 **Need one's head examined** *or* **seen to**: Be acting in a totally irresponsible or stupid manner. □ I think that people who go bathing in the icy seas of winter need their heads seen to (examined).

81/5 **Dotty**: Feeble-minded or slightly crazy. □ That's a dotty idea. □ Gerhard is dotty about his pigeons.

81/6 **Funny/touched**: Insane. *(See also 181/5)* □ Such a shame about her son – he's a bit funny (touched), you know.

81/7 **Wacky**: Crazy or very eccentric (often used approvingly). □ I've just seen the wackiest film. □ Conchita has some really wacky ideas!

81/8 **Potty/loopy/screwy/batty/loony/barmy/mental/cuckoo**: Idiotic, mad or crazy. 'Mental' and 'cuckoo' are generally applied only to people, not to things. □ What a potty (loopy/screwy/batty/loony/barmy) idea! You must be mental (cuckoo) to think of it!

81/9 **Loco/bananas/crackers/bonkers**: Insane or furiously angry. □ You must be loco (bananas etc.) to risk your life unnecessarily. □ When the farmer saw what the birds were doing to his crop, he went bananas.

81/10 **Gaga**: Mad or senile. □ Grandfather is getting slightly gaga.

81/11 **Up the pole**: Mad or crazy. □ The situation in these flats is enough to drive people up the pole.

81/12 **Off one's head/chump/rocker/nut**: Crazy. □ He must be off his chump (head/rocker/nut) to pay so much money for old junk.

81/13 **Plumb crazy** *or* **stark raving mad** *or* **barking mad**: Completely crazy or mad. □ The Nepalese porters believed that the Australian climbers were stark raving mad (plumb crazy/barking mad).

81/14 **Mad as a March hare**: Completely mad or insane. The expression alludes to the frenzied behaviour of mating hares in March. □ My old uncle went clean round the bend – as mad as a March hare by the time he was eighty.

81/15 Nutty (as a fruit cake): (Completely) crazy or mad. □ Owing to inbreeding, the children of several families were nutty as fruit cakes.

81/16 (Clean) round the bend/twist: (Completely) crazy or insane. □ The noise of these drills is enough to drive you round the twist (bend). □ All accusations of fraud against me are clean round the twist (bend).

81/17 A nut-case/head-case/loony/nutter/fruit cake: A madman or insane person. □ Many leading scientists were thought to be nut-cases (fruit cakes/loonies etc.) when they revealed their inventions.

81/18 A loony-bin *or* **a nut-house:** Mental home or psychiatric hospital. □ The gunman was declared insane by the court and sent to a high-security loony-bin (nut-house).

81/19 A funny farm *(US)*: A mental home, usually within its own grounds. □ The film 'One Flew over the Cuckoo's Nest' is about life on a funny farm.

82: STUPIDITY

82/1 Daft as a brush *or* **thick as two short planks:** Very stupid. □ The official was as daft as a brush (was as thick as two short planks) and couldn't understand my explanation.

82/2 There's one born every minute: There is no shortage of fools in the world. □ What a stupid thing he did; there's one born every minute, isn't there?

82/3 **Not see beyond the end of one's nose**:   Have no intelligence or imagination: be very limited in one's outlook. □ It is difficult to convince people who can't see further than their nose that dumping waste in the sea will affect them in the long run.

82/4 **Gormless**:   Stupid and clumsy; witless. □ I'm not employing a gormless person like him.

82/5 **Half-baked**:   Not completely thought-out or planned; foolish. □ That plan is half-baked.

82/6 **Goofy/dopey**:   Stupid. □ Juan is a goofy (dopey) boy.

82/7 **Pig-ignorant**:   Very stupid. □ That was a pig-ignorant thing to say.

82/8 **A blithering/priceless/prize idiot**:   A complete idiot. □ Counter staff dealing with the public on a daily basis usually encounter a blithering (priceless/prize) idiot from time to time.

82/9 **A juggins/dope/nitwit/half-wit/nincompoop/bozo/dim-wit/fat-head/ booby/clot/numskull/blockhead/mutt** (*#US*):   A stupid person; a fool. □ What a juggins (dope/nitwit/booby etc.) she is!

82/10 **Prat/pillock/chump/berk/nana/nelly/wally/prick** (*#??*)/**dick-head** (*#??*):   A stupid person or fool. Being terms of abuse, there is no strict rule as to sex, but these terms are more frequently applied to men (particularly the last two since these allude to the male sexual organ). □ You stupid prat! Didn't you see that car was parked behind you?

82/11 **Silly Billy**:   A fool. 'Billy' is the nickname for 'William', and the term was originally applied to William IV of England who was considered a fool. □ Of course I didn't mean it seriously; you are a silly Billy.

82/12 **A proper Charlie**:   A fool. The term refers to pensioners in the service of Charles I, who were generally thought to lack sense. □ Arlene made a proper Charlie of herself last night.

82/13 **A twerp/twit**:   A stupid or insignificant person.

82/14 **A slob**:   Someone who is stupid, clumsy, untidy, lazy or rude (very often a combination of all or several of these qualities). □ My son-in-law is an utter slob; he won't get a job, and sits around all day watching children's TV or reading comics.

82/15 **A moron**:   A very stupid person. □ Television is making morons of our children.

82/16 **A zombie**:   A person who seems to have no mind or will. The word is a term in voodoo magic for a corpse brought back to life.

82/17 **A goon**:   A stupid person; a hired ruffian. □ You are a goon! □ The underworld boss sent over a couple of goons to beat up the debtor.

82/18 **A bird-brain** *or* **a pea-brain**:   A stupid person; someone with a very small brain. A stupid person or idea may be described as 'bird-brained' or 'pea-brained'. □ That's a pea-brained idea. □ She is a bird-brain.

82/19 **A silly cow/moo**:   Abusive terms for a stupid woman.

82/20 **A bimbo**:   A young, attractive but empty-headed woman. □ The new Miss World is no bimbo; she has a master's degree in economics.

82/21 A **sucker**: Someone who is easily deceived. □ I'd be stupid to buy your overpriced car; go and find yourself another sucker!

82/22 A **mug/muggins**: Someone who is easily deceived or cheated; a fool. □ What do you take me for – a mug or something? These are foreign coins! □ You're a mug (muggins) to go back to your husband knowing he'll beat you again!

82/23 **A mug's game**: An activity that is unlikely to bring profit or reward; something only fools would do. □ Crime is a mug's game. □ Waste disposal is now big business, it's no mug's game!

82/24 A **bright specimen**: Ironic term for a fool. □ The computer was working all right until this bright specimen spilt coffee over it.

82/25 A **duffer**: An inefficient or stupid person. □ Our foremen can usually sort out the duffers in the first few days on the job.

82/26 A **turkey** (#US): A useless or silly person. (See also 18/14)

82/27 A **dunce**: Someone who is slow at learning. □ At school, we used to say that kids in the 'B-stream' classes were dunces.

82/28 A **hill-billy** (US)/a **hick** (#US): A backward rural person. □ We may live in an isolated country area, but we're not hill-billies (hicks).

82/29 A **bumpkin**: A simple or coarse country person. The word comes from the old Dutch 'boomken' meaning a small tree or a small block. This was adopted by the English firstly as a term of abuse for a Dutchman, then it came to mean 'blockhead' – a stupid person.

82/30 A **yokel**: A simple or backward rural fellow. □ A village yokel was leaning against the farm gate and chewing a straw.

82/31 **Scatter-brained/scatty**: Unable to concentrate; absent-minded. □ Xavier had become scatter-brained through years of heavy drinking. □ Yvonne was a lovely girl, but quite scatty.

82/32 Someone **would forget** his **head if it wasn't screwed on (properly)**: Be very forgetful or absent-minded. □ Renate is always forgetting her keys; she'd forget her head if it wasn't screwed on properly.

82/33 **Airy-fairy**: Freely imagined, impractical or foolish. □ Many democratic principles are rejected by governments in developing countries as too airy-fairy for the harsh circumstances there.

82/34 **Harum-scarum**: Wild and reckless; rash and foolish. □ Ahmed has now got a harum-scarum idea about selling our house and emigrating.

83: CLEVERNESS/SENSE

83/1 **Not born yesterday**: No fool; not easy to deceive. □ You can't tell me that this bag of potatoes weighs five kilos; I wasn't born yesterday.

83/2 **Have one's head screwed on (the right way)**: Be intelligent or clever. □ That girl has her head screwed on – she'll probably end up with a first-class degree.

83/3 **Brain before brawn**: Intelligent methods or persons are superior to brute strength or to those who rely solely on it. □ The mechanization of heavy tasks has meant brain before brawn in the work place.

83/4 **There are no flies on** someone: Someone is clever or too astute to be deceived. □ You'd better tell the foreman about your mistake; there are no flies on him and he'll soon find out anyway.

83/5 **An egghead**: An intellectual or person with superior intelligence. □ The water samples were given to some eggheads in the laboratory for analysis.

83/6 **A bright spark**: A clever person; (ironically) someone who erroneously believes himself to be clever. □ At school I wasn't one of the bright sparks that went on to higher education. □ Well, you're a bright spark – you should have seen from the label that the paint isn't waterproof!

83/7 **A clever clogs** *or* **clever boots** *or* **clever dick** *or* **smarty pants** *or* **smart alec** *or* **smart arse** *(#?)*/**ass** *(US#?)*: A conceited know-all or someone who behaves as if he knows everything. □ Abdulla is one of those clever clogs (smart alecs/smarty pants etc.) just out of college who think they know better than older, more experienced engineers.

83/8 **Nifty**: Smart or clever. *(See also 173/7)* □ Lothar knows a nifty trick for opening Yale locks. □ Sofia is nifty with a pair of knitting needles.

83/9 **A dodge**: A cunningly clever trick; an ingenious way of doing something. A 'dodger' is someone skilled in dodges. □ When the fan-belt broke, we used the dodge with the nylon stocking to get the van home. □ That accountant knows a few dodges for avoiding tax.

83/10 **Gumption**: Common sense and initiative. □ What Claire lacks in qualifications, she makes up for in gumption.

83/11 **Horse sense**: The most elementary common sense. □ When you saw the smoke coming from the machine, horse sense should have told you to switch it off.

84: THINK/FORGET

84/1 **Use one's loaf**: Use one's brains; think. □ Use your loaf the next time you light a garden fire on a windy day!

84/2 **Put on one's thinking-cap**: Think about something carefully. □ Building on the waterlogged ground would be difficult, and the engineers went away to put their thinking-caps on.

84/3 **Weigh up** an argument: Assess or consider thoroughly; think about or compare things carefully. □ First we shall have to weigh up the pros and cons of investing money in this project.

84/4 **Jog** someone's **memory**: Stimulate someone's memory. □ The hotel receptionist didn't remember the guest until the detective jogged her memory with a photo of him.

84/5 **Rack one's brains/memory**: Exert one's thinking power; think hard about something. □ Christine racked her memory (brains) for his address.

84/6   **Cast one's mind back**:   Try to remember a past event. □ Filling in the insurance claim was unpleasant, since she had to cast her mind back to the day of the horrific accident.

84/7   **A penny for them!** *or* **a penny for your thoughts!**:   Tell me what you are thinking!; confide your thoughts in me! □ You're looking very serious – a penny for your thoughts!

84/8   **A trip down memory lane**:   A short period of reminiscing over the past or reviving old memories. □ In the evening, the old woman would sit alone with a glass of sherry and take a trip down memory lane. □ That country is forty years behind ours in development, and our visit was a trip down memory lane.

84/9   **Toy with** an idea: Consider a possibility in a casual or half-serious manner. □ For a while he toyed with the idea of joining the navy.

84/10 **Come up with** an idea: Think up, invent or contribute an idea or suggestion □ Several workers have come up with good ideas for reducing wastage.

84/11 Someone's **brain-child**:   Someone's invention or plan. □ The atomic bomb is widely thought to be the brain-child of the team led by Oppenheimer.

84/12 **A brainwave**:   A sudden bright idea. □ While in the bath, Archimedes had a brainwave for calculating the volume of irregular-shaped solids.

84/13 **Cross one's mind**:   Occur to one; have a momentary thought. □ The thought that he was a criminal didn't cross my mind for one moment.

84/14 **Strike** someone: Occur to someone; give an impression or appear. □ Only later did it strike her that the man was not drunk but ill. □ The political situation in that country strikes me as unstable.

84/15 **Seize up**:   (Of the mind) be temporarily incapable of thinking or remembering; go blank. □ At the job interview my mind just seized up and I couldn't even remember where I worked three years ago.

84/16 **Slip one's mind**:   Be overlooked or forgotten by someone. □ I'm sorry I didn't write earlier, it slipped my mind.

84/17 **A memory like a sieve**:   A very poor or forgetful memory. □ Françoise won't remember your name, she's got a memory like a sieve.

85: OPINION/BELIEVE

85/1   **For my money**:   If I had to choose; in my opinion. □ For my money that Japanese video recorder is better than the others.

85/2   **In my book** *or* **to my way of thinking** *or* **to my mind**:   In my opinion. □ To my mind (in my book/to my way of thinking), you should have nothing to do with that scoundrel.

85/3   **From where I'm sitting**:   From my point of view. □ Some politicians have described the economic measures as a success, but it's not like that from where I'm sitting.

85/4 **Figure** (that):   Think or believe. □ He figures that the repair will take two days.

85/5 **Vote** something: Make a suggestion; declare by common consent. □ The visit to the Tower of London was voted a good day out by all who went on it. □ I vote we have lunch now.

85/6 **Grab** someone: Make an impression on someone. □ We'll buy a caravan and go touring, how does that grab you?

85/7 **Say to** something: Give as one's opinion or decision about something. □ What do you say to my new dress? □ What do you say to a cool refreshing beer?

85/8 **Take** something **on board**:   Accept a suggestion; adopt someone's point of view. □ When they reprinted the book, the editors took on board much of the criticism of the first edition.

85/9 **Plump for** someone/something: Choose or vote for whole-heartedly; decide on. □ Of the three job applicants, we plumped for the most experienced. □ We were undecided about the colour of the curtains, but in the end we plumped for red.

85/10 **Latch on to** something: Take in as a good idea; adopt an opinion or course of action as one's own. □ Politicians are latching on to people's worries about the environment by making their policies 'greener'.

85/11 **Drive/get at** something: Intend to convey as a meaning or opinion; imply or mean. □ Some philosophers can talk for an hour without you knowing what they're getting (driving) at. □ Are you suggesting I'm too untidy, or just what are you getting (driving) at?

85/12 **Make out** (that):   Assert or claim; imply. *(Do not confuse with 14/10)* □ Are you trying to make out that I'm a thief?

85/13 **Have a good mind to** do something: Be strongly inclined to do something. □ I've a good mind to stop my son's pocket money until he behaves himself.

85/14 **In two minds**:   Undecided. □ I'm still in two minds about what pattern of wallpaper to buy.

85/15 **Second thoughts**:   A change of mind after reconsideration of a matter. □ On second thoughts, rather than go out, I'll stay at home tonight. □ We were going to rent the flat, but then we had second thoughts.

85/16 **Buy** a story: Believe; accept the truth of. □ That excuse for being late has been tried too often and the boss won't buy it.

85/17 **Lap up** something: Believe or accept eagerly. □ Pop fans in Italy just lap up our music. □ How could you lap up such an obvious lie?

85/18 **Run away with** an idea: Accept an idea too hastily. □ I've allowed people to cross my land several times, but they shouldn't run away with the idea that they have a right of way.

85/19 **Swallow** something **hook, line and sinker**:   Believe something totally, without reservation. □ This thief is cunning and when he tells housewives he is a gas-board official come to check the meter, they swallow his story hook, line and sinker.

85/20 **Take** something **with a pinch of salt:** Believe only part of what is told; allow for (great) exaggeration. □ As an interviewer in the personnel department of a large firm, you soon learn to take the success stories of many job applicants with a pinch of salt.

86: OBSESSION/DETERMINATION

86/1 A **one-track mind:** A mind that can think only of one topic. If used without further qualification, the expression usually signifies an obsession with sex. □ Pedro has a one-track mind and thinks of nothing but football. □ I'm sick of Ilya's dirty jokes, he's got a one-track mind.

86/2 A **hang-up:** An obsession or inhibition. □ Football is not a hobby with him, it's a hang-up. □ Some people have a hang-up about sex.

86/3 **Have a thing about** something: Have an obsession or prejudice about something. □ She has a thing about cats. □ Many of my countrymen have a thing about foreign 'guest workers'.

86/4 **Have a bee in one's bonnet about** something: Have a particular idea that occupies one's thoughts continually. □ Jochen has got a bee in his bonnet about anything to do with the military; he collects army manuals and weaponry, and is always watching war films.

86/5 **A chip on one's shoulder:** A bitter or resentful obsession or prejudice; an obsessive grievance which influences one's attitudes. □ Some Irishmen still bear a chip on their shoulder about the colonization of their country by the English.

86/6 **Hell-bent:** Recklessly determined; obsessed with doing something. □ There are many fanatics hell-bent on overthrowing the government.

86/7 **Dead-set:** Very determined; very opposed to something. □ That runner is dead-set on beating the 2000 metres record. □ Since the arrest of his brother, Luis is dead-set against the police.

86/8 **I'll be damned/blowed if . . .:** Expressions of determination. (*See also 104/2*) □ Gupta is just ungrateful and I'll be damned (blowed) if I'll help him again!

EXERCISES 16: THE MIND

A) Insert a creature or creatures to complete the following sentences.

1) She has a . . . in her bonnet about the dresses she wears.
2) You can't expect anything else from someone so . . . -ignorant.
3) That . . . -brain forgot to tell me.
4) He is as mad as a March . . . .
5) My aunt is old and has . . . in the belfry.
6) This accident would never have happened if you had used your . . . sense.

→

130

7) The passenger then insulted the train conductress by calling her a silly . . . .
8) He is sure to know the answer, there are no . . . on him.
9) The job needs care and skill, it is not as if any . . . can do it.

B) Give as many colloquial synonyms as possible for the definitions below.

1) a backward person from the countryside. 2) a psychiatric hospital. 3) a conceited know-all. 4) in my opinion.

C) Complete the sentences with a male Christian name.

1) You are a silly . . . ; in Japan you must drive on the left, not the right.
2) I felt like a proper . . . for making such a mistake.
3) That smart . . . pretends to know everything.
4) They live in a backward hill- . . . settlement.
5) The clever . . . has ruined everything for us.

D) Replace the underlined adjectives with a colloquial form.

1) She is <u>very</u> crazy.
2) They are <u>very</u> mad.
3) I acted like a <u>complete</u> idiot.
4) She is <u>very</u> set on going on the pilgrimage.

E) Give colloquialisms for the following.

1) a young, attractive but stupid woman. 2) someone who is easily deceived. 3) an intellectual. 4) someone's original invention or idea. 5) an obsession or inhibition. 6) an interval in which one revives past memories.

F) Complete the following colloquialisms with the missing noun(s).

1) They have swallowed our story . . . , . . . and . . . .
2) I have a memory like a . . . and once forgot where I lived.
3) He is as nutty as a . . . .
4) She is as thick as . . . .
5) We'll have to put on our . . .-. . . and devise a solution to the problem.
6) He is illiterate and daft as a . . . .
7) Anyone who would do such a crazy thing must be clean round the . . . .
8) Your suggestion may improve the situation and we shall take it on . . . .

Information

87: INFORM

87/1 **The low-down**: The true facts; the inside information. □ On his arrival in the country, the new diplomat was given the low-down of the political situation there.

87/2 **Gen/dope**: Information. □ The actress was besieged by reporters asking for more dope (gen) on her divorce.

87/3 **Bum-fodder** *or* **bumf**: Documents or papers, especially when containing useless information. 'Bumf' or 'bum-fodder' is a reference to toilet paper. □ We get a lot of advertising bumf (bum-fodder) through the mail.

87/4 **Gen/tee up** someone: Gain information; give information. □ I am all genned (teed) up on the American Civil War. □ I'll tee you up on business opportunities in this region.

87/5 **The nitty-gritty**: The basic facts or crude realities of a matter. □ Let's get down to the nitty-gritty; you simply can't do the job.

87/6 **The nuts and bolts**: The practical details. □ This book explains the nuts and bolts of vegetable gardening.

87/7 **The ins and outs**: The details of an activity or procedure. □ Before you can service your car, you must learn the ins and outs of car maintenance.

87/8 **Get down to brass tacks**: Start to consider the essential facts or practical details. □ We have agreed the basic plan; now let's get down to brass tacks and decide who does what!

87/9 **The size of it**: The basic facts or essentials about a situation or matter. □ The accountant agreed with my assessment of the firm's financial position, saying "That's about the size of it!"

87/10 **Put** someone **in the picture** *or* **fill** someone **in**: Inform someone more fully. □ The heads of departments meet regularly to put each other in the picture (fill each other in) on their activities.

87/11 **Keep** someone **posted**: Keep someone informed. □ The TV announcer promised to keep viewers posted on developments in the White House.

87/12 **Wise up/clue up** (someone): Inform; become aware. □ This firm will have to wise up to the market situation or go out of business! □ We are now clued up on how to go about buying a house.

87/13 **Sock it to me**: Amaze me! Tell me the worst! (*See also 44.1*) □ Come on, Pete – sock it to me; how come you were beaten 16–0?

87/14 **Set** someone **straight**: Inform someone of the true facts. □ He says it is possible to cross the desert alone; someone should set him straight.

87/15 Din/drum/hammer something **into** someone: Force information or facts into a person's mind by continual repetition. □ The only theorem in geometry I still remember is Pythagoras; I had it dinned (hammered/ drummed) into me at school.

87/16 Jungle telegraph *or* **bush telegraph** *or* **grape-vine**: An unofficial way of passing news; rumour and gossip. □ We heard on the jungle telegraph (grape-vine) that redundancies are planned for our company.

87/17 A little (dicky-)bird told me: Jocular way of not disclosing the source of one's information. □ A little dicky-bird told me that you've got engaged.

87/18 Straight from the horse's mouth: (of information) directly from an unquestionably reliable source. □ There's going to be a ministerial reshuffle; I have it straight from the horse's mouth.

87/19 Blind someone **with science**: Overwhelm someone with detailed facts or information; overawe with a display of technical knowledge. □ Don't blind me with science; just tell me how long the car repair will take.

88: FIND OUT

88/1 Suss/suss out something: Investigate or find out. □ That firm is registered in Liechtenstein, and it's difficult to suss out who the actual owners are.

88/2 Get wind of something: Hear a hint or rumour of something; receive a warning, usually from a confidential source. □ The gangsters got wind of the raid and fled the premises before the police arrived.

88/3 Pick someone's **brains**: Get information or advice from someone. □ I've come to pick your brains about the proposed reorganization of the office.

88/4 Do one's homework: Collect the preparatory information for something; prepare the plans or facts before taking action. □ Before going to the job interview, you should do your homework on the firm to give a knowledgeable impression on the day.

88/5 Fly a kite: Carry out a test in order to evaluate people's opinions. □ Maria was keen on a dog but didn't know how her husband would react to the idea, so over dinner she flew a kite by mentioning that guard dogs often prevent burglaries.

88/6 See which the wind blows *or* **. . . the cat jumps**: Find out what people are thinking or what is likely to happen before deciding on a course of action. □ Currency dealers are waiting to see which way the cat jumps (wind blows) on Wall Street before purchasing dollars.

88/7 See how the land lies: Find out more about a situation before deciding to do something; see whether things are favourable or otherwise. □ Let's see how the land lies before we lend them £10,000.

88/8 Put one's finger on something: Identify or find out precisely. □ There's a fault in the central-heating system, but we can't yet put our finger on it.

88/9 **Rumble** someone/something: Detect the truth about someone or something; discover a deception. □ Rosso had been shopping around for weeks with a stolen credit card before a sharp-eyed sales assistant rumbled him.

88/10 **Get wise to** something: Become aware or informed of. □ It didn't take long for the Japanese to get wise to Western technology.

88/11 An **eye-opener**:   A fact or circumstance that enlightens or surprises. □ Carlsen's conviction for armed robbery was an eye-opener for his neighbours, who had always thought of him as an upright man.

88/12 **Get no change/joy out of** someone: Receive no information or help from someone. *(See also 121/7)* □ The police questioned the burglar about his accomplice, but they got no joy (change) out of him.

89: REVEAL

89/1 **Let the cat out of the bag** *or* **give the show away** *or* **spill the beans**: Give away or divulge a secret; reveal a plot. □ Guy Fawkes was caught placing a bomb in the English Parliament after one of the plotters gave the show away (spilled the beans/let the cat out of the bag).

89/2 **Blow** something: Reveal. □ With the arrest of the top-ranking spy, the names of several other agents were blown.

89/3 **Blow the gaff**:   Reveal a secret. We were planning a birthday surprise for Dad, but my younger brother blew the gaff.

89/4 **Blow the whistle on** someone/something: Reveal publicly something illegal or dishonest. □ Sooner or later someone is going to blow the whistle on all this corruption in the city council.

89/5 **Blow** something **sky high** *or* **blow the lid off** something: Reveal a scandal or something sensational. □ The Watergate scandal blew the lid off the Nixon administration (blew the Nixon administration sky high).

89/6 **Let on**:   Reveal a secret. □ Greta has been treated in a clinic for alcoholism, but don't let on when you see her.

89/7 **Blab** (something):   Talk indiscreetly or reveal a secret. □ Don't tell Anwar anything personal, he'll blab everything.

89/8 A **blabbermouth**:   An indiscreet person who reveals confidential information; a tell-tale. □ Tom's a blabbermouth, so don't tell him anything about your love-life!

89/9 **Out with it!**:   Tell the truth! Say what you are thinking! □ Out with it, you've damaged the car haven't you?

89/10 **Spit it out!**:   Say what you are thinking or what you want to say □ This is obviously more than just a social visit, so spit it out!

89/11 **Own up**:   Confess or admit one's guilt. □ Not one of the children would own up to taking the ice-cream from the fridge.

89/12 **Come clean**:   Confess fully; reveal the truth at last. □ The minister was asked to come clean about the government's intention to increase taxes.

89/13 **Break** (news): (Of news) to reveal or become known. □ I have the unpleasant task of breaking the news of the factory closure to the employees. □ The news of the plane crash broke in the early hours of the next morning.

89/14 **Get it off one's chest**: Reveal the cause of one's anxiety. □ If you are upset about something, it is better that you get it off your chest to a friend rather than keep it to yourself.

89/15 **Come out of one's shell**: Reveal one's true character or feelings; overcome one's shyness. □ She always comes out of her shell after a few drinks.

89/16 **That would be telling!**: I can't reveal this confidential information. □ "Who told you about my accident?" "Ah, that would be telling!"

89/17 **My lips are sealed!**: Promise to keep a secret. □ I won't say anything to anyone about this! My lips are sealed . . .

89/18 **Wild horses wouldn't drag it out of me!**: Stronger promise to maintain confidentiality under any circumstances. □ . . . in fact, wild horses wouldn't drag it out of me!

89/19 **Keep it under one's hat**: Keep something secret. □ Inga knew that my husband was having an affair, but she kept it under her hat. □ That's the situation, but keep it under your hat!

89/20 **Mum's the word!**: Say nothing about this! I won't say anything! □ Don't tell him I told you; mum's the word! □ Your secret is safe with me; mum's the word!

89/21 **Hold out on** someone: Conceal something from someone. □ Lately my wife has been acting strangely and I've a feeling she's holding out on me.

90/1   **Twig** something: Realize or understand. □ He hasn't twigged what I'm saying.

90/2   **Cotton on to** *or* **tumble to** something: Understand; become aware of. *(For 'cotton on' see also 107/9)* □ At that time, scientists still hadn't cottoned on (tumbled) to how AIDS spread.

90/3   **Dig** something: Appreciate, enjoy or understand. □ I don't dig classical music. □ Do you dig me?

90/4   **Get** something: Understand. □ I just don't get it, why won't you come?

90/5   **Get the message/drift/picture** *or* **catch on**:   Understand the meaning or what is implied. □ Don't answer the door to that rogue, he might get the message (drift/picture/catch on) and go away.

90/6   **Be with** someone: Understand someone. □ That is how one calculates the area of a circle – is everyone with me so far?

90/7   **Savvy**:   Understand. □ She doesn't savvy. □ The answer is no; savvy?

90/8   **Register** with *or* **sink in** with *or* **click** with someone: Make a mental impression on someone; penetrate; become understood. □ The full danger of their situation still hasn't registered (sunk in/clicked) yet. □ The fact that Ming was dead didn't sink in (click/register) with his family until the next day.

90/9   **The penny drops**:   The meaning of something has at last suddenly become obvious. □ It took Werner a while to understand that he had come to the wrong address, but at last the penny dropped.

90/10 **Have** someone/something **taped**:   Understand someone or something fully; have an organized method of dealing with something. □ Yuri won't trick her, she's got him taped. □ The new secretary had the office routine taped within a week of joining the company.

90/11 **Read** someone **like a book**:   Know exactly what someone is thinking; understand someone's behaviour completely. □ Harry thinks he has fooled me, but I can read him like a book. □ Thanks to information from intelligence sources, the American negotiators at the talks were able to read the Soviet side like a book.

90/12 **Quick** (*or opposite* **slow**) **on the uptake**:   Quick (or slow) to understand. □ You're slow on the uptake today. □ Your son is quick on the uptake at school.

90/13 **Get through to** someone: Make someone understand or realize something. □ It is difficult to get through to some people that they shouldn't bathe on such a polluted beach.

90/14 **Like water off a duck's back**:   Something that has no effect or result. □ I keep telling him not to slam the door, but it's like water off a duck's back.

90/15 **Like talking to a brick wall**:   As if someone refuses to hear or understand at all. □ I'm always asking the landlord to carry out repairs, but it's like talking to a brick wall.

90/16 **Don't get me wrong**: Don't misunderstand me. □ Don't get me wrong, I don't want to interfere in your affairs, just help you.

90/17 **Get hold of the wrong end of the stick**: Completely misunderstand something. □ I once locked myself out, and while I was breaking back into my house through a side window, a policeman got hold of the wrong end of the stick and arrested me.

90/18 **All Chinese/Greek to** someone: Totally incomprehensible to someone; impossible for someone to understand. □ This operating manual is all Chinese (Greek) to me.

90/19 **Not make head or tail of** something: Find it totally incomprehensible. □ We don't have any enemies we know of, yet we keep getting threatening telephone calls; we can't make head or tail of it.

90/20 **Go over one's head** *or* **be above one's head**: Be incomprehensible to someone; be beyond one's capacity to understand. □ Anything to do with algebra goes over my head (is above my head).

90/21 **Mind-boggling**: Causing the mind to become overwhelmed by the great complexity or difficulty of something. □ The extent of the universe is mind-boggling. □ The difficulty of the task is mind-boggling.

90/22 **Stand to reason** *or* **figure** (*US*): Be logical or obvious. □ If he's ill in bed, it stands to reason (it figures) that he can't work. □ Caroline has crashed her car again. That figures (stands to reason) when you consider how badly she drives.

90/23 **Stand up** *or* **hold water** *or* **wash**: (Of an argument) be valid, logical or acceptable. □ That excuse for not paying your bill on time doesn't wash (stand up/hold water) with me.

90/24 **Cast-iron**: (Of an argument) incapable of being refuted or disproved. □ Lawyers had told him that he had a cast-iron claim for damages against the company.

90/25 **Tie in** with something: Agree or be consistent with. □ Those remarks don't tie in with what you said earlier.

90/26 **Add up**: Seem logical or consistent. □ His version of the accident doesn't add up.

90/27 **Put two and two together**: Realize or understand by a process of logic; draw an obvious conclusion. □ When their daughter began phoning secretively and coming home late, they put two and two together and assumed that she had a boy-friend.

91: KNOWLEDGE/SUSPICION

91/1 **Know full well**: Know clearly or without doubt. □ The boys know full well they shouldn't play football near the houses.

91/2 **Know** (a place) **like the back of one's hand**: Know a place very well or intimately. □ I've driven a taxi in Madrid for years, and know the city like the back of my hand.

91/3 **Know one's onions/stuff**: Know one's subject or job thoroughly.
□ That accountant knows his onions (stuff) in tax law.

91/4 **Have** something **at one's fingertips**: Be thoroughly familiar with something. □ I'm looking for someone who has the workings of outboard motors at his fingertips.

91/5 **Versed in** *or* **at home in** *or* **well up in** something: Very knowledgeable or skilled in some art or task. □ To obtain an operating licence for radio transmission, the applicant must be versed (well up/at home) in all aspects of short-wave communication.

91/6 **Know what's what**: Know how something works; know all about something. □ That firm knows what's what in hi-fi equipment.

91/7 **Know a thing or two**: Be knowledgeable or experienced. □ He knows a thing or two about keeping tropical fish.

91/8 **Know the score**: Be aware of the essential facts. □ You know the score already; I don't have any money to lend you.

91/9 **In the know**: Having inside information about something. □ The fewer people who are in the know about our plans, the better.

91/10 **Street-wise**: Familiar with the ways of ordinary people or urban life; quick-witted and cunning. □ Urchins in the slums of Rio de Janeiro quickly learn to be street-wise.

91/11 **A smattering** of something: A slight superficial knowledge about a subject or language. □ She has only a smattering of English.

91/12 **Pick up** knowledge: Acquire knowledge by chance; learn casually.
□ While in the country, I picked up a knowledge of Thai customs.
□ Foreigners don't usually pick up Russian easily.

91/13 **Keep tabs/a tab on** *or* **keep track of** someone/something: Keep under observation; keep oneself informed about someone or something.
□ Customs officers discovered that the lorry was transporting drugs, and kept a tab on it (kept tabs on it/kept track of it) after it left the docks.

91/14 **Not know the first thing about** something: Know nothing at all about something. □ Six months ago, I didn't know the first thing about piloting a helicopter.

91/15 **Not have the foggiest/faintest** *or* **not have a clue**: Have no idea at all.
□ Why he should tell you to come here, I haven't the foggiest (faintest/a clue). □ He claimed to be a plumber, but when I asked him to repair the tap, he hadn't a clue (the foggiest/faintest).

91/16 **Search me!**: I don't know at all! I have no idea! □ "When is she arriving?" "Search me! I haven't a clue."

91/17 **Be a new one on** someone: Be new or unknown to someone. □ That whales eat krill is a new one on me.

91/18 **In the dark**: Having no information about something. □ The press were kept in the dark about what had happened.

91/19 **A dark horse** *or* an **unknown quantity**: A person or thing whose nature, ability or significance is unknown. □ This company is a dark horse (an unknown quantity) among software companies, having grown from

138

nothing very quickly under a relatively unknown director.

91/20 **Not know** someone **from Adam**:   Be unable to recognize someone; not know what someone looks like. □ The actress is well known in her own country, but in America they don't know her from Adam. □ If I'm to meet Mr Levchenko at the airport, you'd better tell me what he looks like, I wouldn't know him from Adam.

91/21 **Not bargain for** something: Not expect something; be unprepared for something. □ We knew that the weather would get worse, but we didn't bargain for a hurricane.

91/22 **A hunch** *or* an **inkling**:   A slight knowledge or suspicion; a feeling based on intuition. □ After finding the remains of a fire near the snow-line, we had a hunch (an inkling) that the Italian climbers had beaten us to the summit.

91/23 **Ring a bell**:   Arouse a vague memory; sound faintly familiar. □ Wait, that name rings a bell!

91/24 **Smell a rat**:   Suspect underhand dealing or foul play; suspect that something is wrong. □ The Volvo was very low-priced and Edouard wanted to buy it, but when he saw some alterations in the car documents, he smelt a rat and backed off from the purchase.

91/25 **Fishy**:   Arousing disbelief or suspicion. □ That's fishy, the neighbours are away on holiday, yet their lights are on. □ Don't believe your uncle, he's always telling fishy stories!

92: STUDY/EXAMS

92/1 **Swot (up)/cram** something: Study hard or intensively. A 'swot' is someone who studies hard or excessively. □ He can't come out tonight, he's cramming (swotting) for his exam tomorrow. □ She's swotting up (cramming) History.

92/2 **Mug/bone up on** something: Learn a subject intensively. □ In the two days before my driving-test, I'll bone up (mug up) on my highway code.

92/3 **Brush/polish up** knowledge: Improve or revive one's former knowledge. □ On my trip to Mexico, I had an opportunity to brush up my Spanish.

92/4 **Learn** something **parrot-fashion**:   Learn uncritically, without thinking; learn by unintelligent repetition. □ Historical trends are more important than learning dates parrot-fashion.

92/5 **Stew/pore over** something: Study something patiently or persistently. □ I spent all the evening poring (stewing) over the firm's accounts.

92/6 **Browse** (through something):   Look through or peruse in a casual or leisurely way. □ While I was browsing through the books in the library, I found that book you were looking for.

92/7 **A bookworm**:   A person who is very fond of reading. □ My son's a real little bookworm – he's always got his nose in a book of some kind or other.

92/8   **A fresher:** A first-year student at college or university. □ I'm going to the freshers' ball tonight.

92/9   **High-falutin:** Pompous; unnatural and affected. □ He is always using high-falutin words that ordinary people can't understand.

92/10   **The three Rs:** The basic school disciplines of Reading, wRiting and aRithmetic. □ Schools must raise the levels of the three Rs.

92/11   **Play hookey** (*#US*) *or* **play truant:** Stay away from school without permission. □ Of the five missing pupils, the teacher reckoned that two were ill and three were playing hookey (truant).

92/12   **Crib** (something): Copy secretly from someone or from hidden notes. □ Sharon's exam results were so unusually good that she was suspected of cribbing.

92/13   **Scrape through:** Only just pass. □ "I scraped through Chemistry. How did Edith do in Maths?" "She only just scraped through."

92/14   **Pass with flying colours:** Pass easily or with distinction. □ He passed Biology with flying colours.

92/15   **Flunk** an exam: Fail an exam. □ The numbers of students flunking Maths has increased dramatically.

92/16   **Plough** someone: Declare that a candidate has failed an exam. □ Ten students were ploughed in Physics this year.

EXERCISES 17: INFORMATION

A) Complete the following phrasal verbs and colloquial phrases by inserting the correct adverb.

1) The boy knew who had committed the theft but he didn't let ... .
2) The colonel will fill you ... on the military situation.
3) I didn't cotton ... to what he meant until much later.
4) She was glad to tell me about it, just to get it ... her chest.
5) I'll tell you a secret if you'll keep it ... your hat.
6) The students are poring ... their books.
7) He picked ... the language in three months.
8) If he knows anything about it, he won't hold ... on us.
9) I can't get ... to him that what he's doing is wrong.
10) The police have been unable to suss ... his whereabouts.
11) That is the rough outline of our plan, now let us get ... to brass tacks.

→

B) Give colloquialisms for the following definitions.

1) documents full of useless information.
2) the basic school subjects of writing, reading and arithmetic.
3) someone who indiscreetly reveals confidential information.
4) a superficial or shallow knowledge of a subject or discipline.
5) an unofficial source of news and gossip.
6) a piece of information that surprises or enlightens.
7) someone whose abilities or nature is unknown.
8) a suspicion based on intuition.
9) someone fond of reading books.

C) Insert an animal or bird to complete the colloquial sentences below.

1) When we asked him for the source of his information, he replied that a little ... had told him.
2) We'll not do anything until we see which way the ... jumps.
3) Your secret is safe with me; wild ... s wouldn't drag it from me.
4) I warned him not to go up the mountain alone, but it was like water off a ... 's back.
5) He offered me a lot of money to transport a parcel to Amsterdam, but when he described the contents as sweets, I smelt a ... .
6) Many actors learn their roles by repetition, ...-fashion.
7) Don't let the ... out of the bag and tell her that I did it.
8) The information is genuine, straight from the ... 's mouth.

D) Replace the underlined phrases with as many colloquial synonyms as possible, paying attention to the tense of the verb and rephrasing where necessary.

1) She <u>failed</u> her Maths exam.
2) They have been <u>studying their English lessons intently</u> all evening.
3) <u>I have no idea at all</u> where she is.
4) He <u>knows a lot about</u> diesel engines.
5) It took him a while before <u>he understood</u> what the foreigner was trying to say.
6) I have been ordered not <u>to reveal the secret</u>.
7) In the car export department, we don't concern ourselves with the <u>basic facts</u> of how the vehicles are assembled.

Language/Conversation

93: TALK/SPEAK

93/1   **Rap:**   To chat. A 'rap' is a chat. □ For a while they stood rapping in the shop entrance. □ We had a good rap.

93/2   **Talk shop:**   Discuss one's work or profession as a subject of conversation; discuss business. □ Don't talk shop at social gatherings!

93/3   **Fire away!** *or* **shoot!** (*US*):   Go ahead with speaking! Begin what you have to say! □ I've got my pencil now, so fire away (so shoot)!

93/4   **The lingo:**   The jargon of a profession or class; a foreign language. □ Our holiday in Greece was nice, but we had trouble with the lingo. □ The computer industry has developed its own special lingo.

93/5   **A buzz word:**   A fashionable jargon word conveying the impression of specialist or inside knowledge. □ Among ecologists, the latest buzz word is 'biodegradable'.

93/6   **A pep-talk:**   A verbal address to boost someone's confidence. □ Once a month, sales staff get a pep-talk from the general manager.

93/7   **Tackle** someone **about** something: Discuss an awkward matter or problem with someone. □ On the staircase, the landlady tackled him about paying his overdue rent.

93/8   **Get on to** someone: Get in contact with; discuss a matter with. □ We got on to the council about having the street drains cleaned.

93/9   **Give** someone **a buzz/ring/bell/tinkle:**   To telephone someone. □ Give him a buzz (tinkle/ring/bell) after five, he'll be in then!

93/10   **Put in a good word for** someone: Speak in favour of someone or something. □ When you call head office in Geneva, put in a good word for our branch here in London!

93/11   **Chip in:**   Interrupt with a remark when someone else is speaking. (*See also 49/16*) □ The politician's speech was continually interrupted by people chipping in with sarcastic comments.

93/12   **Reel/rattle off** something: Recite rapidly or at length. □ At the trade fair, our salesmen spent a week rattling (reeling) off the technical specifications of our equipment.

93/13   **Trot out** something: Bring forward for approval or information; recite rapidly. □ You're always trotting out excuses for not digging the garden! □ At the police station, she trotted out the names of several other people who had been attacked by her neighbour's dog.

93/14   **Dish up** something: Present or bring forward; recite. □ Olaf dished up the usual excuses for being late for work again.

94: EMPTY TALK/JOKE

94/1 **Jaw**: To gossip; to talk long and boringly. A 'jaw' is such a talk or conversation. □ Don't stand around jawing all day!

94/2 **A chin-wag**: A chat. □ The ladies used to meet every Thursday for a chin-wag.

94/3 **Wag one's tongue**: To gossip. □ When people drink, their tongues usually begin to wag.

94/4 **A patter**: Glib talk, chatter or gossip. To 'patter' means to gossip. □ Rudi is fond of the patter but doesn't like the work.

94/5 **Pass the time of day**: Have a friendly talk or gossip. □ She stopped to pass the time of day with the village postman.

94/6 **A crack**: An enjoyable chat or gossip. *(See also 'wisecrack' – 94/17)* □ Anton met his friends in the bar for a beer and a crack.

94/7 **A natter**: A friendly chat or gossip. To chat in a friendly way is to 'natter'. □ Indira visited her neighbour for a natter.

94/8 **Yap**: To chat or gossip, especially in a shrill voice. □ The teacher told the children to stop yapping and to concentrate on the lesson.

94/9 **Tittle-tattle**: Petty gossip or chatter. □ You shouldn't believe all the tittle-tattle you hear!

94/10 **Gas *or* hot air**: Empty talk. □ The trade negotiations were only hot air (gas) that produced no worthwhile agreement.

94/11 **Yackety-yak *or* bla-bla-bla**: Persistent empty talk. □ The speaker went on about how women were less enterprising than men and more suited to repetitive jobs, yackety-yak (bla-bla-bla).

94/12 **Yak/rabbit/witter on**: Chatter idly and persistently; talk continually in a foolish or gossipy manner. □ The old woman yakked (rabbited/wittered) on for an hour about how things were better in her day.

94/13 **Ramble**: Talk or write incoherently; wander unnecessarily from the subject or main theme. □ Instead of telling them what he wanted, he rambled on about the weather.

94/14 **Waffle/flannel**: To talk or write empty phrases in order to conceal one's ignorance. Anything spoken or written in this way is 'waffle' or 'flannel'. □ Having lost his notes on the way to the conference, the speaker was obliged to waffle (flannel) through his speech.

94/15 **Back-chat**: A cheeky reply or objection; a flippant answer. □ You are staying at home tonight to do your homework, and I want none of your back-chat!

94/16 **Crack a joke**: Tell a joke. □ He loves to crack dirty jokes.

94/17 **A wisecrack *or* a crack**: A joke; a witty or clever remark. □ Stop the cracks (wisecracks), this is a serious matter.

94/18 **Corny**: Repeated so often that people are tired of it; well known and empty; not funny. Originally a New York show-business term describing a lower class of unsophisticated audience who were commonly

believed to feed themselves exclusively on corn. *(See also 173/15)*
□ Politicians are always using corny phrases □ I find that comedian's jokes corny. □ I know it sounds corny, but I love you!

95: UNINTELLIGIBLE TALK

95/1 **Pidgin (English):** A barely intelligible jargon of English mixed with another language. The word 'pidgin' is a Chinese corruption of 'business'. In Papua New Guinea, pidgin has achieved the status of a national language. □ As a result of the pidgin of a Chinese waiter, we ended up with a different meal from the one we ordered.

95/2 **Double Dutch:** Incomprehensible talk. □ That lecture on semi-conductors was all double Dutch to me.

95/3 **Gobbledygook:** Incomprehensible jargon (spoken and written); gibberish. □ It took me two whole days to wade through all the gobbledygook on my tax form.

95/4 **Jabber:** Talk rapidly and indistinctly. □ The sailors were jabbering in a foreign tongue. □ Newcomers to the wholesale fish market are often surprised that buyers understand the jabbering of the auctioneers.

95/5 **Garble** speech: To distort or confuse a story or message so that it cannot be easily understood. □ The telex message came through garbled and we couldn't decipher it. □ Refugees from the fighting have given only garbled accounts of the situation in the region, and we may have to wait for a clear picture to emerge.

95/6 **Murder** a language: Speak or write a language very badly. □ Roberto used to murder English before he went on the course.

96: NONSENSE

96/1 **A load of (old) nonsense:** Complete or utter nonsense. One of the colloquialisms for nonsense *(see below)* is usually added. □ That scientific theory is a load of old tripe (cobblers/codswallop etc.).

96/2 **Bunkum/bunk:** Nonsense; ostentatious speech. The word 'bunkum' is derived from the USA county of Buncombe in N. Carolina, whose Congress member spoke needlessly and bombastically. □ What she says is just plain bunkum.

96/3 **Claptrap/hokum:** Nonsense; pretentious talk or showy ideas used only to win applause or approval. □ Aldogan's claim that his family are wealthy landowners in Anatolia is all claptrap (hokum).

96/4 **Poppycock/balderdash:** Nonsense; a jumble of words; idle, senseless talk. □ This report is pure poppycock, so you'd better rewrite it.

96/5 **Tosh/bosh/twaddle:** Rubbish; senseless, feeble and prosy writing or foolish talk. □ That's tosh, so ignore it! □ No wonder Marco failed the exam – he answered question 3 with a load of twaddle.

96/6 **Rot/tommy-rot**: Absurd statement, argument or proposal; nonsense. □ The recession is world-wide and anyone who says otherwise is talking rot.

96/7 **Tripe/hogwash/piffle/guff**: Nonsense; worthless, insincere rubbish; feeble, empty talk. □ You're talking tripe. It's absolute piffle! □ I've never heard so much guff in all my life! Hogwash, all of it!

96/8 **Codswallop/baloney (boloney)**: Nonsense, especially that put forward as serious ideas or information. □ All his chat about buying a new car turned out to be codswallop – he didn't have any money. □ What baloney! We'd never do anything like that.

96/9 **Cobblers/hooey/humbug**: Utter nonsense. □ Oh hooey! Don't expect me to believe a load of cobblers (humbug) like that!

96/10 **Fiddlesticks!**: Generally used as an interjection expressing contemptuous disagreement (as is 'hooey!' *above*, or 'rot!', 'bosh!' and others). □ "Juanita is very good at her job." "Fiddlesticks! She's always making mistakes!"

96/11 **Malark(e)y**: Nonsense; an unfounded story; humbug. (*See also 128/2*) □ Sato trotted out some malarkey about being related to Japanese royalty.

96/12 **Drivel**: Silly nonsense; foolish or childish talk. To 'drivel' is to talk nonsense. □ That shop assistant is a drivelling idiot. □ If I hear any more drivel from you, I'll get really angry!

96/13 **Bullshit** (*#?*)/**bull**: Nonsense; unnecessary tasks or fuss. □ Don't talk bull (bullshit)! □ In my job, you have to put up with a lot of bull.

96/14 **Talk through the back of one's head/neck** *or* **talk through one's hat**: Talk nonsense. □ You're talking through the back of your neck (head)! □ She was talking through her hat!

96/15 **Blether/blather**: Talk or chatter foolishly. 'Blather' or 'blether' is foolish chatter. □ Klaus went on blathering (blethering) about how clever his dog was.

96/16 **Old wives' tale**: An old and foolish belief. □ He claims that predicting the weather by the behaviour of frogs is not just an old wives' tale.

96/17 **Mumbo-jumbo**: Meaningless ritual; words or actions that are deliberately obscure in order to mystify or confuse people. □ Some people regard spiritualism as superstitious mumbo-jumbo.

97: TALK A LOT/LOUDLY

97/1 **Rattle away nineteen to the dozen**: Talk rapidly and continually. □ The tourist guide rattled away nineteen to the dozen about the history of the pyramids.

97/2 **Talk one's head off**: Talk too much; talk endlessly. □ The announcer talked his head off, and I thought the concert would never start.

97/3 **Talk the back/hind legs off a donkey:** To talk endlessly. (*See also 150/11*) ☐ My wife can talk the hind (back) legs off a donkey.

97/4 Have **the gift of the gab:** Be good at talking; have a talent for talking fluently or eloquently. ☐ A talk-show host on TV must have the gift of the gab.

97/5 **Blarney:** Smooth talk that flatters and deceives. ☐ With blarney like that, he could sell ice-cream to Eskimos.

97/6 Talk **till one is blue in the face:** Make a great but futile effort to convince someone of something. ☐ You can argue your political opinion till you are blue in the face, I won't accept it! ☐ Tamara begged until she was blue in the face, but the soldier wouldn't give her her child back.

97/7 **Not get a word in edgeways:** Be unable to say anything owing to someone else monopolizing the conversation or speaking continually. ☐ One speaker at the public meeting kept on talking and wouldn't let anyone else get a word in edgeways for over an hour.

97/8 **Beat about the bush:** Discuss a subject without coming to the point; make lengthy and irrelevant comments. ☐ Stop beating about the bush and tell me if I've passed the exam!

97/9 **Thrash** something **out:** Discuss something at length; consider thoroughly. ☐ The two companies got together and thrashed out the details of the planned merger.

97/10 **Go on about** something: Talk lengthily about something. ☐ He's always going on about his new car. ☐ Don't go on about the curtains looking dirty, I'll wash them tomorrow!

97/11 **A chatterbox:** A talkative person. ☐ My sister is a chatterbox on the phone.

97/12 **A windbag** *or* **a gasbag:** Someone who irritates people with lengthy talk. ☐ That politician is a windbag (gasbag).

97/13 **Shoot (one's mouth) off** *or* **sound off** *or* **spout:** Talk loudly and indiscreetly; be loud and unpleasantly noticeable. ☐ Beate is a Jehovah's Witness and is always shouting her mouth off (spouting/sounding off/shooting off) about the sins of others.

97/14 **Holler** (*US*): To shout or yell. A 'holler' is a shout. ☐ The crane driver hollered to the men below to stand clear. ☐ If you need me, just give a holler; I'll be in the yard!

98: COMPLAIN

98/1 **Grouse/grouch/gripe/beef:** To grumble. The grumble itself is a 'beef', a 'grouse', a 'grouch' or a 'gripe'. ☐ He likes to beef (grouch/gripe/grouse) about the weather. ☐ One of our customers in the restaurant has a gripe (beef/grouse/grouch) about his meal being cold.

98/2 **Bellyache:** To grumble. ☐ What's he bellyaching about now?

98/3 **Whinge/winge/yammer:** Complain persistently and irritatingly. ☐ You shouldn't go abroad if you want to winge (whinge/yammer) about other people's countries.

98/4 **Misery-guts** (*#?*): An unpleasant person who is always complaining. □ Fred's an old misery-guts tonight – I can't think what's got into him!

99: KEEP QUIET

99/1 **Shut up like a clam** *or* **clam up**: Refuse obstinately to talk or say anything. □ The film star was quite happy to give the reporter an interview, but when he mentioned her private life, she shut up like a clam (clammed up).

99/2 **Put a sock in it** *or* **belt up** *or* **cut the cackle**: Be quiet; shut up. □ Why don't you put a sock in it (belt up/cut the cackle)!

99/3 **Shush!**: Hush!; be quiet! Shush! The baby's asleep.

99/4 **Pipe down**: Cease talking; become less noisy or insistent. □ Please tell your son to pipe down; I can't hear the film!

99/5 **Dry up**: Cease talking or run out of words. □ The new chairman attempted an impromptu speech, but dried up almost immediately.

99/6 **Not a peep from** someone: Not a sound from someone. □ I don't want to hear a peep more from you this evening. □ When the baby began to cry, she gave him a bottle and there wasn't a peep more from him.

99/7 **Not say a dicky-bird**: Not utter a word. □ She didn't say a dicky-bird all evening.

100: TALK CLEARLY/FRANKLY

100/1 **Call a spade a spade**: Speak plainly or bluntly. □ Excuse the forceful language, but where I come from we call a spade a spade!

100/2 **Not mince matters** *or* **not mince one's words**: Speak plainly or bluntly. □ The new president didn't mince matters (. . . his words) and declared that the country was facing the threat of war.

100/3 **Make no bones about** something: Speak frankly about something; speak without reserve □ Lehmann makes no bones about his previous criminal convictions.

100/4 **Lay it on the line** *or* **give it to** someone **straight**: Speak frankly. □ I'll lay it on the line (I'll give it to you straight), tthe company doesn't need your services any more.

100/5 **Not put too fine a point on it**: Express something bluntly or plainly. □ Not to put too fine a point on it, our financial situation is shit!

100/6 **Talk turkey** (*#US*): Talk in a frank or businesslike way. □ The conference on world health proved an excellent opportunity for delegates from the super-powers to talk turkey on other mutual problems in a non-political atmosphere.

100/7 **Have it out with** someone: Settle a problem with someone by frank discussion. □ The warehouse is continually delivering the goods late; I'll have it out with their manager this afternoon.

101: SET CONVERSATIONAL PHRASES

101/1 **Speak/talk of the devil!:** Said humorously when the person under discussion unexpectedly appears. The full phrase is 'speak of the devil and he will appear'. □ Karen has gained a place in the national athletics team. Why, speak of the devil, here she comes now!

101/2 **Look what the cat's brought in!** *or* **look what the wind's blown in!:** Humorous or impolite way of saying that someone has arrived. □ Look what the cat's brought in (the wind's blown in), it's that conceited fellow again!

101/3 **It's a small world!:** Expression of surprise at meeting someone in an unexpected place. □ Petra! It's a small world – I never thought I'd see you here! Long time no see!

101/4 **Long time no see!:** It's a long time since we met.

101/5 **How's tricks?:** How are things? □ How's tricks? Have you become a father yet?

101/6 **Ta!** *(pr. 'tar'):* Thank you! *(Do not confuse with 'ta-ta' 101/20)*

101/7 **Come again!:** Please repeat what you said! □ Come again, I didn't hear you because of that train passing!

101/8 **Between you, me and the gate-post:** Confidentially between the two of us. □ Between you, me and the gate-post, our boss is sexually harassing the secretaries.

101/9 **Bless you!:** Said to someone who has just sneezed.

101/10 **Any road:** Anyhow; anyway. □ I don't want to go out tonight, any road it's raining.

101/11 **As it were**: So to speak; in a manner of speaking. □ Mr Wu hasn't arrived because he has been, as it were, detained; between you and me, arrested.

101/12 **By rights**: If the proper thing were done; normally in such cases. □ After such a serious crash, by rights I should be dead now. □ By rights, you should have taken the money you found to the police.

101/13 **Look here!**: Pay attention; I'm not joking. □ Look here, I won't tolerate your misbehaviour!

101/14 **Not to worry**: There is no problem or cause for concern. □ "I've locked my key in the car!" "Not to worry, I can get the door open with a screwdriver and some wire."

101/15 **Come to think of it** *or* **come to that**: When I think about it; since you mention it. □ Come to think of it (Come to that), I need a haircut too.

101/16 **Look who's talking!**: You have (or that person has) no right to say that. □ You say I'm greedy, well – look who's talking, you never stop eating!

101/17 **You are a one!**: You are a dear!; you are amusing! □ Flowers for me? You are a one! □ Gone and got all dirty again? You are a one!

101/18 **Or else!**: Added to a command to signify a threat. □ Do it! Or else!

101/19 **Are there bears in the woods?** *(US)* **or do bears shit in the woods?** *(US) (#?)*: (In reply to a question) Of course! Naturally! □ "Do you wish you were back home away from this war?" "Do bears shit in the woods?"

101/20 **Toodle-oo!/Ta-ta!** *(pr. 'tar-tar')*: Goodbye! *(See also 101/6 for 'ta')*

101/21 **I must love you and leave you!**: I must say goodbye now.

101/22 **Nope!**: No! □ "Did you enjoy the film?" "Nope! I didn't." □ "Have the goods we ordered arrived yet?" "Nope!"

101/23 **Yep!/yeah!** *(pr. 'yair')*: Yes!

102: ADDRESSES

102/1 **Sunshine**: Endearing or sarcastic term of address. □ Come on, sunshine – don't worry about it. □ Watch out, sunshine; one more mistake and you're in trouble!

102/2 **Love/lover**: Endearing term of address to someone of the opposite sex, often used by someone quite unknown to the person so addressed. □ Sorry love (lover), I don't know where the street is, I'm a stranger here myself.

102/3 **Ducky**: Dear; familiar or endearing term of address.

102/4 **Sweetie-pie/honey**: Darling. □ Be a honey and turn the TV on – I'm too tired to move.

102/5 **Kid/sonny**: Condescending address to a boy or youth by an older person. □ Now look here, sonny, you'd better do what I say – remember I'm the one with the experience in this job.

102/6 Squire/guv/governor: Sir; respectful terms of address to one's superiors.

102/7 Pop: Term of address to an elderly man. Literally it means 'father'.

102/8 Mate/matey: Friend; familiar form of address to one's equals.

102/9 Old chap/bean: Familiar terms of address to a man.

102/10 Mac *(US)*: Casual address to a man whose name one doesn't know. □ Say, mac – where's the nearest drugstore?

102/11 Buster *(US)*: Aggressive or disrespectful term of address to someone. □ Listen buster, if you don't tell the truth, I will get angry!

102/12 Folks: Casual address to a group of people. *(See also 165/12)* □ The driver got into the bus, and turning to the passengers said, "OK folks, let's go!".

103: OATHS/EMPHASIS

103/1 Blast (it)!/damn (it)!/drat!/bother!: Oaths expressing annoyance or disappointment. □ Blast it (Bother etc.), my tyre is punctured!

103/2 Dratted *or* **confounded:** Annoying or unpleasant. □ The dratted (confounded) window won't shut!

103/3 Blinking/flaming/blooming/flipping/blasted/perishing/blessed: Annoying, nasty or unpleasant; extremely. □ What a blooming (flaming etc.) impudent thing to say to anyone! □ It's blinking (flipping etc.) hot in here.

103/4 Damned *(#?)*/**frigging** *(#?)*/**fucking** *(#??)*/**bloody** *(#?)*/**goddamn** *(#?)*: Cursed or unpleasant; extremely. □ I've told you already, pass me the frigging (bloody etc.) spanner! □ That's a frigging (bloody) crazy idea! □ This drill is no damned (frigging/goddamn etc.) good!

103/5 Swear like a fish-wife/trooper: Swear forcefully or vulgarly. □ When she's angry, she can swear like a fish-wife (trooper).

103/6 Excuse my French!: Excuse my bad language! □ Excuse my French, but it was damned annoying!

103/7 You can put that in your pipe and smoke it!: Phrase appended to an angry remark to add emphasis to it. □ Tell Jung he's a rogue and I'll have no more commercial dealings with him, so he can put that in his pipe and smoke it!

103/8 The heck/on earth/the devil/the blazes/the dickens/the deuce/the hell: Added to an interrogative pronoun (why/when/how etc.) for emphasis. □ Why on earth (the hell/the dickens etc.) didn't you tell me earlier? □ What the deuce (the heck/on earth etc.) are you doing here?

103/9 Old: Used for emphasis in a friendly or casual manner. □ Good old Franz! □ Come with us, you can do your homework any old time! □ Any old TV won't do, we must have one with teletext and remote control. □ My wife criticizes me for any old reason.

103/10 Like: Meaningless expletive appended to a question or sentence in order to lessen its emphasis. The use of this term is regarded by many people as uneducated. □ Why do you say that, like? □ Where are you going, like? □ The countryside there is nice, like.

104: EXCLAMATIONS OF AMAZEMENT

104/1 Shiver me timbers!/stone the crows!/cor blimey!/crikey!/holy cow!/ hell's bells!/holy mackerel!/holy smoke!: Exclamations of astonishment. □ Shiver me timbers (Crikey/Cor blimey/Stone the crows etc.), the kitchen is on fire!

104/2 Well blow me!/I'll be blowed/bless my soul!/I'll be jiggered!/well I never!: Exclamations of amazement. □ Well blow me (I'll be blowed/ bless my soul etc.) it's Marcel from Rouen come to visit us!

104/3 Fancy that!/just fancy!/can you beat that!/it just goes to show!: Exclamations of amazement at some feat or some amazing occurrence. □ Fancy that (Can you beat that etc.)! – a dog that drinks beer!

104/4 Goodness gracious (me)!/good heavens!: Exclamations of surprise. □ Goodness gracious me (good heavens) there's a man drowning near the jetty!

104/5 Great Scott!: Exclamation of surprise. The reference is to General Winfield Scott, a hero of the Mexican-American war in the mid 19th century.

104/6 By Jove/Jingo/George!/gum!: Exclamations of astonishment or determination. □ By gum (George/Jove/Jingo), I've won first prize! □ By Jove (gum/George/Jingo) I'll do my best!

104/7 Crumbs!: Exclamation of dismay or surprise. □ Crumbs, I've forgotten my wallet in the shop!

104/8 Golly!/gosh!/gee whiz! *(US)*: Mild exclamations of surprise. □ Gee whiz (Golly/Gosh etc.) it's a real eagle! I've never seen one in the wild before.

104/9 Wow!/Coo!: Expressions of astonishment and admiration. □ Wow (Coo)! The Hoover Dam is certainly massive.

104/10 Whoops! *or* **Oops(-a-daisy)!:** Exclamation on falling, slipping or making an obvious mistake. □ Whoops ! (Oops!/Oops-a-daisy!) I nearly slipped. □ Whoops! (Oops-a-daisy!) I've dropped the cup. □ Oops! (Whoops!) I keyed in the wrong number.

104/11 Yippee! *or* **whoopee!:** Exclamation of excitement or joy. □ Yippee (Whoopee)! I've got the job!

104/12 Have/did you ever!: Exclamation of surprise; have you ever seen or heard such a thing! □ Have you ever! No-one but he would wear such outrageous clothes!

104/13 You don't say!: Exclamation of surprise at something said. □ You don't say! Can a cheetah really run that fast?

104/14 **Get away!** *or* **go on with you!**: Exclamations of surprise or disbelief at what has been said. □ Get away (Go on with you), no-one can can stay under water that long!

104/15 **For Christ's/heaven's/goodness'/God's sake**: Exclamations of surprise and annoyance. □ For goodness' (God's/heaven's/Christ's) sake don't drive so fast in the rain!

104/16 **For crying out loud!/for Pete's sake!/for the love of Mike!**: Exclamations of surprise and annoyance. □ For Pete's sake (For crying out loud/For the love of Mike)! – what have you done to your hair? □ For the love of Mike (For crying out loud etc.), who's left the bath dirty again?!

104/17 **Shucks!**: Exclamation of amazed disgust or disbelief. □ Shucks, you're not really going to dismiss me!

104/18 **Yuk!**: Exclamation of disgust. From it comes an adjective, 'yucky' (*see 70/5*). □ Yuk! I'm not eating that – it looks horrible!

104/19 **Phew!/Strewth!**: Exclamations of wonder, surprise, relief or discomfort. □ Phew! That's a beautiful diamond ring. □ Phew! It's hot in here. □ Strewth! That car almost ran me over.

104/20 **Ouch!**: Exclamation of sudden pain! □ Ouch! I've just pricked my finger on something.

104/21 **Gob-smacked/flabbergasted**: Amazed or astonished. □ We were gob-smacked (flabbergasted) when we heard that our son had been arrested for burglary.

104/22 **You could have knocked me down with a feather!**: I was amazed or astounded. □ When the museum curator said that the old painting I had inherited was extremely valuable, you could have knocked me down with a feather!

EXERCISES 18: LANGUAGE/CONVERSATION

A) Complete the following sentences with a person, a creature or a nationality.

1) He has a foul mouth and swears like a . . . .
2) There was interference on the phone and when she spoke, all I heard was double . . . .
3) Holy . . .! The boat has sprung a leak!
4) Look what the . . .'s brought in! I haven't seen you in years!
5) For the love of . . ., stop annoying me!
6) Speak of the . . ., here he comes now!
7) "Were you frightened when the robber threatened you with a gun?" "Are there . . . s in the woods?"

→

8) When the policeman entered the bar, everyone shut up like a . . . .
9) We shall have to talk . . . and agree the practical details of the deal.
10) Excuse my . . . , I didn't mean to swear!

B) Give colloquialisms for the definitions listed below.

1) the jargon of a given profession, or a particular foreign language.
2) empty talk or writing intended to conceal ignorance.
3) a witty remark or joke.
4) empty or foolish ritual.
5) an old foolish belief.
6) a talkative person.
7) smooth deceptive talk.
8) badly spoken English heard in parts of the Far East.
9) petty gossip.

C) From the module, find as many synonyms as possible to replace the underlined phrases.

1) I phoned you last night but you weren't at home.
2) He is talking nonsense.
3) Stop grumbling and get on with your work!
4) We spent the afternoon chatting over cups of coffee.

D) Using colloquial exclamations and phrases from the module, what would you say . . .

1) to someone who has just sneezed?
2) to thank someone?
3) when leaving someone?
4) when you wish the speaker to repeat his words?
5) to tell someone forcefully to shut up?
6) to express your disgust at something horrible?
7) to express great and sudden joy?
8) to ask someone to treat what you are about to say as confidential?
9) to request or allow someone to commence speaking?

E) Insert a part or parts of the body to complete the following sentences.

1) That is nonsense, don't talk through the back of your . . . !
2) He is always shooting his . . . off about how rich he is.
3) I shouted until I was blue in the . . . , but she appeared not to hear.
4) Some people at the meeting said nothing, yet others talked their . . . off.
5) They just stood there wagging their . . . while I was busy.
6) The old woman can talk the . . . . . . off a donkey.

153

Emotions [A]

105: AGREEMENT/APPROVAL

105/1 **You bet:** You may be sure; Certainly! □ "Are you going to the baseball final?" "You bet!"

105/2 **Now you're talking!:** I welcome that offer or suggestion. □ "How about a trip to the seaside?" "Now you're talking!"

105/3 **That's more like it!:** That is more acceptable or nearer the truth; I welcome that suggestion. □ That's more like it, so you did break the window after all! □ That's more like it; you're learning quickly how to swim! □ That's more like it, of course I'll have a beer with you!

105/4 **Rather!/not half!/and how!:** Emphatically yes; very much so. □ "Do you like the present I gave you?" "Rather (And how/Not half)!" □ "He'll be punished for doing that." "Not half (Rather/And how)!"

105/5 **You can say that again!** *or* **you're telling me!** *or* **I'll say!:** I totally agree with you; yes indeed. □ "Sorry my shoes are dirty." "You can say that again (You're telling me/I'll say)!"

105/6 **More's the pity!:** That is sadly true; that only makes matters worse. □ "Your child may have a serious physical handicap but he's very intelligent." "More's the pity, for it makes him all the more aware of his defects."

105/7 **Hear! hear!:** I agree. □ "I think the club chairman should resign." "Hear! Hear!" □ "Let's stop work for the day!" "Hear! Hear!"

105/8 **Okey-doke!/right(y)-oh!/right you are!:** All right; OK! □ "Get me a sandwich while you are at the shops." "Okey-doke! (Righty-oh etc.)!"

105/9 **You're on!:** I accept your proposition or wager. □ "I bet you he can't do it!" "You're on!" □ "I can deliver as much timber as you want at that price!" "You're on!"

105/10 **Done!:** (in reply to an offer) I accept!

105/11 **Fair enough!:** That is a reasonable or satisfactory proposition!

105/12 **Put it (right) there!:** Let's shake hands in agreement! □ You've got yourself a deal! Put it right there!

105/13 **Easy:** Willing (without being particularly keen); having no objections. Beware the use of "I'm easy" in North America, where it will be understood to mean that you are available for sex. □ "Want to go for a drive?" "I'm easy!"

105/14 **Game:** Willing; having the spirit or energy for something. □ He's always game for a laugh. □ The journey will be difficult and I don't know whether she is game enough for it.

105/15 **Be my guest!**: I have no objection: you are welcome. ▫ "May I come in and use your telephone?" "Be my guest!"

105/16 **Sign on the dotted line**: Agree to something in writing; sign a written agreement. ▫ The estate-agent wants us to buy the house, but we still haven't signed on the dotted line yet.

105/17 **Give the green light** *or* **give the thumbs-up**: Give agreement or approval for a project or plan to go ahead. ▫ We can't give the builders the green light (the thumbs-up) until all the tenants have vacated the block.

105/18 **That's the stuff!/attaboy!/good show!**: An exclamation of admiration, approval or encouragement; well done! ▫ "Our team has won again." "That's the stuff (Attaboy/Good show)!"

105/19 **Bully for** someone: Expression of approval or admiration of someone's actions or performance; bravo; well done! The expression may also be used ironically to suggest indifference or lack of interest. ▫ Bully for you, you ran a great race! ▫ "Caroline is extremely well mannered and dresses impeccably." "Well, bully for her!"

105/20 **Swear by** something: Have great confidence or trust in something; approve very much of something. ▫ She swears by old-fashioned remedies for curing colds.

105/21 **Hold with** something: Approve of something. ▫ Not all criminals hold with violence. ▫ I don't hold with throwing litter.

106: TOLERATE/SUPPORT

106/1 **Stand for** *or* **wear** something: Accept or tolerate. ▫ The boss won't wear (stand for) your continual late arrival at work.

106/2 **Not take** something **lying down**: Not accept something objectionable in a passive manner or without protest. □ The ANC stated that it wouldn't take the injustices of South African apartheid lying down.

106/3 **Stomach** something: Tolerate or endure something. □ Many American soldiers in Vietnam were unable to stomach the carnage and later they showed chronic distress symptoms.

106/4 **Lump/stick** something: Put up with, or tolerate something unpleasant. □ Many tourists can't lump (stick) the heat here at this time of year.

106/5 **Like it or lump it**: There is no choice but to endure an unpleasant situation. □ There is nothing you can do about the noise if you live near an airport; it's like it or lump it.

106/6 **Bear with** someone: Show patience or tolerance towards someone. □ A computer fault at the passport office resulted in long delays in the issue of travel documents, and staff were continually requesting applicants to bear with them.

106/7 **The worm will turn**: Even the smallest, most unimportant person will retaliate if the limit to his patience or tolerance is reached. □ He won't put up with being teased by everyone at work for much longer – eventually the worm will turn and he'll get his own back on them.

106/8 **The end of one's tether**: The limit of one's endurance or patience. □ The teachers are at the end of their tether with your son's behaviour. □ I'm reaching the end of my tether with this noise every night.

106/9 **Hold no brief for** something: Refuse to support or defend something. □ A spokesman for the Libyan government said that his country held no brief for terrorists. □ I hold no brief for whaling.

106/10 **Stick/stand up for** something: Defend or support someone or something. □ The few brave people that stood (stuck) up for democracy are now in jail. □ When I was small, my elder brother used to stick (stand) up for me.

106/11 **Root for** something *(US)*: Support or encourage enthusiastically. □ Mussolini was a clever demagogue and his speeches always got the crowds rooting for him. □ The German footballers had the whole country rooting for them in the World Cup.

106/12 **Try it on**: Do something experimentally, to see if it will be tolerated. □ The captain of the Japanese trawler told the coastguards who confiscated his catch that he was just trying it on in US coastal waters. □ Natasha is a pretty girl and men are always trying it on with her.

106/13 **Stake** someone *(US)*: Support financially or materially. □ The Contra rebels feared that the US would stop staking them after the Nicaraguan elections.

107: LIKE/POPULARITY

107/1 **Fancy** something/someone: To like or find attractive. *(See 122/1)* □ Do you fancy a coffee? □ That girl fancies you.

156

107/2 **Feel like** something: Be in the mood for something. □ I feel like leaving now. □ We felt like something to eat.

107/3 **I could do with** something: I would benefit from, or feel better for something. □ I could do with some help.

107/4 **I could do without** something: I would benefit or feel better without something. □ I could do without your sarcastic comments! □ I could do without these bills right now.

107/5 **Tickle** someone's **fancy**: Arouse a liking in someone; appeal to, or charm someone. □ The car tickled my fancy, so I bought it.

107/6 **Be soft on** or **have a soft spot for** something: Have a feeling of affection towards a person or thing. □ She has a soft spot for (is soft on) chocolates. □ He is soft on (has a soft spot for) blondes.

107/7 **Take to** something **like a duck to water** or . . . **in a big way**: Develop a (great) liking or ability for something. The 'duck to water' expression more usually applies to ability than to liking. □ We have taken to the new house in a big way. □ She has taken to skiing in a big way (like a duck to water). □ Maya has taken to him in a big way (has really taken to him).

107/8 **Go a bundle on** something/someone: Like immensely. □ Children go a bundle on the fun park. □ As soon as Emilio saw the new teacher, he went a bundle on her.

107/9 **Cotton on to** or **take a shine to** something (*US*): Develop a liking for someone or something. (*For 'cotton on', see also 90/2*) □ It was during his stay on a farm that Stepan began to cotton on (take a shine) to animals. □ I've cottoned on (taken a shine) to early-morning swimming.

107/10 **A blue-eyed boy/girl**: Someone's favourite. □ He is teacher's blue-eyed boy. □ Paula thinks she can do what she likes, just because she's the blue-eyed girl of the boss.

107/11 **Catch on**: Become popular (*See also 90/5*) □ European soccer is catching on fast in the USA. □ Somehow I don't think that dress fashion will catch on with the public.

108: ADMIRE/LOVE

108/1 **Click with** someone: Be a success with; make a favourable impression on someone. □ He has clicked with her.

108/2 **Hit it off** with someone: Get on well with a person. □ The couple didn't hit it off with one another (hit it off together).

108/3 **Struck on** someone: Impressed with; liking. □ Tamara is not at all struck on him.

108/4 **Have a crush on** someone: Be infatuated with someone. □ Lots of girls used to have a crush on Elvis Presley.

108/5 **All over** someone: Excessively attentive towards someone. □ She is all over him.

108/6 **A yen for** something: A longing or ardent desire for. □ The sailors had a yen for home. □ For years I've had a yen to go to the Himalayas.

108/7 **Nuts/nutty/potty about** something/someone: Mad about; infatuated with. □ I am nuts (nutty/potty) about her. □ Otto is nuts (potty/nutty) about boats.

108/8 **Hooked/gone on** something/someone: Mad about; infatuated with. □ The children are gone (hooked) on ice-cream.

108/9 **Think that the sun shines out of** someone's **backside/arse** (*#?*): Think very highly of someone; admire someone greatly or excessively. □ She thinks that the sun shines out of his backside (arse).

108/10 **Think that** something **is the best thing since sliced bread**: Think very highly of something; admire someone above all others. □ Juan thinks (that) she is the best thing since sliced bread. □ For my son, video games are the best thing since sliced bread!

108/11 **Think the world of** something: Love something or someone. □ The old lady thinks the world of her dog.

108/12 **Fall for** someone: Fall in love with. □ My daughter fell for an American serviceman.

108/13 **Head over heels in love**: Passionately or hopelessly in love. □ He fell head over heels in love with Sabina. □ That young couple are head over heels in love.

108/14 **Be bitten by** (*or* **have**) **the love bug**: Be in love. □ She's been bitten by (she has) the love bug.

108/15 **Puppy love**: Adolescent or immature love. □ Before he met Anneliese, all the other girls had just been puppy love.

108/16 **A heart-throb**: Someone venerated by the opposite sex; an idol. □ Rudolph Valentino was one of the early heart-throbs in films.

108/17 **An old flame**: A former sweetheart or love. □ She is one of Reiner's old flames.

109: ENTHUSIASM

109/1 **At the drop of a hat**: Eagerly and immediately; suddenly and without warning. □ Most unemployed people are not lazy, they would accept work at the drop of a hat. □ The main supports on the bridge are weak and could collapse at the drop of a hat.

109/2 **Keen as mustard**: Extremely keen or enthusiastic. □ After their long training, the astronauts were as keen as mustard to be launched into space.

109/3 **Gung-ho**: Exuberantly or aggressively enthusiastic. □ The military were gung-ho about sending troops to the trouble spot.

109/4 **Raring to** do something: Enthusiastic about something. □ I'm raring to meet my pen-friend for the first time. □ Competitors on the long-distance car rally are raring to go.

109/5 **Dying to/for** something: Extremely eager or keen to; longing for something. ☐ I'm dying for a cool drink. ☐ My mother is dying to meet you in person. ☐ During the meeting I was dying to go to the toilet.

109/6 **Go overboard:**   Become excessively enthusiastic. ☐ I told him that he would probably be promoted, but not to go overboard just yet as it wasn't certain.

109/7 **Sold on** something: Keen on. ☐ My wife is not sold on the idea of moving house.

109/8 **Turn** someone **on:**   Arouse someone's enthusiasm or interest. ☐ At first I wasn't keen on getting a satellite TV dish, but a look at the programmes on offer really turned me on. ☐ Some men get turned on by women in short skirts.

109/9 **Turn** someone **off:**   Dampen someone's enthusiasm; cause someone to lose interest. ☐ I could never be a nurse; the sight of blood turns me off.

109/10 **Snap up** something: To take or accept eagerly. ☐ All the bargains in the sale had been snapped up before we got there. ☐ In this region, skilled men seeking work are soon snapped up.

109/11 An **eager beaver:**   An enthusiastic person; a diligent worker. ☐ When the foreman arrived in the morning at the apprentice-training workshop, the eager beavers were already at work. ☐ My daughter's trip is not till next week, but the eager beaver has her bags packed already.

109/12 A **buff** (*US*):   An enthusiast. (Do not confuse with a 'Buff', who is a member of the 'Buffs' or 'Buffaloes' – a fraternal organization similar to the 'Freemasons'.) ☐ The shop caters for computer buffs. ☐ This film can be recommended to all buffs.

109/13 A **real one for** something: Someone who is enthusiastic about something. ☐ My brother is a real one for sport. ☐ He's a real one for chasing the girls.

109/14 A . . . **fiend** (*pr. 'feend'*):   A whole-hearted enthusiast or addict for something. ☐ Helmut is a fresh-air fiend; he leaves the windows open all the time. ☐ My wife has become a slimming fiend; our meals are now all low-calorie.

109/15 A/the **bug:**   A great enthusiasm or craze. ☐ Travelling can become a bug. ☐ After talking to a professional, I got the golf-bug.

EXERCISES 19: EMOTIONS (A)

A) Complete the following sentences with the missing word or phrase.

1) Her application for a study grant has been given the . . . and she will start college in September.
2) They couldn't . . . the pressures of city life and went to live in the country.
3) The boy has the train-spotting . . . and can't stay away from railway stations.
4) The two of them are . . . over . . . in love.
5) She adores him and thinks that the . . . . . . out of his backside.
6) At first we didn't enjoy Indian cooking, but now we have taken to it in a . . . .
7) When the girl saw the speaking doll, it really tickled her . . . .
8) My car has been in the workshop for a simple repair far too long and I'm at the end of my . . . with the garage.
9) They think that wind surfing is the best thing since . . . .

B) Give a colloquial term or expression to fit the following definitions.

1) immature love.
2) a person who enjoys special favour or privileges with someone.
3) an enthusiast.
4) a very enthusiastic person.
5) an idol adored by the opposite sex.
6) become excessively enthusiastic.

C) Replace the underlined phrases with as many colloquial synonyms as possible.

1) He is infatuated with the girl next door.
2) They are extremely keen to help us.
3) "Did you enjoy your vacation?" "I certainly did!"
4) "Make four photocopies of this document!" "All right!"

D) Insert an adverb (*up/to/on* etc.) to complete the sentences below.

1) Stop using vulgar words! I don't hold . . . swearing.
2) Bear . . . me a couple of days and I'll do the job on Friday!
3) My son is not sold . . . the idea of becoming a farmer like me.
4) He wouldn't like digging your garden; heavy work turns him . . . .
5) I advertised a flat to rent and it was snapped . . . by the first caller.
6) In many holiday resorts street sellers often try it . . . by asking exorbitant prices from unsuspecting tourists.
7) They are walking hand in hand; it looks as if he has really hit it . . . with her.

160

Emotions [B]

110: REFUSAL/DISAPPROVAL/DISLIKE

110/1 **Not on your nelly!**: A derisive refusal; I refuse categorically! □ "Will you lend me your car?" "Not on your nelly!"

110/2 **Not for all the tea in China!**: I wouldn't do it for anything. □ I wouldn't apologize to him for all the tea in China.

110/3 **Not likely!/no fear!/no way!/nothing doing!/like hell!** (#?)/**like fuck!** (#??): That is impossible!; I refuse! □ Drive to that notorious area at night?; not likely (nothing doing/no way/no fear/like hell)! □ No way (Like hell) will I pay for the damage – it was your fault!

110/4 **Not have** something: Refuse to accept or tolerate something. □ As for this continual misbehaviour, I'm not having it (any)!

110/5 **Over my dead body!**: Not if I can prevent it! I would die rather than allow it! □ Sell my firm to him? Over my dead body!

110/6 **Give the thumbs-down** to something: Reject a plan or course of action. □ A last-minute computer failure forced mission control to give the thumbs-down to the rocket launch.

110/7 **Tut-tut!**: Exclamation of mild annoyance or disapproval. □ Tut-tut, she's late for her appointment!

110/8 **I like that!**: Ironic expression of disapproval. □ Well I like that, they've gone and left without me!

110/9 **Don't mind me!**: Ironic disapproval of a continuing activity. □ The taxi driver turned to the two lovers who were in a passionate embrace on the back seat of his car and quipped 'Don't mind me!'

110/10 **. . . If you please!**: Ironic disapproval of someone's unreasonable or excessive conduct. □ He accused me, if you please, of poisoning his cat! □ For installing the telephone, they charged me not the normal rate, but three times that, if you please!

110/11 **Sticky** about something: Raising objections; objectionable. □ The landlord can be very sticky about cooking in the rooms.

110/12 **Steady on!**: Expression of disagreement with unreasonable comments or actions. □ Steady on, I didn't say that! □ Steady on! If everyone wasted water like you, there would be none left for drinking.

110/13 **What's the 'we' bit?**: I object to being included in your plans or comment. □ What's the 'we' bit? I'm not going anywhere tonight!

110/14 **My foot/eye!**: Expressions of disagreement or total disbelief. Nonsense! Rubbish! □ "You're a rich man now!" "Rich man, my foot (my eye)!" □ "We have time to finish our meal." "My eye! The train goes in two minutes!"

161

110/15 **Come on!** *or* **come off it!** *or* **get off it!** *or* **get along with you!**: Expressions of disbelief and impatience or annoyance. □ Oh come on (come off it) – you know that's not true! □ Get along with you! I've no time to waste in arguing about it.

110/16 **But me no buts!** *or* **no buts about it!**: Do not raise objections! The matter is decided! □ But me no buts (No buts about it), you'll do as I say!

110/17 **Not on**: Not acceptable or practicable. □ The farmers are complaining that low-level flying by the air force is not on during the lambing season. □ Laying electricity cables to such a remote spot is not on; it would be too expensive.

110/18 **Not done**: Not socially acceptable. □ In many Islamic countries, kissing in a public place is just not done.

110/19 **Turn one's nose up at** *or* **look down one's nose at** something: Scorn or reject someone or something as inferior. □ Before the arrival of writers such as Chaucer, the English aristocracy, who wrote mainly in Latin or Norman French, looked down their noses (turned their noses up) at the use of Saxon English.

110/20 **Take a dim view of** something: Disapprove of something. □ The authorities here in Thailand take a very dim view of drug smuggling.

110/21 **Not** someone's **cup of tea** *or* **not** someone's **scene**: Not what someone likes or finds interesting. □ Shooting ducks for fun is not my cup of tea (not my scene).

110/22 **Allergic to** something: Having a strong dislike for something. □ Antonio is allergic to work. □ I am allergic to arrogant people.

110/23 **There's no love lost between** them/us: Mutual dislike. □ They may be brothers but there's no love lost between them.

110/24 **Hate** someone's **guts**: Hate someone intensely. □ The people applaud the dictator's speeches out of fear, secretly they hate his guts.

110/25 **The 'V'-sign** *or* **a two-fingered gesture** *or* **the finger sign** (*US*): An offensive sign of refusal or disapproval made with two forked fingers; a 'fuck off' sign (*See 110/30 below*) □ The driver hooted at a careless pedestrian who made the 'V'-sign (a two-fingered gesture/the finger sign) in retaliation.

110/26 **To moon**: Express disapproval or contempt by baring the buttocks to someone. □ It was a rough football match, and one player was even sent off for mooning at the crowd.

110/27 **A raspberry**: A vulgar sound imitating the breaking of wind. The term is also used figuratively to express a rude or impolite refusal. □ Children from the other school down the road make raspberries at us. □ I've applied for ten jobs and got only raspberries in reply.

110/28 **Go and take a running jump!** *or* **go and chase yourself!** *or* **drop dead!** *or* **go to blazes!/go to pot!**: Offensive expressions of refusal, disapproval or contempt. (*But see 18/9 for 'Go to pot' meaning 'fail'*) □ Jakob had fallen out with his girl-friend and when he asked her to come back to him, she told him to go and take a running jump (go and chase himself/drop dead etc.)!

110/29 You **can stuff/stick/shove** it **up** your **jumper/arse** (*#??*) *or* **shove it!/stuff it!**: Abusive refusals of an offer or suggestion. □ Buy his old motorbike? No way! He can stuff it up his jumper (arse)! □ Stuff it, Pete – that's a really stupid idea!

110/30 **Up yours** (*#??*) *or* **sod/naff/fuck/piss/bugger off!** (*#??*) *or* **get knotted/ stuffed!** (*#??*): Abusive expressions of strong refusal or disapproval. (*See also 144/14*)

111: BORE/IRRITATE/ANNOY

111/1 **Have had a bellyful**: Be sick of, or completely bored with something. □ I've had a bellyful of problems with my car and I'm going to sell it.

111/2 **Fed up to the back teeth with/of** something: Very sick of something; exceedingly discontented or displeased. □ The firm is fed up to the back teeth with/of customer complaints about this make of pram.

111/3 **Sick and tired**: Very sick of something; nearing the end of one's patience. □ Physically handicapped people are sick and tired of being treated as second-class citizens.

111/4 **Chock-a-block** *or* **chocker**: Very sick of something. (*See also 148/1*) □ People at the bus-stop are continually using my garden as a litter-bin; as for cleaning up after them, I'm chocker (chock-a-block).

111/5 **Bore** someone **stiff**: Bore someone exceedingly. □ Working in an office would bore me stiff. □ I was bored stiff the whole journey.

111/6 **Bore the pants off** someone: Bore someone exceedingly. □ Circus performances bore the pants off me.

111/7 **Cheese** someone **off** *or* **brown** someone **off** *or* **piss** someone **off** (*#??*): Bore someone completely; exasperate. □ The job is OK, what cheeses (browns/pisses) me off is commuting the long distance every day.

111/8 **Dull as ditchwater**: (of a thing) very dull and boring; (of a person) completely lacking vitality. □ The book is as dull as ditchwater.

111/9 **A drag** *or* **a bind**: A boring person or thing; a nuisance. □ What a drag (bind) having to work on such a fine day! □ I don't enjoy it when your brother stays with us; he really is a bind (drag).

111/10 **Pain in the neck/arse** (*#?*): An annoying person or thing; a source of continuous annoyance. □ I'm on 24-hour call and find the night call-outs a pain in the neck (arse).

111/11 **A crashing bore**: An exceedingly boring person or thing. □ The party was a crashing bore.

111/12 **Enough to drive you to drink**: A continuous and unbearable annoyance. □ Living in that vandalized tower block is a nightmare and enough to drive you to drink.

111/13 Get under someone's **skin:** Annoy or interest someone greatly. □ His squeaky voice gets under my skin. □ Lorenzo thinks Agnes is fantastic, she's really got under his skin.

111/14 Rub someone **up the wrong way:** Irritate or repel someone by one's actions. □ Staff must be polite at all times so as not to rub the customers up the wrong way.

111/15 Get someone's **goat** *or* **get on** someone's **wick:** Annoy someone. □ We firemen don't mind the fires; what gets our goat (gets on our wick) are the hoax alarms.

111/16 Get up someone's **nostrils/nose:** Irritate strongly. □ Bossy officials really get up my nostrils (nose).

111/17 Drive/send someone **up the wall:** Annoy greatly or anger. □ My neighbour gives violin lessons at home and the screeching is driving (sending) me up the wall.

111/18 Bug someone: Annoy or irritate. □ Something is obviously bugging him. □ The thought that he could have prevented the accident bugs him continually.

111/19 Badger someone: Pester or annoy continually. □ Mrs Malik is still in a state of shock and doesn't wish to be badgered by press reporters.

111/20 What gets me: What irritates or annoys me. □ What gets me is that she didn't even say thank you.

111/21 What's biting/eating you?: What is annoying or irritating you? □ What's biting (eating) him this morning?

111/22 Cussedness: Annoying stubbornness or obstinacy; nastiness. □ Schmidt has nothing to lose by letting you use the shed, but he refuses out of pure cussedness.

111/23 Bitchy: Spiteful or bad-tempered (usually said of a woman, who would be called a 'bitch'). To 'bitch' is to make spiteful or nasty remarks. □ She made bitchy remarks about her husband, saying he hadn't as good a job as her neighbour's.

111/24 Uptight: Nervously tense or annoyed. □ The prospect of dismissals has made everyone in the factory uptight.

111/25 Niggly: Finding fault with petty details; irritating. □ Why be so niggly about a few small spelling mistakes?

111/26 Pesky (#US): Annoying. □ I was delayed by a pesky traffic cop. □ The national park is full of pesky bears that beg and steal food from campers.

111/27 Huffy *or* **in a huff** *or* **miffed:** Annoyed or offended. □ Grandmother is in a huff (huffy/miffed) because we haven't visited her for a month.

112: ANGER

112/1 Have the hump *or* **be humpty:** Have a fit of depression or annoyance. □ What's he got the hump (What's he humpty) about this time?

112/2 As cross (as two sticks): (Very) angry. □ Her father is as cross as two sticks about what she's done.

112/3 Rile/nark someone: Annoy or anger. □ I was really narked (riled) by what he said. □ Don't nark (rile) him, whatever you do!

112/4 Hopping mad *or* **livid:** Furiously angry. □ Mother will be hopping mad (livid) when she sees what a mess you've made!

112/5 Shirty/ratty: Annoyed or angry. □ Don't get so shirty (ratty) with me!

112/6 Steamed up: Angry or upset. □ He is steamed up about what you said. □ She is all steamed up about losing the money.

112/7 Hot under the collar: Angry, resentful or embarrassed. □ The mere mention of her ex-husband's name can make her hot under the collar.

112/8 On the warpath: Angry and seeking a quarrel or trouble. □ I told you not to borrow Lothar's car without asking, now he's on the warpath.

112/9 Like a bear with a sore head: In a very bad mood or temper. □ Watch what you're doing in the office today, the boss is like a bear with a sore head!

112/10 Have/get the screaming habdabs: Have a fit of furious anger or rage. □ Cheng will get (have) the screaming habdabs when he hears of this.

112/11 In a paddy: In a rage; very angry. □ She gets into a paddy about the slightest untidiness. □ The shareholders are in a paddy and demanding the resignation of the board.

112/12 Throw a tantrum: (Usually of a child) have an outburst of bad temper. □ As a young girl, Elke was always throwing tantrums.

112/13 Throw a wobbly: Have an outburst of annoyance or anger. □ If he had done that to me, I would have thrown a wobbly as well.

112/14 **See red:** Become suddenly filled with anger. □ Cruelty to animals always makes me see red.

112/15 **Have a fit** *or* **go off the deep end** *or* **flip one's lid** *or* **fly off the handle:** Become uncontrollably angry; lose one's temper. □ When he heard the news, he had a fit (went off the deep end/flipped his lid etc.).

112/16 **Do one's nut/block:** Become very angry. (*See 176/Body Parts for alternative colloquialisms for 'head'*) □ You'd better go and repair the leak now, the tenant is doing his nut (block) over the phone and has called three times today.

112/17 **Blow's one's stack/top** *or* **blow a fuse** *or* **hit the ceiling/roof:** Become uncontrollably angry. □ When Hitler heard of his defeat at Stalingrad, he blew his stack (blew a fuse/hit the ceiling etc.).

112/18 **Cut up rough/nasty:** Become extremely or violently angry. □ Traffic wardens can all tell stories of motorists who've cut up rough (nasty) when they were fined for illegal parking.

112/19 **Keep your hair/shirt on!:** Don't lose your temper! Don't get angry!

112/20 **Get** someone's **dander/back/monkey up:** Make someone angry or aggressive; provoke. □ Foreign tourists who show a lack of respect for the customs here get the local people's dander (backs/monkey) up.

112/21 **Get on the wrong side of** someone: Anger someone; lose someone's favour or good will; have someone as an enemy. □ Gomez is a powerful man in this country, and you would be well advised not to get on the wrong side of him.

112/22 **I could kick myself!:** I am angry with myself for having made an obvious mistake or missed an opportunity. □ The invention was first offered to my firm, but I turned it down. Later, when it became a great success, I could have kicked myself.

113: CONFUSED/UPSET/NERVOUS

113/1 **Flummox** someone: Baffle or confuse someone. □ Keep calm and don't let the examiners flummox you!

113/2 **Rattle** someone: Agitate, confuse or make nervous. □ I get rattled easily when people ask me questions while I'm speaking.

113/3 **Bamboozle** someone: Mystify, confuse or deceive. □ Detectives were bamboozled by the apparent lack of motive for the crime.

113/4 **Fluster** someone: Make someone nervous or confused. □ The young violinist got flustered by the audience and played several wrong notes.

113/5 **(All) at sea:** Confused; not knowing how to proceed □ I've never used this machine before and I'm all at sea as to operating it.

113/6 **Put** someone **off** his **stroke:** Distract, disconcert or confuse someone. □ I'm sorry about the mistakes, a row with my wife this morning has put me off my stroke.

113/7 Off-putting: Disconcerting, distracting or confusing. □ Constant coughing in the library is very off-putting for other readers. □ Political reports about my intended holiday destination were very off-putting.

113/8 Throw someone: Disconcert. □ I answered all the questions without hesitation, but the last one threw me for a few minutes.

113/9 Put someone **out:** Disconcert; annoy or inconvenience. □ His rudeness really put me out. □ I'll do it gladly, you're not putting me out at all.

113/10 Tie someone **in knots:** Baffle or confuse someone. □ Without a lawyer to represent you in court, the prosecution will tie you in knots.

113/11 Get one's wires crossed: Become confused and misunderstand. □ I'm not talking about Dieter, you've got your wires crossed somewhere.

113/12 Not know whether one is coming or going: Be completely confused or upset. □ I was so busy at the office, at times I didn't know whether I was coming or going.

113/13 Mixed-up: Emotionally confused; having problems with behaviour and adjusting to society. □ Kurt is not an evil boy, he's just mixed-up.

113/14 Shake someone **(up):** Shock, disturb or upset someone. □ Martin's divorce really shook him up. □ The news that President Kennedy was dead shook the world.

113/15 Get (oneself) worked up: Become excited or upset. □ Don't get yourself worked up over his impudence!

113/16 Get one's knickers in a twist (#?): Become confused or upset. □ If the police start asking questions, keep calm – don't get your knickers in a twist and say the wrong thing!

113/17 Cut up: Very distressed or upset. □ Mrs Yakima is still very cut up about her husband's death.

113/18 In a tizzy/stew/flap or **het up:** In a state of nervous agitation or confusion; angry or emotional. □ Don't get into a tizzy (into a stew/into a flap/het up); the pilot knows perfectly well how to land in fog.

113/19 Keyed up or **wound up:** Nervously tense or excited. □ We can't delay the race too long, the competitors are all wound up (keyed up).

113/20 On tenterhooks: In a state of nervous suspense or strain. □ The film 'Psycho' had me on tenterhooks the whole time. □ It's impossible to enjoy the summer holidays if you're on tenterhooks waiting for exam results.

113/21 Have the jitters or **be jittery/jumpy:** Be in a state of nervous fright. □ My wife had the jitters (was jumpy/jittery) last night and kept thinking she could hear a burglar downstairs.

113/22 A jitterbug: A nervous person, especially someone who spreads alarm. □ The doctors keep telling her that there's nothing wrong with her child; she's just a jitterbug.

113/23 Have butterflies in one's tummy/stomach or **have the collywobbles:** Be nervously apprehensive; have an attack of nervousness before an important event. □ Many people have the collywobbles (butterflies in their stomach) when they visit the dentist.

EXERCISES 20: EMOTIONS (B)

A) Insert a body part or organ to complete the following sentences.

1) She is fed up to the back ... with cleaning up after them.
2) "The exam was very easy." "Easy, my ... ! I found it difficult."
3) Keep your ... on! There's no need to get angry.
4) She is a pain in the ... with her stupid questions.
5) I detest that man, he really gets up my ... .
6) I wonder what has angered him – he's like a bear with a sore ... .
7) If you come home late again, you'll get your parents' ... s up.
8) They are arch-enemies and hate each other's ... .
9) The children waiting to be inoculated had butterflies in their ...
   when they saw the size of the doctor's needle.
10) His arrogant manner gets under my ... .

B) Replace each of the underlined phrases with as many colloquial
synonyms as possible.

1) He <u>became furiously angry</u> when he heard the news. 2) "Give him
the money he wants!" "<u>I refuse completely!</u>" 3) We were
<u>extremely bored</u> with the rainy weather during our vacation.
4) Dolores <u>became very upset</u> when she saw that her flat had been
burgled. 5) <u>Don't make her angry!</u> 6) At school, technical
subjects were <u>not something that I found interesting</u>.

C) Give colloquialisms for the following definitions.

1) a vulgar sound expressing refusal or disapproval. 2) a boring person
or thing. 3) a vulgar gesture with two forked fingers. 4) a nervous
person who spreads alarm. 5) I am very angry with myself! 6) the
baring of buttocks to someone as a sign of contempt. 7) an
exclamation of mild annoyance or disapproval.

D) Complete the sentences below with the corresponding adverb (*in/out/
up* etc.).

1) The boss got hot ... the collar when he heard of your blunder.
2) He came to apologize, but she told him to stick his apology ... his
   jumper.
3) The result of the ballot was about to be announced, and all the
   candidates for election were ... tenterhooks.
4) In the past, some managers used to look ... their noses at manual
   workers.
5) During the Emir's visit, we will avoid any mention of the democratic
   movement in his country so as not to rub him ... the wrong way.
6) Hypocrites like him get ... my wick.
7) The long speech bored the pants ... most of the audience.
8) I wouldn't mind a cup of coffee, but don't put yourself ... for me!

168

Emotions [C]

114: FRIGHT

114/1   **Scared stiff** *or* **shit-scared** (*#?*):   Very frightened. □ As we were crossing the field, a bull suddenly began to run towards us – we were scared stiff (shit-scared), I can tell you!

114/2   **In a blue funk**:   In a state of terror or extreme fear. □ I'm in a blue funk about parachuting for the first time.

114/3   **Get the wind up** *or* **put the wind up** someone *or* **put the frighteners on** someone: To be afraid; frighten someone. □ He got the wind up when he heard the police car coming. □ She put the wind up her boyfriend when she told him she was pregnant. □ The drug case was held in New York to make it more difficult for Chicago gangsters to put the frighteners on witnesses.

114/4   **Scare the living daylights out of** someone *or* **scare the pants off** someone *or* **scare the hell/shit** (*#?*)**out of** someone: Give someone a great fright; terrify. □ The sight of the Mongol hordes advancing over the steppe scared the living daylights out of (the pants off/the hell out of) Russian peasants. □ The thud of the two cars crashing scared the hell out of me.

114/5   **Have kittens**:   Be very nervous or frightened. □ I don't know how you could remain so calm during the thunderstorm – I was having kittens!

114/6   **Give** someone **quite a turn**:   Give someone a nasty fright or shock. □ You shouldn't creep up on people like that – you gave me quite a turn!

114/7   **Give** someone **the creeps**:   Arouse in someone a feeling of fear or nervous dislike. The adjective is 'creepy'. □ Films about the Holocaust and concentration camps give me the creeps. □ Children used to find the old woman creepy and kept away from her.

114/8   **Give** someone **the willies**:   Arouse in someone a feeling of fear or terror. □ Spiders give her the willies.

114/9   **Enough to make your hair curl**:   Very frightening. □ The speed of the bus on the mountain road was enough to make your hair curl.

114/10   **Hairy**:   Dangerously frightening; terrifying. □ My first encounter with a wild crocodile was a hairy experience.

114/11   **Make** someone's **hair stand on end**:   Terrify someone. □ During our stay in Beirut, we saw things that made our hair stand on end.

114/12   **Spooky**:   Ghostly and frightening. □ Churchyards can be spooky places at night.

114/13 Shoo!: Sound used to frighten away animals. The verb is 'shoo away'. □ Every day I have to shoo away cats from around my bird table.

115: BRAVERY/COWARDICE

115/1 Spunk: Courage or bravery. *(See also 189/6)* 'spunky' means brave or courageous. □ That man has got spunk (is spunky).

115/2 Guts: Courage and determination. The corresponding adjective is 'gutsy'. □ The civilian population doesn't have the guts (isn't gutsy enough) for a long war with heavy casualties.

115/3 Grit: Courage and endurance. The adjective is 'gritty'. □ Marathon runners need grit (need to be gritty).

115/4 Bottle: Bravery or courage. □ He hasn't the bottle to do it. □ You need bottle to be a stunt man.

115/5 The bulldog breed: The courageous type. The bulldog is the symbol of British bravery and perseverance. □ The army needs men of the bulldog breed.

115/6 A yellow streak: Cowardice in someone's character. □ I always knew he had a yellow streak.

115/7 Yellow(-bellied) *or* **lily-livered:** Very cowardly. □ Knut is a yellow-bellied (lily-livered) deserter from the army.

115/8 A chicken *or* a **scaredy-cat:** A coward or someone who is easily frightened. 'Chicken' is also an adjective meaning cowardly. □ Motor racing is not for chickens (scaredy-cats). □ You say you don't want to do it, but I think you're just chicken (just a chicken/a scaredy-cat).

115/9 Chicken out (of something): Withdraw cowardly. □ At school he used to chicken out of sports involving rough physical contact. □ 'The Four Feathers' is a classic film about a 19th-century English army officer wrongly accused of chickening out of the war in Sudan.

115/10 Get cold feet: Be afraid or reluctant to act. □ Public protest over the proposed bill has made the government get cold feet and withdraw it.

115/11 Cut and run: Run away before one loses what one has already gained. □ On the basis of gloomy economic forecasts for the company, most of the large investors have decided to cut and run by selling their shares.

116: COMPOSURE/INHIBITION

116/1 Keep one's pecker up: Stay cheerful; not allow oneself to become depressed or disheartened. Avoid the use of this phrase in Canada and the U.S.A., where 'pecker' is a slang word for 'penis'. □ If the team keep their pecker up in the second half of the game, they can still catch up and win.

116/2 Keep a stiff upper lip: Suppress all emotion; show determination in facing problems. □ No matter what happens, keep a stiff upper lip!

116/3 Keep one's cool: Remain calm. □ It's sometimes difficult to keep your cool when you're dealing with rude people.

116/4 Keep one's wits about one: Remain mentally alert and ready to act. □ When his van skidded into the canal, the driver kept his wits about him and waited till the water had almost filled the cabin before opening the doors to escape.

116/5 Keep a level head: Remain mentally well balanced and sensible. □ When currency dealing becomes hectic, brokers must keep a level head.

116/6 Not bat an eyelid: Show no sign of emotion; remain totally calm. □ The murderer didn't bat an eyelid as the death sentence was read out by the judge.

116/7 Snap out of it: Recover quickly from a mood or fit of emotion; regain one's composure quickly. □ The girl was crying hysterically and the man shook her several times, telling her to snap out of it.

116/8 Cool it: Calm down; not become excited. □ The meeting was becoming chaotic and emotional, so the chairman told those present to cool it.

116/9 Cool as a cucumber: Very calm and unemotional. □ When fire broke out in the house, Jutta remained as cool as a cucumber and got her children out before phoning the fire brigade.

116/10 Unflappable: Remaining calm in any crisis; completely unemotional. □ A conference interpreter must translate instantaneously and remain unflappable for hours at a time.

116/11 Dead-pan: (Of a face) expressionless or showing no emotion. □ The funeral procession was led by the undertaker's men with dead-pan faces.

116/12 **A poker face:** A face that does not reveal thoughts or feelings, or a person with such a face. 'Poker-faced' describes this person. The derivation is from 'poker', a card game in which keeping an expressionless face may help you win. □ She sat poker-faced throughout the meeting, and surprised everyone with her eventual summary.

116/13 **Hard-boiled:** Unfeeling or hard-hearted. □ Lawyers have to deal with people's problems every day and can sometimes appear very hard-boiled.

116/14 A **smoothie:** A pleasantly polite and calm person who doesn't reveal his true emotions. □ Their public relations adviser is a smoothie.

116/15 A **cool cat** *or* a **cool customer:** A calm person; someone not easily excited. □ You can't wind him up – he's a cool cat (customer)!

116/16 **Simmer down:** Become less agitated or excited; calm down. □ Tell the children to simmer down! □ The company still intends to dump its waste at sea; they are just waiting for public protests to simmer down.

116/17 **Bottle/cork up** one's emotions: Restrain or suppress one's emotions. □ Policemen have to be impartial and keep their emotions corked (bottled) up. □ Famine aid workers see so much suffering, they have to bottle (cork) up their feelings to remain sane.

116/18 **Break the ice:** Overcome someone's shyness or reserve; create a much less formal atmosphere. □ The tribe were nomads and suspicious of foreigners, especially Westerners, so it took a while to break the ice.

117: HAPPINESS/FUN

117/1 **In (a) fine fettle:** In a good mood. □ Judging from the way he's joking, he must be in (a) fine fettle today.

117/2 **Buck up:** Make someone more cheerful; become more cheerful or feel better. *(See also 182/1)* □ Here's a cup of coffee to buck you up! □ Rana has been feeling poorly, but she's bucking up now.

117/3 **Thrilled to bits** *or* **over the moon:** Very pleased or excited. □ She is thrilled to bits (over the moon) with her exam results.

117/4 **On top of the world** *or* **on cloud nine** *(US):* Very pleased or happy. □ I feel on top of the world (on cloud nine) today.

117/5 **(As) pleased as Punch:** Very pleased. □ Milla is (as) pleased as Punch with her birthday present.

117/6 **(As) happy as Larry:** Very happy. □ We are as happy as Larry in our new home.

117/7 **Cock-a-hoop:** Happy and rejoicing. □ Everyone was cock-a-hoop that the war had ended.

117/8 **Tickled pink** *or* **tickled to death:** Very pleased or amused. □ I was tickled pink (to death) that I had got the contract in the face of such powerful competition.

117/9 Chuffed: Pleased or happy. □ Bjorn is feeling really chuffed that he has been accepted as a club member.

117/10 In stitches: Laughing uncontrollably. □ That comedian had me in stitches.

117/11 Split one's sides laughing: Laugh uncontrollably. □ Farid split his sides laughing when he saw the state of her hair.

117/12 Laugh up one's sleeve: Laugh secretly at someone's misfortune; be secretly pleased with oneself. □ The Russians offered their sympathies over the Challenger rocket disaster, but they were probably laughing up their sleeves, since it had set the USA back years in the space race.

117/13 Grin like a Cheshire cat: Grin widely from ear to ear. The expression was coined by Lewis Carroll in his book 'Alice in Wonderland'. □ On hearing the news, he grinned like a Cheshire cat.

117/14 Warm the cockles of someone's **heart:** Make someone glad or happy. □ It warmed the cockles of my heart to see my native country again after so many years abroad.

117/15 A bundle/barrel of laughs/fun: A lot of laughs or fun. □ He is a barrel of laughs (bundle of laughs/barrel of fun/bundle of fun). □ The day at the seaside was a barrel of fun (bundle of laughs etc.).

117/16 A scream or **a riot:** An extremely amusing person or thing. □ The film comedy was a riot (a scream). □ You must meet Estelle, she's a scream (riot).

117/17 Priceless: Very amusing or funny. □ That is a priceless joke. □ The sight of him falling into the water was priceless.

117/18 A sight for sore eyes: A very pleasing and welcome sight. □ After a week in the desert, the oasis was a sight for sore eyes.

117/19 Music to someone's **ears:** Very pleasing news. □ The news of the pay-rise was music to my ears.

117/20 A whale of a time or **a rare/high old time:** An exceedingly good time. □ Everyone had a whale of a time (rare old time/high old time) at Disney World.

117/21 Let it all hang out or **let one's hair down:** Relax and enjoy oneself. □ You work too much; you should let your hair down (let it all hang out) once in a while!

117/22 Have a ball: Enjoy oneself immensely. □ The children from the city had a ball at the summer camp.

117/23 Have a field day: Have great and enjoyable success; revel in victory over an opponent or in someone's failure. A 'field day' was a military term for a day allocated to field manoeuvres. □ The scientist knew that if he published his theory without conclusive proof, his critics would have a field day. □ The Finnish ski-jumpers had a field day, winning ten medals.

117/24 Lark about or **horse around:** Have energetic or boisterous fun; carry out pranks. □ The swimming-pool attendant told the youths to stop larking about (horsing around) on the springboard.

117/25 Horseplay: Energetic or boisterous play. □ His accident was the result of horseplay at work.

117/26 High jinks: Spirited enjoyment. □ High jinks are to be expected from students at the end of term.

117/27 Get a kick/buzz out of something: Get a thrill out of something. □ Some perverse teenagers get a kick (buzz) out of vandalism. □ I get a kick (buzz) out of photographing rare birds.

117/28 For kicks: For thrills or enjoyment. □ Some go pot-holing for scientific reasons but I do it for kicks.

117/29 For the hell of it: For reckless thrills. □ He drove the car as fast as it would go for the sheer hell of it. □ She steals from shops not out of need, but for the hell of it.

118: SADNESS/DEPRESSION

118/1 Blubber: Weep noisily. □ Stop blubbering, the situation is not as bad as that. □ Our baby blubbered all night.

118/2 Turn on the waterworks: Weep. □ At her daughter's wedding, she turned on the waterworks.

118/3 A cry-baby: Someone who weeps easily without good reason.

118/4 A sob-story: A sad story meant to arouse sympathy. □ Most rich people receive letters telling sob-stories and asking for money.

118/5 A tear-jerker: Something calculated to produce tears. □ The film is a real tear-jerker. □ The song contest was the usual mixture of pop, ballad and tear-jerker.

118/6 Mush: Feeble sentimentality. The adjective is 'mushy'. □ Sad music makes her mushy. □ That author's books are all mush.

118/7 Soppy: Foolishly or sickly sentimental. □ Don't get soppy! □ The film is too soppy for my taste.

118/8 A sourpuss: A person who is always sour-tempered, dispirited or moping. □ Don't ask Susan to come – she's such a sourpuss.

118/9 In the doldrums/dumps: In very low spirits; feeling depressed. □ He's been in the dumps (doldrums) ever since he failed his exam.

118/10 Have the heebie-jeebies/blues *or* **feel blue:** Be depressed. □ We're taking him on holiday with us to stop him getting the heebie-jeebies (blues/feeling blue).

118/11 Have a thin time: Have a wretched or unhappy time. □ I had a thin time when I was unemployed.

118/12 Down in the mouth: Looking unhappy or miserable. □ You're looking down in the mouth, what's the matter?

118/13 Pull/make a face as long as a fiddle: Look very unhappy or depressed. □ When Konrad heard the bad news, he pulled (made) a face as long as a fiddle.

118/14 **A long streak of misery**:   A person of sad or miserable appearance (usually, but not necessarily, someone who is also tall and thin). □ Have you seen the new storeman? He looks like a long streak of misery to me!

118/15 **Get** someone **down**:   Make someone depressed or sad. □ Working away from his home and family for long periods got him down.

118/16 **Put the damper on** something: Reduce someone's enthusiasm or enjoyment. □ It was the country's Independence Day, but the news of the president's death put a damper on the celebrations.

118/17 **Spoil-sport** or **kill-joy** or **party-pooper**:   Someone who spoils the enjoyment of others. □ It can't be time to go home yet, and anyway I'm enjoying myself – don't be a spoil-sport (kill-joy/party-pooper) and leave now.

119: CARE/WORRY

119/1 **Not give a hang/brass farthing/hoot/fig/tinker's cuss/monkey's (toss)**:   Not care at all. □ I don't give a brass farthing (fig/tinker's cuss etc.) what he says. □ This government doesn't give a monkey's (hang etc.) about old-age pensioners.

119/2 **Not give two hoots/pins**:   Not care in the least. □ Some day-trippers don't give two hoots (two pins) about the damage they cause in the countryside.

119/3 **Not give a toss/damn/fuck** *(#??)/***shit** *(#??)*:   Vulgar or abusive expression of lack of care. □ I don't give a damn (toss etc.) what people think about me!

119/4 **No skin off** someone's **back/nose**:   Be no cause for concern, or not matter since one is not involved; not care about something since one has nothing at all to lose by it. □ I don't care if he's driving without insurance, it's no skin off my nose (back).

EXERCISES 21 – EMOTIONS (C)

A) In the following comparative sentences, insert a noun or adjectival phrase expressing the great extent of the emotion.

1) Even under intense pressure, he remained as calm as a . . . . .
2) The little girl was thrilled to . . . with her new doll.
3) When the children heard that their trip to the zoo had been cancelled, they pulled faces as long as a . . . .
4) We are pleased as . . . with the new flat.
5) He grinned like a . . . . . . when he saw that he had fooled us.
6) The children were as happy as . . . playing on the beach.
7) I am tickled . . . to have passed my exams with honours.

→

175

B) Give colloquialisms for the definitions below.

1) someone who spoils the pleasure of others.
2) someone who is always bad-tempered or depressed.
3) an unemotional person who always remains calm.
4) a coward.
5) an amusing person or thing.
6) someone who cries very easily.
7) a very polite and outwardly pleasant person who keeps his true emotions hidden.
8) energetic and rough pranks or play.
9) a depressing story intended to arouse sympathy.
10) spirited enjoyment or fun.

C) Replace each underlined word or phrase with as many colloquial synonyms as possible.

1) He hadn't the courage to jump into the sea to save the boy.
2) When the cyclist rang his bell to pass the woman, he gave her a great fright.
3) Some people don't care at all what happens in other countries.
4) We enjoyed ourselves immensely on holiday.
5) He is very depressed today.

D) Complete the following sentences with a part of the body or an adjectival phrase containing a part of the body.

1) You can dig for worms in my garden if you wish, it's no . . . off my . . . .
2) I know that you have many problems, but keep a stiff upper . . . !
3) She shouted hateful abuse at him, but he didn't even bat an . . . .
4) The sight of so many happy children warmed the cockles of her . . . .
5) When profits fell drastically, several investors got cold . . . and sold their shares in the company.
6) In the exam room, it is important to keep a level . . . and not get confused.
7) Several passers-by saw the youth attack and rob the old lady, but they were too . . . . - . . . to help her.
8) That horror film made my . . . stand on end.

176

Behaviour

120: FAWNING/FLATTERY

120/1 **Suck up to** someone *or* **toady to** someone: Behave with exaggerated respect to someone in the hope of personal advantage or gain. □ Kjeld is always sucking up (toadying) to royalty.

120/2 **Lick** someone's **boots**:   Behave in a servile or excessively flattering manner. □ When the general is here, all the officers lick his boots.

120/3 **Kowtow to** someone: Behave slavishly or with an exaggerated respect to someone. The word is derived from the Chinese 'k'o-t'ou' meaning to show respect for officials by kneeling and touching the ground with one's forehead. □ The ambassador said that his country would not kowtow to the USA.

120/4 **Yes sir, yes sir three bags full (sir)!**:   Said of someone who is excessively servile or anxious to please. □ Staff used to criticize the boss when he was away, but when he returned, it was all yes sir, yes sir, three bags full (sir)!

120/5 **Crawler/creeper/boot-licker/arse-licker** *(#?)***/toady**:   A person who behaves in an excessively submissive or flattering way.

120/6 **Butter** someone **up** *or* **soft-soap** someone: Flatter someone. □ Don't try to soft-soap me (butter me up) because I won't lend you the money.

120/7 **Smarmy**:   Excessively or annoyingly flattering or polite. □ Kyoko was all smarmy and wanted me to help her.

121: INDULGE/PLEASE

121/1 **Mollycoddle** someone: Pamper someone; show great kindness or indulgence towards a person. □ Children who have been mollycoddled can later have difficulties coping with the pressures of life.

121/2 **Go easy on** someone: Have consideration for someone; treat a person kindly or leniently. □ At school, teachers went easy on Elena since they were aware of her difficult home circumstances.

121/3 **Be a sucker for** someone/something: Be always unable to resist the attractions of something or someone. *(See also 82/21)* □ She's a sucker for well-dressed salesmen. □ He's a sucker for antiques.

121/4 **A soft touch** *or* a **push-over**:   Someone who readily gives way to the requests of others, especially for money or favours. □ The child is spoilt; he knows his mother is a soft touch (a push-over).

121/5 **A sport:** Someone who indulges or pleases others. □ Be a sport and lend me your bike!

121/6 **You can't win!:** There is no way of achieving success or pleasing people. □ After failing to convince my son to stop smoking with the health argument, I resorted to threats, but you just can't win!

121/7 **Get no change/joy out of** someone: Fail to get satisfaction from someone. (See also 88/12) □ I asked Mr Rivero to stop lighting garden fires so close to my house, but I got no joy (change) out of him.

122: CONCEIT/AFFECTATION

122/1 **Think no small beer of oneself** *or* **think one is the bee's knees/the cat's whiskers** *or* **fancy oneself:** Have a very high opinion of oneself. (*See also 67/4*) □ Since Heike won a place at university to study Law, she thinks she is the bee's knees.

122/2 **Too big for one's boots:** Conceited; having an exaggerated opinion of oneself. □ Mr Tranelli has no right to order more senior staff around; he's getting too big for his boots.

122/3 **Get on one's high horse:** Assume an arrogant attitude of moral superiority. □ Don't get on your high horse with me, I knew you when you were still in your nappies!

122/4 **Stuck-up/toffee-nosed/snooty:** Snobbish; arrogant and showing contempt for others. □ At first, a few toffee-nosed (snooty/stuck-up) managers objected to sharing the same canteen as workers, but it is now clear that staff relations have benefited.

122/5 **A stuffed shirt:** A snobbish, pompous person who is usually incompetent or unimportant. □ It's no good putting a stuffed shirt like him to work on the shopfloor – he'd soon get up our noses.

122/6 **An ego-trip:** An activity undertaken only for the selfish purpose of self-expression or personal pleasure, without regard for the benefit of others. □ The dictator's palace had every luxury in spite of the fact that his poverty-stricken country couldn't afford such a massive ego-trip.

122/7 **La-di-da:** Having an affected manner or pronunciation; snobbish. □ Peter the Great scorned la-di-da courtiers and surrounded himself with practical people who could build up Russia.

122/8 **Arty-farty:** Displaying exaggerated and affected artistic style or interests. □ The new monument was criticized as being too arty-farty for the city's practical image.

122/9 **Camp:** Effeminate or affected; exaggerated in style or dress. □ His clothes are too camp. □ The room was painted pink and had camp furniture.

122/10 **A namby-pamby:** A person lacking positive character; an effeminate or affected person. □ The army is no place for namby-pambies.

123: SECRECY/CONCEALMENT

123/1 **Hush-hush:** Kept very secret. □ That scientist is engaged in hush-hush work for the government.

123/2 **Hugger-mugger:** Secretly. *(See also 30/10)* □ People are protesting about the hugger-mugger transport of nuclear missiles through the county.

123/3 **Cloak-and-dagger:** Secretive; involving dramatic adventures in spying. □ John Le Carre is a cloak-and-dagger author. □ The firm is very cloak-and-dagger about its manufacturing process.

123/4 **Keep** something **under (tight) wraps:** Keep in concealment or in great secrecy. □ The prototype of the new car is being kept under tight wraps until the motor show next month.

123/5 A **deep one:** A secretive person; someone who hides his true feelings and whose mentality is not easy to understand. □ Maria is a deep one – I've known her for years and yet I don't really know her, if you know what I mean!

123/6 **Paper over the cracks:** Seek to conceal faults or disagreement. □ The Shah of Iran tried to paper over the cracks in his regime with a show of wealth and by arresting those who publicly opposed him.

123/7 **Fudge:** Something improvised or put together in a dishonest manner to conceal faults. To act in this way is to 'fudge'. □ The report of the committee investigating the use of torture by police was declared a fudge by civil rights groups. □ You've made a fudge of repairing the vase you broke and Mother is sure to notice it when she gets back!

123/8 **Sweep** something **under the carpet:** Not mention something embarrassing or unpleasant; seek to hush up or conceal something. □ The existence of his illegitimate child was simply swept under the carpet.

123/9 **Salt away** something: Store away; hoard. □ That businessman has salted away a lot of money abroad to evade the taxman.

124: CHEEK

124/1 **Lip/buck**:   Impudence; cheeky remarks. □ Don't give me any of your lip (buck)!

124/2 **Gall/nerve**:   Impudence. □ What gall (What a nerve) Uwe's got, saying that about his own mother!

124/3 **Sauce**:   Impudence; racy or indecent. The adjective is 'saucy'. □ You've got some sauce asking for a pay-rise after all the blunders you've made at work. □ The film is full of saucy scenes and jokes.

124/4 **Sarky**:   Sarcastic or impudent. □ I'm doing my best and I want none of your sarky remarks about my work.

124/5 **Get fresh**:   Become very forward or impudently bold; become amorously impudent. □ Don't get fresh with me, I've already told you I had nothing to do with it. □ The girl gave the tipsy man a slap in the face when he started getting fresh with her.

124/6 A **cheeky monkey**:   A cheeky person. □ You're a cheeky monkey!

125: ECCENTRIC/STRANGE/FUSSY

125/1 **Way-out/far-out**:   Unusual or strange in an exaggerated way. □ He is way-out (far-out) in dress and hair-style. □ Doing something so dangerous without good reason is way-out (far-out).

125/2 A **kook** *(US)*:   An eccentric or strange person. The corresponding adjective is 'kooky'. □ Who's the kook in the corner, the one with a light bulb dangling from his ear?

125/3 An **oddball** *or* a **weirdy/weirdo**:   An eccentric person.

125/4 A **screwball** *or* a **crackpot**:   A crazy or very eccentric person. □ Some people say he's a weirdo – I'd go further and call him a screwball.

125/5 **Zany**:   Comically funny or eccentric; crazy. □ He is a zany comedian. □ That's a zany idea!

125/6 **Rum**:   Strange or odd. □ That's very rum, he should have been here by now. □ The plan sounds rum, but it might work.

125/7 **Pernickety/finicky**:   Excessively choosy; too particular or fussy about something. □ Grandfather is pernickety (finicky) about his food. □ She can be pernickety (finicky) about colours.

126: AGGRESSION/MANLINESS

126/1   **Pushy**:   Self-assertive. □ The salesman was very pushy but I didn't buy anything.

126/2   **Cut-throat**:   Intense and merciless. □ Our company is faced with cut-throat competition.

126/3   **Come on strong**:   Act powerfully or aggressively. □ He came on strong with threats. □ They are coming on strong about our company's alleged use of their trade mark and are suing us in several countries.

126/4   **Butch**:   Tough-looking or masculine; aggressively assertive. The word is frequently applied to the 'male' partner in a lesbian relationship. □ It is very butch to be seen walking with large aggressive dogs. □ I'd not be too sure about her, I reckon she's a bit butch.

126/5   **Macho**:   Showing manly courage or virility. An abbreviation of the Spanish word 'machismo'. □ Body-building is for macho men. □ 'Rambo' is a macho film.

127: GOOD BEHAVIOUR

127/1   **Play one's cards right**:   Behave with good judgement. □ If you play your cards right at work, you might get promoted.

127/2   **Watch/mind one's language**:   Be careful what one says. □ Mind (watch) your language, you shouldn't swear in public places!

127/3   **Mind one's Ps and Qs**:   Be careful what one says or does. In the 16th and 17th centuries, drinking-bills in taverns were marked in 'p' for pint and 'q' for quart (two pints). The letters are easily confused, and it was thus important to count the Ps and Qs exactly when paying one's bill. □ We're meeting the bank manager today and we need the loan, so mind your Ps and Qs.

127/4   **Remember oneself**:   Behave with suitable dignity, especially when one has already acted in an undignified manner. □ In church he blew his nose loudly and his wife told him to remember himself.

127/5   **Not put a foot wrong**:   Behave very correctly. □ Since leaving prison, Teshima hasn't put a foot wrong.

127/6   **Keep one's nose clean**:   Stay out of trouble. □ The boy was warned that if he didn't keep his nose clean, he would be expelled from school.

127/7   **Play ball** *or* **play the game**:   Co-operate with someone; go along with, or aid a decision. □ The Americans moved several warships into the trouble spot, hoping that the Russians would play ball (play the game) and not protest.

127/8   **Shape up**:   Improve one's conduct or attitude. □ Competition has increased, and if these old-style managers don't shape up, they'll have to leave the company.

127/9 **Turn over a new leaf:** Abandon one's previous bad manners or conduct; improve one's behaviour. □ When Antoine got married, he stopped drinking and turned over a new leaf.

127/10 **Mend one's ways:** Improve one's manners or behaviour. □ Vitali is too old to mend his ways.

127/11 **That's** someone **all over!:** That is typical of someone's behaviour. □ Angelika is so kind, that's her all over! □ I'm sorry he tricked you, but that's him all over.

128: BAD BEHAVIOUR

128/1 **(Get) up to no good:** (become) involved in mischief. □ Every time she leaves the house, her children get up to no good. □ I am sure the man loitering near that car is up to no good.

128/2 **Shenanigans/goings-on/capers/malark(e)y:** Mischievous conduct or misbehaviour; high-spirited behaviour. (*See also 96/1 'malarkey'*)
□ Some of our agents are cheating the company and we will have to put an end to these shenanigans (goings-on/capers/this malarkey).
□ Someone should tell Mr Brockman's wife of his goings-on (malarkey/ shenanigans/capers) with his secretary.

128/3 **A bad egg:** A person of bad character; a rogue. □ The police commissioner stated that his force would make every effort to rid themselves of bad eggs.

128/4 **A scallywag/scamp:** A rascal or mischievous person. □ My son is a young scallywag (scamp) – but most boys are, I suppose!

128/5 **Stroppy/bolshy:** Difficult to deal with; rebellious or uncooperative. □ Don't get stroppy (bolshy) with me, do as I say!

128/6 **Draw the line** at something: Set a limit to what is acceptable or tolerable. □ I don't mind using the tax law to my advantage, but I draw the line at fraud. □ It may seem ridiculous that your income is just above the requirements for legal aid, but the government must draw the line somewhere.

128/7 Not know **what came over one:** Not know what impulse caused one to misbehave or do something rash. □ The shoplifter told the judge that she didn't know what came over her when she saw the high-heeled shoes. □ What came over you to be so rude?

128/8 **Don't come the . . . with me!:** Don't behave like someone or something. □ Don't come the bully with me! □ You have no authority to order anyone about, so don't come the high-and-mighty with me!

129: IMITATE/COPY

129/1 **Take a leaf out of** someone's **book:** Follow someone's example; copy a person's behaviour. □ You aren't diligent enough; you should take a leaf out of your cousin's book!

129/2 **Jump/climb on the bandwagon** *or* **get in on the act:** Follow the example of something successful; imitate popular opinion for the sake of personal advantage. □ When it became clear that goods marked 'environment-friendly' were selling well, other firms started jumping on the bandwagon (getting in on the act).

129/3 **A copy-cat:** A person who copies the actions of others. □ Police refused to give details of the robbery for fear of 'copy-cat' crime. □ Top fashion designs are often stolen by copy-cats who mass-produce them under their own cheaper brand names. □ My teacher accused me of being a copy-cat in the school test.

129/4 **Like sheep:** Easily led or influenced; inclined to imitate blindly the behaviour of others. □ If you can get a famous investor to put money into your company, the rest will follow like sheep.

129/5 **A spoof/send-up:** A humorous imitation. □ The play is a send-up (spoof) of 18th-century monarchy. □ The film 'Casablanca' has generated many send-ups (spoofs).

130: REPUTATION/CREDIT/IMPRESSION

130/1 **His name is mud/dirt:** He is in disgrace, disliked or not in favour. □ Her name is now dirt (mud) with her family.

130/2 **In** someone's **bad books:** Not in favour with someone. □ I'm still in Ilse's bad books for what I said about her.

130/3 **In** someone's **good books:** In favour with someone. □ Matthias wants to stay in the management's good books, so he hasn't joined the strike.

130/4 **In the dog house:** In disgrace; held in contempt. □ That politician has been in the dog house since his removal from office for accepting bribes.

130/5 **Have egg on one's face:** Be humiliated; look foolish. □ Critics of the scientific theory had egg on their faces when it was proved correct.

130/6 **Cut a poor figure:** Make an unfavourable impression. □ The league champions cut a poor figure in their match today. □ Mr Shimoda sounded impressive over the phone, but when I met him in person he cut a poor figure.

130/7 **Make an exhibition of oneself:** Make oneself appear ridiculous; make a fool of oneself. □ Sybille got drunk at the wedding reception and made an exhibition of herself in front of all her relatives.

130/8 **I wouldn't put it past** someone: He is capable of it. □ I wouldn't put it past our aunt to exclude you from her will.

130/9 Live something down: Live in such a way that a scandal or disgrace is forgotten. □ We could never live it down that our father was a murderer. □ It will take a long time to live this defeat down.

130/10 Go down as someone/something: Be remembered or recorded as. □ Napoleon went down as one of the greatest generals in history. □ This day will go down as a day of shame for our family.

130/11 Someone's track record: A past history or career. □ The new manager has a good track record in the plastics industry. □ The death penalty has a poor track record as a deterrent for murder.

130/12 The talk of the town: A person or thing that has given rise to gossip; a fashionable and much-recommended place. □ The scandal has become the talk of the town with the neighbours. □ The new shopping centre has become the talk of the town.

130/13 Drop names: Casually mention the names of famous people in connection with something, in order to create a favourable impression. This activity is 'name-dropping'. □ Salesmen were told to drop the names of a few famous clients when promoting the service. □ Don't believe his name-dropping; he has never met anyone from the royal family.

130/14 Rest on one's laurels: Cease to strive for further success or fame; rely solely on one's past achievements, reputation or credit with someone. □ Our company is successful, but we cannot rest on our laurels and must continually seek to develop new products.

130/15 You've got to hand it to someone: One must give someone credit or praise for something. □ Anja failed again, but I've got to hand it to her, she tries hard.

130/16 Take one's hat off to someone: Give someone credit or praise for something. □ I take my hat off to the soldiers that died for freedom.

130/17 A feather in someone's cap: An achievement that one can be proud of. □ This long tunnel is a feather in the cap of the engineers who built it. □ If you pass the exam, it will be another feather in your cap.

130/18 Earn Brownie points: Do good deeds in order to win recognition or favour. A 'Brownie' is a junior member of an organization for girls similar to the Scouts, which encourages girls to be good citizens. □ If the government increases pensions, it will earn a few Brownie points with elderly voters.

130/19 Smelling of roses: Having the appearance of total blamelessness; of apparently irreproachable character, nature or conduct. □ Signal defects were blamed for the train crash, but the driver wasn't exactly smelling of roses either. □ The businessman was suspected of dealing illegally in weapons and was given a security check, but he came out of it smelling of roses.

131: CAUTIOUS/UNSUSPECTING

131/1 **Cagey:** Wary or sly; suspicious. □ The old wolf was cagey and didn't touch the poisoned lamb carcass.

131/2 **Play it by ear:** Proceed cautiously and gradually, going by one's instincts or results. □ Irmgard had never worked in an editorial office before, and had to play it by ear until she understood the routine.

131/3 **Pussyfoot:** Act cautiously; avoid committing oneself. □ Stop pussyfooting around and get the job done. □ I didn't pussyfoot and told him what I thought of him.

131/4 **Catch** someone **on the hop** *or* **catch** someone **with his trousers down** *or* **catch** someone **napping:** Catch someone completely unawares or unprepared. □ The town authorities were caught on the hop (with their trousers down/napping) by the winter weather, and had not enough grit and salt for the roads. □ Nato generals promised that they would not be caught napping (with their trousers down/on the hop) by a potential aggressor.

131/5 **Spring** something **on** someone: Produce or do something unexpectedly or suddenly; surprise someone with something. □ We sprang a birthday party on my sister. □ The enemy is not yet defeated; they can still spring an unpleasant surprise on us.

131/6 **(Like a bolt) out of the blue:** Totally unexpectedly. □ The news of his death came like a bolt out of the blue. □ The factory had plenty of work but then, out of the blue, we all received our dismissal notices.

EXERCISES 22 – BEHAVIOUR

A) Insert the missing nouns in the following sentences.

1) I asked him to park his car elsewhere but I got no . . . out of him.
2) The two men became friends again and all their past differences were swept under the . . . .
3) Mr Nyman resolved to clean the house while his wife was out, in order to earn a few . . . points.
4) The decision to open the Berlin Wall came like a . . . out of the . . . .
5) The youth was an idle student but he promised his parents that he would turn over a new . . . .
6) The Italian clothes designer was world-famous and other designers copied his dresses and suits slavishly like . . . .
7) The collapse of the firm was blamed on depressed market conditions, but the management wasn't smelling of . . . either.

→

8) Most hunters obey the rules and draw the . . . at shooting protected species.
9) The directors of the firm wanted to reduce the workforce but they were afraid that the trade unions wouldn't play . . . .
10) Two years ago in this region, there was only one farmer cultivating mushrooms on a large scale; now many others have jumped on the . . . .

B) Give colloquialisms for the definitions below.

1) a snobbish, pompous and incompetent person.
2) someone who copies what other people do.
3) an effeminate or affected person lacking positive character.
4) a servile person who behaves in an extremely submissive or flattering way.
5) a person or thing that has become a common topic of discussion.
6) a personal achievement that is worthy of pride.
7) someone who is easy to convince or overcome.
8) an eccentric person.
9) impudence or cheek.
10) a rogue or someone of bad character.

C) Replace the underlined phrases with as many colloquial synonyms as possible.

1) He is always <u>fawning to</u> his superiors.
2) She <u>has a very high opinion of herself</u>.
3) The police raid caught the gangsters <u>completely unawares</u>.
4) <u>Be careful what you say</u> in their presence, they are important people!
5) On New Year's Eve two revellers were injured during drunken <u>pranks</u> on the bridge.

D) From the module, give an adjective or noun answering the meaning of the following idiomatic descriptions.

1) A snob who thinks no small beer of himself is . . . (*adjective*).
2) A project that is kept under tight wraps is . . . (*adjective*).
3) A weak attempt by a political party to paper over cracks in its ranks is a . . . (*noun*).
4) Someone who is always soft-soaping another person is . . . (*adjective*).
5) A scallywag who will accept no control is . . . (*adjective*).
6) A physically tough man who is always coming on strong is . . . (*adjective*).

Things/Animals/Weather

132: TRANSPORT

132/1 **A tub**: A ship. □ This old tub is not seaworthy.

132/2 **A crate/kite**: An aircraft. □ Can this old crate (kite) still fly?

132/3 **A chopper** or a **whirlybird**: A helicopter. □ Air-sea rescue have sent out a chopper (whirlybird) to pick up the injured sailor.

132/4 **A crock**: An old or worn-out vehicle or ship. □ Do you think this old crock will keep going for the entire journey?

132/5 **A jalopy**: A battered old car. □ Whose jalopy's that parked outside?

132/6 **A banger**: A noisy old car. □ The first car I ever had was an old Ford banger.

132/7 **A run-about**: A car for short journeys. □ This small car is a good run-about for the shops and getting to work.

132/8 **A hot-rod**: A motor vehicle modified to have extra power and speed. □ Hot-rod racing on the streets should be banned.

132/9 **Soup/beef up** an engine: Increase the power or performance of an engine. □ The robbers' get-away car had a souped-up (beefed-up) engine.

132/10 **Wheels**: A vehicle or car. □ Have you got wheels (any wheels)?

132/11 A **Roller**/a **Jag**/a **Merc** (pr. 'merk'): Abbreviations for a Rolls-Royce, a Jaguar, a Mercedes – makes of car. □ We got married in a Roller.

132/12 A **juggernaut**: A large long-distance lorry. □ Our main street is too small for juggernauts.

132/13 **The Chunnel**: An abbreviation for the Channel Tunnel uniting England and France.

133: HOUSES/PREMISES

133/1 **Bricks and mortar**: A house or houses; buildings. □ Bricks and mortar are a safe investment. □ We've bought our own bricks and mortar.

133/2 **Jerry-built**: Speedily constructed out of inferior quality materials. This type of construction work is called 'jerry-building' and the person doing it is a 'jerry-builder'. □ Those houses were jerry-built and must now be demolished.

133/3 A **doss house** or a **flop house** (#US): Any low-class premises for sleeping; a cheap lodging house. □ The tramps spend the night in a doss house (flop house) run by the Salvation Army.

133/4 **A dive:** A place with a bad reputation; premises which are not respectable in character or appearance. □ The hotel was too expensive, so I spent the night in a cheap dive.

133/5 **A fire-trap:** A building without sufficient safe exits in the event of a fire. □ The fire department closed the dance-hall down because it was a fire-trap.

133/6 **Digs** *or* **a pad:** Lodgings; a temporary rented room or flat. □ It is difficult to find digs (a pad) in this town, most cheap accommodation has been taken up by students.

133/7 **A bed-sit(ter):** A bed-sitting room; a single room used for both living and sleeping in.

133/8 **Mod cons:** Modern conveniences or comforts like a modern kitchen or bathroom. □ It's a house with all the mod cons.

133/9 **Des. res.** (*pr. 'dez-rez'*): A desirable residence; a nice house or place to live. □ I'm looking for a des. res. near my place of work.

133/10 **A clip-joint:** A club or bar charging outrageously high prices. □ I'm not going into that bar – it looks like a clip-joint.

133/11 **The flicks** *or* **the pictures:** The cinema. □ There's a good film on at the flicks (pictures).

133/12 **A lab:** A laboratory. □ Theo is in the language-lab.

134: TECHNICAL TERMS

134/1 **A (one-armed) bandit:** A gambling-machine operated by inserting a coin and pulling down an arm-like handle. □ How much have you lost on the (one-armed) bandits?

134/2 **A fruit machine:** A coin-operated gambling-machine, often using symbols represented by different fruits. □ Tony's just won the jackpot on that new fruit machine in the pub!

134/3 **The blower:** The telephone. □ Get on the blower and tell the doctor I'm ill!

134/4 **A mike:** Microphone. □ The speaker's mike is not working.

134/5 **A ghetto-blaster:** A large portable stereo radio on which very loud pop music is played. □ Installation teams shouldn't work in a customer's house with their ghetto-blasters on, it gives a bad impression.

134/6 **A tranny:** A transistor radio. □ I heard it on the tranny.

134/7 **A bug:** A small concealed microphone or other listening-device. To 'bug' a room or premises is to install such listening devices. Also, a technical fault, especially in a computer program. □ Specialists were called in to clean the embassy of bugs. □ We can't run the program yet, it's still full of bugs.

188

134/8 **A box of tricks**: A complex technical device or piece of apparatus. □ My brother has bought a new box of tricks – the very latest in audio technology.

134/9 **A gadget** *or* a **gizmo** *(US)*: A small mechanical device or tool. □ This kitchen has all the latest labour-saving gizmos (gadgets).

134/10 **A contraption**: A strange device or machine. □ Early aviators invented many contraptions to defy gravity, most of which never left the ground.

134/11 **A job**: A machine or other technical object. □ Your computer is out of date, there are new jobs that can handle data much faster. □ I flew to Sydney in one of these supersonic jobs.

134/12 **A widget**: Jocular term for a small indefinite technical unit such as a screw or washer. □ If the company collapses, the firms that supply their widgets will also be in trouble.

134/13 **A bird** *(#US)*: A satellite. □ The 'Ariane' rocket has just put a telecommunications bird into orbit.

134/14 **Ammo**: Ammunition. □ The soldiers have run out of ammo.

134/15 **A nuke**: A nuclear weapon. To 'nuke' means to hit with a nuclear weapon. □ During the Vietnam War, some American generals wanted to nuke Hanoi. □ We want no nukes based near our village.

134/16 **Juice**: Electricity or petrol. □ We've just moved into the flat and the juice isn't on yet. □ Have we enough juice in the tank to get there?

134/17 **Turps**: Turpentine. □ Thin the paint with turps or a turps substitute such as white spirit.

135: UNDEFINED THINGS

135/1 **So-and-so**: Expression used in place of a person's name. *(See also 171/2)* □ When you meet a client, you first say good morning Mr or Mrs so-and-so. □ "Who told you that?" "Oh, so-and-so!"

135/2 **Thingumajig/thingumabob/thingummy/thingy**: Substitutes for a name or thing one cannot remember. □ I saw thingummy (thingy etc.) in the post office yesterday.

135/3 **A what-do-you-call-it**: A substitute for an object or thing one cannot remember. □ It's not a radio, it's a what-do-you-call-it.

135/4 **What's-his-name**: A substitute name for a person's name one has forgotten. □ I have just been talking to what's-her-name.

135/5 **Stuff**: Unnamed things or personal belongings. □ I've a lot of stuff in my flat. □ That wine is strong stuff! □ Lately, the films on TV have been all repeat stuff.

135/6 **Traps**: Personal belongings. □ Can I leave my traps here while I go around town?

135/7 **Gear/clobber**: Equipment or belongings *(See also 172/3)* □ The cupboard is full of his clobber (gear).

135/8   **Bits and pieces** *or* **odds and ends**:   Various isolated or unimportant items. ◻ The renovation is almost completed and there are just a few odds and ends (bits and pieces) to be done. ◻ There is still no clear picture of events in that country; we are just getting odds and ends (bits and pieces) of information from different sources.

135/9   **Paraphernalia**:   Numerous small pieces of equipment or belongings. ◻ He has all the paraphernalia for underwater diving.

135/10   **And stuff** *or* **and all that jazz** *or* **and suchlike**:   And other such things. ◻ Gina studies botany, you know – plants and stuff (and all that jazz/and suchlike).

135/11   **And whatnot**:   And many other things. ◻ The luxury house has ten bedrooms, a swimming-pool and whatnot.

135/12   A **hodge-podge/hotch-potch/rag-bag/mishmash**:   A jumble or confused mixture. ◻ The government consisted of a rag-bag (hotch-potch etc.) of coalition parties with widely differing policies.

135/13   A **knick-knack**:   Any small ornamental article. ◻ The Cairo bazaar was full of 'touristy' knick-knacks.

136: TELEVISION/MEDIA

136/1   A **(goggle-)box/telly/tube** (*US*):   A television-set. ◻ What's on the box (tube/telly) tonight?

136/2   **Zap**:   To change television channels with a remote-control device or 'zapper'. ◻ In New York, insomniacs can spend the night zapping from one TV channel to another.

136/3   A **soap opera** *or* **soap**:   A sentimental series of films, dealing with the everyday lives or dramas of a family, street or community. ◻ As soon as she gets home she turns on the TV to watch her favourite soap.

136/4   A **sitcom**:   Situation comedy; a comedy in which the humour comes from the misunderstandings and embarrassment of the characters. ◻ It's the funniest sitcom on the box at the moment.

136/5   A **fly-on-the-wall documentary**:   A documentary film showing the smallest details or events of people's lives, as if seen by an invisible observer. ◻ Did you see that fly-on-the-wall documentary about an out-of-work miner last night?

136/6   **The beeb**:   Colloquial or familiar term for the BBC. ◻ We often tune in to the Beeb.

136/7   A **blue movie**:   An indecent or pornographic film.

136/8   A **video nasty**:   A horror film on video. ◻ Blue movies should be shown late at night, but it's not so easy to stop children watching video nasties at any time of day.

136/9   A **whodunit**:   A detective film or book where the identity of the murderer or criminal is revealed at the end of the plot. ◻ There's nothing I like better than a good whodunit.

136/10 **A girlie-mag**: A magazine containing pictures of naked or semi-naked female bodies and articles intended for male readers.

136/11 **A rag**: Derogatory description of a newspaper, sometimes used casually. □ It was in the local rag last week – didn't you read it?

136/12 **A tabloid**: A popular, cheap and usually sensational newspaper with pages that are half the size of larger papers.

136/13 **An agony aunt**: A TV, radio or newspaper journalist running an 'agony column', which answers questions from the public about personal matters or complaints.

136/14 **A couch potato**: A lazy person who spends all his or her free time watching television uncritically. □ Jane was in danger of turning into a couch potato when she was resting at home after her operation.

136/15 **A gig**: An engagement for a single performance of a jazz band or pop group. □ The group has a gig in Hamburg next week.

137: SEARCH/FIND/OBTAIN

137/1 **Cast about for** something: Search or look for. □ Our firm is casting about for a new production manager.

137/2 **Chase up** something: Investigate and find. □ The clerk went away to chase up my file in the records department.

137/3 **Come by** something: Obtain. □ Police asked him how he came by the TV. □ In Saudi Arabia, alcohol is hard to come by.

137/4 **Dig/dredge up** something: Obtain or find; discover by investigation. □ Where did you dig (dredge) up that old gas mask? □ We dug (dredged) up a lot of information about the town from the newspaper archives.

137/5 **Ferret out** something: Discover by energetic searching. □ Mr Huang's wife has hired a private detective to ferret out his whereabouts. □ He rummaged through the box of assorted screws and ferreted out one of the exact size needed.

137/6 **For keeps**: For permanent possession; permanently. □ Ria didn't loan me her pocket calculator, she gave it to me for keeps. □ When we're married, you'll be mine for keeps.

137/7 **Finders keepers!**: Said when someone claims possession of an object by right of finding it. □ I found the money and I'm not taking it to the police; finders keepers!

137/8 **Happen on to** something: Discover or find by chance. □ I happened on to a real bargain at the used-car sale. □ Cheap flats are not easy to find, but you've happened on to a good thing there.

137/9 **Drum up** support: Obtain or enlist support or assistance through vigorous effort. □ We went from door to door, drumming up cash for the charity appeal. □ No candidate for presidency has yet drummed up enough votes to be certain of victory.

137/10 **Easy come, easy go**: Money or possessions can be spent or lost as easily as they were earned or obtained. □ On the first race I won £50, but then I lost it all on the second – easy come, easy go!

137/11 **Bag** something: Take possession of; lay claim to. □ A new group of children arrived in the dormitory, and there was a race to bag the top beds of the double bunks.

138: AVAILABLE

138/1 **On tap**: Always available (like tapwater). □ If any company needs extra labour, there are plenty on tap at the employment agency. □ I have large amounts of cash on tap through a credit agreement with the bank. □ Fred always has an excuse on tap for arriving late.

138/2 **On one's hands**: Available in excess; as an unwanted responsibility. □ Now that I'm retired, I have a lot of free time on my hands. □ My cat has just had kittens, and now I've seven cats on my hands.

138/3 **How are you fixed for . . .?**: What is the situation as regards the availability of something. □ How are you fixed for money? □ How are the stranded travellers fixed for overnight accommodation?

138/4 **Good for** something: Having available as a resource; able to pay or undertake. □ The old man declared that he was good for another ten years yet. □ If you want a loan, he's good for a hundred dollars. □ The car is good for another 10,000 kilometres.

138/5 **Fresh out of** something: Without a supply of something after having just sold or used up what remained. □ The shop is fresh out of bread; the last loaf was sold five minutes ago.

138/6　**Up for grabs**: Available for anyone to take or exploit. □ The removal of building restrictions means that the countryside around our towns is up for grabs.

138/7　**Up one's sleeve**: Concealed and available for use; in reserve. □ They haven't beaten me yet, I still have a few tricks up my sleeve. □ I've told you the whole truth and I've kept nothing up my sleeve.

138/8　**Another/a second string to one's bow**: A second or other means of achieving one's means; a resource in reserve on which one can draw. The reference is to archers who carry a second string for their bows. □ Yasmeen is a typist, but she's learning word processing to give herself a second string to her bow. □ Executives with a foreign language have another string to their bow.

138/9　**To hand**: Within reach; easily available. □ Hold the line a second, I haven't a pen to hand. □ We'll have to repair the light ourselves, there isn't an electrician to hand in the factory.

138/10　**Not grow on trees**: Not be freely or easily available. □ Money doesn't grow on trees. □ We'll have to advertise in the national press for staff, since specialists of this calibre don't grow on trees.

139: PASTIMES/LEISURE

139/1　**A fad**: A craze or hobby, especially when short-lived. □ His latest fad is stamp-collecting.

139/2　**A kick**: An interest or activity. □ The gymnasium has everything for the body-building kick.

139/3　**Go in for** something: Engage in an activity. □ He doesn't go in for sport. □ I don't go in for criticizing my country.

139/4　**Be into** something: Be actively interested or participating in. □ She's really into classical music.

139/5　**Dabble in** something: Occupy oneself casually with. □ Sophie dabbles a little in supernatural phenomena, but she doesn't take it seriously.

139/6　**Potter/mess around**: Work on trivial tasks in a leisurely relaxed way. □ At weekends, he potters (messes) around in boats. □ Karen is messing (pottering) around in the garden.

139/7　**Do one's own thing**: Follow one's personal interests or urges; do as one likes. □ Pressures of work leave me no time to do my own thing.

139/8　**Unwind**: Relax after a period of work or tension. □ After work, I unwind with slow music.

139/9　**Put one's feet up**: Relax, in a chair or on a couch, after a period of work. □ When she gets home in the evening she puts her feet up for half-an-hour before cooking a meal.

139/10　**A snap/snapshot**: A photograph taken informally or casually. To 'snap' someone or something is to take a casual photo. □ Here are our holiday snaps (snapshots). □ I snapped her standing in front of the fountain.

139/11 **Say 'cheese'!:**   Request for a person or persons to smile, so that their photo can be taken.

139/12 **Soccer:**   An abbreviation for 'Association' football – i.e. the game played in many countries, by eleven-a-side teams with a round ball. The word originated in the English public schools when there came a need to differentiate between this game and rugby football (*139/13*) □ Manchester United plays soccer; London Welsh plays rugger.

139/13 **Rugger:**   An abbreviation for rugby football. □ Rugger is a rougher game than soccer.

139/14 **DIY** (*pr. 'dee-eye-why'*):   An abbreviation for do-it-yourself; work done by the amateur handyman. □ I'm no good at DIY.

139/15 **A radio ham:**   An amateur operator of a long-distance radio transmitter/receiver. □ The ship's distress signal was picked up by a radio ham over 2,000 miles away.

139/16 **Swim like a brick:**   Swim very badly; be unable to swim. □ I'm not going out of my depth – I swim like a brick!

139/17 **A busman's holiday:**   Leisure time spent doing something similar to one's usual occupation. □ I'm a fishmonger during the week, so this pike-angling trip is something of a busman's holiday for me.

139/18 **A hop:**   An informal dance. □ I'm going to the hop tonight.

139/19 **Scrape the fiddle:**   Play the violin, usually in an unprofessional manner. □ Sherlock Holmes used to scrape the fiddle for relaxation.

139/20 **Plonk (on) the piano:**   Play the piano, usually in an amateurish way. □ After a few drinks in the bar she usually starts plonking on the piano and we sing a song or two.

139/21 **Doodle:**   Draw aimlessly while thinking about something else. □ Throughout the lecture, she sat doodling and looking out the window.

140: ANIMALS

140/1 **A creepy-crawly:**   Any small crawling insect. □ Life on the camp site was made unbearable by an invasion of creepy-crawlies.

140/2 **A tiddler:**   Any small fish. □ Children used to catch tiddlers in that stream.

140/3 **A critter:**   A creature or animal. □ The dog just lay there still, and it was obvious the poor critter was dead.

140/4 **A varmint** (*US*):   A mischievous animal or person. □ Foxes are a nuisance; that's the third time the varmints have stolen my hens.

140/5 **A bunny:**   A child's term for a rabbit. □ Look at all the bunnies in the field!

140/6 **A mog/moggie:**   A cat.

140/7 **A pooch:**   A small dog.

140/8　**A mutt**:　A dog, especially a mongrel. *(See also 82/9)*

140/9　**A bow-wow**:　Child's term for a dog.

140/10　**A porker**:　A pig.

140/11　**A gee-gee**:　A horse. □ He's always betting on the gee-gees.

140/12　**A nag**:　An (old) horse. □ The hay cart was pulled by an old nag.

140/13　**A moo-cow**:　Child's term for a cow.

140/14　**A chimp/hippo/rhino/budgie**:　Diminutives for chimpanzee, hippopotamus, rhinoceros, budgerigar . . . there are many abbreviations such as these.

141: WEATHER/CLIMATE

141/1　**Not fit to turn a dog out**:　Very stormy or cold. □ It's not fit to turn a dog out tonight.

141/2　**A nip in the air**:　A chill in the air.

141/3　**Nippy/parky**:　Rather cold or chilly. □ In England, by late September there's often a nip in the air; in November it can get really parky.

141/4　**Perishing**:　Very cold. □ It's perishing on deck.

141/5　**Cold enough to freeze the balls off a brass money *or* brass monkey weather**:　Extremely cold or freezing. □ It's cold enough to freeze the balls off a brass monkey. □ It's brass monkey weather outside.

141/6　**Boiling *or* sweltering**:　Uncomfortably warm. □ Open a window, it's boiling (sweltering) in here!

141/7　**Baking/sizzling/scorching**:　Very hot. □ The summer was baking (boiling/scorching).

141/8　**A scorcher**:　A very hot day. □ It's a scorcher today.

141/9　**Spit** (with rain):　Rain lightly; drizzle. □ Take your raincoat, it's starting to spit!

141/10　**Pour/bucket/belt/teem (down) *or* chuck it (down)**:　Rain heavily. □ It's pouring (bucketing/belting/teeming/chucking it) down.

141/11　**Rain cats and dogs**:　Rain very heavily. □ It rained cats and dogs the whole day.

141/12　**A wash-out**:　An event which is cancelled or stopped owing to rain. *(See also 18/26)* □ The athletics competition was a wash-out.

141/13　**Get a ducking/soaking/drenching**:　Get wet through. □ We got a drenching (ducking/soaking) on the way here.

141/14　**Sopping wet *or* wringing wet**:　Very wet. □ My clothes are sopping (wringing) wet.

141/15　**A pea-souper**:　A dense fog with very low visibility. □ All flying has been cancelled because of a pea-souper.

EXERCISES 23 – THINGS/ANIMALS/WEATHER

A) Give colloquialisms for the following definitions.

1) an old car.
2) a cheap, low-class lodging house.
3) a complex technical device or apparatus.
4) an expression used in place of a person's name that one has forgotten.
5) a popular newspaper of the sensational type with pages which are half the size of larger more serious newspapers
6) a second skill or means of achieving one's goal.
7) an informal dance.
8) a helicopter.
9) the telephone.
10) electricity or petrol.

B) Give as many colloquial synonyms as possible for the definitions below.

1) a jumble or confused mixture.
2) an undefined thing or object.
3) to rain heavily.
4) the TV set.

C) Replace the underlined phrases with colloquialisms from the module.

1) Where did you <u>find</u> that book?
2) He is <u>working in a leisurely manner</u> in the garage.
3) <u>What is her situation regarding the supply</u> of floppy discs?
4) We <u>photographed</u> some magnificent animals on our safari holiday.
5) <u>I am not interested in</u> cricket.
6) He <u>can't swim at all</u>.
7) He <u>found her address by searching</u> in the Paris phone directory.
8) I have no opportunity to <u>relax</u>.
9) This firm has realized that skilled staff <u>are not freely available in large numbers</u>, and has started an in-house training scheme.
10) <u>The weather is extremely cold</u>.

D) Give colloquial terms for the following:

1) an animal or creature. 2) a dog. 3) a crawling insect. 4) a small fish. 5) a cat. 6) a horse. 7) a pig.

E) List as many colloquial <u>abbreviations</u> as you can find in the module. These should include living creatures, things, names of products and so on, and not all have been described as abbreviations in the text.

Movement/Places

142: ARRIVE/MEET

142/1 **Blow in**: Arrive casually or unexpectedly. □ My daughter thinks she can blow in at any time of the night. □ I'm glad you've blown in, you're just in time for coffee.

142/2 **Roll up**: Arrive casually or arrive in a vehicle. □ I inquired at the bar whether Marc had rolled up yet. □ He rolled up in an expensive car.

142/3 **Turn up**: Make one's appearance; arrive. □ We had a date, but she didn't turn up.

142/4 **Surface**: Make one's appearance after a long absence; wake up or regain consciousness. □ After a year, the man wanted by Interpol surfaced in Mexico. □ Alain drank a lot that evening and didn't surface till late the next morning.

142/5 **Drop in/by** someone: Pay a casual visit. □ I'll drop by (in) tonight, to see if she is all right. □ Nice of you to drop by (drop in on us).

142/6 **Bump into** someone: Meet by chance. □ Can you guess who I bumped into in the supermarket today?

142/7 **Wind up** somewhere: Finally come to a place. □ If Raoul goes on stealing, he'll wind up in prison. □ After three days' journey on foot, we wound up at the village where the monastery was situated.

143: WALK/GO

143/1 **Pop/slip/nip**: Come or go quickly, suddenly or unexpectedly. □ I'll pop (nip/slip) over to the shops for some sugar. □ We must pop (nip/slip) off now!

143/2 **Hoof it/leg it**: Go on foot. □ There's no bus to the youth hostel, so you'll have to leg (hoof) it.

143/3 **On Shanks's mare/pony**: On foot; using one's legs. □ Our car broke down, so we covered the last two miles on Shanks's pony (mare).

143/4 **On the hoof**: Moving around or as one goes along. □ During the mid-day break, many city workers can be seen eating sandwiches on the hoof.

143/5 **Foot-slogging**: Walking or marching. □ The hikers spent a week foot-slogging in the hills.

143/6 **Yomp**: March across open country carrying one's equipment. □ To get to the river, we had to yomp through the woods carrying our canoes.

143/7 **Traipse**: Walk wearily. □ We've been traipsing round the town all day looking for bargains in the shops.

143/8 **Mooch**: Walk slowly and aimlessly. □ He spent the day mooching around the beach.

143/9 **Mosey/tootle/toddle**: Walk in a casual or leisurely way. □ I'll mosey (tootle/toddle) off home now to get my dinner.

143/10 **Trot**: Walk or go. □ She trotted down to the bus-stand.

143/11 **On the go/trot**: Continually busy or moving around; active. □ There's plenty to do here, we're always on the trot (go).

143/12 **Waltz**: Move gaily or casually. □ On hearing the good news, he waltzed off to tell his friends.

143/13 **Swan**: Go in a leisurely majestic way, like a swan. Also, to travel aimlessly or at someone else's expense. □ The bride-to-be swanned down the aisle of the church. □ "Where's Mike?" "He's swanned off to New York for a few days, again – he always seems to be away on business, but I don't think he does very much."

143/14 **Gallivant**: Go around in search of pleasure. □ They spent the night gallivanting around night-clubs.

143/15 **Toing and froing**: Coming and going. □ The contract involved much toing and froing between America and Asia.

143/16 **Knock around**: Go around or associate with. (*See also 145/3 below*) □ I don't like the people she knocks around with. □ Have you seen Hans knocking around anywhere?

143/17 **On your travels**: While you were on the move or going around. □ If you see the head storekeeper on your travels, tell him that a new delivery has arrived!

143/18 **Make a beeline**: Go directly or rapidly towards. □ When our bus got to the hotel, some of the travellers made a beeline for the bar.

143/19 **Follow one's nose**: Go straight ahead. □ The museum is straight ahead, just follow your nose for two hundred metres.

143/20 **String/tag along**: Accompany. □ When we heard that the Japanese tourists were going to visit a crocodile farm, we decided to string (tag) along out of interest.

143/21 **Dog** someone: Follow persistently or closely. □ My ex-boyfriend has been dogging my steps all day. □ His business was dogged by financial set-backs.

143/22 **Gangway!**: Make way! Step out of the way! □ Gangway! We must get this man to hospital immediately.

144: LEAVE/RUN AWAY/DISAPPEAR

144/1 **Hit the road/trail** (*US*): Depart. □ It's time we hit the trail (road) or we won't get there on time.

144/2 **Run/hop along** *or* **get on**: Leave. □ You'd better be running along (hopping along/getting on) now!

144/3 **Shove/push off**: Go away. □ We can't stay any longer, we'll have to push (shove) off. □ Katia told him to shove (push) off and stop bothering her.

144/4 **Dash off**: Leave hurriedly. □ Enzo is always dashing off when I want to speak to him.

144/5 **Make tracks**: Go away; head for. □ I'll have to make tracks shortly. □ When the storm started, we made tracks for shelter.

144/6 **Skedaddle** *or* **scarper**: Run away. □ You'd better scarper (skedaddle) before you get into trouble!

144/7 **Hook it** *or* **skip** *or* **split**: Go away hastily or secretly. □ When the police arrived on the scene, the thieves had already hooked it (split/skipped).

144/8 **Show a clean pair of heels**: Run away or escape. □ The boys who were stealing apples showed a clean pair of heels when they saw the farmer.

144/9 **Do a bunk** *or* **vamoose**: Run away. □ I told him to vamoose (do a bunk). □ The cashier did a bunk (vamoosed) with the bank's money.

144/10 **Up sticks**: Go and live somewhere else. □ The volcano eruption forced many Filipino families to up sticks.

144/11 **Do a vanishing trick** *or* **make oneself scarce**: Run away or disappear. □ That fraudster sets up false companies to get people's money, and then does a vanishing trick (makes himself scarce).

144/12 **Scat!** *or* **get lost!**: Go away!

144/13 **Scram/hop it/buzz off/beat it/clear off**: Go away. These verbs are usually, but not always, found in the command form or imperative (Scram! Hop it! etc.) □ They didn't wait, they just buzzed off (scrammed/cleared off/beat it/hopped it) without us.

144/14 **Fuck off** (*#??*)/**piss off** (*#??*)/**bugger off** (*#??*): Vulgar expressions similar to above, meaning 'to go away'.

144/15 **Bang goes** something: Said when something disappears quickly. □ Here's the money for the car repair and bang goes a week's salary. □ Olaf got an unfavourable work assessment from his superior, and bang went his chances of promotion.

144/16 Something **has walked**: Something has disappeared or has been stolen. □ I left my bag in the changing-room, but it seems to have walked.

145: TRAVEL/DISTANCE

145/1 **Go places**: Travel widely. □ As an airline stewardess, you can go places.

145/2 **Get around**: Travel or move about a lot. □ Travelling salesmen get around a lot in the course of their work.

145/3 **Knock around/about:** Travel widely somewhere. □ The old sea captain had knocked around (about) the world.

145/4 **Live out of a suitcase:** Be continually travelling; be hardly ever at home. □ Travel couriers must enjoy living out of a suitcase.

145/5 **Have itchy feet:** Travel a lot or have an urge to travel. □ Young people often have itchy feet and want to see something of the world before they get older.

145/6 **A globetrotter:** Someone who travels all over the world, more often as a tourist. □ He used to be a globetrotter, but since getting married he can't afford to travel so much.

145/7 **A drifter:** An aimless person; a tramp or someone who frequently changes his job or home. □ Don't think of employing him – he's an out-and-out drifter and you'll soon be looking for someone else.

145/8 **Take in** a place: Include a place in one's travel plans; visit a place en route. □ The Egypt trip takes in the pyramids and the Aswan dam.

145/9 **Do** somewhere: Visit or see the sights. □ Europe is a small place for some American tourists, who do Berlin, Rome and Paris in a week.

145/10 **Hop** (over): Make a short quick trip. □ Let's hop over to Paris for the weekend.

145/11 **Thumb a lift:** Hitch-hike; travel by requesting lifts with one's thumb. □ The last bus has gone, we'll have to try and thumb a lift. □ It is forbidden to thumb lifts on the motorway!

145/12 **Under one's own steam:** By one's own means of transport. □ The Bangladeshi girls were offered hotel work in Saudi Arabia, but had to get to Riyadh under their own steam.

145/13 **Jet-lag:** Delayed tiredness after a long air flight, owing to local time differences. □ I'm still suffering from jet-lag. (I'm still jet-lagged.)

145/14 **Burn up** the road/miles: Travel or cover a great distance quickly. □ During our tour of South America, we burnt up an awful lot of road (miles).

145/15 **A stone's throw:** A short distance. □ The beach is only a stone's throw from the hotel.

145/16 **As the crow flies:** In a straight line. □ The village is only three kilometres from here as the crow flies, but seven by road.

145/17 **On** someone's **doorstep:** Very close. □ The city is modern and we have beautiful countryside on our doorstep.

146: CARRY/FORCEFUL MOVEMENT

146/1 **Lug/hump** something: Carry something heavy or cumbersome. □ Leave your bags here, it will save you humping (lugging) them around the town!

146/2 **A piggyback:** A ride on someone's shoulders and back. □ A fireman gave the old lady a piggyback to get her out of the burning house.

146/3   **Give a bunk-up**: Push someone up with one's body; allow one's body to be used as a ladder. □ In order to get into the football ground without tickets, fans were giving one another bunk-ups over the perimeter fence.

146/4   **Chuck/sling**: Throw. □ Chuck (sling) me that telephone directory!

146/5   **Heave**: Throw something heavy. □ He then heaved a brick through my window.

146/6   **Yank**: Pull forcefully with a sudden sharp tug. □ The door was jammed, and when I tried to open it, I yanked off the handle.

146/7   **Bung**: Throw or push without great care. □ Bung your rucksacks in the dormitory and report to the hostel warden! □ I had sunburn, so I bunged on some skin lotion.

146/8   **Stick**: Put without great care. □ Stick the box down there!

146/9   **Pop**: Put quickly. □ Just pop it in the oven for five minutes and it's ready to eat!

146/10   **Slam/jam on** brakes *or* **slam/slam down**: Apply brakes forcefully; hence, switch or throw something on or down with great force. □ When he saw the cyclist through the fog, the driver slammed (jammed) on his brakes. □ She slammed down the phone when she heard who was speaking.

146/11   **Slap-bang**: Forcefully; headlong. □ The jewel thief ran out of the shop, slap-bang into a passing policeman.

146/12   **Hit the deck**: Fall or throw oneself to the ground. □ As soon as the gunfire started, the hotel residents all hit the deck.

146/13   **Splosh**: Splash; fall heavily into water or any liquid. □ On catching sight of the heron, the frog sploshed into the pond.

146/14   **Flump/plump**: Fall down heavily or wearily. □ Immediately on arriving home from work, Helga would flump (plump) down into an armchair with a glass of sherry.

146/15   **Come a cropper**: Fall heavily. *(See also 18/5)* □ The motorcyclist hit the badger and wobbled on for twenty metres before finally coming a cropper in a ditch.

146/16   **Geronimo!** *(US)*: Exclamation when jumping or throwing something from a height. The exclamation is attributed to American parachutists who used it before jumping from planes. □ One of the house-breakers shouted 'Geronimo!' and threw a large beam down from the roof.

147: PLACES

147/1   **The drink/briny**: The sea. □ The sailor fell from the boat into the briny (the drink).

147/2   **Davy Jones's locker**: The graveyard of sailors and ships at the bottom of the sea. □ The 'Titanic' and most of its passengers and crew lie now in Davy Jones's locker.

147/3 **The (herring-)pond:** The Atlantic. □ My brother lives over the herring-pond in Canada.

147/4 **Down under:** Countries in Australasia, most commonly Australia and New Zealand. □ The family emigrated down under to New Zealand.

147/5 **Oz:** Australia. □ Alice Springs is at the centre of Oz.

147/6 **The Emerald Isle:** Ireland. Owing to heavy rainfall and the resulting very green grass, Ireland is said to resemble the colour of an emerald.

147/7 **Uncle Sam:** The USA and its people. □ We're going on holiday to Uncle Sam.

147/8 **The Old World:** Europe, Asia and Africa as distinct from the Americas. □ My grandmother in Chicago told me about how she entered America from the Old World many years ago.

147/9 **A sunspot:** A place with a sunny climate. □ Most tourists are looking for cheap sunspots.

147/10 **A jumping-off place:** A starting-point for a tour or journey. □ Nairobi is a good jumping-off place for a tour of Southern Africa.

147/11 **Hail from** somewhere: Originate or have come from a place. □ This is Torger, he hails from Bergen in Norway.

147/12 **Put** a place **on the map:** Make a place famous or important. □ A disastrous nuclear accident put the sleepy Ukrainian town of Chernobyl on the map.

147/13 **A stamping-ground:** The haunt or usual place of action of a person or animal. □ Simone spends most afternoons in her favourite stamping-ground, the city library.

147/14 Someone's **neck of the woods:** An area or place that someone knows well. □ Inquiries about exports to Syria are dealt with by our Middle East department, that's their neck of the woods.

147/15 **A dump:** A dull or unattractive place. □ That town is not worth a visit, it's a dump.

147/16 **A hole/the pits:** A small or dark or wretched place. □ The building in which the family lives is a rat-infested tenement; it's a hole (the pits).

147/17 **Left, right and centre:** Everywhere and continually. □ During the siege of Leningrad civilians were dying of hunger left, right and centre.

147/18 **All over the place/shop:** Everywhere. *(See also 30/11)* □ When I was in the merchant navy, I travelled all over the shop (place). □ There were locusts all over the shop (place).

147/19 **Take a pew:** Take a seat or place. □ Take a pew in the waiting-room and listen for your number to be called!

147/20 **Plonk oneself (down)** *or* **park oneself:** Take a place or sit down. □ Let's plonk ourselves down (park ourselves) on that section of the river bank, it looks like a good place to catch fish.

147/21 **A backwater:** A place unaffected by new ideas or progress. □ Our town is a cultural backwater.

147/22 **A backwoods**: A remote or backward area. □ You only need drive twenty kilometres from the city centre and you're in the backwoods.

147/23 **The back of beyond** *or* **the middle of nowhere**: A very remote area. □ For many Westerners, the remote Saharan town of Timbuktu in Mali has come to signify the back of beyond (the middle of nowhere).

148: CROWDED

148/1 **Jam-packed/chock-full/chock/chocker-a-block**: Crowded into a very small space; full to bursting point. □ During the rush hour, trains in Tokyo are jam-packed (chock-a-block etc.).

148/2 **Crammed/packed like sardines**: Crowded very closely together. □ The beach was tiny and bathers were crammed (packed) like sardines.

148/3 **Sandwiched** between: Crowded or pressed between. □ The accused arrived at the court room sandwiched between two officers. □ Our house is sandwiched between a factory and a garage.

148/4 **No room to swing a cat**: Very small and cramped; very little free space available. 'Cat' here refers not to the animal but to a cat-o'-nine-tails, a nine-thonged whip used to flog disobedient seamen. The flogging took place on deck because the cabins were usually too small to swing the whip. □ He can't stay in my flat, I've no room to swing a cat there.

148/5 **Poky**: Small and cramped. □ That's a high rent for a poky room.

EXERCISES 24 – MOVEMENT/PLACES

A) Complete the following sentences with the missing noun.

1) When the fight broke out in the bar, we made a . . . for the exit.
2) The town hall is only a . . . 's throw from the station.
3) As the water rose, people living on the islands of the river delta had to up . . . and move to the mainland.
4) I don't know that region of the country, it's not my . . . of the . . . .
5) Have you seen André on your . . . ?
6) The factory site is ideal for our firm, since we would have a large potential market on our . . . .
7) We can't buy any more furniture for our flat, for we have no room to swing a . . . already.
8) The nuclear reactor was built in the middle of . . . , far from the nearest centre of population.

B) Give colloquialisms for the definitions below.

1) the USA and its people. 2) delayed tiredness caused by long-distance travel in jet aircraft. 3) the Atlantic Ocean. 4) Australia. 5) a place with a sunny climate. 6) a vagrant or person who continually travels around aimlessly. 7) travelling in a straight line. 8) a ride on someone's shoulders or back.

C) Replace the underlined phrases with as many colloquial synonyms as possible.

1) We decided not to take the bus, but to <u>go on foot</u> instead.
2) The boat was <u>crowded to bursting point</u> with refugees.
3) Last night someone <u>threw</u> a brick through our window.
4) It is getting late and I must <u>leave</u> now.
5) The thieves <u>ran off</u> when the alarm sounded.
6) <u>Take a seat</u> there and wait for your number to be called!

D) Complete the following sentences with the appropriate adverb or adverbial expression.

1) As a result of the collision, four people wound . . . in hospital.
2) I read the letter . . . the hoof, while making my way to the office.
3) She is an invalid and can't get to the shops . . . her own steam.
4) After the pop concert in the park, there was litter scattered . . . . . . the place.
5) The royal visit will take . . . an old people's home and a new housing estate.
6) They said they were going to pick blackberries and asked me if I wanted to tag . . . .
7) The snack-bar is very busy and staff are always . . . the go.

Eating/Drinking

149: FOOD

149/1 **Chow/grub/nosh:** Food. □ Let's get some nosh (chow/grub)!

149/2 **Din-dins:** Jocular or child's term for 'dinner'. □ I'm off to have my din-dins.

149/3 **Elevenses:** Light refreshments at about 11 am.

149/4 **A bite:** A small quick meal or snack. □ I feel like a bite.

149/5 **A square meal:** A substantial and satisfying meal. □ It's no good living on snacks; you should get a square meal into you!

149/6 **A tuck-in/blow-out:** A large meal or period of eating well. □ We had a tuck-in (blow-out) over Christmas.

149/7 **A slap-up meal** *or* **a spread:** A first-class or lavish meal. □ The retiring chairman was given a slap-up meal (spread) on his last day at the firm.

149/8 **Junk food:** Low-quality food, especially from take-away restaurants and kiosks.

149/9 **Stodgy:** Heavy and difficult to digest. □ Puddings are too stodgy for me!

149/10 **Piping hot:** Very hot. □ The water is piping hot.

149/11 **Stone-cold:** Cold as stone. □ The tea will be stone-cold by now.

149/12 **Bangers and mash**: Sausages and mashed potato.

149/13 **A spud**: A potato.

149/14 **Spud-bashing**: The period of potato-peeling, especially for a group of people. □ In the army, we all took turns at spud-bashing.

149/15 **A gob-stopper**: A large mouth-filling sweet.

149/16 **A chippie**: A shop or kiosk selling chips or pommes-frites.

149/17 **Rustle up** a meal: Prepare or get together a meal. □ We don't have much in the fridge, but I think I can rustle up something.

149/18 **Whip up** a meal: Prepare a meal quickly. □ The cook is busy whipping up lunch.

150: EATING

150/1 **Keep body and soul together**: Eat enough to stay alive. □ I've been working all day non-stop, so I'll have a sandwich, just to keep body and soul together.

150/2 **Grab** a meal: Have a quick meal. □ I'll just grab some breakfast before leaving.

150/3 **Tuck in** *or* **dig in** *or* **get stuck in**: Eat, or start eating heartily.
□ There's your dinner, so tuck in (dig in/get stuck in)! □ I'd like to tuck (dig/get stuck) into a juicy steak.

150/4 **Tackle** a meal: Eat or find room for a meal. □ I'm still a bit sea-sick and couldn't tackle dinner right now.

150/5 **Demolish** a meal: Eat up. □ I demolished the whole cake on my own.

150/6 **Polish off** food: Eat up quickly. □ Don't polish off all the food before we get there!

150/7 **Gobble up/down** *or* **wolf/hog/shovel down**: Eat up greedily and quickly. □ I've never seen anyone gobble up (wolf down/scoff etc.) so much for breakfast.

150/8 **Put away** food: Consume; eat or drink. □ She put away three bars of chocolate and two cans of cola.

150/9 **A good trencherman**: A hearty eater; a person with a large appetite and liking for food. □ Your wife is a good trencherman.

150/10 **Eat like a horse** *or* **eat one's head off**: Eat excessively. □ People suffering from bulimia eat like a horse (eat their heads off) in secret.

150/11 Able to **eat the hind/back legs off a donkey**: Able to eat an excessive amount. *(See also 97/3)* □ Bruno can eat the back (hind) legs off a donkey.

150/12 **A bottomless pit**: A person who can eat endlessly.

150/13 **A gannet**: Someone with a large appetite, as has the gannet (a sea bird).

150/14 **A greedy guts** *(#?)*: A greedy person.

150/15 **His eyes are bigger than** his **belly**: Out of greed, he attempts to eat more than he can take or manage. □ No wonder you feel ill, your eyes are bigger than your belly!

150/16 **A free loader**: A person who eats and drinks at the expense of others. □ We want no free loaders in this house, so go out and earn your keep like everyone else!

150/17 **Have a sweet tooth**: Be fond of sweet or sugary food. □ Theresa has a sweet tooth and puts on weight easily.

150/18 **Dunk** food: Dip food into a liquid, such as gravy or tea. □ Dunking biscuits into coffee is not considered good etiquette.

150/19 **Feel free!**: Help yourself to the food!

150/20 **Burp**: Belch or send up stomach wind through the mouth, especially after eating or drinking. □ Katsumi burped and all the dinner guests looked at him.

151: APPETITE/HUNGER

151/1 **Yum-yum!**: An exclamation of pleasure at the thought of eating.

151/2 **Yummy/scrumptious**: Delicious or tasty. □ That recipe sounds scrumptious (yummy). □ There was lots of yummy (scrumptious) food.

151/3 **Mouth-watering**: Appetizing. □ The stall was full of mouth-watering melons and exotic fruits.

151/4 **Make** someone's **mouth water**: Arouse a person's appetite. □ The smell of baking pies makes my mouth water.

151/5 **I could eat a horse!**: I am ravenously hungry!

151/6 **I could murder** something: Have a great appetite or thirst for something. □ I could murder a pizza and a glass of beer.

151/7 **Peckish**: Slightly hungry. □ Colette kept a choc-bar in her desk in case she felt peckish between meals.

151/8 **Famished/starving**: Ravenously hungry. □ Is dinner ready?, I'm famished (starving).

151/9 **Off one's oats**: Having lost one's appetite for food. □ My brother has flu and he's off his oats today.

152: DRINKS

152/1 **Char/cha**: Tea. □ I'll make a cup of char.

152/2 **A cuppa**: A cup of tea. □ Want a cuppa?

152/3 **Brew up**: Make some tea. □ The apprentice was told to brew up for his workmates.

152/4 **Pop**: Fizzy drinks or lemonade; beer. (*See 155/3 below*) □ The girl asked for a bottle of pop.

152/5　**A jar**:　A glass of beer. □ He's gone to the bar for a few jars.

152/6　**Plonk**:　Cheap or inferior wine.

152/7　**Booze**:　Alcoholic drink. □ Egon spends all his money on booze.

152/8　**The hard stuff**:　Strong alcohol or drink. □ I do drink beer, but not the hard stuff like whisky.

152/9　**Jungle-juice** *or* **rot-gut**:　Strong alcohol, especially the cheap varieties.

152/10　**Hooch**:　Crude alcoholic liquor. The Hoochinoo were Alaskan Indians who distilled a particularly rough but strong liquor.

152/11　**Moonshine**:　Illegally distilled or smuggled alcoholic liquor. □ Many farmers in this region make their own moonshine.

152/12　**Scrumpy**:　Rough cider.

152/13　**Tot/snifter**:　A small measure of spirits or strong alcohol.

152/14　**On the rocks**:　(Of a drink) served undiluted, with ice-cubes. □ Give me a vodka on the rocks!

152/15　**Bubbly/shampers**:　Champagne. □ The best bubbly (shampers) is reputed to come from France.

152/16　**A chaser**:　A drink taken after a drink of another kind. □ After coffee they had a brandy chaser.

152/17　**A nightcap**:　A hot or alcoholic drink taken at bedtime.

152/18　**One for the road**:　A final drink before departing.

152/19　**Spike** a drink:　Increase the alcoholic content of a drink by pouring in something stronger, especially when done without the knowledge of the drinker. □ After he failed the breathalyser-test, the drunken motorist claimed that someone in the bar had spiked his lager with vodka.

152/20　**Stand** a drink:　Pay for someone's drink; treat someone to a drink. □ If you've no money, I'll stand you a few beers.

152/21　**A shout**:　A person's turn to buy a round of drinks. □ It's your shout, Erich bought the last round!

152/22　**Say when!**:　Say when I've poured in enough! The reply is usually given as 'When!'. □ Would you like water in your whisky? Yes? Say when!

153: DRINKING/THIRST

153/1　**Wet one's whistle**:　Take a drink (usually alcoholic). □ I'm off to wet my whistle.

153/2　**Crack a bottle**:　Drink up a bottle. □ Let's crack a few bottles of wine to celebrate your engagement.

153/3　**Down/sink** a drink:　Drink up or swallow. □ Dirk downed (sank) seven litres of beer last night.

153/4　**Toss off** *or* **knock back**:　Drink up or swallow rapidly. □ He calmly tossed off (knocked back) the glass of whisky and requested another.

153/5　**A swig**:　A mouthful of liquid or a swallow. ☐ The three men were taking swigs out of the same schnapps bottle.

153/6　**The local**:　The local bar usually frequented by someone. ☐ This bar is my local. ☐ He's gone to the local.

153/7　**The boozer**:　A bar. *(See also 155/6 below)* ☐ Just think, instead of doing this, I could have been in the boozer right now.

153/8　**Drink like a fish**:　Drink excessively.

153/9　**Drink** someone **under the table**:　Beat someone in a contest to drink the most alcohol. ☐ The captain was renowned as a hard drinker who could drink any sailor under the table.

153/10　**Swill down** a drink:　Drink greedily in large quantities. ☐ She swilled down three pints of cider in three minutes.

153/11　**Beer/wine-swilling**:　Given to drinking beer in large quantities. ☐ We must protect the city against lager-swilling football hooligans.

153/12　**Tank up**:　Fill one's stomach with drink. ☐ They've gone to the bar to tank up. ☐ Shimoda goes home every evening tanked up.

153/13　**Bottoms up!** *or* **chin-chin!** *or* **down the hatch!**:　Cheers!; request or encouragement to empty one's glass.

153/14　**Dying/gasping** for a drink *or* **parched**:　Very thirsty. ☐ It was so hot, I was dying (gasping) for a drink (I was parched).

154: CELEBRATION

154/1　**Throw a party**:　Hold or give a party. ☐ I'm throwing a birthday party tonight.

154/2　**A house-warming**:　A party to celebrate the occupation of a new home.

154/3　**A hen-party/night**:　A party or evening for women only. ☐ The restaurant doesn't allow men in on hen-nights.

154/4　**A stag-party/night**:　A party or evening for men only, often on the night before the groom's wedding.

154/5　**Gate-crash**:　Enter a private party or celebration without an invitation. A 'gatecrasher' is an uninvited guest.

154/6　**A do**:　A party or entertainment. ☐ The neighbours had a really big do to celebrate their silver wedding.

154/7　**A knees-up**:　A lively party with dancing.

154/8　**A rave-up** *or* a **wingding** *(#US)*:　A lively or wild party. ☐ At college, we had a rave-up (wingding) every weekend.

154/9　**Whoop it up**:　Engage in noisy revelry or celebration. ☐ Granny spends every winter in Spain, whooping it up with the other pensioners.

154/10　**Out on the town**:　Out celebrating or seeking pleasure in town. ☐ We're going out on the town tonight.

154/11　**Paint the town red**:　Go on a drunken outing in town; visit several bars or night-clubs in drunken revelry. The expression dates back to an April night in 1873 when the Marquis of Waterford and his drunken friends daubed red paint on public places.

154/12 **On the razzle** *or* **on the spree**: Out for enjoyment. (*For 'spree', see also 55/5*) □ Birthdays are a good excuse to go on the razzle (spree).

155: DRUNKENNESS

155/1 **Dutch courage**: False courage obtained by drinking alcohol. □ The accused had first drunk a bottle of whisky for Dutch courage before committing the murder.

155/2 **Hit the bottle**: Drink alcohol heavily. □ After a domestic row, he went away and hit the bottle.

155/3 **On the pop/bottle**: Drinking beer ('pop') or alcohol ('bottle') heavily. □ Chao is a completely different person when he's on the pop (the bottle).

155/4 **Tipple**: Drink habitually, especially alcohol or wine. The person doing this is a 'tippler', and 'tipple' is also the drink. □ My wife tipples while I'm at work. □ What's your tipple? Beer, whisky, a glass of wine?

155/5 **Boozy**: Habitually drinking. □ He's one of these boozy types.

155/6 A **boozer**: A habitual drinker or drunk. (*See also 153/7*)

155/7 A **wino/plonky/piss-artist** (*#?*)/**lush** (*#US*): A drunkard or alcoholic.

155/8 **Tiddly**: Tipsy; slightly drunk. □ I'm feeling tiddly after that glass of cognac.

155/9 **Have had one over the eight** *or* **a drop too many**: Be slightly drunk; have drunk too much. □ When Gitte has had a drop too many (one over the eight), she would tell her life story to a complete stranger.

155/10 **Tight/high**: Drunk; intoxicated.

155/11 A **skinful**: Enough alcohol to make a person very drunk. □ He must have drunk a skinful to do something so foolish.

155/12 **Well-oiled** *or* **half-seas-over**: Drunk. □ By ten-o'clock he was well oiled (half-seas-over).

155/13 **Canned/stoned/stewed/pickled/sloshed/sozzled/pissed** (*#?*)/**soused/ plastered**: Drunk. □ He got canned (stoned/pissed etc.) in the bar. □ His wife warned him not to come home pickled (sloshed etc.).

155/14 **Smashed/blotto/paralytic/legless**: Very drunk. □ He can't get home on his own, he's smashed (blotto/paralytic/legless).

155/15 Drunk **out of one's senses/mind**: Madly or foolishly drunk. A colloquialism for 'drunk' is often used with this. □ The bandsmen were pissed out of their minds (senses) and couldn't play the tune.

155/16 **Stinking drunk/steaming drunk**: Very drunk.

155/17 **Drunk as a newt**: Very drunk. The newt or salamander walks in an unstable wobbly way on land, as if drunk. The colloquialism is often reinforced by replacing 'drunk' with one of its synonyms above, e.g. 'pissed as a newt'.

155/18 **Drunk as a lord:** Very drunk. A slightly more formal version of 'drunk as a newt'.

155/19 **On the tiles:** Stay out late for enjoyment, usually drinking heavily. □ We spent a night on the tiles.

155/20 **A piss-up** (*#?*): A bout of heavy drinking.

155/21 **A bender:** A bout of very heavy drinking. □ When Jürgen was dismissed from his job, he went on a bender.

155/22 **Have the DTs** (*pr. 'dee-tees'*): Suffer from delirium tremens, a form of delirium caused by heavy drinking and characterized by shaking and illusions. □ When she gets the DTs, she can't even hold a glass in her hand.

156: SOBRIETY/SOBER UP

156/1 **A teetotaller:** A person abstaining totally from alcoholic drinks. □ Don't offer Julia any wine, she's a teetotaller.

156/2 **Stone-cold sober** *or* **sober as a judge:** Completely sober. □ I thought Torsten was drunk, but he was sober as a judge (stone-cold sober).

156/3 **On the (water-)wagon:** Abstaining from alcohol. □ I've been on the wagon (water-wagon) three months now.

156/4 **A hang-over:** A severe headache or other unpleasant side-effects from drinking a lot of alcohol. □ Much work-time is lost through hang-overs.

156/5 **The morning after (the night before):** A morning when one suffers the unpleasant side-effects of heavy drinking on the previous evening. □ He's not feeling well this morning? It's probably the morning after the night before. □ I've got that morning-after feeling.

156/6 **A mouth like the bottom of a parrot's cage:** A dry, bitter mouth after a period of drinking. □ I had a mouth like the bottom of a parrot's cage this morning.

157: SMOKING

157/1 **Baccy:** Tobacco. □ I've got no baccy for my pipe.

157/2 **A drag:** A puff at a cigarette or pipe. □ The soldier gave the wounded man a few drags at his cigarette.

157/3 **A smoke:** A cigarette or cigar. □ He's always asking for smokes.

157/4 **A tab/fag/ciggy/butt** (*US*): A cigarette. □ The car floor was covered in fag (tab/ciggy/butt) ends. □ Want a fag (tab/ciggy/butt)?

157/5　**A gasper:**　Jocular (and now somewhat dated) name for a cigarette. □ Ignacio runs around with a gasper hanging from his mouth.

157/6　**A rollie:**　A self-rolled cigarette.

157/7　**A chain-smoker:**　A person who smokes one cigarette after another in continuous succession.

157/8　**Smoke like a (factory) chimney:**　Smoke excessively. □ Carmen smokes like a chimney (factory chimney).

158: DRUGS

158/1　**Dope:**　Drugs. □ Several athletes have been suspended for taking dope. □ The mountain trail was used by dope-smugglers.

158/2　**Grass/weed/pot:**　Marijuana. □ He sometimes smokes grass.

158/3　**A joint/reefer:**　A marijuana cigarette. □ Pass me the joint.

158/4　**Coke:**　Cocaine.

158/5　**Hash:**　Hashish.

158/6　**Acid:**　The drug LSD.

158/7　**Speed:**　An amphetamine drug.

158/8　**A fix:**　An addict's injection or dose of narcotic drugs. □ Addicts will steal or even kill for a fix.

158/9　**A trip:**　A visionary experience caused by a drug.

158/10　**A junkie:**　A drug addict.

158/11　**A pusher:**　A person who sells (pushes) drugs; a drug dealer.

158/12　**Freak out:**　Have hallucinations from narcotic drugs.

158/13　**Cold turkey:**　A sudden withdrawal of narcotic drugs from an addict as a form of treatment. □ Going 'cold turkey' has unpleasant side-effects.

EXERCISES 25 – EATING/DRINKING

A) From the module, insert a colloquial verb of action or motion to complete the following sentences.

1) She . . . up a meal for the family while her husband did the cleaning.
2) He . . . back two large vodkas to recover from the shock.
3) She is . . . a birthday party next week.

→

4) When he is depressed, he . . . the bottle.
5) Let's . . . the town red to celebrate your promotion!
6) I repaired her puncture, and in return she . . . me a drink in the bar.
7) Who has . . . off the strawberries I left in the fridge?
8) I've had no time to . . . a meal all day.
9) Rather than wait for the latecomers to arrive, let's . . . in to the dinner before it gets cold.

B) Give colloquialisms for the definitions below.

1) a potato. 2) a person who eats or drinks at the expense of others. 3) a good, hearty eater. 4) cheap or inferior wine. 5) tea. 6) crude alcoholic liquor. 7) champagne. 8) false courage induced by drinking alcohol. 9) someone who smokes continually. 10) the sudden withdrawal of drugs as a form of treatment.

C) List as many colloquial synonyms as possible for the underlined words or phrases.

1) During the dinner break, I get my <u>food</u> in the canteen.
2) The tourists were <u>very drunk</u> on cheap wine.
3) He stopped working to light up a <u>cigarette</u>.
4) The children <u>greedily ate up their</u> meal and ran out to play.

D) Name the types of party or celebration described below.

1) any party or organized celebration.
2) an evening party for men only.
3) an evening party for women only.
4) a party to celebrate moving into a new house or flat.
5) a lively party with dancing.
6) a wild party.

E) Replace the following underlined superlatives with more colloquial descriptions of excess or extreme.

1) We had an <u>excellent lavish</u> meal in that restaurant.
2) The coffee was <u>very hot</u>.
3) Your dinner has become <u>very cold</u>, I'll warm it in the oven.
4) He eats <u>excessively</u>.
5) She smokes <u>excessively</u>.
6) Yesterday he was drunk, but today he is <u>extremely sober</u>.
7) After last night's party, I had a <u>very dry and bitter mouth</u> this morning.
8) I <u>am very hungry</u>.
9) He is as drunk as <u>it is possible to be</u>.

213

Life/Death

159: LIVE

159/1   **Alive and kicking:** Very much alive and active. □ Grandfather is ninety-four, but still very much alive and kicking.

159/2   **Hang out** somewhere: Have one's home or residence somewhere; spend one's time somewhere. □ The doctor hangs out in the cottage at the end of the road. □ Where do you usually hang out during the day?

159/3   **In all my born days:** In all my life. □ In all my born days, I have never seen such a thing.

159/4   **See how the other half lives:** Experience the life style of a different social class. □ We spent one night in a top hotel frequented by millionaires and film stars, just to see how the other half lives.

159/5   **Civvy Street:** Civilian life, as opposed to life in the army. □ In the USSR, the end of the 'Cold War' created problems of housing and work, as thousands of soldiers came on to Civvy Street.

159/6   **Live up to** principles: Live or behave in accordance with rules or principles. □ Top managers often preach pay restraint to workers, without living up to it themselves.

159/7   **Live it up:** Live in a lively extravagant way. □ The robbers are now living it up in South America.

159/8   **You can't take it with you!:** One may as well enjoy one's personal possessions while one lives. □ Before Mrs Morita died, she used up all her savings on round-the-world cruises, following the motto that you can't take it with you.

159/9   **Sow one's wild oats:** Lead a wild, undisciplined life in one's youth before settling down and becoming more steady. Wild oats are weeds deceptively similar to real oats, and to sow them would be wasting one's time with a worthless occupation. □ Giorgio was middle-aged and clean-living, having sown his wild oats during a nomadic youth.

159/10 **Lead the life of Reilly:** Live an easy life of plenty. □ The old man used to complain about how hardened criminals were leading the life of Reilly in gaol.

159/11 **A dog's life:** A life of misery and harassment. □ I've so many problems, it's a dog's life.

159/12 **Get by:** Manage to survive or get what one needs. □ We just get by on my husband's wage. □ In Algeria, you can usually get by in French if you don't know Arabic.

159/13 Make ends meet: Keep one's expenditure within one's income; live within one's means. □ Many people on fixed incomes are finding it increasingly difficult to make ends meet.

159/14 Keep one's head above water: Earn just enough money to cover one's expenditure or live. □ Our business has a small turnover, but we still manage to keep our heads above water.

159/15 Keep the wolf from the door: Ward off hunger or starvation; survive in spite of debts or expenditure. □ Her divorce settlement amounted to a million dollars, which should keep the wolf from the door for a while.

159/16 Eke (*pr. 'eek'*) **out a living** *or* **scrape a living:** Be just able to exist or make a living; survive with difficulty. □ The islanders eked out (scratched/scraped) a living by fishing and growing potatoes.

159/17 Scrape along: Just manage to survive. □ We have to scrape along on our pensions.

159/18 Rough it: Do without ordinary comforts; live in rough or primitive conditions. □ When the river overflowed its banks and flooded the town, many families had to rough it temporarily in emergency tents.

159/19 Fend for oneself: Look after oneself or survive. □ My husband will have to fend for himself while I'm in hospital.

159/20 In a rut: Leading a settled, stable but boringly predictable life. □ I was getting into a rut, commuting to a nine-to-five job from a house in the suburbs, so I decided to get out of it and emigrate to Canada.

159/21 Live in a fool's paradise: Live a life of happiness that is based on illusion and could collapse at any time; live in temporary or insecure prosperity. □ Several states in the Arabian Gulf have realized that to rely solely on oil for income would be to live in a fool's paradise.

159/22 Live in Cloud-Cuckoo-Land: Live in an imaginary world that bears no relation to reality. □ If you think he'll do it, you're living in Cloud-Cuckoo-Land!

160: YOUTH

160/1 A tot: A small child. □ We have organized a play-group for tots.

160/2 A toddler: A child who has only recently learned to walk.

160/3 A nipper: A young boy or girl. □ That was a long time ago and you were still a nipper.

160/4 A kid/kiddie: A child. □ There is nowhere for the kids (kiddies) to play in this neighbourhood.

160/5 A teeny-bopper: A young immature teenager.

160/6 A whipper-snapper: A young insignificant person who behaves like an important person. □ I'll have no whipper-snapper telling me what to do!

160/7 A brat: An ungrateful, unpleasant or naughty child. □ Mrs Estrupp's children are all brats.

161: OLD/THE PAST

161/1   **Getting on:** Advanced in years. □ My parents are getting on now.

161/2   **Getting on for** *or* **pushing** *or* **knocking:** Approaching the age of. □ He must be getting on for (pushing/knocking) fifty by now.

161/3   **(On) the wrong side of forty:** Over forty years of age. □ I'm (on) the wrong side of forty.

161/4   **Have known/seen better days:** Be no longer in good condition owing to old age. □ My car has seen better days.

161/5   **Have had one's day:** Have had one's most successful period behind one in the past; be on the decline. □ I've had my day; it's time to retire from work. □ Communism has had its day.

161/6   **Past it:** Too old to be able to do something; old and useless. □ I used to be able to walk up that hill, but I'm past it now. □ My spin-drier is past it.

161/7   **Put out to grass:** Make someone retire because of age. □ Mr Tanaka told his boss that at fifty he was too young to be put out to grass.

161/8   **Long in the tooth:** Rather old. □ I'm a bit long in the tooth to take up cycling as a hobby.

161/9   **Be no (spring) chicken:** Be no longer young. □ Sanchez may be old to get married, but his bride is no spring chicken either.

161/10   **Have had a good innings:** Have had a long life or career. An 'innings' is a cricketing term for the period a player spends batting and scoring runs. □ My business partner decided that he'd had a good innings, and that he would retire.

161/11   **There's life in the old dog yet:** Be still full of energy in spite of old age. □ Don't think I'm too old to swim that river, there's life in the old dog yet.

161/12   **An oldie:** An old person or thing.

161/13   **A geezer:** Rather unkind name for a person or old man. □ He's just a bad-tempered old geezer.

161/14   **An old codger:** Rather unkind term for an old fellow. □ The silly old codger won't open his door to anyone.

161/15   **An old dodderer:** An old person, especially someone trembling with age or infirmity.

161/16   **An old bag** *or* **an old trout:** An objectionable or unpleasant old woman.

161/17   **An old fogey:** A person with old-fashioned ideas; an old grumbler. □ Our company needs to replace the old fogies in top management with young blood.

161/18   **A fuddy-duddy:** A pleasantly old-fashioned person who is unable to accept new ideas. □ My parents are fuddy-duddies.

161/19   **Old hat:** Something that is old-fashioned or out-of-date; something uninteresting or too well known through long use. □ That joke is old hat. □ Weekly newspapers tend to contain a lot of old hat.

161/20 **Olde-worlde** (*pr. 'oldy-worldy'*):   Having an old-fashioned atmosphere or appearance, especially when artificially created; reminiscent of the past or a bygone age. □ Gouda in Holland has an olde-worlde town centre with its Renaissance churches and medieval merchants' houses.

161/21 **Take** someone **back**:   Remind a person of a past time or event. □ That song takes me back to my youth.

161/22 **Drag up** the past: Revive some scandal or problematic issue that had been forgotten. □ Many young Germans resent people continually dragging up their country's Nazi past.

162: DIE

162/1 **Be on one's/its last legs**:   Be on the verge of collapse or death. □ The old man is on his last legs. □ The company is almost bankrupt and on its last legs.

162/2 **Live on borrowed time**:   Be liable to die at any moment. □ A year ago, the doctor gave Marcel only six months to live, so he's living on borrowed time now.

162/3 **Have one foot in the grave**:   Be very old or near to death. □ She is ill with cancer and has one foot in the grave.

162/4 **A goner**:   A person or thing that is dead, doomed or ruined. (*See also 18/17*) □ Any crash at that speed and all passengers are a goner. □ If my business doesn't win this contract, I'm a goner.

162/5 **Have had it**:   Be near death; be irreparable or no longer usable. (*See also 18/17 and 76/15*) □ After being left in the rain, the transistor radio had had it. □ There is no chance of the patient's recovery; she's had it, I'm afraid.

162/6 **Have had one's chips**:   Die; be defeated or suffer. □ No one could have survived a plane crash like that; the passengers have certainly had their chips. □ If the city falls to the enemy, we'll have had our chips.

162/7 **Curtains for** someone: Death or the end for someone. (*See also 18/18*) □ If you fall from this height, it's curtains for you.

162/8 Someone's **number is up**:   Someone is going to die, suffer or be punished. □ Those poor children are infected with AIDS and their numbers are up. □ When the police arrested the burglar he knew his number was up.

162/9 Someone's **days are numbered**:   Someone has not long to live or remain in a present position. □ After that scandal, his days as a member of parliament are numbered. □ The illness has got worse and her days are now numbered.

162/10 **Kick the bucket**:   Die. The expression probably alludes to the bucket on which a suicidal person stands before kicking it away to hang himself. □ With my heart condition, I could kick the bucket at any time.

162/11 **Snuff it/buy it**: Die or be killed. □ Many World War I soldiers snuffed it (bought it) in the trenches.

162/12 **Give up the ghost** *or* **pop off** *or* **peg out**: Die. □ My old dog quietly popped off (gave up the ghost/pegged out) in the night.

162/13 **Come to a sticky end**: Come to an unpleasant end or death; be punished or suffer. □ The climber came to a sticky end on the north wall of the Eiger. □ One day that rogue will be caught and come to a sticky end.

162/14 **Swing**: Be executed by hanging. □ I believe that all murderers of policemen should swing.

162/15 **Push up (the) daisies**: Be dead. □ My uncle is no longer with us, he's pushing up the daisies.

162/16 **Dead as a dodo** *or* **dead as mutton** *or* **dead as a door-nail**: Dead beyond doubt; incapable of being revived or brought back to life. The dodo was a large non-flying bird on Mauritius that became extinct in the 18th century. □ That snake can't bite you, it's as dead as a dodo (dead as mutton/as a door-nail).

162/17 **A stiff**: A corpse or dead body. □ All stiffs from road accidents are taken to the county morgue.

163: KILL

163/1 **Send** someone **to kingdom come**: Send to the next world; kill or destroy. □ If the ammunition factory were to explode, it would send half the neighbourhood to kingdom come.

163/2 **Do in** *or* **polish off** *or* **finish off** someone: Kill or ruin. □ Nazar threatened to do me in for taking his girlfriend. □ Cheap foreign imports are polishing off (finishing off/doing in) our industry.

163/3 **Rub out** *or* **bump off** *or* **take out** or **waste** *(US)* *or* **snuff** someone: Kill or murder. □ The dictator was taken out (bumped off/rubbed out/wasted/snuffed) by an army officer during a military parade.

163/4 **Do away with** *or* **get shot of** someone: Kill or get rid of. □ The 'Yakuza' are Japanese gangsters who often do away with (get shot of) their rivals in ritualized murders.

163/5 **A hit man**: A hired murderer or assassin.

163/6 **A hit list**: A list of people to be murdered; a list of things against which action is to be taken. □ One of the terrorists had a hit list of top judges. □ The government has a secret hit list of schools which are to be closed.

163/7 **End it all**: Commit suicide. □ As the illness progressed, she decided to end it all under a train.

163/8 **Top oneself**: Commit suicide, usually by hanging. □ Enrique threatened to top himself if she should leave him.

163/9   **Put** an animal **down** *or* **put** an animal **to sleep**:   Have an animal
destroyed.   □ If we can't find homes for the stray cats, they are put
down (put to sleep).

EXERCISES 26 – LIFE/DEATH

A) Complete the following sentences with the missing noun.

1) He had wasted his youth sowing his wild . . . .
2) At the age of 85, Mr Gomez has had a good . . . already.
3) Ricardo is no longer with us, he's pushing up . . . in the cemetery.
4) The use of valves in radios will soon be as dead as . . . .
5) If he believes that his health will not be affected by heavy smoking,
he is living in a fool's . . . .
6) She is getting a bit long in the . . . to go camping.
7) After twenty years in the same boring job, he had got into a . . . .
8) I won't tell you how old I am, but I'm no spring . . . .

B) Give colloquialisms for the definitions below.

1) civilian life compared to life in the army. 2) a hired murderer.
3) something that is old and well known or boring. 4) a person with
old-fashioned ideas. 5) over 40 years of age. 6) an unpleasant old
woman. 7) a young immature teenager. 8) having an old-fashioned
atmosphere or appearance. 9) very much alive and active. 10) a
pleasant life of luxury.

C) Replace the underlined words or phrases with as many colloquial
synonyms as possible.

1) He is <u>approaching</u> 65 now.
2) She <u>died</u> last night.
3) The feud between the two men reached the stage where one
threatened to <u>kill</u> the other.
4) The family <u>just managed to survive</u> on four small rice fields.
5) The injured woman <u>is near to death</u>.

D) Complete the following phrases or phrasal verbs with the missing
adverb.

1) He has a flat in Milan, that's where he hangs . . . .
2) The dog is too old and sick, and will have to be put . . . .
3) You should live . . . to your principles!
4) That old photo certainly takes me . . . !
5) If he crashes at that speed, then his number is . . . .
6) He wasted all the money he had received on living it . . . .

Society

164: FRIENDSHIP/ASSOCIATION

164/1 **A fair-weather friend**: A superficial friend, whose friendship extends only to the good times. □ Don't count upon fair-weather friends!

164/2 **A pal/chum/mate/buddy**: A friend. □ I went out with a few mates (buddies/pals/chums).

164/3 **A side-kick** (*US*): A close associate; a member of a group or pair.

164/4 **A crony**: A close friend or companion; a partner, especially in crime. □ Keep away from that gangster and his cronies!

164/5 **Chum/pal up** with someone: Become friends with. □ The two of us palled (chummed) up at work. □ I refuse to pal (chum) up with him.

164/6 **Pally/chummy/matey** with someone: Very friendly with. □ He is pally (chummy/matey) with the boss.

164/7 **Hob-nob with** *or* **rub shoulders with** someone: Socialize or associate with someone. □ She hob-nobs with royalty. □ In the course of my work, I've rubbed shoulders with many criminals.

164/8 **Keep in with** someone: Remain on good or friendly terms with someone; keep a person's favour or good will. □ Such influential people could be useful to you later, so keep in with them!

164/9 **One of the boys**: An accepted member of a group or association. □ With Los Angeles street gangs, tattooing signifies who is one of the boys.

164/10 **Hail-fellow-well-met with**: Very friendly towards strangers. □ David's a very hail-fellow-well-met sort of person; you'll like him.

164/11 **Get on (with)**: Enjoy a friendly relationship with someone. □ We get on reasonably well with our new neighbours.

164/12 **Get on like a house on fire**: Get on extremely well together. *(See also 22/12)* □ My son has got on like a house on fire with the pupils at his new school.

164/13 **A get-together**: A social gathering. □ We are organizing a get-together of new tenants in the block.

164/14 **Thick as thieves**: Strongly bonded to each other by friendship or association. □ If you have a problem with one gypsy, you have problems with all of them, they are as thick as thieves.

164/15 **In cahoots with** someone: In league with; acting in close association or conspiracy with. □ In this city, many policemen are in cahoots with organized crime.

164/16 **Friends at court**: Friends or associates in influential places who can help one. □ Marcus got his job through friends at court.

164/17 **Pull strings/wires**: Use one's influence, often secretly, in favour of oneself or another person. □ There is a long waiting-list for membership of that club and the only way to join quickly is to pull strings (wires).

164/18 **Scratch my back and I'll scratch yours!**: If you promote my interests or do me a favour, I will do likewise!

164/19 **Back-scratching**: The granting of favours in return for a reciprocal service. □ The politician got to the top of the party not through merit, but by back-scratching.

164/20 The **old-boy network**: A class or persons from a shared and privileged educational background, usually from private schools, who promote each other's interests. □ In several developing countries, the civil service is riddled with nepotism and the old-boy network.

164/21 **Jobs for the boys**: The granting of jobs or positions to persons of the same social class or group. □ It must be jobs for the boys – the boss is a Freemason and so are his new sales and finance directors.

164/22 **Not let the side down**: Do one's best for the group or association to which one belongs; justify the trust placed in oneself by a group. □ In our family, there is a tradition of sons taking over the farm from their fathers, and I hope my son won't let the side down.

164/23 **Rub off on** someone: (Of mental qualities or behaviour) transfer to someone casually through close association. □ We own a bar, and we hope that the bad language our children often hear won't rub off on them.

165: THE FAMILY

165/1 **Hubby**: Someone's husband. □ What does hubby think of the idea? □ Wives can bring their hubbies along.

165/2 **Pa/papa**: Father. 'Papa' is an informal term used with, or by children. □ I'll ask Pa (Papa) tonight.

165/3 **Dad/daddy** *or* **Pop**: Father. 'Daddy' is a child's term. □ Don't forget to tell your dad (daddy/pop).

165/4 The/someone's **old man**: Someone's father; (occasionally) husband. □ Here comes your old man.

165/5 The/someone's **missus**: Someone's wife. □ That woman is his missus. □ I can't wait to tell the missus.

165/6 **Ma/mam(my)/mum(my)**: Mother. 'Mammy'/'mummy' is a child's term. □ This little girl has lost her mum (ma) in the crowd.

165/7 **Gran(ny)/Gran(d)ma**: Grandmother.

165/8 **Gran(d)pa**: Grandfather. □ We're going to visit gran (granny) and granpa.

165/9 **Our kid**: My younger brother. □ Our kid is still at school.

165/10 **Sis**: Shortened colloquial form of 'sister'. □ He's got a little sis.

165/11 **In-laws**: A person's relatives by marriage. □ Some of my in-laws helped me set up in business.

165/12 Someone's **folks**: Someone's family, parents or relatives. □ Give my regards to your folks when you get back home!

166: DISSOCIATION/UNFRIENDLY

166/1 **Give** someone **the cold shoulder**: Be deliberately unfriendly towards someone. □ I had a row with my uncle and now he's giving me the cold shoulder.

166/2 **Give** someone **the brush-off**: Reject someone sharply; snub. □ Nathalie slammed the door in my face. I think she's giving me the brush-off.

166/3 **Send** someone **to Coventry**: Refuse to speak to, or associate with someone. During the English Civil War (1642–1646) the most difficult royalist prisoners were sent to Cromwell's stronghold at Coventry. □ The strike-breaker was sent to Coventry by his work-mates.

166/4 **Have no truck with** someone: Have no dealings with someone. □ Many countries of the British Commonwealth had no truck with the apartheid regime in South Africa.

166/5 **Not touch** someone/something **with a barge-pole** or . . . **ten-foot pole** (*US*): Refuse to have anything to do with something. □ The stolen jewellery can be easily identified, and no reputable dealer would touch it with a barge-pole (with a ten-foot pole).

166/6 **Give** someone/something **a wide berth**: Refuse to have anything to do with something or someone; keep a person at a safe distance. □ He is very angry with you and you should give him a wide berth.

166/7 **Avoid** someone/something **like the plague**: Stay well away from something abhorrent or harmful. □ Since Wolfgang was bitten, he avoids dogs like the plague.

166/8 **Not be seen dead** (doing/with/in): Avoid something shameful or distasteful. □ Veronika wouldn't be seen dead in a bikini, she's too fat.

166/9 **Send** someone **packing**: Send someone away abruptly. □ Kazimir came asking me for money again, but I sent him packing.

166/10 **Freeze** someone **out**: Exclude from business or social dealings. □ The large companies are trying to freeze out small businesses.

166/11 (Leave) someone **out in the cold**: Ignore or neglect. □ One by one, Honneker's former supporters in East Germany denounced him, and soon the party chief was left out in the cold.

166/12 **Opt out of** something: Choose not to participate in something. □ Muslim children often opt out of Christian morning services in schools.

166/13 **Keep oneself to oneself**: Avoid meeting people or socializing. □ The Amish are a religious sect in the USA that keep themselves to themselves, in order to keep out harmful modern influences.

166/14 **I'm all right, Jack!**: The motto of a selfish individual who would promote his own interests even to the detriment of his friends or others. □ At a time of mass unemployment, those in work shouldn't adopt an 'I'm all right, Jack!' attitude.

166/15 A **bad mixer**: Someone who is unsociable or who doesn't get on well with others (as opposed to 'a good mixer').

166/16 A **drop-out**: A person who abandons a course of study or conventional society. □ He's a high-school drop-out. □ Life in the city is so hectic, it's enough to make you live as a drop-out on a desert island.

166/17 A **lone wolf** *or* a **loner**: A person who lives alone and prefers not to associate with others.

166/18 A **one-man band/show**: Someone who refuses help or does everything alone. □ My business is a one-man band (one-man show), because I can't afford to employ staff.

166/19 **On one's tod/toddy**: On one's own; unaided or unaccompanied by others. □ I prefer to work on my tod (toddy).

167: HIERARCHY/SOCIAL STATUS

167/1 **The pecking order**: The order of importance in a given social group or hierarchy. □ Mr Cabrillo got a higher salary increase than you, because he's higher in the pecking order.

167/2 Someone's **opposite number**: A person holding a similar position to someone in another group or organization. □ The American Secretary of State got on the hot-line to speak to his opposite number in the Kremlin.

167/3 **Pull rank**: Make unfair use of one's senior rank or status to demand obedience or obtain privileges. □ Councillors who are not on official business have no right to borrow a car and shouldn't attempt to pull rank with attendants in the city car-pool.

167/4 **Kick** someone **upstairs**: Promote a person to a nominally higher position, which is in fact less influential, in order to get rid of him or her. □ The production engineer had only a few years to retirement but was making serious mistakes, so he was kicked upstairs to a desk job where he could do no damage.

167/5 The **upper crust**: The aristocracy or upper layers of society. □ High-ranking army officers and communist party officials belonged to the upper crust of Soviet society.

167/6 A **Colonel Blimp**: An extremely conservative person, opposed to reform; a pompous establishment figure. □ Women's suffrage had always been opposed by Colonel Blimps.

167/7 **A double-barrelled name**:   A surname composed of two separate family names, sometimes linked by a hyphen. □ He has one of those double-barrelled names, Worthington-Smithe or something like it.

167/8 **The jet-set**:   Wealthy people who make frequent air journeys between social and business events. This activity is described as 'jet-setting' and the person, a 'jet-setter'.

167/9 **Rank-and-file** *or* **grass roots**:   Ordinary members of a political party or other group. □ Policies approved by the party leadership are not always popular with the rank-and-file (grass roots).

167/10 **Plebs**:   Colloquial form of 'plebeians' or the lower social classes. □ Since Isolde was promoted, she doesn't talk to us plebs any more.

167/11 **A rat-race** *or* **dog-eat-dog**:   A ruthless, ambitious race for positions and social status. □ I didn't like working for that company – it was dog-eat-dog (a rat-race) all the time.

167/12 **Keep up with the Joneses**:   Strive to remain on the same social level as one's neighbours, or at least give that appearance. □ When neighbours started adding conservatories to their houses, we decided to keep up with the Joneses and commissioned one ourselves.

167/13 **Peer pressure**:   Pressure to imitate the conduct of members of the same age group or social class as oneself. □ Peer pressure forces many teenagers into drugs and crime.

167/14 **Upset the apple-cart**:   Upset the established order or hierarchy; spoil a situation or someone's plans. □ It looked like a good year for the travel industry, and then the Gulf crisis upset the apple-cart.

167/15 **Rock the boat**:   Upset the plans or progress of one's group. □ OPEC has fixed oil-prices for the year and will take action against any member country that rocks the boat by undercutting them.

168: CONTROL/RULE/SUBMIT

168/1 **Call the shots** *or* **run the show**:   Make the decisions; be in control. □ After Britain's withdrawal in 1997, the Chinese authorities will call the shots (run the show) in Hong Kong.

168/2 **Rule the roost**:   Be the dominant person or authority. □ At home, it's his wife that rules the roost.

168/3 **The top dog**:   The master or victor; the chief person in a group. □ That manager is top dog in the sales division.

168/4 **Have** someone **in the palm of one's hand** *or* **have** someone **under one's thumb**:   Have someone completely under one's influence. □ I have him in the palm of my hand (under my thumb); he'll do as I say.

168/5 **Like putty in** someone's **hands**:   Easily influenced or controlled by someone. □ When he turns on the charm, she's like putty in his hands.

168/6 **Twist** someone **around one's little finger**:   Be able to control a person's actions or compel someone to obey. □ Rasputin was reputed to have magic powers and could twist the Czarina around his little finger.

168/7 **Have** someone **by the short and curlies** *or* **have** someone **over a barrel** *or* **have** someone **on toast:** Have someone at one's mercy or at a hopeless disadvantage. □ The economic boycott against the former Rhodesia had the country by the short and curlies (over a barrel).

168/8 **Eat humble pie:** Submit humbly or make a humble apology. The expression dates back to the 11th century when the innards or 'umbles' of a deer were fed to the servants or menials. □ The boxer boasted that he would win the fight easily; after his defeat he had to eat humble pie.

168/9 **Knuckle under:** Yield or submit to someone. □ The government will not knuckle under to terrorism.

168/10 **Toe the line:** Conform to the requirements of one's group or party, especially under compulsion. □ Under Brezhnev, Eastern European countries were forced to toe the Russian line.

168/11 **Hen-pecked:** Dominated by a nagging wife. □ Salim can't make any decision without consulting his wife, he's too hen-pecked.

168/12 An **underdog:** A person, organization or country in an inferior or subordinate position. □ Our country is poor and can only export raw materials, which makes us the underdog when it comes to trading with the industrialized world.

168/13 A **stooge:** A person whose actions are entirely controlled by another. □ At the conference, it was claimed that the presidents of several countries in Central America were stooges of the USA.

EXERCISES 27 – SOCIETY

A) Complete the following sentences with a proper noun (i.e. the name of a person, city etc.) or a hyphenated expression.

1) He is honest and wouldn't touch stolen property with a . . . - . . . .
2) They buy a new car every year to impress their neighbours and keep up with the . . . .
3) Some people have an I'm-all-right- . . . philosophy of life and care only about themselves.
4) He is too familiar with complete strangers, who sometimes find his . . . - . . . - . . . - . . . attitude amusing.
5) Many workers remain silent about misconduct by colleagues, so as not to upset the . . . - . . . and spoil relations with them.
6) He is a typical . . . - . . . husband and does everything his wife says.
7) My neighbours are not speaking to me for some reason, and I think that I've been sent to . . . .
8) He knew some former pupils from his old school who worked in the firm, and got the job through the . . . - . . . network. →

225

B) Give colloquialisms for the definitions below.

1) the granting of favours to someone in return for services.
2) a husband.
3) someone who lives alone and does not associate with others.
4) the order of importance in a hierarchy.
5) a surname made up of two separate family names.
6) someone who does everything by himself, without help from others.
7) the ordinary members of an organization.
8) a ruthless race for jobs or prestige.
9) the person who does the same job as you, but for a different company.
10) a person whose actions are completely under the control of another.

C) Replace the underlined word or phrase with as many colloquial synonyms as possible.

1) Luc is a <u>friend</u> of his.
2) Small shopkeepers like ourselves cannot compete with large supermarkets, which <u>have us at their mercy</u>.
3) He once craved for alcohol, but now he <u>avoids it completely</u>.

D) Complete the following colloquial similes with a word or phrase from the module.

1) At work he is well liked by staff, and gets on like a ... ... with the customers.
2) Few policemen would testify in court against another; they are as thick as ... .
3) Air-travel makes her ill, and she avoids it like the ... .
4) The teacher controls his pupils well and they are like ... in his ... .

E) Replace the underlined text with a phrasal verb (i.e. a verb + adverb) or an adverbial expression.

1) He did it <u>on his own</u> without any help.
2) The landlord is demanding that we vacate our flat, but we have a right to stay and we won't <u>give in</u> to pressure.
3) My parents sent me to a different school where they hoped that the more diligent attitude to study would <u>influence</u> me.
4) I want to <u>remain on friendly terms</u> with them, so I can't do what you ask.
5) They don't socialize with our neighbours and keep <u>themselves apart</u>.
6) Some fishermen who catch more fish than their legal quota are able to sell the catch by acting <u>in league</u> with port officials.

MODULE

28

People/Clothes

169: NATIONALITY/RACE

169/1   A **Chink** (*#??*): A Chinese person.

169/2   A **Nip** (*#??*)/a **Jap** (*#?*): A Japanese person.

169/3   A **gook** (*#??*) (*#US*): An oriental person, especially someone of Chinese or Japanese appearance.

169/4   A **Yank/Yankee** (*#?*): An American. The term is thought to be a corruption of 'Jan Kaas', a contemptuous nickname given by English settlers in America to Dutchmen.

169/5   A **Russky** (*#?*): A Russian.

169/6   A **Kiwi**: A New Zealander.

169/7   An **Aussie**: An Australian.

169/8   A **pom/pommie**: In Australia and New Zealand, a term for a Briton, especially a recent immigrant.

169/9   A **Limey** (*US*): US term for a Briton. Lime-juice used to be issued to British sailors in order to prevent scurvy, a vitamin-deficiency disease.

169/10   A **Jock**: A Scotsman.

169/11   A **Taff**: A Welshman.

169/12   A **Paddy** (*#?*)/a **Mick** (*#?*): An Irishman.

169/13   An **Eyetie** (*#??*): An Italian.

169/14   A **dago** (*#??*): A person from Southern Europe.

169/15   A **wop** (*#??*): A person from Southern Europe, especially an Italian.

169/16   A **wog** (*#??*): A foreigner, especially if coloured or from the Middle East.

169/17   A **wet-back** (*#?*) (*#US*): An illegal immigrant from Mexico, especially one that enters America by crossing the Rio Grande on the Mexican border.

169/18   A **darky** (*#??*)/**coon** (*#??*): A negro.

169/19   A **honky** (*#?*) (*#US*): A negro term for a white person. The name derives from a colloquial term for a Hungarian immigrant in the USA.

169/20   A **Yid** (*#??*)/**sheeny** (*#US*) (*#??*)/**kike** (*#US*) (*#??*): A Jewish person.

169/21   A **Jew boy** (*#??*): A Jewish male.

169/22   A **Jerry/Kraut** (*#??*): A German.

169/23   A **Polack** (*#??*): A Pole.

169/24   A **Frog/Froggie** (*#??*): A Frenchman.

227

170: PERSONS

170/1   A **chap/guy**:   A man. □ Okay guys (chaps), let's go! □ A guy (chap) gave me a lift here.

170/2   A **wallah**:   A person employed or concerned in a specific task or occupation. □ Those men are plumbing wallahs.

170/3   **Yours truly**:   Me or myself. □ Guess who they chose: yours truly!

170/4   **Number one**:   Oneself. □ Tibor doesn't care who gets a seat in the train, as long as number one does.

170/5   A **brick**:   A kind-hearted person. □ You're a brick for helping me out.

170/6   A **live wire**:   An energetic, lively person who is full of initiative.

170/7   A **son-of-a-gun**:   Humorous term for a person. □ The son-of-a-gun has beaten me in golf again.

170/8   A **dog** or a **bod** or a **beggar**:   (Used in combination with an adjective) a person. □ He's a sly dog (beggar/bod). □ She's a lucky beggar (dog/bod). □ They are dirty dogs (beggars/bods).

170/9   A **sea dog**:   An experienced sailor. □ I'm no sea dog, I always feel ill on boats.

170/10   A **tough cookie/baby**:   A physically or mentally hard person. □ He has a reputation among businessmen as a tough cookie (baby) who always gets the best price.

170/11   A **rough diamond**:   A good-natured but rough-mannered person.

170/12   A **rubberneck** (*#US*):   An inquisitive person or a gaping sightseer. To behave in this manner is to 'rubberneck'. □ A crowd of rubbernecks stood watching the demolition of the building.

170/13   **Who is** someone **when** he's **at home?**:   Request for information about someone, with the suggestion that the person is not so important or famous as is claimed. □ "She must be good, she has a reference from Doctor Schuhmacher personally." "Well, who's he when he's at home?"

170/14   **Man or beast**:   Anyone. Usually preceded by 'no good to' or 'useless to'. □ This stuff's no good to man or beast – throw it away!

170/15   **Joe Public/Joe Bloggs** or **the man in the street**:   An ordinary or average person. □ Inflation always hits the man in the street (Joe Bloggs/Joe Public) hardest.

170/16   **Tom, Dick and Harry**:   Ordinary people; people taken at random. □ If the story gets into the newspapers, every Tom, Dick and Harry will know about it.

171: NEGATIVE TYPES OF PERSON

171/1   A **son-of-a-bitch** (*#??*):   An unpleasant person.

171/2 A **so-and-so**: (To avoid using a vulgar or nasty word) an unpleasant or objectionable person. (*See also 135/1*) □ I loaned him my camera, and the so-and-so has lost it.

171/3 **Get** (*#??*)/**Git** (*#??*)/**creep**/**bastard** (*#??*)/**wanker** (*#??*)/**mother-fucker** (*#US*) (*#??*): An unpleasant person. □ The git (bastard/creep/get etc.) played a dirty trick on me.

171/4 A **jerk** (*US*): A stupid or insignificant person.

171/5 A **waster**: A useless or good-for-nothing person. □ Alfonso doesn't want to work, he's just a waster.

171/6 A **punk**: A worthless person; a young ruffian. (Do not confuse with a fan of punk rock music.) □ The liquor store was raided by a couple of punks.

171/7 An **ugly customer** *or* a **nasty piece of work**: An unpleasant and potentially violent person. □ His bodyguard is a nasty piece of work (an ugly customer).

171/8 A **bogyman**: An imaginary man feared by children; an unpleasant nuisance. □ During the Suez crisis, President Nasser of Egypt became the bogyman of France and England.

171/9 A **perisher**: An annoying person or thing. □ The perisher forgot to tell me about the meeting.

171/10 A **blighter**: An annoying person. □ Those little blighters have been stealing from your garden again.

171/11 A **rotter** *or* a **toe-rag**: A nasty or contemptible person.

171/12 A **bounder**: A dishonest or badly mannered person. □ The bounder didn't keep his part of the deal.

171/13 A **squirt**: A small, unimportant but cheeky or arrogant person.

171/14 A **sod** (*#?*): Abusive term for a person. □ He's a stupid sod.

171/15 A **cuss**: An awkward or difficult person.

171/16 A **bird/fish/customer**: An unusual person. □ He's a strange bird (customer/ fish).

171/17 A **specimen**: An unusual or pathetic individual. □ You're a useless specimen – you can't even wash up without breaking something.

171/18 A **shower**: A contemptible or pathetic person or persons. □ Is this shower the only men you could hire for the job?

171/19 A **stick-in-the-mud**: A person who is excessively conservative and lacks initiative; someone unwilling to adopt new ideas.

171/20 A **drip**: A weak or boring person.

171/21 A **(spineless) wimp**: A feeble and ineffective person; someone lacking energy and initiative.

171/22 A **sissy**: An effeminate or cowardly person.

171/23 A **softie**: A person who is physically weak or not hardy; a soft-hearted person. □ In business, you can't afford to be a softie.

171/24 A **tomboy**: A girl who enjoys energetic activities more usually associated with boys.

171/25 A **floozy/floosy/floozie/floosie**: Whichever way you may see it spelt, it is a disreputable woman.

171/26 A **do-gooder**: A person who is well-meaning in trying to promote social work or reform, but who is unrealistic or interfering. □ Many missionaries in the third world are do-gooders who destroy ancient civilizations under the guise of introducing Western forms of religion.

171/27 A **back-seat driver**: A person with no responsibilities who is keen to give orders to someone who has. □ The problem with working in public places is that you always get back-seat drivers giving you advice.

171/28 **Old Nick**: Nickname for the Devil or Satan.

172: CLOTHES/DRESS ACCESSORIES

172/1 **Beetle-crushers**: Large shoes or boots with thick soles.

172/2 **Clod-hoppers**: Large heavy shoes.

172/3 **Clobber/gear**: Clothes (*See also 135/7*).

172/4 **Togs**: Clothes. □ I've bought some new togs.

172/5 **Glad rags**: Dress clothes or clothes for special occasions. □ Put on your glad rags for the dance tonight.

172/6 **Best bib and tucker**: A person's best clothes. The 'bib' and 'tucker' were items of clothing worn before 1700. □ The guests arrived in their best bib and tucker.

172/7 **Sunday best**: A person's best clothes kept for Sunday use. □ The whole village put on their Sunday best for the fair.

172/8 A **get-up/rig-out**: A suit, outfit or costume. □ We don't have the right get-up (rig-out) for climbing in cold conditions. □ He was dressed in a flashy get-up (rig-out).

172/9 **Hand-me-downs**: Second-hand clothes worn previously by other members of the family. □ As a young girl I never had a new dress; all I got were hand-me-downs from my older sisters.

172/10 **Long johns**: Underpants or knickers with long legs. □ In winter, many old people put on their long johns.

172/11 **Undies**: Women's underwear. □ I'll pack a fresh change of undies in the suitcase.

172/12 **Panties**: Short knickers for children or women.

172/13 **Frillies**: Light frilly female underwear.

172/14 A **nightie**: A women's nightdress.

172/15 **Drag**: Women's clothing worn by men, especially transvestites. □ Several of the bar's customers were in drag.

172/16 **Run up** clothes: Make quickly by sewing. □ The tailor will run me up a new suit. □ Mother ran up some new curtains.

172/17 **Bags**: Trousers, especially of the loose-fitting kind. □ I've spilled coffee on my bags.

172/18 A **dog-collar**: A stiff detachable collar worn by clergymen.

172/19 A **lid**: A hat. □ The wind blew his lid off.

172/20 A **woolly**: A knitted woollen garment.

172/21 A **pinny**: A pinafore or apron. □ Put on a pinny for the washing-up!

172/22 A **mac**: A mackintosh raincoat.

172/23 A **brolly**: An umbrella.

172/24 A **hanky**: A handkerchief.

172/25 **Sparklers**: Diamonds.

172/26 **Rocks**: Large precious stones. □ The princess was laden with rocks.

173: DRESS/LOOKS/FASHION

173/1 **Kit** someone **out**: Supply the dress or equipment needed for a particular activity or situation. □ We landed in snowy Alaska still kitted out for the streets of sunny California.

173/2 **Tog** oneself **up/out**: Dress or dress smartly. □ Why are you all togged-up (togged out)?

173/3 **Doll/toff** oneself **up**: Dress smartly. □ There's no need to toff (doll) yourself up for the party.

173/4 **Dressed (up) to the nines**: Dressed very elaborately or to perfection.

173/5 **Dressed to kill**: Dressed very showily or attractively. □ You're dressed to kill tonight.

173/6 **Jazz up** someone/something: Brighten up the appearance of oneself or something. □ He has jazzed himself up for the dance. □ The shop front is too dull, we must jazz it up a little.

173/7 **Posh**: Very smart *(See also 53/7)* □ She's looking very posh.

173/8 **Snazzy/natty/nifty**: Smart; stylish. *(For 'nifty', see also 83/8)* □ I've bought a snazzy (natty/nifty) suit.

173/9 **Swanky**: Boastfully smart or expensive. □ The Hashimoto family are very swanky people. □ The Plaza hotel had a swanky marble entrance.

173/10 **Fetching**: Attractive. □ That is a fetching dress.

173/11 **Trendy/funky/hip**: Stylish or fashionable; up to date. □ Trendy (funky/hip) clothes need not be expensive.

173/12 **All the rage**: Temporarily very popular or fashionable. □ Mini-skirts were all the rage in the 'sixties.

173/13 **Be in**: Be fashionable. □ That colour is not in this year.

173/14 **Be out**: Be out of fashion or unpopular. □ That hair style went out some time ago.

173/15 **Square**: Old-fashioned or conventional; lacking a taste for fashion. Someone of this nature is a 'square'. □ My father is a square.

173/16 **Corny**: Unimaginative; crude and old-fashioned. *(See also 94/18)* □ A lot of Eastern European fashion is too corny for Western tastes.

173/17 **A bobby-dazzler**: A person or thing that is extremely good-looking, fashionable or smart. □ Saskia is a beautiful girl, a real bobby-dazzler.

173/18 **A fancy pants** *or* a **dude** *(US)*: A dandy; someone characterized by showiness or display in clothes. □ He looks a proper dude (fancy pants) in that suit.

173/19 **A slicker**: A stylish townsman with a smooth but deceptive manner; a very civilized and worldly person.

173/20 **Scruffy**: Shabby and untidy. □ You can't go out looking scruffy.

173/21 **Look as if one has been in the wars**: Look bedraggled or have minor injuries. □ When her son returned from playing with the other boys, he looked as if he had been in the wars.

173/22 **Down-at-heel** *or* **out-at-elbows**: Shabbily dressed; wearing worn-out clothing or shoes. □ Some students on small grants are a little down-at-heel (out-at-elbows).

173/23 **A scarecrow**: A badly-dressed person.

173/24 **There's egg on your chin!**: Warning to a man that his trouser fly or slit is open and that he should zip or button up. *(Do not confuse this set expression with the idiom 'have egg on one's face' – see 130/5)*

173/25 **War paint**: Skin make-up. □ My sister is upstairs putting on her war paint.

232

174: NOISY/QUIET

174/1   **Not able to hear oneself think**:   Not able to concentrate or think owing to loud noise. □ The road-works outside the office were so loud that I couldn't hear myself think.

174/2   **Kick up a din/racket/hullabaloo**:   Make a loud continuous noise; create an uproar. □ Can't you come home at night without kicking up a racket (hullabaloo/din) and waking everyone?

174/3   **Raise the roof**:   Arouse tremendous and noisy applause or laughter. □ Some of his jokes raised the roof.

174/4   **Belt out** music: Sing or play something loudly. □ The band belted out a tune. □ His hi-fi equipment is belting out pop songs.

174/5   **Able to hear a pin drop**:   Said when there is total or sudden silence somewhere. □ Even when the aircraft's engines are at full power, you can hear a pin drop in the cabin. □ When I mentioned his name, everyone looked at me and you could hear a pin drop.

175: DIRTY/CLEAN

175/1   **Mucky**:   Dirty or filthy. 'Muck' is dirt or filth. □ Don't get yourself mucky!

175/2   **Gunge**:   A sticky or messy mass of a substance; oily fat. □ The sink outlet is blocked with gunge.

175/3   **Gooey**:   Wet and sticky. □ Asphalt on the roads becomes gooey on hot days.

175/4   **Grubby**:   Dirty; unwashed. □ Her furniture was grubby. □ I'll have to wash first, I'm still grubby from work.

175/5   **Grotty**:   Dirty and unpleasant. (*See also 70/3*) □ I couldn't live in such a grotty house.

175/6   **Sleazy/seedy**:   Dirty, untidy or immoral in appearance. (*For 'seedy', see also 181/1*) □ She's a barmaid in a sleazy night-club.

175/7   **Crawling**:   Covered with insects such as lice or fleas; infested with vermin. □ After one night in that dirty hostel, I was crawling.

175/8   A **litterbug** *or* a **litter-lout**:   A person who carelessly throws litter on the street or in the countryside.

175/9   A **tide-mark**:   A line between the washed and unwashed parts of a person's body; a dirty line in a bath showing the level of water used.

175/10 **Squeaky clean**:   So clean that it squeaks when rubbed; of irreproachable past and conduct. □ My kitchen floor is squeaky clean. □ The party leader must be squeaky clean.

175/11 **Spick and span**:   Neat and clean; new-looking. □ It took me a day to get the house spick and span for visitors.

175/12 **Shipshape**:   In good order or tidy. (*See also 182/4*) □ I try to keep my room shipshape.

EXERCISES 28 – PEOPLE/CLOTHES

A) If the colloquial questions below were put to someone of that nationality, would he or she <u>probably</u> be offended? Answer 'Yes' or 'No' , and give a non-colloquial alternative for that nationality. Are you . . .

1) a Chink?   2) an Aussie?   3) an Eyetie?   4) a Froggie?
5) a Kiwi?   6) a Taff?   7) a Nip?   8) a Limey?
9) a Kraut?   10) a Polack?

B) Give colloquialisms for the following persons.

1) someone who carelessly throws litter around.
2) an energetic lively person.
3) an ordinary average person.
4) an unpleasant nuisance.
5) the Devil.
6) ordinary people.
7) an energetic girl who behaves like a boy.
8) a good-hearted but rough-mannered person.
9) a person who gives unwanted advice about something in which he or she is not involved.
10) oneself or one's own interests.

C) Replace the underlined word or phrase relating to dress with as many colloquial synonyms as possible.

1) The man was <u>very smartly dressed</u>.
2) She had a <u>very smart</u> dress on.
3) The children were <u>dressed in worn-out clothes</u>.
4) I've bought some new <u>clothes</u>.

D) Complete the second clause of the following sentences with a colloquial word (antonym) or phrase meaning the opposite of the first clause.

1) That man is a tough cookie, but his friend is a . . . .
2) My neighbour's kitchen is grubby, but mine is . . . .
3) That suit is trendy, but this one is . . . .
4) In the old factory you couldn't hear yourself think, but in this new one you can . . . .
5) His work colleagues are all dudes, yet he dresses like a . . . .

E) Give colloquialisms for the following items of clothing or dress accessories.

1) a suit, outfit or dress. 2) an apron. 3) an umbrella. 4) diamonds.
5) second-hand clothes previously worn by other family members.
6) large heavy shoes. 7) loose-fitting trousers. 8) one's best clothes.

The Body

176: BODY PARTS

176/1 **A gob/trap/cake-hole:** A mouth. □ Shut your gob (trap/cake-hole)!

176/2 **A kisser:** A mouth or face. □ I punched him in the kisser.

176/3 **A mush/mug/dial/puss:** A face. □ He had an ugly mug (dial etc.).

176/4 **A block/bonce/noggin/noddle:** A head. □ I bumped my noggin (bonce/noddle) against the beam.

176/5 **A conk:** A nose or head. □ He got hit on the conk.

176/6 **A hooter/beak/snoot:** A nose. □ She has a long snoot (beak/hooter).

176/7 **Peepers:** Eyes. □ She has beautiful blue peepers.

176/8 **Choppers** or **gnashers** (*pr. 'nashers'*): Teeth or false teeth. (*See 189/2 for 'chopper'*) □ I'd like to get my choppers (gnashers) into a juicy steak. □ He puts his choppers (gnashers) into a glass of water every night.

176/9 **Lugs:** Ears. □ She's had her lugs pierced for ear-rings.

176/10 **A ticker:** Heart. □ He has a weak ticker.

176/11 **A tummy:** Stomach. □ I sometimes get tummy-trouble on holiday.

176/12 **A paw/mit:** Hand. □ Keep your paws (mits) off my property!

176/13 **A peg/pin:** Leg. □ The footballer injured his left peg in training.

176/14 **A trotter:** Foot. □ She has difficulty remaining on her trotters.

176/15 **Tootsies:** Toes. □ Don't step on my tootsies!

176/16 **A botty:** Child's or jocular term for the buttocks. □ The mother told the child she would smack his botty if he was naughty again.

176/17 **A backside/butt** (*US*)/**bum** (*#?*)/**arse** (*#?*)/**ass** (*US*) (*#?*)/**fanny** (*US*) (*#?*): The buttocks. □ Get your butt (arse etc.) over here fast! (*Do not confuse the American term 'fanny' meaning 'buttocks' with the UK variant – see 189/8*)

177: NAKEDNESS/HAIR

177/1 **In the raw** *or* **in one's birthday suit** *or* **in the altogether:** Naked. □ When the fire-alarm sounded, he ran out of his hotel room in the altogether (in his birthday suit/in the raw).

177/2 **Starkers** *or* **stark naked:** Completely naked. □ We had to strip starkers (stark naked).

177/3 **Not have a stitch on:** Be completely naked; have no clothes on.

177/4 **Skinny-dipping**: Naked bathing or swimming.

177/5 **Thin on top**: Balding. □ He was thin on top at a very early age.

177/6 **Bald as a coot** *or* **bald as a billiard-ball**: Completely bald. □ He is a good hairdresser, although he's as bald as a coot (billiard ball) himself.

177/7 **A tash**: Moustache. □ He had a long drooping tash.

178: PHYSIQUE/LOOKS

178/1 **Tubby/podgy/dumpy**: Short and fat.

178/2 **Roly-poly**: Plump or fat; well rounded.

178/3 **A pot-belly**: A large extending stomach or a person with such a stomach. □ He has a pot-belly from drinking too much.

178/4 **A corporation**: A large stomach or belly. □ He can't button the jacket round his corporation.

178/5 **A spare tyre**: A thick layer of fat around the waist.

178/6 **Middle-age spread**: An increased waistline that often comes with middle age. □ She has middle-age spread.

178/7 **Well stacked**: (Of a woman) buxom; having large breasts.

178/8 **A beanpole/lamppost**: A lanky person; someone who is tall and thin.

178/9 **Thin as a rake**: Extremely thin. □ The prisoner was as thin as a rake.

178/10 **Skinny**: Very thin.

178/11 **A shrimp**: A very small person.

178/12 **A titch**: A small person or animal. The corresponding adjective is 'titchy'.

178/13 **Vital statistics**: The measurements of a woman's bust, waist and hips.

178/14 **Tough as old boots**: Physically tough or able to endure hardship.

178/15 **Hard as nails**: Physically or mentally tough. □ That sailor is used to all weathers, he's as hard as nails. □ The negotiators at the arms-reduction talks were as hard as nails.

178/16 **Husky**: Big and strong; burly.

178/17 **Be no oil painting**: Be ugly. □ He is no oil painting.

178/18 **Be ugly as sin** *or* **be plug-ugly** *or* **have a face like the back of a bus**: Be extremely ugly. □ His wife is as ugly as sin (is plug-ugly etc.).

178/19 **An old hag** *or* **an old witch**: An ugly old woman.

178/20 **Bonny**: Good-looking or beautiful. □ She's a bonny girl. □ That's a bonny dress.

178/21 **Stunning**: Extremely attractive. □ She is stunning.

178/22 **A dish** *or* **a cutie**: An attractive girl. The corresponding adjectives are 'dishy' and 'cute'.

178/23 **A looker**: An attractive woman. □ She's a looker.

179: SLEEP

179/1   **Hit the sack/hay** *or* **turn in**:   Go to bed. □ It's time to hit the sack (hit the hay/turn in).

179/2   **Get one's head down** or **get some shut-eye**:   Get some sleep. □ I got some shut-eye (got my head down) for an hour or two on the train.

179/3   **Kip**:   To sleep. A 'kip' is a colloquial word for sleep. □ We kipped in a barn for the night. □ I had a good kip.

179/4   **Sleep like a log/top**:   Sleep very soundly. □ "How did you sleep?" "Like a log! (Like a top!)."

179/5   **Not sleep a wink**:   Not sleep at all. □ I didn't sleep a wink last night.

179/6   **A night owl**:   Someone who stays up late or who doesn't go to bed until the early hours of the morning.

179/7   **Snatch forty winks**:   Take a short sleep especially during the day. □ After dinner she sometimes snatches forty winks.

179/8   **Nap/snooze**:   Take a short sleep. A short sleep is a 'nap' or a 'snooze'. □ He's napping (snoozing/taking a nap etc.) in the sitting room.

179/9   **A catnap**:   A very short sleep.

179/10   **Drop/nod off**:   Fall asleep. □ She's nodded (dropped) off watching TV.

179/11   **In the land of Nod**:   Asleep. □ The children are upstairs in the land of Nod.

179/12   **Shake down** *or* **crash out**:   Sleep in an improvised bed. □ Last night I shook down (crashed out) on a sofa at a friend's house.

179/13   **Sleep rough**:   Sleep in a rough improvised bed, especially out of doors. □ In many cities, homeless people sleep rough on the pavements.

179/14   **Flake out**:   Fall asleep from exhaustion or faint. □ When I got to the hotel room, I just flaked out on the bed.

179/15   **Lie in**:   Lie idly in bed late in the morning. This inactivity is called a 'lie-in'. □ On Sunday mornings, I always lie in (have a lie-in).

179/16   **Rise and shine!**:   Command to get out of bed in the morning.

180: TIRED

180/1   **Fagged out/done/dead-beat/bushed/jiggered/all-in/whacked/fit to drop/shattered/tuckered out** *(US)*:   Tired out; exhausted. □ I'm fagged out (fit to drop/dead-beat etc.) after that journey.

180/2   **Shagged** *(#?)*/**knackered** *(#?)*/**pooped** *(#?)*:   Terms of a more colloquial or vulgar nature for being tired out or exhausted.

180/3   **The worse for wear**:   Exhausted or injured. *(See also 71/7)* □ After a rough journey, we arrived the worse for wear.

180/4   **Out of puff**:   Out of breath. □ I'm out of puff after that walk.

181: UNWELL/ILL/INJURED

181/1 **Rough** *or* **under the weather** *or* **out of sorts** *or* **ragged around the edges/seedy**: Unwell or depressed. □ I'm feeling a bit rough (out of sorts/under the weather/ragged around the edges/seedy) today.

181/2 **Groggy** *or* **woozy** (*US*): Weak and unsteady, especially after an illness; dizzy or dazed, especially after drinking alcohol. □ All that wine has made her groggy (woozy). □ I've recovered from the flu, but I'm still feeling slightly groggy (woozy).

181/3 **Run-down**: Weak, exhausted or depressed; lacking energy or vitality. □ She is feeling run-down.

181/4 **Off-colour**: Not in the best of health. □ You look rather off-colour.

181/5 **Funny**: Slightly unwell. (*See also 81/6*) □ If you're feeling funny, you'd better sit down for a while.

181/6 **Pass out**: Faint. □ One soldier passed out after standing to attention for over an hour in the sun.

181/7 **Down with** *or* **laid up with** an illness: In bed with an illness. □ My son is down (laid up) with the measles.

181/8 **The shakes**: A fit of shaking. □ He has the shakes from drinking too much.

181/9 **Shake like a leaf**: Shake vigorously with fear, illness or cold. □ During my illness, I was shaking like a leaf.

181/10 **Dodder**: Tremble or walk in an unsteady fashion owing to age or illness (*See also 161/15*) □ A week after his accident, he was still weak and doddering.

181/11 **The curse**: Menstruation; a woman's period.

181/12 **A zit**: A pimple or acne spot. □ Her face is covered in zits.

181/13 **Catch one's death of cold**: Catch a severe cold. □ Put on a coat or you'll catch your death of cold!

181/14 **A stinker of a cold** *or* **a stinking cold**: A very bad cold. □ I've caught a stinker of a cold (a stinking cold).

181/15 **A jab**: An injection with a syringe, or an inoculation. □ Before you travel to Africa, you should get some jabs against tropical diseases.

181/16 **Gammy**: Lame or defective. □ He has a gammy arm from a childhood accident. □ The table has a gammy leg.

181/17 **Crack up**: Have a physical or mental breakdown. □ Working with asbestos can cause your health to crack up. □ He cracked up under the stress of his job.

181/18 **Do oneself a mischief**: Injure oneself. □ Don't try to lift the trunk without help, you could do yourself a mischief!

181/19 **Sick as a parrot/dog**: Very sick or unwell. □ The sea-food made her as sick as a dog (parrot). □ After realizing that I had paid a lot of money for nothing, I was as sick as a parrot (dog).

181/20 Throw/heave/fetch up *or* **puke:** Vomit. □ After seeing the dead car-crash victim, I had to fetch up (puke/heave up/throw up).

181/21 Spew one's guts out: Vomit violently. □ During the flight, I was air-sick and spewed my guts out.

182: RECOVERY/GOOD HEALTH

182/1 Buck/perk/pick up: Regain vitality or strength; recover health. (*For 'buck up', see also 117/2*) □ Nadeem was ill for a week, then he started to buck (pick /perk) up.

182/2 A pick-me up: A tonic to restore health or relieve depression. □ Aspirin and alcohol are common pick-me-ups.

182/3 On the mend: Improving in health or condition. □ The patient is on the mend.

182/4 Shipshape: In good health (*See also 175/12*) □ I'm feeling shipshape.

182/5 In the pink *or* **a picture of health:** In very good health; having a healthy complexion or appearance. □ She is in the pink (is a picture of health).

182/6 Right as rain/nails: Completely recovered from an illness. □ I had flu, but now I'm right as rain (nails).

182/7 Fit as a fiddle *or* **fighting fit** *or* **sound as a bell:** Very fit or healthy. □ You have to be fit as a fiddle (fighting fit/sound as a bell) to work as a scaffolder. □ The doctor gave me a check-up and told me that I was sound as a bell (fighting fit etc.).

182/8 The daily dozen: Daily exercises. □ The old man attributed his long age to the daily dozen.

183: SENSES

183/1   **Vibes:**   Mental or emotional vibrations. □ Religious music gives me pleasant vibes.

183/2   **Switched on:**   Alert to what is happening; up-to-date. □ You should subscribe to that magazine if you want to stay switched on in the world of politics.

183/3   **Not miss a trick:**   Be alert to everything. □ Trust him to know about it first, he doesn't miss a trick.

183/4   **Keep one's eyes skinned/peeled:**   Watch carefully; be observant or alert. □ The sailors kept their eyes peeled for land on the horizon.

183/5   **Have a gander/dekko:**   Have a look. □ My seat is near the porthole and if you come here, you can get a gander (dekko) of Tokyo from the air.

183/6   **Get a load/cop of** something: Take a look at, or notice of something; listen to. □ Get a load of that (Cop that)!, it's the biggest spider I've ever seen. □ Get a load of (Cop) this beautiful music!

183/7   **Clap/set eyes on** something: Catch sight of; see. □ I don't know who he is, I've never clapped (set) eyes on him in my life.

183/8   **The once-over:**   A rapid inspection or superficial examination. □ I haven't read the book properly, I've only given it the once-over.

183/9   **A going-over:**   An inspection *(See also 42/5)* □ Customs officials gave the suspect lorry a thorough going-over.

183/10   **Stand/stick out a mile** *or* . . . **like a sore thumb:**   Be clearly noticeable or visible. □ It stood out a mile (stuck out like a sore thumb) that he was telling a lie.

183/11   **Crystal-clear:**   Extremely clear or obvious. □ The meaning of the poem is crystal-clear.

183/12   **Specs/goggles:**   Spectacles; glasses. □ She needs specs (goggles) for reading.

183/13   **Four-eyes:**   Abusive term for someone who wears spectacles.

183/14   **Blind as a bat:**   Completely blind or (jocularly) very short-sighted. □ I'm blind as a bat without my glasses.

183/15   **Gawp:**   Stare stupidly. □ The villagers had never seen a hovercraft before, and they stood around gawping at it.

183/16   **Catch** something: Manage to hear or see. □ Sorry, I didn't catch what you said. □ We didn't catch the TV film last night.

183/17   **Deaf as a (door)post:**   Completely deaf or (jocularly) very hard of hearing. □ You may have to ring the door-bell several times because the old lady is as deaf as a post.

183/18   **Have a frog in one's throat:**   Be unable to speak, except in a hoarse voice. □ I've caught cold and have a frog in my throat.

183/19   **Killing** someone: Causing pain. □ I've been rushing around all day and my feet are killing me.

183/20 **Snug as a bug (in a rug)**: Very snug, cosy or comfortable. □ We're snug as a bug (snug as a bug in a rug) in our new flat.

183/21 **Comfy**: Comfortable. □ Make yourself comfy in an armchair.

183/22 **B.O.**: Body odour; an unpleasant smell of body sweat. □ I use deodorants to avoid B.O. □ He has B.O.

183/23 **Hum** *or* **reek**: Give off an unpleasant smell or stink. □ My socks are beginning to hum (reek). □ That cheese really reeks (hums).

183/24 **Pong**: To stink. A 'pong' is a stink or nasty smell and the corresponding adjective is 'pongy'. □ She had ten cats in the house and the whole place ponged.

183/25 **Whiff/niff** (something): To smell something or emit a smell. A 'whiff' or a 'niff' is a smell, and the corresponding adjectives are 'whiffy' and niffy'. □ Take a niff (whiff) at this flower. □ You can whiff (niff) the smell of cooking from here.

183/26 **Stink to high heaven**: Stink horribly. □ After cleaning the drain, I stank to high heaven.

184: TOILET/EXCRETA

184/1 **See a man about a dog** *or* **spend a penny** *or* **pay a call/visit**: Go to the toilet. □ The touring coach stopped in the wood to allow the passengers to spend a penny (see a man about a dog/pay a visit/pay a call).

184/2 **Powder one's nose**: Go to the ladies' toilet. □ She's gone to powder her nose.

184/3 **Pee/piddle**: To urinate. A 'pee' and a 'piddle' are nouns for urine or the act of urination. □ Someone has peed (piddled) in the lift.

184/4 **A wee(-wee)**: Child's term for the act of urination or urine.

184/5 **A leak/slash**: Urination. □ He's having a slash (taking a leak).

184/6 **Be taken/caught short**: Be caught by a sudden need to go to the toilet at an unfavourable moment. □ I was taken (caught) short on the bus.

184/7 **Do one's business**: Defecate. □ The neighbour's dog has done its business on our lawn.

184/8 **A privy/loo/jakes/khazi/lav/bog(s)**: The lavatory, toilet or WC. □ Where is the jakes (khazi/bog etc.) in this building?

184/9 **The John/gents**: The gentlemen's toilets. □ He's in the John (gents).

184/10 **The plumbing**: The lavatory installation.

184/11 **Crap/poop/shit**: Empty the bowels or defecate. Also nouns meaning excrement or nonsense. □ You're talking crap (shit)!

184/12 **A turd**: A lump of excrement, or a term of abuse for a despicable person. □ There was a huge dog-turd on the pavement.

184/13 **The shits/runs**: Diarrhoea. □ Eating unwashed fruit can give you the runs (shits).

184/14 **Fart** *or* **let off**:   Pass wind through the anus.

184/15 **Snot**:   A slimy discharge from the nose. The adjective 'snotty' can also mean immature. □ Marco has a snotty nose from his cold. □ They are just snotty kids, and shouldn't be taken seriously.

EXERCISES 29 – THE BODY

A) Complete the following sentences with the missing part of the colloquialism.

1) I didn't sleep a . . . all night.
2) The teacher apologized for speaking hoarsely, saying that she had a . . . in her throat.
3) It is . . . clear to me why this accident happened.
4) On naturist beaches, the bathers run around in their . . . suits.
5) Keep your eyes . . . for a post box – there must be one here somewhere!
6) His waistline had expanded and now he had a spare . . . .
7) We've not . . . eyes on her in a month.
8) I'll snatch . . . winks before the plane lands.
9) He has caught his . . . of cold on that fishing trip.
10) Far from being unfit, he is a . . . of health.

B) Give colloquialisms for the definitions below.

1) someone who doesn't go to bed until the early hours of the morning.
2) a very small person.
3) a lanky person.
4) a pimple or acne spot on the skin.
5) naked swimming.
6) an injection against disease or inoculation.
7) a tonic to liven someone up.
8) spectacles or glasses.
9) the measurements of a woman's bust, waist and hips.
10) a rapid inspection of something.

C) Replace the underlined word or phrase with as many colloquial synonyms as possible.

1) It is late and I'm going to bed.
2) He is very ugly.
3) We were exhausted after our journey.

→

242

4) She is feeling <u>unwell</u> today.
5) The meat began to <u>smell unpleasantly</u> in the sun.
6) He is in the <u>toilet</u>, but will be right back.

D) Complete the following comparative sentences with the missing noun or phrase.

1) The peasant had worked outdoors in the fields all his life and was as tough as ... .
2) Mr Akira is as bald as a ... .
3) On the first night of the expedition, we were exhausted and slept like a ... .
4) If you can't read that sign, you must be blind as a ... .
5) The woman had a pretty figure, but unfortunately she had a face like the ... .
6) The baby was fast asleep in her cot, snug as a ... .
7) I was ill for a month, but now I'm right as ... .
8) She was unhurt when we dragged her from the crashed car, but she was shaking like a ... .
9) The fish didn't agree with me, and I was as sick as a ... later.
10) She went on a diet and now she is as thin as a ... .
11) You'll have to speak louder, for she is as deaf as a ... .
12) The fact that they had been keeping animals in the flat stood out like a ... .

E) Replace the following underlined body parts with colloquial terms.

1) My <u>ears</u> are cold.
2) She has a nice pair of <u>legs</u>.
3) If you had used your <u>head</u>, this mistake wouldn't have happened.
4) The book jacket had the marks of someone's dirty <u>hands</u> all over it.
5) Get off your <u>buttocks</u> and get some work done!
6) You should have your <u>teeth</u> checked by a dentist.
7) He had a large cigar in his <u>mouth</u>.
8) My <u>feet</u> are sore after shopping around town.
9) Fatty foods are supposed to be bad for the <u>heart</u>.
10) His <u>face</u> was black with soot.

Marriage/Sex

185: COURTING

185/1 A **blind date**: An arranged social engagement or meeting between two persons of the opposite sex who haven't met before.

185/2 A **heavy date**: An arranged meeting or date with serious sexual intentions.

185/3 **Go wenching**: Go out in search of sex with women. A 'wench' is an old term of abuse for a low-class woman.

185/4 **Go steady**: Go about regularly with someone of the opposite sex, with the possible intention of marriage; be courting on a regular basis. □ They are going steady now. □ He is going steady with her.

185/5 **Stand** someone **up**: Fail to keep an arranged appointment or social engagement. □ She stood me up.

185/6 **Pick** someone **up**: Flirt or begin an affair with someone. □ I picked up my future wife at a dance.

185/7 **Chat** someone **up** *or* **get off with** someone: Chat to someone in a flirty manner; become friendly with someone, especially after attracting him or her deliberately. □ Men always try to chat her up (get off with her).

185/8 **Give** someone **the glad eye**: Look invitingly towards someone of the opposite sex. □ She's been giving me the glad eye all night.

185/9 **Make sheep's eyes at** someone: Gaze at someone lustfully or amorously. □ He makes eyes at me every time I see him.

185/10 **Make a pass at** someone: Try to attract sexually; make a sexual advance, especially involving touching. □ He made a pass at her.

185/11 A **wolf whistle**: A whistle by men in admiration of a woman's looks. □ Building workers made wolf whistles at women on the street below.

185/12 A **catcall**: Vulgar shouting by men at women. (Do not confuse with a 'catcall' at a theatre or meeting, which is a loud shout of disapproval.) □ The drunken youths made catcalls at women in the carpark.

185/13 **Play gooseberry**: Be an unwelcome companion to a pair of lovers. □ I don't want to play gooseberry, so I'll leave now.

186: MARRIAGE

186/1 **Mr Right**: The right man to marry. □ She is waiting for Mr Right to come along.

186/2 **Hook** someone *or* **get one's hooks/claws into** someone: Win a partner for oneself; catch a husband or wife. □ Watch out, she's trying to hook (get her claws into) you!

186/3 **Pop the question**: Propose marriage. □ Where did your husband pop the question?

186/4 **Take the plunge**: Decide to get married; take a bold decisive step. □ That old bachelor has finally decided to take the plunge.

186/5 **Tie the knot** *or* **get hitched** *or* **get spliced**: Get married. □ He's not ready to get hitched (get spliced/tie the knot) just yet.

186/6 **Shotgun-wedding**: A speedy enforced wedding, usually because of the bride's pregnancy.

186/7 **Shack up with** someone: Live together or cohabit with someone. □ He has shacked up with her.

186/8 **Live in sin**: (Used jocularly) live together without being married. □ They are living in sin.

186/9 A **common law wife/husband**: A partner who is legally recognized as man or wife, after a period of living together without being married.

186/10 A **gym-slip mum**: A single mother of school age. A 'gym-slip' is a sleeveless tunic worn by girls at school.

186/11 A **tug-of-love**: A dispute by divorced or separated parents over the custody of a child or children.

186/12 Someone's **'ex'**: Someone's former husband or wife. □ I saw my 'ex' today with another woman.

186/13 **On the shelf**: Past marriageable age. □ Until he came along, she had always thought of herself as an old maid on the shelf.

187: SEXUALITY

187/1 **Fruity**: Sexually suggestive. □ Our boss sometimes gets fruity with the secretaries.

187/2 **Randy** *or* **horny**: Lustful or eager for sex.

187/3 **Kinky**: Bizarre or eccentric, especially in sexual behaviour. □ Partner-swopping is really kinky. □ She wore a kinky night-dress.

187/4 A **sex-kitten**: An attractive, sexually active woman.

187/5 A **sex-pot**: A sexy person (especially a woman).

187/6 A **sugar daddy**: An older man who associates with much younger women.

187/7 A **toy boy**: A younger man who associates with much older women.

187/8 A **cradle-snatcher**: An older person who associates with a much younger person of the opposite sex.

187/9 A **fancy man**: A boyfriend, especially of the playboy type.

187/10 **Talent**:   Good-looking people of the opposite sex. □ There is plenty of talent at the disco.

187/11 A **bit of all right** *or* **hot stuff** *or* a **dolly**:   An attractive woman or girl. *(For 'hot stuff', see also 7/11)* □ She is hot stuff (a dolly/a bit of all right).

187/12 A **bit of skirt**:   A woman.

187/13 A **bint/chick/bird**:   A young woman, especially an attractive one.

187/14 A **broad** *(#US)*:   A woman or prostitute.

187/15 A **moll**:   A prostitute or woman of loose morals, especially when she is the girlfriend of a criminal.

187/16 A **good-time girl**:   A woman who lives for pleasure, especially of the sexual kind.

187/17 A **cock-teaser** *(#??)*:   A woman who flaunts her sexuality in the presence of men.

187/18 A **scrubber**:   A woman, especially one of loose morals.

187/19 A **tart/trollop/hussy**:   A woman of immoral character; a prostitute.

187/20 A **hooker** *(US)*:   A prostitute.

187/21 A **call-girl**:   A prostitute who accepts appointments by telephone.

187/22 **On the game**:   Involved in, or living by prostitution. □ She must be on the game to afford such expensive things.

187/23 A **rent boy**:   A young male prostitute.

187/24 A **pimp/pander**:   A man who procures clients for prostitutes.

187/25 **Straight**:   Heterosexual; not homosexual.

187/26 **Bent/gay**:   Homosexual. *(For 'bent', see also 35/1)*

187/27 A **gay/fairy/queer/pansy/faggot** *(#US)***/nancy-boy/puff/poof/ponce**:   A male homosexual.

187/28 A **queen**:   A male homosexual, especially an elderly one.

187/29 A **dyke** *(#US)*:   A lesbian.

187/30 A **flasher**:   A man who exposes himself to women in public places.

187/31 A **streaker**:   A person, male or female, who runs naked in public places or at large events to attract attention.

187/32 A **peeping Tom**:   A man who secretly watches people undressing or engaging in sexual activities. □ You should keep your curtains drawn at night – there's a peeping Tom in the neighbourhood!

188: THE SEXUAL ACT

188/1 **Kiss-and-tell-all**:   Said of someone who relates in public his or her sexual exploits with well-known people. □ He threatened to sue the newspaper for printing a kiss-and-tell-all story by a former girlfriend.

188/2 **Petting** *or* **groping**:   Serious sexual caressing.

188/3 A **slap and tickle**:   Light-hearted sexual caressing.

246

188/4 **Smooch/snog/neck:** Kiss and caress. □ They were snogging (necking/ smooching) in the park.

188/5 **A smacker:** A loud kiss.

188/6 **A clinch:** A tight embrace. □ The couple were in a clinch.

188/7 **A dirty weekend:** A weekend trip for the purposes of sex.

188/8 **Carry on with** someone: Have sexual relations with someone, especially immorally or secretly. □ She is carrying on with another woman's husband.

188/9 **Nookie** *or* **(a bit of) how's-your-father:** Sexual intercourse. □ They went home early from the party to have a bit of how's-your-father.

188/10 **Wham, bam, thank you ma'am** *(US)*: A single act of sexual intercourse solely for the purpose of gratification.

188/11 **Score/make it/do it/have it off** *or* **have it away** (with someone): Have sexual intercourse. □ He scored (made it/did it etc.) with her.

188/12 **Get laid** *or* **get one's oats** *or* **get one's leg over:** Have sexual intercourse. □ He got laid (got his oats/got his leg over) last night.

188/13 **A lay:** An act of intercourse; a person with whom one has sexual intercourse. □ She's a good lay.

188/14 **Screw/shaft/bop** *(US)*/**bonk/hump/shag/fuck/stuff** someone: (Of a man) to have sexual intercourse with a woman. □ He has bopped (shagged/screwed etc.) a lot of girls.

188/15 **Sleep around:** Have several casual sexual relations with different partners. □ In order to prevent the spread of AIDS, people are advised not to sleep around.

188/16 **Get one's end away:** (of a man) have sexual intercourse. □ All he wants is to get his end away.

188/17 **Have a bit on the side:** Have a secret sexual relationship with someone other than one's marriage partner; have extra-marital sex. □ Several married men in this office are having a bit on the side.

188/18 **A gang-bang:** Sexual intercourse between a woman and several men.

188/19 **A blow job:** An act of oral sex on a man; fellatio.

188/20 **A knocking-shop:** A brothel or house of prostitutes.

188/21 **Knock up** a girl: Make pregnant. □ He knocked her up.

188/22 **Get** a girl **into trouble:** Make a girl pregnant. □ He has got her into trouble.

188/23 **Join the pudding club:** Become pregnant. □ She has joined the pudding club.

188/24 **Have a bun in the oven** or **be in the family way:** Be pregnant. □ She has a bun in the oven (She's in the family way).

188/25 **On the pill:** Taking the birth-control or contraceptive pill. □ The doctor asked her if she was on the pill.

188/26 **A blob/Johnnie/rubber** *or* a **French letter:** A condom or preservative.

188/27 **The clap:** Venereal disease; disease of the sexual organs.

189: MALE AND FEMALE ORGANS

189/1 **Goolies/balls/nuts/bollocks**: Testicles.

189/2 A **prick/cock/knob/willie/dick/chopper/dong** (#*US*) or an **old man**: The penis or male sexual organ.

189/3 **A hard-on**: (Have or get) a hard or erect penis. □ He had a hard-on.

189/4 **Come**: Have an orgasm. □ She didn't come.

189/5 **Come one's load**: Ejaculate. □ He came his load.

189/6 **Spunk**: Semen or sperm.

189/7 **Toss/jerk off** or **wank**: (Of a man) masturbate.

189/8 A **crumpet/pussy/cunt/fanny**: The vagina or female sexual organ.

189/9 **Bristols/boobs/tits/knockers/bumpers**: Female breasts. □ She has a nice pair of boobs (bristols etc.).

EXERCISES 30 – SEX

A) Replace the underlined phrases with colloquialisms, rephrasing where necessary.

1) My aunt is 50 and past marriageable age.
2) My husband proposed marriage on a day-trip to Copenhagen.
3) Stella is making a living by prostitution.
4) They have started living together.
5) They are courting each other regularly.
6) She is his unmarried but legally recognized wife.
7) She often wears sexually eccentric clothes.
8) He has made his young girlfriend pregnant.

B) Give colloquialisms for the following definitions.

1) a man who watches others undressing or engaging in sexual activity.
2) a single unmarried mother of school age.
3) the man who would make a good husband.
4) light-hearted sexual caressing.
5) a male whistle of admiration for a woman.
6) an older man who associates with much younger women.
7) a young man who associates with much older women.
8) a sexy woman.
9) a young male prostitute.
10) a condom.

C) Replace the underlined phrase with as many synonyms as possible.

1) The couple were kissing in the park.
2) They got married in June.
3) His wife is pregnant.

Answers

Where a single answer could be any one of two or more colloquialisms, these are divided by an oblique [/]. If a question poses two separate answers (as in Mod. 3, Ex. A/5), these will be divided by a full colon [:] – see also Mod. 1, Ex. D, where the abbreviation (*coll*) = colloquial use.

MODULE 1

A) 1) tied up / hard at it / at full stretch / fully stretched. 2) went all out / pulled out all the stops / did their level best / leant over backwards / bent over backwards. 3) didn't lift a finger. 4) bone idle / a lazybones. 5) landed. 6) burn the midnight oil. 7) knocked off. 8) spade work. 9) skiving / shirking / scrimshanking. 10) marching orders / cards. 11) a workaholic. 12) a cushy number. 13) tooth and nail.

B) 1) bacon. 2) beans. 3) plum. 4) loaf. 5) donkey. 6) beaver. 7) hammer : tongs. 8) hook : crook.

C) 1) polished off. 2) elbow grease. 3) nobody's business. 4) gone to great lengths. 5) pull your socks up. 6) explored every avenue.

D) 1) made an unnecessary detour: (*coll*) made a great effort. 2) she was naked: (*coll*) she had free time. 3) a plateful of food: (*coll*) a lot of work. 4) he hasn't got the goods or means of transport: (*coll*) he cannot keep his promise. 5) bound up: (*coll*) busy.

E) 1) in. 2) away. 3) under. 4) down. 5) off. 6) on.

MODULE 2

A) 1) all the tricks of the trade / the drill / the ropes. 2) what it takes. 3) shift for myself. 4) razz(a)matazz / razzle-dazzle. 5) take small misfortunes in your stride. 6) licked / snookered / stymied / stumped. 7) bite off more than she can chew. 8) red tape. 9) wobbly / rusty / dusty. 10) fluff it / botch it / louse it up / screw it up / foul it up / muck it up. 11) fix me up with a car / lay on a car for me.

B) 1) a Jack tar. 2) a chippie. 3) a sparky / a spark. 4) a shrink. 5) a cowboy. 6) a Jack of all trades. 7) a charlady / a Mrs Mop. 8) a girl Friday. 9) a rookie / a greenhorn. 10) a gaffer.

C) 1) beyond me. 2) under her belt. 3) up-market. 4) junk mail. 5) cut out for the job. 6) for the life of me. 7) through his paces. 8) backroom boys.

D) 1) hand. 2) bull. 3) fingers. 4) monkey. 5) hand. 6) fist / hand. 7) hand.

E) 1) They have made a hash of their work. 2) couldn't do anything for toffee/for nuts. 3) Bad organization has fouled/mucked/loused/screwed up our delivery schedule.

MODULE 3

A) 1) worked wonders / worked magic. 2) stuck it out. 3) stuck to their guns. 4) on the right track. 5) got off to a flying start : bogged down. 6) the proof of the pudding. 7) wangled me a parking permit. 8) went like a bomb / went over big / was a smash hit / hit the jackpot / scored a bull's eye. 9) never looked back. 10) pay off. 11) romped home / won hands down. 12) pipped at the post.

B) 1) soldier. 2) uncle. 3) yuppies. 4) kid. 5) horse. 6) rabbit. 7) bull.

C) 1) keep the ball rolling. 2) get our foot in the door. 3) we're getting nowhere fast. 4) hanging on like grim death. 5) make out with. 6) sort itself out. 7) muddling through.

D) 1) scored a bull's eye / hit the jackpot. 2) come out in the wash / sort themselves out. 3) going great guns / winning / well away. 4) notched up / chalked up. 5) bucked the trend. 6) come off. 7) made good. 8) licked / knocked the spots off / slaughtered / made mincemeat of / ran rings around.

MODULE 4

A) 1) foot. 2) faces. 3) ears. 4) turkey. 5) goose. 6) feet. 7) duck. 8) legs. 9) feet. 10) dogs.

B) 1) boob(oo) / howler / bloomer. 2) gone under / gone bust / gone to the wall / folded (up) / gone down the tube / gone down the drain / gone down the Swanee. 3) torn it / done it. 4) take the rough with the smooth. 5) swings and roundabouts / snakes and ladders. 6) lay off! / knock it off! / cut it out! / pack it in! / give it a rest! / give over! / leave off! / leave be! 7) kick. 8) good riddance! 9) a wash-out. 10) in the lurch. 11) I am through with her. 12) jacked in / chucked in.

C) 1) back to square one. 2) like a hot potato. 3) barking up the wrong tree. 4) dropped a brick / dropped a clanger. 5) gone to pot / gone to the dogs. 6) washed-up.
D) 1) a dead-beat / a dead loss. 2) an also-ran. 3) a has-been. 4) an off-day. 5) a cop-out. 6) a slip / a slip-up.

MODULE 5

A) 1) in a jiffy / in a mo / in a tick. 2) all along the line. 3) on the trot / on end. 4) off the top of my head. 5) like the clappers / like mad / like crazy / like billy-o / like blazes / like a house on fire / like greased lightning. 6) like wildfire / like the clappers / like mad / like crazy / like billy-o / like blazes / like a house on fire / like greased lightning / hell for leather. 7) spanking / rattling. 8) shilly-shally / drag our feet / dither / faff around. 9) pigs might fly. 10) pronto. 11) in store / in the pipeline. 12) 'Jack Robinson'.
B) 1) a slowcoach / a slowpoke. 2) a flash in the pan / a nine days' wonder. 3) a quickie. 4) yonks / ages / donkey's years. 5) the home stretch / the home straight. 6) pie in the sky / a pipe-dream. 7) the year dot.
C) 1) donkey. 2) cows. 3) snail. 4) horses. 5) pigs. 6) chickens.
D) 1) in less than no time / in no time. 2) more times than someone has had hot dinners. 3) half the time. 4) in the nick of time. 5) chucking-out time.
E) 1) month. 2) hour. 3) second. 4) moment. 5) yonks / ages / donkey's years. 6) day. 7) mo / tick / jiffy.

MODULE 6

A) 1) gave me the run-around / messed me around / jerked me around / mucked me around. 2) standing on her head / with one hand tied behind her back. 3) hit several snags. 4) strings attached. 5) ironed out. 6) fought City Hall. 7) broken the back of. 8) put me through the mill. 9) go in at the deep end / jump in at the deep end. 10) is out on a limb.
B) 1) a hiccup / a rub / a hitch. 2) teething troubles. 3) a Catch-22 situation. 4) a tough nut to crack / a handful / a stinker / a teaser. 5) a hot potato. 6) everything in the garden is lovely / everything is a bed of roses / everything is hunky-dory.
C) 1) beer. 2) peaches and cream. 3) apple pie. 4) cake. 5) pie. 6) jam. 7) soup. 8) nut.
D) 1) pie / falling off a log / ABC. 2) snip / doddle / cinch / piece of cake / push-over / breeze. 3) a jam / a spot / a pickle / the soup / Queer Street. 4) lumbered / saddled / stuck. 5) pushed / put / pressed.
E) 1) plain sailing. 2) open-and-shut. 3) messing me around. 4) not out of the woods yet. 5) half the battle. 6) batting on a sticky wicket.

MODULE 7

A) 1) an argy bargy / a bust-up / a slanging-match. 2) stand-up. 3) hugger-mugger / topsy-turvy / higgledy-piggledy. 4) a fine how-d'ye-do. 5) hoo-ha / carry-on. 6) ding-dong.
B) 1) patched up. 2) thrown a spanner in the works. 3) raised Cain / raised up a hell of a stink / kicked up a hell of a stink / kicked up a rumpus / made a song-and-dance / made a to-do. 4) off his own bat. 5) bone to pick. 6) at loggerheads. 7) passes the buck. 8) hold the fort.
C) 1) monger / merchant. 2) dog. 3) pigeon / baby. 4) cat : pigeon. 5) fish. 6) Murphy / Sod. 7) fish.
D) 1) song and dance. 2) sixes and sevens. 3) hammer and tongs. 4) dead and buried.
E) 1) a fusspot. 2) a busybody / a nosy parker. 3) hassle. 4) aggro. 5) a storm in a teacup. 6) trouble at t'mill.

MODULE 8

A) 1) a mole. 2) a cat-burglar. 3) a fire-bug. 4) a road-hog. 5) a pig. 6) fly-tipping. 7) a jay-walker. 8) a kangaroo court. 9) rat on someone. 10) do bird.
B) 1) knocked off / whipped / nicked / pinched / swiped / ripped off / lifted. 2) Bill / Law / fuzz / boys in blue / coppers / cops. 3) pulled in / run in / nicked / nabbed / copped / pinched. 4) the clink / the nick / the jug / the quod / the can / the slammer. 5) shopped / ratted on / grassed on / squealed on / split on / snitched on / sung on / coughed on.
C) 1) a lager-lout. 2) a fence. 3) a minder. 4) a dick / a private eye. 5) a beak. 6) a screw. 7) a gaolbird (jailbird) / an old lag. 8) a supergrass. 9) a mugger. 10) the Mob.
D) 1) had fallen off the back of a lorry. 2) launders hot money. 3) greased the security guard's palm / gave the security guard a back-hander. 4) cased the joint. 5) red-handed. 6) went straight / never left the straight and narrow. 7) set him up / framed him. 8) He has a clean slate and doesn't appear in the mug-shots.

MODULE 9

A) 1) letter. 2) brass. 3) penny. 4) furniture. 5) jacket. 6) hinge. 7) anchor. 8) house. 9) pot. 10) cauliflower. 11) handle.

B) 1) bigwig / big noise / big gun / big shot / big nob. 2) Lady Muck / her nibs. 3) riff-raff / low life. 4) bouncer. 5) a toff / a swell. 6) a bruiser. 7) Mr Big.

C) 1) hit him for six / knocked him into the middle of next week. 2) smack me in the chops / clock me. 3) put the nut on. 4) beat the living daylights out of him / knocked the stuffing out of him / knocked his block off / skinned him alive / gave him a drubbing/tanning/hiding/lathering/walloping/whaling/pasting. 5) cuffed the boy / clipped the boy. 6) a scrap / a punch-up / a brawl. 7) set about / laid into / weighed into / pitched into / waded into / lammed into. 8) clobbered / walloped / whaled.

D) 1) the sixty-four thousand dollar question. 2) fetched him one / gave him one / let him have it / walloped him / whaled him. 3) into the middle of next week. 4) all chiefs and no Indians / *(less correctly)* all cowboys and no Indians. 5) hit for six. 6) duffed up / did over. 7) the name of the game. 8) frogmarched away / manhandled away.

MODULE 10

A) 1) back. 2) skin : teeth. 3) neck. 4) head. 5) teeth. 6) head. 7) foot. 8) neck. 9) ear. 10) arm.

B) 1) on. 2) under. 3) in. 4) back. 5) out. 6) on. 7) at. 8) out. 9) on. 10) off.

C) 1) scot-free. 2) nit-picking. 3) what-for. 4) second-guess. 5) talking-to / dressing-down / ticking-off. 6) mud-slinging / muck-raking.

D) 1) the carrot and the stick. 2) a fall guy / a whipping boy / a scapegoat. 3) flak. 4) a dose of one's own medicine. 5) a glutton for punishment. 6) a close shave.

E) 1) get out. 2) wiped / mopped. 3) carry. 4) come down. 5) jump. 6) knocking / slamming / bashing. 7) hauled.

MODULE 11

A) 1) bread / lolly / dough. 2) pig in a poke. 3) hot cakes. 4) nest-egg. 5) bean. 6) chicken-feed / peanuts. 7) white elephant. 8) gravy train. 9) fat cat.

B) 1) nicker / quid / smacker. 2) buck / smacker. 3) a grand. 4) a rake-off. 5) the damage. 6) a skinflint. 7) a snip. 8) a punter. 9) cadger / scrounger / bum / sponger. 10) a rainy day.

C) 1) shoe-string. 2) money-bags. 3) rock-bottom. 4) tight-fisted / *(more vulgarly)* tight-arsed. 5) money-spinner. 6) knock-down. 7) hard-up. 8) whip-round. 9) never-never. 10) sky-high.

D) 1) flogged. 2) fetch. 3) chipped in. 4) top up. 5) fork out / shell out / stump up / cough up. 6) set me back / knocked me back. 7) touch for / tap for. 8) blued / blown.

MODULE 12

A) 1) herring. 2) possum. 3) marine. 4) cock : bull. 5) monkey. 6) cleaner. 7) fox.

B) 1) a cheap skate. 2) a sly boots. 3) a con-man / a sharper / a twister. 4) a wide boy. 5) the real McCoy. 6) a white lie. 7) a raw deal. 8) a fix / a put-up job. 9) bogus / phoney. 10) eyewash / window dressing. 11) a fly-by-night firm.

C) 1) cooking. 2) spinning. 3) fell *or* fall. 4) pull. 5) leading.

D) 1) out. 2) on. 3) down. 4) up. 5) on. 6) through. 7) up.

E) 1) gypped you / diddled you / rooked you / fleeced you / stung you / screwed you / done you / had you / ripped you off / conned you / seen you coming. 2) palm off. 3) pulling the wool over your eyes / taking you in /taking you for a ride / putting one across you / slipping one across you / hoodwinking you / foxing you. 4) skulduggery / funny business / monkey business / jiggery-pokery / hocus-pocus. 5) having him on / joshing him / taking the mickey out of him / *(vulgar)* taking the piss out of him. 6) not above board / not fair and square / not kosher / not on the level / not fair dos.

MODULE 13

A) 1) to be going on with / to be getting on with. 2) jacked up / hiked. 3) in a nutshell. 4) the world and his wife. 5) the daddy / the mammy / the father / the mother. 6) when it comes to the crunch / when the chips are down / at the end of the day. 7) bang / slap-bang. 8) make a mountain out of a molehill. 9) it's better than a slap in the eye / face / *(more vulgarly)* it's better than a kick up the arse.

B) 1) straw. 2) lock, stock, barrel. 3) wool. 4) ground : muck. 5) trowel. 6) barrel. 7) kitchen sink. 8) biscuit / cake. 9) sausage.

C) 1) the whole caboodle / the whole shebang / the whole boiling. 2) thumping / thundering / whacking / walloping / dirty. 3) tiddly / piffling / trifling / piddling. 4) bags / loads / stacks /

251

pots / oodles / no end / any amount.   5) dead-on / bang on.   6) sod all / sweet Fanny Adams / sweet F.A.

D) 1) give : take.   2) pushed / pressed / strapped.   3) coming.   4) overshot / overstepped.   5) crawling.   6) piling.

MODULE 14

A) 1) candle.   2) kettle : fish.   3) bag.   4) pin.   5) door.   6) peg.   7) chalk : cheese.   8) ball.

B) 1) a lemon.   2) a crock.   3) gremlins.   4) a U-turn.   5) the odd-man-out.   6) the spitting image.   7) even Stephen(s)/Steven(s) / level pegging.

C) 1) in / up.   2) out.   3) on.   4) in.   5) up.   6) up.   7) on.   8) up.   9) up.

D) 1) moves.   2) do.   3) join.   4) touch.   5) skin.   6) driving.

E) 1) a spanker / a stunner / a peach / a belter / a corker / a smasher / a humdinger / a knock-out / the cat's whiskers.   2) crummy / crappy / grotty / lousy / yucky.   3) bust / up the spout / clapped out / duff / bum / dud / knackered / (*vulgar*) buggered.   4) six of one and half a dozen of the other / six and two threes / it's as broad as it's long.

MODULE 15

A) 1) wood.   2) devil.   3) cheese / lines.   4) books.   5) wedge.   6) Dutchman.   7) cherry.   8) boat / bus.   9) boots / bottom dollar.   10) cookie.

B) 1) a flutter.   2) Hobson's choice.   3) a fluke.   4) a spin-off.   5) a cliff-hanger.   6) a toss-up.   7) a no-hoper.   8) a jinx.   9) the bottom line.   10) a knee-jerk reaction.

C) 1) down.   2) on.   3) up.   4) off.   5) down.   6) on.   7) out.   8) on.   9) up.

D) 1) have a go/shot/bash/whirl/whack/crack/stab / try my hand.   2) haven't an earthly / haven't a ghostly / haven't (*or* don't stand) a cat/dog in hell's chance / haven't (*or* don't stand) a snowball's chance in hell / a fat chance.   3) clinched / struck / swung / wrapped up / sewn up.   4) sure as eggs (is eggs) / that is a dead-cert / you can bet your bottom dollar / you can bet your boots / I'm telling you / take it from me / make no mistake about it.

E) 1) play.   2) skating.   3) jumped.   4) pushing.   5) run.   6) eat.

MODULE 16

A) 1) bee.   2) pig.   3) bird.   4) hare.   5) bats.   6) horse.   7) cow / moo.   8) flies.   9) turkey.

B) 1) bumpkin / hill-billy / yokel / hick.   2) nut-house / loony-bin / funny-farm.   3) clever clogs / clever boots / clever dick / smarty pants / smart alec / (*vulgar*) smart arse / bright spark.   4) to my mind / to my way of thinking / in my book / for my money / from where I'm sitting.

C) 1) billy.   2) charlie.   3) alec.   4) billy.   5) dick.

D) 1) plumb.   2) stark raving / barking.   3) priceless / prize / blithering.   4) dead.

E) 1) a bimbo.   2) a sucker / a mug / a muggins.   3) an egghead.   4) someone's brain-child.   5) a hang-up / a bee in someone's bonnet.   6) a trip down memory lane.

F) 1) hook, line, sinker.   2) sieve.   3) fruit-cake.   4) two short planks.   5) thinking-caps.   6) brush.   7) twist / bend.   8) board.

MODULE 17

A) 1) on.   2) in.   3) on.   4) off.   5) under.   6) over.   7) up.   8) out.   9) through.   10) out.   11) down.

B) 1) bumf / bum-fodder.   2) the three Rs.   3) a blabbermouth.   4) a smattering of something.   5) the jungle telegraph / the bush telegraph / the grape-vine.   6) an eye-opener.   7) a dark horse / an unknown quantity.   8) a hunch / an inkling.   9) a bookworm.

C) 1) bird / dicky-bird.   2) cat.   3) horse.   4) duck.   5) rat.   6) parrot.   7) cat.   8) horse.

D) 1) was ploughed in / flunked.   2) swotting (up) their English lessons / cramming their . . . / mugging up on their . . . / boning up on their . . . / stewing over their . . . / poring over their . . . 3) I haven't the foggiest / I haven't the faintest / I haven't a clue / I am in the dark as to / I wouldn't know / Search me.   4) is versed in / is well up in / is at home in / knows what's what in / knows a thing or two about / knows his onions in / knows his stuff in / has diesel engines at his fingertips.   5) he twigged / he cottoned on to / he tumbled to / he got / he dug / the penny dropped / it registered (with him) / it clicked (with him) / it sunk in (with him).   6) blow the gaff / let the cat out of the bag / give the show away / spill the beans / let on / blab.   7) nitty-gritty / ins and outs / nuts and bolts.

MODULE 18

A) 1) trooper / fish-wife.   2) Dutch.   3) cow / mackerel.   4) cat.   5) Mike.   6) devil.   7) bear.   8) clam.   9) turkey.   10) French.

B) 1) the lingo. 2) waffle / flannel. 3) a crack / a wisecrack. 4) mumbo-jumbo. 5) an old wives' tale. 6) a chatterbox / a gasbag / a windbag. 7) blarney. 8) pidgin English. 9) tittle-tattle.

C) 1) gave you a ring / buzz / bell / tinkle. 2) bunk / bunkum / baloney / humbug / poppycock / hooey / codswallop / guff / tosh / balderdash / malarkey / piffle / fiddlesticks / hokum / hogwash / cobblers / twaddle / tommy-rot / rot / bosh / tripe / drivel / bullshit / bull / claptrap / through the back of his head/neck / through his hat. 3) grousing / grouching / griping / beefing / bellyaching / w(h)ingeing / yammering. 4) nattering / passing the time of day / wagging our tongues / having a crack / having a chin-wag.

D) 1) Bless you! 2) Ta! 3) Toodle-oo! / Ta-ta! / I must love you and leave you! 4) Come again! 5) Put a sock in it! / Belt up! / Shush! / Cut the cackle! / Pipe down! 6) Yuk! 7) Yippee! / Whoopee! 8) Between you, me and the gate-post. 9) Fire away! / Shoot!

E) 1) neck. 2) mouth. 3) face. 4) head. 5) tongues. 6) back/hind legs.

MODULE 19

A) 1) thumbs-up / green light. 2) stomach / lump / stick. 3) bug. 4) head : heels. 5) sun shines. 6) big way. 7) fancy. 8) tether. 9) sliced bread.

B) 1) puppy love. 2) a blue-eyed boy *or* a blue-eyed girl. 3) a buff / a fiend for something. 4) an eager beaver. 5) a heart-throb. 6) go overboard.

C) 1) has gone a bundle on / has fallen for / is struck on / has a crush on / is nuts about / is potty about / is nutty about / is hooked on / is gone on / thinks the world of / is head over heels in love with. 2) keen as mustard / dying / raring. 3) You bet! / Rather! / Not half! / I'll say! 4) Okey-doke! / Righty-oh! / Right you are!

D) 1) with. 2) with. 3) on. 4) off. 5) up. 6) on. 7) off.

MODULE 20

A) 1) teeth. 2) eye / foot. 3) hair. 4) neck / (*vulgar*) arse. 5) nostrils / nose. 6) head. 7) back. 8) guts. 9) stomachs / tummies. 10) skin.

B) 1) became cross as two sticks / became hopping mad / became livid / got the screaming habdabs / had a fit / threw a wobbly / saw red / threw a tantrum / went off the deep end / flipped his lid / flew off the handle / did his nut / did his block / blew his stack / blew his top / blew a fuse / hit the ceiling / hit the roof / got into a paddy / was like a bear with a sore head. 2) Not on your nelly! / No fear! / No way! / Not likely! / Nothing doing! / Not for all the tea in China! 3) bored stiff / chocker / chock-a-block / fed up to the back teeth / cheesed off / browned off / (*vulgar*) pissed off. 4) got herself worked up / was shaken up / was cut up / got into a stew / got into a tizzy / got into a flap / got het up. 5) Don't rile her! / Don't nark her! / Don't get on her wrong side! / Don't get her dander up! / Don't get her monkey up! / Don't get her back up! 6) not my scene / not my cup of tea.

C) 1) a raspberry. 2) a drag / a bind / a crashing bore / a pain in the neck (*vulgar*) a pain in the arse. 3) the V-sign / a two-fingered gesture. 4) a jitterbug. 5) I could kick myself! 6) mooning. 7) tut-tut! / I like that!

D) 1) under. 2) up. 3) on. 4) down. 5) up. 6) on. 7) off. 8) out.

MODULE 21

A) 1) cucumber. 2) bits. 3) fiddle. 4) Punch. 5) Cheshire cat. 6) Larry. 7) pink / to death.

B) 1) a spoil-sport / a kill-joy / a party-pooper. 2) a sourpuss. 3) a cool cat / a cool customer. 4) a chicken / a scaredy-cat. 5) a scream / a riot / a bundle of laughs / a barrel of laughs. 6) a cry-baby. 7) a smoothie. 8) horseplay. 9) a sob-story. 10) high jinks.

C) 1) bottle / spunk / guts. 2) scared the living daylights out of her / scared the pants off her / scared the hell out of her / gave her quite a turn. 3) give a hang / give a brass farthing / give a hoot / give two hoots / give two pins / give a fig / give a monkey's / give a tinker's cuss or / (*vulgar*) give a toss. 4) had a whale of a time / had a rare old time / had a high old time / had a bundle of fun / had a barrel of fun / had a ball / let our hair down / let it all hang out. 5) is in the doldrums / is in the dumps / is down in the mouth / has the heebie-jeebies / has the blues / is feeling blue.

D) 1) skin : back / nose. 2) lip. 3) eyelid. 4) heart. 5) feet. 6) head. 7) yellow-bellied / lily-livered. 8) hair.

MODULE 22

A) 1) change / joy. 2) carpet. 3) Brownie. 4) bolt : blue. 5) leaf. 6) sheep. 7) roses. 8) line. 9) ball / the game. 10) bandwagon.

B) 1) a stuffed shirt. 2) a copy-cat. 3) a namby-pamby. 4) crawler / creeper / boot-licker / toady / (*vulgar*) arse-licker. 5) the talk of the town. 6) a feather in someone's cap. 7) a soft touch / a push-over. 8) an oddball / a weirdo / a weirdy / a kook / a screwball / a crackpot. 9) lip / buck / gall / nerve / sauce. 10) a bad egg.

C) 1) sucking up to / toadying to / kowtowing to / licking the boots of. 2) thinks she is the bee's knees / fancies herself / thinks no small beer of herself / thinks she is the cat's whiskers. 3) on the hop / napping / with their trousers down. 4) Mind your Ps and Qs / Watch your language / Mind your language / Remember yourself / Play your cards right. 5) shenanigans / malarkey / goings-on / capers.

D) 1) stuck-up / toffee-nosed / snooty. 2) hush-hush / cloak-and-dagger. 3) fudge. 4) smarmy. 5) bolshy / stroppy. 6) butch / macho.

MODULE 23

A) 1) a crock / a jalopy / a banger. 2) a doss house / a flop house. 3) a box of tricks / a gadget / a gizmo. 4) what's-his-name / what's-her-name / so-and-so. 5) a tabloid. 6) another string to one's bow. 7) a hop. 8) a chopper / a whirlybird. 9) the blower. 10) juice.

B) 1) hodge-podge / hotch-potch / rag-bag / mishmash. 2) thingy / thingummy / thingumabob / thingumajig / what-do-you-call-it. 3) rain cats and dogs / pour (down) / bucket (down) / belt (down) / teem (down) / chuck it (down). 4) the (goggle-)box / the tube / the telly.

C) 1) ferret out / dig up / dredge up / happen on to. 2) pottering around / messing around. 3) How is she fixed for. 4) snapped. 5) I am not into / I don't go in for. 6) swims like a brick. 7) chased up / ferreted out / dug up. 8) unwind. 9) don't grow on trees / are not on tap. 10) It's cold enough to freeze the balls off a brass monkey! / It's brass-monkey weather!

D) 1) varmint / critter. 2) a mutt / (*small dog*) a pooch / a bow-wow. 3) a creepy-crawly. 4) a tiddler. 5) a mog / a moggie. 6) a nag / a gee-gee. 7) a porker.

E) Roller; Jag; Merc; the Chunnel; bed-sit; mod cons; des. res.; lab; mike; tranny; ammo; nuke; turps; telly; soap; sitcom; the Beeb; mag; soccer; rugger; DIY; chimp; hippo; rhino; budgie.

MODULE 24

A) 1) beeline. 2) stone. 3) sticks. 4) neck : woods. 5) travels. 6) doorstep. 7) cat. 8) nowhere.

B) 1) Uncle Sam. 2) jet-lag. 3) the (herring-)pond. 4) Oz / down under. 5) a sunspot. 6) a drifter. 7) as the crow flies. 8) a piggyback.

C) 1) hoof it / leg it / go on Shanks's mare / go on Shanks's pony. 2) jam-packed / chock-full / chocker / chock-a-block. 3) chucked / slung / heaved. 4) hit the road / hit the trail / make tracks / shove off / push off / dash off / toddle off / tootle off / mosey off. 5) scarpered / skedaddled / hooked it / split / skipped / showed a clean pair of heels / did a bunk / vamoosed / did a vanishing trick / made themselves scarce / cleared off / beat it / buzzed off / scrammed / hopped it. 6) take a pew / park yourself / plonk yourself (down).

D) 1) up. 2) on. 3) under. 4) all over. 5) in. 6) along. 7) on.

MODULE 25

A) 1) rustled / whipped. 2) knocked. 3) throwing. 4) hits. 5) paint. 6) stood. 7) polished. 8) grab. 9) dig / tuck.

B) 1) a spud. 2) a free loader. 3) a good trencherman. 4) plonk. 5) cha / char. 6) hooch / jungle-juice / rot-gut. 7) bubbly / shampers. 8) Dutch courage. 9) a chain-smoker. 10) cold turkey.

C) 1) chow / nosh / grub. 2) tight / high / well-oiled / half-seas-over / canned / stoned / stewed / pickled / sozzled / sloshed / pissed / soused / plastered / smashed / blotto / paralytic / legless / steaming drunk / stinking drunk / drunk out of their minds / drunk out of their senses / drunk as a newt / drunk as a lord. 3) fag / ciggy / gasper / tab / butt / (*self-rolled*) rollie. 4) gobbled up/down / wolfed down / hogged down / shovelled down / scoffed.

D) 1) a do. 2) a stag-party / stag-night. 3) a hen-party / hen-night. 4) a house-warming. 5) a knees-up. 6) a rave-up / a wingding.

E) 1) (a) slap-up. 2) piping hot. 3) stone-cold. 4) like a horse / his head off. 5) like a factory chimney. 6) sober as a judge / stone-cold sober. 7) a mouth like the bottom of a parrot's cage. 8) am famished / am starved / could eat a horse. 9) as a newt / as a lord.

MODULE 26

A) 1) oats. 2) innings. 3) daisies. 4) a dodo / mutton. 5) paradise. 6) tooth. 7) rut. 8) chicken.

B) 1) Civvy Street. 2) a hit man. 3) old hat. 4) a fuddy-duddy. 5) the wrong side of forty. 6) an old trout / an old bag. 7) a teeny-bopper. 8) olde-worlde. 9) alive and kicking. 10) the life of Reilly.

C) 1) getting on for / pushing / knocking. 2) kicked the bucket / snuffed it / bought it / gave up the ghost / popped off / pegged out. 3) do in / polish off / finish off / rub out / bump off / take out /

snuff / waste / do away with / get shot of.   4) scrape along / eke out a living / scrape a living / scratch a living / just get by / just keep the wolf from the door / just make ends meet / just keep their heads above water.   5) has one foot in the grave / is living on borrowed time / is on her last legs / is a goner / has had it / has had her chips.

D) 1) out.   2) down.   3) up.   4) back.   5) up.   6) up.

MODULE 27

A) 1) barge-pole / ten-foot pole.   2) Joneses.   3) Jack.   4) hail-fellow-well-met.   5) apple-cart.   6) hen-pecked.   7) Coventry.   8) old-boy.

B) 1) back-scratching.   2) hubby.   3) a lone wolf / a loner.   4) the pecking order.   5) a double-barrelled name.   6) a one-man band.   7) the rank and file.   8) a rat-race / dog-eat-dog.   9) my opposite number.   10) a stooge.

C) 1) pal / chum / mate / buddy / side-kick / (*friend in crime etc.*) crony.   2) have us by the short and curlies / have us over a barrel / have us on toast / have us in the palms of their hands / have us under their thumbs.   3) wouldn't touch it with a barge-pole / gives it a wide berth / avoids it like the plague / wouldn't be seen dead with it.

D) 1) house on fire.   2) thieves.   3) plague.   4) putty in his hands.

E) 1) on his tod / on his toddy.   2) knuckle under.   3) rub off on.   4) keep in.   5) themselves to themselves.   6) in cahoots.

MODULE 28

A) 1) Yes : Chinese (*The term 'Chinaman' is also sometimes considered offensive*).   2) No : an Australian.   3) Yes : an Italian.   4) Yes : a Frenchman.   5) No : a New Zealander.   6) No : a Welshman.   7) Yes : Japanese (*without the indefinite article 'a'*).   8) No : an Englishman.   9) Yes : a German.   10) Yes : a Pole.

B) 1) a litter-lout / a litter-bug.   2) a live wire.   3) Joe Public / Joe Bloggs / the man in the street.   4) a bogyman.   5) Old Nick.   6) Tom, Dick and Harry.   7) a tomboy.   8) a rough diamond.   9) a back-seat driver.   10) number one.

C) 1) togged up / dolled up / toffed up / dressed to the nines / dressed to kill.   2) natty / nifty / snazzy / posh / swanky / fetching.   3) down-at-heel / out-at-elbows.   4) togs / clobber / gear.

D) 1) a (spineless) wimp / a sissy / a softie.   2) spick and span / shipshape / squeaky clean.   3) square / corny.   4) hear a pin drop.   5) scarecrow.

E) 1) get-up / rig-out.   2) a pinny.   3) a brolly.   4) sparklers.   5) hand-me-downs.   6) clod-hoppers / beetle-crushers.   7) bags.   8) one's Sunday best / one's best bib and tucker / one's glad rags.

MODULE 29

A) 1) wink.   2) frog.   3) crystal.   4) birthday.   5) skinned / peeled.   6) tyre.   7) clapped / set.   8) forty.   9) death.   10) picture.

B) 1) a night owl.   2) a titch / a shrimp.   3) a beanpole / a lamppost.   4) a zit.   5) skinny-dipping.   6) a jab.   7) a pick-me-up.   8) goggles / specs.   9) her vital statistics.   10) the once-over.

C) 1) hitting the sack / hitting the hay / getting my head down / getting some shut-eye / getting some kip.   2) is no oil-painting / has a face like the back of a bus / is as ugly as sin.   3) fagged out / dead-beat / done / jiggered / all-in / whacked / fit to drop / shattered / bushed / tuckered out / (*vulgar*) shagged / knackered / pooped.   4) seedy / rough / out of sorts / ragged around the edges / under the weather.   5) whiff / pong / niff / hum / reek.   6) privy / loo / jakes / khazi / lav / bogs / bog / john / gents.

D) 1) old boots.   2) coot / billiard-ball.   3) log / top.   4) bat.   5) back of a bus.   6) bug in a rug.   7) rain / nails.   8) leaf.   9) parrot / dog.   10) rake.   11) doorpost.   12) sore thumb.

E) 1) lugs.   2) pegs / pins.   3) block / bonce / noggin / noddle.   4) paws / mits.   5) backside / butt / bum / arse / ass.   6) choppers / gnashers.   7) gob / trap / cake-hole / kisser.   8) trotters.   9) ticker.   10) mug / dial / mush / kisser / puss.

MODULE 30

A) 1) on the shelf.   2) popped the question.   3) on the game / a hooker.   4) shacked up together.   5) going steady.   6) common-law wife.   7) kinky.   8) got his young girlfriend into trouble / knocked up his young girlfriend.

B) 1) a peeping Tom.   2) a gym-slip mum.   3) Mr Right.   4) slap and tickle.   5) a wolf whistle.   6) a sugar daddy.   7) a toy boy.   8) a sex-pot / a sex-kitten.   9) a rent boy.   10) a blob / a johnnie / a French letter / a rubber.

C) 1) snogging / smooching / necking.   2) took the plunge / tied the knot / got hitched / got spliced.   3) has joined the pudding club / has a bun in the oven / is in the family way.

255

Index

small beer of oneself 122/1
beetle-crushers 172/1
beggar 170/8
bell, give a bell (phone) 93/9; ring a bell 91/23; sound as a bell 182/7
bells, pull the other one, it's got bells on 60/10
bellyache (complain) 98/2
bellyful, have had a bellyful 111/1
belt, under one's belt 7/17
belt, belt (speed) 22/24; belt (hit) 41/6; belt down 141/10; belt out (noise) 174/4; belt up (shut up) 99/2
belter, a belter 67/1
bend, clean round the bend 81/16
bender 155/21
bent bent (criminal) 35/1; bent (homosexual) 187/26
berk 82/10
berth, give a wide berth 166/6
bet, you bet! 105/1
better, go one better 68/14
beyond, beyond so. 8/2
bib, best bib and tucker 172/6
biff (hit) 41/9
big, go over big 15/2; in the big time 15/5; Mr Big 38/4
bigwig 38/2
Bill, the Bill 36/1; fit/fill the bill 74/3
billiard-ball, bald as a billiard-ball 177/6
billy, silly billy 82/11
billy-o, like billy-o 22/13
bimbo 82/20
bind, a bind (bore) 111/9
bingo 15/28
bint 187/13
bird, bird (person) 171/16; bird (girl) 187/13; bird (satellite) 134/13; do bird 37/17; a little bird told me 87/17
bird-brain 82/18
birthday, in one's birthday suit 177/1
biscuit, that takes the biscuit 66/4
bit, a bit of all right 187/11; bits and pieces 135/8; a bit of skirt 187/2; what's the 'we' bit 110/13
bitchy 111/23
bite, a bite (meal) 149/4
bite, bite off more than one can chew 8/9; two bites at the cherry 76/5; what's biting so. 111/21
blab, 89/7
blabbermouth 89/8
bla-bla-bla 94/11
blarney 97/5
blast, blast it! 103/1

blasted 103/3
blather 96/15
blazes, the blazes 103/8; go to blazes! 110/28; like blazes 22/13
blazing, a blazing row 32/1
bless, bless you! 101/9; well bless my soul! 104/2
blessed 103/3
blether 96/15
blighter 171/10
Blimp, colonel Blimp 167/6
blind, blind date 185/1
blink, on the blink 71/18
blinking 103/3
blithering, blithering idiot 82/8
blob 188/27
block, block (head) 176/4; do one's block 112/16; knock so.'s block off 42/9
blockhead, 82/9
bloody 103/4
bloomer (mistake) 17/2
blooming 103/3
blotto 155/14
blow, blow (reveal) 89/2; to blow (money) 55/9; well blow me! 104/2; blow in 142/1; a blow job 188/19
blowed, I'll be blowed 104/2; I'll be blowed if (determined) 86/8
blower 134/3
blow-out 149/6
blubber 118/1
blue, to blue (money) 55/9
blue, in a blue funk 114/2; blue movie 136/7; feel blue 118/10; like a bolt out of the blue 131/6
blue-eyed, blue-eyed boy/girl 107/10
blues, the blues 118/10
blurb 12/7
b.o. 183/22
board, above board 61/3; take on board 85/8
boat, in the same boat 73/12; miss the boat 76/14; rock the boat 167/15
Bob, Bob's your uncle 15/27; cost a few bob 53/2
bobby-dazzler 173/16
bod 170/8
body, over my dead body! 110/5; keep body and soul together 150/1
boffin 11/15
bog(s) 184/8
bog, bog down 14/13
bogus 59/29
bogyman 171/8
boil, boil down to 80/19
boiling, boiling (hot) 141/6; the whole boiling 64/22
bollicking, a bollicking 45/1

bollocks, (testicles) 189/1; make a bollocks of 9/11
boloney 96/8
bolshy 128/5
bomb, bomb (money) 49/21; go like a bomb 15/1; a bomb 18/14; drop a bomb 31/21
bombshell, come as a bombshell 31/21
bonce 176/4
bone, have a bone to pick with 32/10; make no bones about 100/3; bone idle 5/2
bone, bone up on 92/2
bonk, bonk (hit) 41/12; bonk (sex) 188/14
bonkers 81/9
bonny 178/20
boob(oo) (mistake) 17/1
boobs 189/9
booby 82/9
book, bring to book 44/10; call so. everything in the book 47/8; go by the book 61/11; in my book 85/2; in so.'s bad books 130/2; in so.'s good books 130/3; read so. like a book 90/11; throw the book at so. 45/11
bookie 11/9
bookworm 92/7
boot, the boot 6/4; the boot is on the other foot 72/12; lick so.'s boots 120/2; put the boot in 44/15; too big for one's boots 122/2; can bet your boots 79/4; clever boots 83/7; tough as old boots 178/14
boot-licker 120/5
booze 152/7
boozer, boozer (bar) 153/7; boozer (person) 155/6
boozy 155/5
bop (sex) 188/14
borrowed, live on borrowed time 162/2
bosh 96/5
botch 9/8
bother, bother! 103/1
bothered, cannot be bothered 5/9
bottle, bottle (courage) 114/4; on the bottle 155/3; hit the bottle 155/2
bottle, bottle up (emotions) 116/17
bottom, bet your bottom dollar 79/4; the bottom line 80/20
bottoms, bottoms up! 153/13
botty 176/16
bounce (cheque) 57/10
bouncer 40/1
bound, bound to 79/9
bounder 171/12
bowl, bowl along 22/25

bow-wow 140/9
box, box (TV) 136/1; box of tricks 134/8
boys, the boys in blue 36/2; one of the boys 164/9; jobs for the boys 164/21
bozo 82/9
brain, brain before brawn 83/3; pick so.'s brains 88/3
brain-child 84/11
brainwave 84/12
brand, brand new 67/14
brass, brass (money) 49/2; top brass 38/1; get down to brass tacks 87/8; not give a brass farthing 119/1; brass monkey weather 141/5; cold enough to freeze the balls off a brass monkey 141/5
brat 160/7
brawl 40/2
bread, bread (money) 49/2; so.'s bread and butter 1/22; quarrel with one's bread and butter 1/23
break (luck) 75/4; (chance) 76/1
break, (be revealed) 89/13
breathe, breathe down so.'s neck 43/6
breeze, a breeze 26/3
brew, brew 24/7; brew up 152/3
brick, brick (person) 170/5; drop a brick 17/5; like talking to a brick wall 90/15; swim like a brick 139/16
bricks, bricks and mortar 133/1; come down on so. like a ton of bricks 44/7
bricky 11/4
bridges, not cross bridges before one comes to them 24/2
brief, hold no brief for 106/9
bright, bright and early 21/6
brill 67/10
bring, bring sth. off 15/17
briny, the briny 147/1
bristols 189/9
British, the best of British! 75/9
broad, a broad (woman) 187/14; it's broad as it is long 73/6
broke, flat/stony broke 52/4
brolly 172/23
brown, brown so. off 111/7
brownie, earn brownie points 130/18
browse 92/6
bruiser 40/8
brush, brush up (improve) 92/3
brush-off, give so. the brush-

off 166/2
bubbly 152/15
buck, buck (dollar) 49/10; buck (cheek) 124/1; the buck stops here 33/14; pass the buck 33/15; turn a quick buck 49/10
buck, to buck sth. 15/20; buck so. up (cheer) 117/2; buck up (health) 182/1
bucket, kick the bucket 162/10
bucket, bucket down 141/10
buckle, buckle (down) to 4/1
buckshee, 54/9
budding 24/8
buddy 164/2
budgie 140/14
buff 109/12
bug, bug (microphone/fault) 134/7; the bug (craze) 109/15; the love bug 108/14; snug as a bug in a rug 183/20
bug, bug so. 111/18
bugger, bugger all 63/9; bugger off! 110/30; (leave) 144/14
buggered (defective) 71/3; I'll be buggered 104/2
bull, bull (nonsense) 96/13; like a bull in a china shop 9/4; score a bull's-eye 15/7
bulldog, the bulldog breed 115/5
bulldoze, bulldoze into 43/11
bullshit 96/13
bully, bully for so. 105/19
bum (defective) 71/5; bum (bottom) 176/17
bum, bum around 5/8; bum (beg) 57/2
bumf, 87/3
bum-fodder, 87/3
bump, bump into 142/6; bump off 163/3
bumper (large) 65/1
bumpers 189/9
bumpkin 82/29
bun, have a bun in the oven 188/25
bunch, the pick of the bunch 68/9
bundle, bundle (money) 49/21, a bundle of laughs/fun 117/15; go a bundle on 107/8
bung, bung (put) 146/7; bunged up 71/16
bunk, bunk (nonsense) 96/2; do a bunk 144/9
bunkum 96/2
bunk-up, give a bunk-up 146/3
bunny 140/5
burn, burn up (distance) 145/14; money to burn 51/5
burp 150/20

burton, go for a burton 71/11
bus, miss the bus 76/14; a face like the back of a bus 178/18
bush, bush telegraph 87/16; beat about the bush 97/8
bushed 180/1
business, business end 1/30; like nobody's business 4/24; put business so.'s way 3/10; unfinished business 32/11; not be in business of 33/4; have no business to 33/6; do one's business 184/7
busker 11/14
busman, busman's holiday 139/17
bust, a bust (raid) 36/10
bust, bust (broken) 71/1; don't bust yourself 4/29; go bust 18/12, bust (arrest) 36/8
buster 102/11
bust-up (quarrel) 32/7
busybody 33/19
but, no buts about it 110/16; but me no buts 110/16
butch 126/4
butt, butt (bottom) 176/17; butt (cigarette) 157/4; work one's butt off 2/3
butter, butter so. up 120/6
butter-fingers 9/3
butterflies, butterflies in one's stomach/tummy 113/23
buy, buy (believe) 85/16; buy it (die) 162/11
buzz, give a buzz (phone) 93/9; get a buzz out of 117/27
buzz, buzz off 144/13
buzz-word 93/5

caboodle, the whole caboodle 64/22
cackle, cut the cackle 99/2
cadge 57/2
cagey 131/1
cahoots, in cahoots 164/15
Cain, raise Cain 31/1
cake, a piece of cake 26/4; go like hot cakes 56/2; that takes the cake 66/4 ; have one's cake and eat it 76/6
cake-hole 176/1
call, have no call to 33/6; pay a call (WC) 184/1
call, call it a day 1/3
call-girl 187/21
camp (effeminate) 122/9
can, the can (jail) 37/12; carry the can 46/2
candle, not hold a candle to 68/7
canned 155/13
capers 128/2
capital 67/10
cards, one's cards 6/5; on the

cards 76/17; play one's cards right 127/1

carpet, sweep under the carpet 123/8

carpeting, a carpeting 45/4

carrot, the carrot and the stick 44/18

carry, carry on with so. 188/8

carry-on 31/6

case, case a joint 34/7

cash, cash in on 50/5

cast, cast one's mind back 84/6; cast about for 137/1

cast-iron, 90/24

cat, set the cat among the pigeons 32/16; more than one way to skin a cat 72/8; not a cat in hell's chance 76/23; see which way the cat jumps 88/6; let the cat out of the bag 89/1; look what the cat's brought in! 101/2; rain cats and dogs 141/11; no room to swing a cat 148/4

cat-burglar 35/11

catcall 185/12

catch, catch it 46/6, catch so. out 17/11; catch on (understand) 90/5; catch on 107/11; catch (hear) 183/16

catch-22, a catch-22 situation 29/18

catnap 179/9

cauliflower, cauliflower ear 41/24

ceiling, hit the ceiling 112/17

cert, a dead cert 79/3

cha (tea) 152/1

chain-smoker 157/7

chalk, different as chalk and cheese 72/2; not by a long chalk 72/4

chalk, chalk up 15/8

champion (excellent) 67/10

change, get no change out of (information) 88/12; get no change out of (indulgence) 121/7

chap, chap 170/1; old chap 102/9

char, char (tea) 152/1; charlady 11/7

charlie, a proper charlie 82/12

chase, go and chase yourself! 110/28; chase up sth. 137/2

chaser (drink) 152/16

chat, chat up 185/7

chatterbox, 97/11

cheap, on the cheap 54/7

cheese, hard cheese 75/16; say 'cheese' 139/12

cheese, cheese so. off 111/7

Cheshire, grin like a Cheshire cat 117/13

chest, get it off one's chest

89/14

chick 187/13

chicken, chicken (coward) 115/8; chicken out 115/9; be no (spring) chicken 161/9; chicken feed 49/20

chickens, so.'s chickens have come home to roost 46/15; not count one's chickens before they're hatched 24/3

chiefs, too many chiefs and not enough Indians 38/10

child, child's play 26/1

chimney, smoke like a (factory-) chimney 157/8

chimp 140/14

chin-chin 153/13

Chinese, all Chinese 90/18

Chink 169/1

chin-wag 94/2

chip, a chip off the old block 73/4; have a chip on one's shoulder 86/5

chip, chip in (money) 49/16; chip in (speak) 93/11

chippie (chip shop) 149/16

chippy (job) 11/3

chips, when the chips are down 66/1; have had one's chips 162/6

chivvy 2/11,

chock-a-block (fed-up) 111/4; (full) 148/1

chocker (fed-up) 111/4; (full) 148/1

chock-full 148/1

chop, the chop 6/4; chop chop! 22/9

chopper (helicopter) 132/3; chopper (penis) 189/2

choppers 176/8

chops, a smack in the chops 41/19

chow 149/1

Christ, for Christ's sake 104/15

chronic 70/7

chuck, chuck (throw) 146/4; chuck in (stop) 19/12; chuck it down 141/10

chucking-out, chucking-out time 21/22

chuffed 117/9

chum, a chum 164/2

chum, chum up with 164/5

chummy 164/6

chump, a chump (fool) 82/10; off one's chump 81/12

Chunnel 132/13

churn, churn out 64/17

ciggy 157/4

cinch, (easy) 26/3,

city, fight City Hall 28/5

Civvy, Civvy Street 159/5

clam, shut up like a clam 99/1

clam, clam up 99/1

clanger, drop a clanger 17/5

clap, the clap 188/28

clap, clap in jail 37/13

clapped, clapped out (defective) 71/4

clappers, like the clappers 22/20

claptrap 96/3

claws, get one's claws into so. 186/2

clean, come clean 89/12

cleaners, take so. to the cleaners 58/8

clear, in the clear 37/11

clear, clear off 144/13

click, click with (understand) 90/8; click with (impress) 108/1

cliff-hanger 78/9

clinch, a clinch 188/6

clinch, clinch a deal 79/20

clink 37/12

clip, clip joint 133/10

clip (hit) 41/20

cloak-and-dagger 123/3

clobber, clobber (belongings) 135/7; clobber (clothes) 172/3

clobber (hit) 41/5

clock, clock (hit) 41/2; clock up 22/27

clod-hoppers 172/2

clogs, clever clogs 83/7

clot 82/9

cloud, on cloud nine 117/4

cloud-cuckoo-land 159/22

clout, clout (hit) 41/9; pack clout 38/5

clover, in clover 51/11

club, join the club! 73/13

clue, not have a clue 91/15

clue, clue up 87/12

coach, drive a coach and horses through 71/20

coals, haul so. over the coals 45/12

coast, the coast is clear 78/5

cobblers 96/9

cock (penis) 189/2

cock-a-hoop 117/7

cock-and-bull, cock-and-bull story 60/2

cock-eyed 71/14

cockles, warm the cockles of so.'s heart 117/14

cock-teaser 187/17

cock-up, 9/10

codger, old codger 161/14

codswallop 96/8

coke (cocaine) 158/4

cold, knock cold 41/16; get cold feet 115/10; out in the cold 166/11

collar, hot under the collar 112/7

collywobbles, have the collywobbles 113/23

come, as they come 66/20; come off (succeed) 15/22; come off (occur) 80/14; how come . . . ? 80/2; come up with (idea) 84/10; come again! 101/7; come to think of it 101/15; come to that 101/15; come on! 110/15; come off it! 110/15; not know whether one is coming or going 113/12; come on strong 126/3; not know what came over one 128/7; don't come the . . . with me! 128/8; come by (obtain) 137/3; come (sex) 189/4

come-back, have no come-back 29/16

come-uppance, get one's come-uppance 46/11

comfy 183/21

coming, get what is coming to one 46/11, have it coming 46/9; see so. coming 58/7, have another thing coming 79/8

commercial 12/3

common, common as muck 64/14; common-or-garden 64/15; common law wife/husband 186/9

computer-hacking 34/22

con, (fraud) 58/1

confounded 103/2

conk (nose) 176/5

conk, conk out 71/9

contraption 134/10

coo, coo! 104/9

cook, cook the books 58/12; cook up (invent) 60/4

cooked (fail) 18/15

cookie, a tough cookie 170/10; the way the cookie crumbles 75/13

cooking, what's cooking? 80/9

cool, a cool sum 49/19; a cool cat/customer 116/15; keep one's cool 116/3

cool, cool it 116/8

coon, 169/18

coot, bald as a coot 177/6

cop, a fair cop 36/11; not much cop 69/7; get a cop of 183/6

cop, cop (arrest) 36/7; cop it 46/6; cop out 18/34

coppers, coppers (police) 36/2; going for coppers 54/5

cops 36/2

cop-shop 36/5

copy-cat 129/3

cor, cor blimey! 104/1

cork, cork up (emotions) 116/17

corker, a corker 67/1

corner, corner the market 12/14

corners, cut corners 22/30

corny (talk) 94/18; corny (old-fashioned) 173/15

corporation (stomach) 178/4

cotton, cotton on to (understand) 90/2; cotton on to (like) 107/9

cough, cough (reveal) 36/20; cough up 55/2

count, out for the count 41/17

Coventry, send to Coventry 166/3

cow, silly cow 82/19; holy cow! 104/1

cowboys, 9/5

cows, till the cows come home 20/5

crack (excellent) 67/5

crack, a crack (attempt) 77/1; a fair crack of the whip 61/8; a crack (chat) 94/6; a crack (joke) 94/17; paper over the cracks 123/6

crack, crack down on 44/8; not all that sth. is cracked up to be 69/6; crack a joke 94/16; crack a bottle 153/2; crack up 181/17

crackers (crazy) 81/9

cracking, cracking 67/8; at a cracking pace 22/17; get cracking 22/1

crackpot 125/4

cradle-snatcher 187/8

cram (learn) 92/1

crap 184/11

crappy 70/2

crash, crash out 179/12

crashing, a crashing bore 111/11

crate (plane) 132/2

crawler 120/5

crawling, crawling (dirty) 175/7; crawling with 64/12

crazy, like crazy 22/16

creek, up the creek 29/6

creep (person) 171/3

creeper 120/5

creeps, 114/7

creepy-crawly 140/1

crib (copy) 92/12

cricket, not cricket 61/2

crikey 104/1

critter 140/3

crock (defective) 71/6; (vehicle) 132/4

crony 164/4

crook (criminal) 35/2

crooked 35/1

crop, crop up 80/13

cropper, come a cropper (fail) 18/5; come a cropper (fall)

146/15

cross, cross as two sticks 112/2

cross, cross one's mind 84/13

crow, stone the crows! 104/1; as the crow flies 145/16

crown (hit) 41/3

crumbs, crumbs! 104/7

crummy 70/2

crumpet 189/8

crunch, when it comes to the crunch 66/11

crush, have a crush on 108/4

crust, upper crust 167/5

cry, a far cry from 72/5

cry-baby 118/3

crying, for crying out loud! 104/16

crystal, not have a crystal ball 24/13; crystal clear 183/11

cuckoo, (crazy) 81/8

cucumber, cool as a cucumber 116/9

cuff, cuff (hit) 41/21; off the cuff 21/17; on the cuff 57/4

cum, sth. cum sth. 68/12

cunt 189/8

cup, not so.'s cup of tea 110/21

cuppa 152/2

curse, the curse 181/11

curtains (fail) 18/18; curtains (death) 162/7

cushy, a cushy number 1/27

cuss (person) 171/15

cussedness 111/22

customer, customer (person) 171/16; an ugly customer 171/7

cut, a cut above 68/3

cut, cut it (out) 19/2; cut it fine/close 21/8; cut and run 115/11; be cut up about 113/17; cut up rough/nasty 112/18

cut, cut out (ability) 7/13; have one's work cut out 28/7

cutie 178/22

cut-throat 126/2

dabble, dabble in 139/5

dad 165/3

daddy, daddy 165/3; the daddy of all 65/8

daft, daft as a brush, 82/1

dago 169/14

daily, daily dozen 182/8

daisies, push up daisies 162/15

damage, (cost) 55/14

damn, damn it! 103/1; not give a damn 119/3

damned, damned 103/4; I'll be damned if (determined) 86/8

damnest, do one's damnest 4/10

damper, put the damper on 118/16

dander, get so.'s dander up 112/20

dark, in the dark 91/18

darky 169/18

dash, dash off (work) 1/12; dash off (leave) 144/4

Davy, Davy Jones's locker 147/2

day, all in a day's work 1/18; that'll be the day! 24/11; in all my born days 159/3; have had one's day 161/5; have seen better days 161/4

daylight, daylight robbery 58/10

daylights, beat the living daylights out of 42/10; scare the living daylights out of 114/4

dead, dead (very) 66/23; dead easy 26/11; dead beat (tired) 180/1; dead and buried 32/19; drop dead! 110/28; not be seen dead in 166/8

dead-beat, a dead-beat 18/22; dead-end, dead-end job 1/24

dead-on 66/25

dead-pan 116/11

dead-set 86/7

deal, (no) big deal! 39/13; raw deal 61/6

death, hang on like grim death 13/8; catch one's death of cold 181/13

debunk 61/15

decent, a decent amount 62/3

deck, hit the deck 146/12

deep, jump in at the deep end 28/14; go off the deep end 112/15; a deep one 123/5

dekko, have a dekko 183/5

deliver the goods 1/17,

demolish, demolish a meal 150/5

dent, make a dent in (money) 53/9

depth, out of one's depth 8/3

deserts, get one's just deserts 46/11

des. res. 133/9

deuce, the deuce 103/8

devil, the devil to pay 46/18; the devil's own luck 75/3; the devil 103/8; luck of the devil 75/3; talk of the devil 101/1

dial (face) 176/3

diamond, rough diamond 170/11

dice, no dice 75/12

dicey 78/1

dick, dick (penis) 189/2; (detective) 36/4; a clever dick 83/7

dickens, the dickens 103/8

dick-head 82/10

dicky (defective) 71/15

dicky-bird, not say a dicky-bird 99/7

diddle, diddle so. 58/2

diddy 65/12

die, straight as a die 61/13

dig, have a dig at 47/6

dig, (understand) 90/3; dig up 137/4; dig in (eat) 150/3

digs 133/6

dilly-dally 23/3

dim, take a dim view of 110/20

dim-wit 82/9

din, din into 87/15; kick up a din 174/2

din-dins 149/2

ding-dong 32/2

dinky (small) 65/11

dirt, dirt cheap 54/1; so.'s name is dirt 130/1

dirty, do the dirty on so. 59/23; dirty great 65/4

dish, (girl) 178/22

dish, dish out 62/4; dish up 93/14

distance, go the distance 13/9

ditch (abandon) 19/13

ditchwater, dull as ditchwater 111/8

dither 23/1

dive, a dive (place) 133/4

DIY 139/14

do, do (organize) 10/6; do (arrest) 36/8; do (visit) 145/9; do (party) 154/6; do so. (defraud) 58/6; do over (beat) 42/6; do (be suitable) 74/6; could do with 107/3; could do without 107/4; do in (kill) 163/2; do away with (kill) 163/4; do it with so. (sex) 188/11

doc 11/24

doctor, just what the doctor ordered 74/1

dodder 181/10

dodderer, old dodderer 161/15

doddle, a doddle 26/2

dodge 83/9

dodgy 78/2

dodo, dead as a dodo 162/16

dog, dog (person) 170/8; sea dog 170/9; work like a dog 2/1; a dog's breakfast/dinner 30/4; not a dog's chance 76/23; in the dog house 130/4; not fit to turn a dog out 141/1; a dog's life 159/11; life in the old dog yet 161/11; top dog 168/3; sick as a dog 181/19; go to the dogs 18/9

dog, dog so. 143/21

dog-collar 172/18

dog-eat-dog 167/11

do-gooder 171/26

dogsbody 11/19

doing, take a bit of doing 28/9; anything doing 80/10; nothing doing! 110/3

doldrums, in the doldrums 118/9

dole, on the dole 6/8

dole-wallah 5/7

doll, doll up 173/3

dollop, a dollop 62/2

dolly 187/11

done, done! 105/10; done (tired) 180/1; that's done it 18/19; not done 110/18

dong (penis) 189/2

donkey, donkey work 2/7; donkey's years 20/1; talk the hind legs off a donkey 97/3; eat the hind legs off a donkey 150/11

doodle 139/21

door-nail, dead as a door-nail 162/16

doorpost, deaf as a doorpost 183/17

doorstep, on so.'s doorstep 145/17

dope, dope (drugs) 158/1; a dope (fool) 82/9; dope (information) 87/2

dopey 82/6

dose, go through like a dose of salts 22/14; a dose of one's own medicine 45/13

dosh, 49/2

doss, doss house 133/3

dot (hit) 40/9

dot, the year dot 20/4; on the dot 21/10

dotted, sign on the dotted line 105/16

dotty 81/5

double, at the double 22/11

double-barrelled, double-barrelled name 167/7

double-cross 59/26

dough, (money) 49/2

down, down and out 52/11; down on one's luck 75/14; get so. down 118/15; send so. down 37/15; down under (Australia) 147/4; down with (ill) 181/7

down, down a drink 153/3

downhill, go downhill 18/1

down-market 12/13

drag, drag (clothes) 172/15; a drag (bore) 111/9; drag (smoke) 157/2

drag, drag up (revive) 161/22

drain, down the drain (fail) 18/10; money down the drain 55/10

drat, drat! 103/1

261

dratted 103/2
draught, feel the draught 53/12
drawing board 18/27
dredge, dredge up 137/4
drenching, get a drenching 141/13
dressed, dressed to kill 173/5; dressed to the nines 175/4
dressing-down 45/3
dribs, dribs and drabs 63/13
drift, get the drift 90/5
drifter 145/7
drill, the drill 7/3
drink, the drink (sea) 147/1; drive so. to drink 111/12
drip, a drip (person) 171/20
drive, drive at (mean) 85/11
drivel 96/12
drop, a drop in the ocean 63/5; a drop too many 155/9
drop, drop it (stop) 18/3; drop so. in it/the shit 29/9; drop in/by 142/5; drop off 179/10
drop-out 166/16
drubbing (beating) 42/1
drum, drum into 87/15; drum up 137/9
dry run 7/20
dry, dry up 99/5
DTs, have the DTs 155/22
duck, dead duck 18/20; lame duck 53/14; sitting duck 26/10; like water off a duck's back 90/14; take to sth. like a duck to water 107/7
ducking, get a ducking 141/13
ducky (address) 102/3
dud 71/5
dude 173/17
duff (defective) 71/5
duff, duff up 42/6
duffer 82/25
dummy, dummy run 7/20
dump (place) 147/15
dumps, in the dumps 118/9
dumpy 178/1
dunce 82/27
dunk 150/18
dust, dust so.'s jacket 42/7
dusty, dusty in 8/14
Dutch, go Dutch 49/15; double Dutch 95/2; Dutch courage 155/1
Dutchman, I'm a Dutchman if 79/7
dyed-in-the-wool 66/21
dying, dying to/for 109/5; dying for a drink 153/14
dyke 187/29

ear, play it by ear 131/2
earful, an earful 45/6
ears, collapse around one's ears 18/13; up to one's ears in (work) 3/3; up to one's ears in (debt) 57/9
earth, cost the earth 53/1; on earth 103/8
earthly, no earthly good/use 71/21; not an earthly 76/22
easy, be easy (agree) 105/13; easy does it! 23/10; go easy on so. 121/2; easy come, easy go 137/10
easy-peasy 26/11
eat, what's eating so. 111/21
edge, the edge on (advantage) 68/13
edgeways, not get a word in edgeways 97/7
egg, a bad egg 128/3; have egg on one's face 130/5; egg on so.'s chin 173/23
eggs, sure as eggs is eggs 79/1
ego-trip 122/6
eight, one over the eight 155/9
eke, eke out a living 159/16
elbow grease 4/19
elbows, out at elbows 173/21
elephant, white elephant 53/13
elevenses 149/3
emerald, the emerald isle 147/6
end, at a loose end 3/12; on end 20/13; not the end of the world 38/21; no end of 64/2; make ends meet 159/13; at the end of the day 66/12; on the receiving end 46/7; get one's end away 188/16
end, end it all 163/7
enough, enough to be getting/going on with 62/5
even-handed 61/10
ever, ever so 66/16; have/did you ever! 104/12
Ex, so.'s Ex 186/12
exhibition, make an exhibition of oneself 130/7
eye, my eye! 110/14
eyelid, not bat an eyelid 116/6
eye-opener 88/11
eyes, up to one's eyes in (work) 3/3; up to the eyes in (debt) 57/9; his eyes are bigger than his belly 150/15; clap/set eyes on 183/7
Eyetie 169/13
eyewash 59/31

face, fall flat on one's face 18/7; laugh on the other side of one's face 46/17; talk till one is blue in the face 97/6
fad 139/1
faff, a faff 30/4; faff around 23/5
fag (cigarette) 157/4
fagged, fagged out 180/1

faggot 187/27
faintest, not have the faintest 91/15
fair, fair and square 61/5; fair dos 61/4; fair-to-middling 69/4; fair enough! 105/11
fair-weather, fair-weather friend 164/1
fairy 187/27
fall, fall through 18/6; fall for sth. (believe) 59/9; fall for 108/12
fall, fall guy 46/5
family, in the family way 188/25
famished 151/8
fancy, fancy pants 173/17; fancy man 187/9
fancy, tickle so.'s fancy 107/5
fancy, fancy that!/just fancy! 104/3; fancy sth. 107/1; fancy oneself 122/1
fanny, fanny (buttocks) 176/17; fanny (vagina) 189/8; sweet Fanny Adams 63/10
far-out 125/1
fart, fart 184/14; fart around 5/8
fashion, spend money like it was going out of fashion 55/6
fast, pull a fast one 59/14
fat, fat cat 51/7; fat chance 76/24; a fat lot 63/8
fat-head 82/9
father, the father of all 65/8
fear, no fear of 79/11; no fear! 110/3
feather, another feather in so.'s cap 130/17; you could have knocked me down with a feather! 104/22
federal, make a Federal case of sth. 31/19
feel, feel like (want) 107/2
feet, drag one's feet 23/4; rushed off one's feet 3/5; have itchy feet 145/5; put one's feet up 139/9
fence (criminal) 35/13
fences, rush one's fences 22/31
fend, fend for oneself 159/19
ferret, ferret out 137/5
fetch, fetch so. one 41/10; fetch a price 56/4; fetch up 181/20
fetching 173/9
fettle, in a fine fettle 117/1
few, a good few 64/4
fib 60/5
fiddle, on the fiddle 58/14; a face as long as a fiddle 118/13; fit as a fiddle 182/7; scrape the fiddle 139/19
fiddle, fiddle so. 58/13
fiddlesticks 96/10

fiddly 28/13

field, have a field day 117/23

fiend, (enthusiast) 109/14

fig, not give a fig 119/1

fight, put up a good fight 4/26

fighting, a fighting chance 76/2; fighting fit 182/7

figure, cut a poor figure 130/6

figure, (think) 85/4; (be logical) 90/22

fill, fill in for 1/6; fill so. in (beat up) 42/6; fill so. in (inform) 87/10

finders, finders keepers 137/7

fine, a fine (mess) 30/1

finger, get/pull one's finger out 4/17; have a finger in the pie 33/7; not lay a finger on 41/26; not lift a finger 4/28; put one's finger on sth. 88/8; twist so. round one's little finger 168/6

fingers, all fingers and thumbs 9/1; work one's fingers to the bone 2/3; keep fingers crossed 75/8

fingertips, have at one's fingertips 91/4

finicky 125/7

finish, finish off (kill) 163/2

fink 36/24

fire, fire (dismiss) 6/3; fire away! (speak) 93/3

fire-bug 35/12

fire-trap 133/5

fireworks (trouble) 31/12

first, first come, first served 21/4

fish, a fish (person) 171/16; other fish to fry 33/8; big fish in a small pond 76/11; other (good) fish in the sea 76/9; drink like a fish 153/8

fish-wife, swear like a fish-wife 103/5

fishy 91/25

fit, fit to drop 180/1

fix, fix sth. (fraud) 59/17; fix so. 44/5

fix, a fix (fraud) 59/18; a fix (drugs) 158/8; in a fix 29/1

fixed, how are you fixed for ...? 138/3

fix-up 10/4

fizzle, fizzle out 18/4

flabbergasted 104/21

flak (criticism) 47/10

flake, flake out 179/14

flame, an old flame 108/17

flaming 103/3

flannel (talk) 94/14

flap, in a flap 113/18

flash, flash in the pan 20/9

flash, flash money around 55/7

flasher 187/30

flat, flat broke 52/4; flat out 22/21

fleece, fleece so. 58/4

flicks 133/11

flies, no flies on so. 83/4

fling, have one's last fling 21/21

flipping 103/3

flog, (sell) 56/1

floor, floor so. 8/7, wipe the floor with so. 44/3

floozy 171/25

flop, flop 18/14; flop house 133/3

fluff (bungle) 9/8

fluke 75/2

flummox 113/1

flump (fall) 146/14

flunk, 92/15

flush, (rich) 51/1

fluster 113/4

flutter, a flutter (bet) 77/11

fly, not hurt a fly 78/10

fly, let fly 41/1

fly-by-night, fly-by-night trader 58/18

flying, get off to a flying start 14/2; pass with flying colours 92/14

fly-on-the-wall 136/5

fly-posting 34/20

fly-tipping 34/19

fob, fob sth. off on so. 58/9

fogey, old fogey 161/17

foggiest, not have the foggiest 91/15

fold, fold (up) (fail) 18/11

folks, (address) 102/12; (family) 165/12

foot, get/put a foot in the door 14/1; put one's foot down 44/9; put one's foot in it 17/5; put one's best foot forward 22/7; my foot! 110/14; not put a foot wrong 127/5; have one foot in the grave 162/3

foot, foot the bill 55/12

foot-slogging 143/5

fork, fork out 55/2

fort, hold the fort 33/13

foul, foul up 9/9,

four-eyes 183/13

fox, fox so. 59/2

frame, frame so. 37/6

frame-up 37/5

freak, freak out 158/12

free, feel free 150/19; a free loader 150/16

freebie 12/5

free-for-all 40/5

freeze, freeze out 166/10

French, excuse my French! 103/6; French letter 188/27

fresh, get fresh 124/5; fresh out of sth. 138/5

fresher 92/8

Friday, girl Friday 11/12

friends, friends at court 164/16

frigging 103/4

frighteners, put the frighteners on 114/3

frillies 172/13

frisk 36/14

frog(gie) 169/24; have a frog in one's throat 183/18

frogmarch 40/17

front, up front 21/1

fruit, fruit machine 134/2; fruit cake 81/17

fruity 187/1

fry, small fry 39/1

fuck, fuck all 63/9; like fuck! 110/3; fuck off! (refusal) 110/30; fuck off (leave) 144/14; not give a fuck 119/3; fuck so. 188/14

fucking 103/4

fuddle-duddy 161/18

fudge, a fudge 123/7

full, know full well 91/1

funeral, be so.'s funeral 33/2

funky 173/10

funny, funny (crazy) 81/6; funny (unwell) 181/5; funny business 59/20; funny farm 81/19

furniture, be a part of the furniture 39/5

fuse, blow a fuse 112/17

fusspot 31/9

fuzz 36/2

gab, gift of the gab 97/4

gadget 134/9

gaff, blow the gaff 89/3

gaffer 11/20

gaga 81/10

gall (cheek) 124/2

gallivant 143/14

galore 64/6

game, game (willing) 105/14; game (plan) 59/21; the game is up 59/22; easy game 26/9; two can play at that game 73/8; play the game 127/7; on the game 187/22

gammy 181/16

gander, have a gander 183/5

gang-bang 188/18

gangway, gangway! 143/22

gannet 150/13

gaolbird 37/20

garble 95/5

garden, everything in the garden is lovely 25/2; lead up the garden path 59/3

gas (talk) 94/10

gasbag 97/12

gasper (cigarette) 157/5

gasping 153/14**

gate-crash 154/5

gate-post, between you, me and the gate-post 101/8

gauntlet, run the gauntlet 78/6

gawp 183/15

gay 187/26; a gay 187/27

gear 135/7, gear (clothes) 172/3

gee, gee whiz 104/8

gee-gee 140/11

geezer 161/13

gen, 87/2

gen, gen up 87/4

gents 184/9

George, by George! 104/6

geronimo, geronimo! 146/16

get (person) 171/3

get, get (understand) 90/4; get through to 90/13; don't get me wrong 90/16; get at (criticize) 47/13; get at (cheat) 59/16; get up to no good 128/1; get so. down 118/15; get away with 15/19; get in (work) 1/11; get it (suffer) 46/6; get one's own back 44/11; what gets me 111/20; get nowhere fast 14/14; get there 14/7; get so. off 37/10; get at (mean) 85/11; get on to so. (speak to) 93/8; get away! 104/14; get off it! 110/15; get along with you! 110/15; get on (leave) 144/2; get on with (friendship) 164/11; get around (travel) 145/2; get by 159/12; get off with so. 185/7

getting, be getting on (old) 161/1; getting on for (an age) 161/2

get-together 164/13

get-up 172/8

ghetto-blaster 134/5

ghost, give up the ghost 162/12

ghostly, not a ghostly 76/22

gig 136/15

gimmick 12/4

girlie-mag 136/10

git 171/3

give, give so. it 41/10; give over (stop) 19/3, give or take 62/8

gizmo 134/9

glad, glad rags 172/5; give the glad eye 185/8

globetrotter 145/6

glorify 67/17

glutton, glutton for punishment 46/8

gnashers 176/8

go, go (energy) 4/21; make a go of sth. 15/16; right from the word 'go' 20/16; have a go at (criticize) 47/5; have a go 77/2; give it a go 77/3; on the go 143/11

go, go down well 15/3; go over big 15/2; go under 18/11; gone and done it 17/6; as things go 80/16; go on about 97/10; go on with you! 104/14; go down as 130/10; go in for 139/3

goalposts, move the goalposts 72/11

goat, get so.'s goat 111/15

gob 176/1

gobble, gobble down 150/7

gobbledygook 95/3

gob-smacked 104/21

gob-stopper 149/15

god, for god's sake 104/15

goddamn 103/4

goggle-box 136/1

goggles 183/12

going, hard/heavy going 28/15; while the going is good 75/7

going-over (beating) 42/5; going-over (look) 183/9

goings-on 128/2

gold, good as gold 67/13

golly, golly! 104/8

gone, gone on sth. 108/8

goner, a goner (failure) 18/17; a goner (die) 162/4

good, good for 138/4

goodness, for goodness' sake 104/15

good-time, good-time girl 187/16

gooey 175/3

goof, a goof 17/3; goof it 17/4, **goofy** 82/6

gook 169/3

goolies 189/1

goon 82/17

gooseberry, play gooseberry 185/13

gormless 82/4

gosh, gosh! 104/8

governor 102/6

GP (doctor) 11/25

grab (opinion) 85/6; grab a meal 150/2

grabs, up for grabs 138/6

gracious, goodness gracious me! 104/4

grade, make the grade 74/11

graft (work) 2/5; (bribery) 34/15

grand, (money) 49/11

grandmother, don't teach your grandmother to suck eggs 68/8

gran(d)ma 165/7

gran(ny) 165/7

gran(d)pa 165/8

grape-vine, on the grape-vine 87/16

grapple, grapple with 4/5

grass (drugs) 158/2; put out to

grass 161/7; the grass roots 167/9

grass, grass on so. 36/19

gravy, gravy train 50/10

grease, grease so.'s palm 34/16

Greek, all Greek 90/18

green, green (inexperienced) 8/16; give the green light 105/17

greenhorn 8/16

gremlins 71/19

grind, daily grind 1/25; hard grind 2/6; grind to a halt 23/9

gripe 98/1

grit (courage) 115/3

gritty 115/3

groggy 181/2

groovy 67/11

groping 188/2

grotty (poor) 70/3; (dirty) 175/5

grouch 98/1

ground, suit so. down to the ground 74/4

grouse (complain) 98/1

grub 149/1

grubby 175/4

guess, it's anybody's guess 79/21

guessing, keep so. guessing 79/22

guest, be my guest! 105/15

guff 96/7

gum, up a gum tree 29/4; by gum! 104/6

gumption 83/10

gun, big gun 38/3; jump the gun 22/32; go great guns 14/6; stick to one's guns 13/3

gunge 175/2

gung-ho 109/3

gunning, be gunning for 44/14

guts, guts (courage) 115/2; sweat one's guts out 2/2; hate so.'s guts 110/24; greedy guts 150/14; have so.'s guts for garters 44/7; spew one's guts out 181/21

gutsy 115/2

guv 102/6

guy 170/1

gym-slip, gym-slip mum 186/10

gyp 58/2

habdabs, the screaming habdabs 112/10

hacking, computer hacking 34/22

hag, old hag 178/19

hail, hail from 147/11

hail-fellow-well-met 164/10

hair, keep your hair on! 12/19; enough to make your hair curl 114/9; make so.'s hair stand on end 114/11; let one's hair down 117/21

hairs, split hairs 32/15

hairy 114/10

half, not half (very) 66/17; not half! 105/4; see how the other half lives 159/4

half-baked 82/5

half-seas-over 155/12

half-wit 82/9

halves, do things by halves 1/15

ham, radio ham 139/15

ham-fisted 9/2

ham-handed 9/2

hammer, hammer and tongs (energy) 4/16; hammer and tongs (quarrel) 32/3

hammer, hammer into 87/15

hand, dab hand 7/8, keep one's hand in 7/18; hand over fist 22/29; old hand 7/6; do sth. with one hand tied behind one's back 26/13; turn one's hand to 4/6; win hands down 16/10; try one's hand 77/4; know like the back of one's hand 91/2; on one's hands 138/2; to hand (available) 138/9

hand, you've got to hand it to so. 130/15

handful, a handful (problem) 28/2

handle, have a handle to one's name 38/11; fly off the handle 112/15

hand-me-downs 172/9

handy, come in handy 67/18

hang, the hang 7/1; not give a hang 119/1

hang, hang around 23/15; hang on 23/12; let it all hang out 117/21; hang out (live) 159/2; hang out for sth. 13/4

hang-over 156/4

hang-up 86/2

hanky 172/24

hanky-panky 59/20

happen, happen on to sth. 137/8

hard, hard at it 3/7; hard luck 75/15; hard stuff (drink) 152/8; have a hard on 189/3

hard-boiled 116/13

hard-up 52/6

harum-scarum 82/34

has-been 18/24

hash, hash (drug) 158/5; make a hash of 9/11

hassle 31/15

hat, I'll eat my hat if 79/7; keep it under one's hat 89/19; talk through one's hat

96/14; at the drop of a hat 109/1; take one's hat off to 130/16; old hat 161/19

hatch, down the hatch! 153/13

have, have so. (defraud) 58/6; have had it 18/17 (failure); have had it (die) 162/5; have had it (chance) 76/15; have it in for so. 44/14; have it out with 100/7; have so. up (in court) 37/1; have so. on (hoax) 60/9; not have sth. (disapprove) 110/4; have it away/off with so. 188/11

havoc, play havoc with 30/16

haywire, go haywire 71/17

head, do sth. standing on one's head 26/13; bite so.'s head off 45/14; heads will roll 46/10; off one's head 81/12; need one's head examined/seen to 81/4; not right in the head 81/2; forget one's head if not screwed on 82/32; have one's head screwed on 83/2; not make head nor tail of 90/19; be above so.'s head 90/20; go over so.'s head 90/20; talk through the back of one's head 96/14; talk one's head off 97/2; head over heels in love 108/13; eat one's head off 150/10; keep one's head above water 159/14; get one's head down 179/2

head-case 81/17

head-shrinker 11/10

healthy (large) 64/8

hear, hear! hear! 105/7

heart-throb 108/16

heat, if you can't stand the heat, get out of the kitchen 43/4; turn on the heat 43/3

heave (throw) 146/5; heave up 181/20

heaven, good heavens! 104/4; for heaven's sake 104/15; stink to high heaven 183/26

heavy, heavy mob 40/9; a heavy date 185/2

heck, the heck 103/8; what the heck! 39/12; a heck of a 65/7

heebie-jeebies 118/10

heel, down at heel 173/21

heels, cool one's heels 23/16; show a clean pair of heels 144/8

heist 34/3

hell, the hell 103/8; hell for leather 22/15; all hell broke loose 31/13; hell's bells! 104/1; come hell or high water 28/17; like hell 22/15; play hell with 30/16; raise

hell 31/1; like hell! 110/3; what the hell! 39/12; a hell of a 65/7; scare the hell out of 114/4; for the hell of it 117/29

hell-bent 86/6

hen-party 154/3

hen-pecked 168/11

herring, a red herring 59/32

het, het up 113/18

hiccup, a hiccup 27/2

hick 82/28

hiding (beating) 42/1

higgledy-piggledy 30/10

high, high (drunk) 155/10; be for the high jump 46/9

high-falutin 92/9

hike, (raise) 62/10

hill-billy 82/28

hilt, up to the hilt 66/14

hinge, hinge on sth. 38/17

hip (fashionable) 173/10

hippo 140/14

hit, hit man 163/5; hit list 163/6

hit, hit it off with 108/2

hit-and-run 34/13

hitch, a hitch 27/3

hitched, get hitched 186/5

hob-nob 164/7

Hobson, Hobson's choice 76/7

hock, in hock 57/8

hocus-pocus 60/20

hodge-podge 135/12

hog, go the whole hog 66/3

hog, hog down 150/7

hogwash 96/7

hokum 96/3

hold, hold down (job) 1/5; hold out (last) 62/6; hold it 23/13; hold on 23/12; hold out on 89/21; hold with 105/21

hole, a hole (place) 147/16; make a hole in (expense) 53/9; need like a hole in the head 71/22

holes, pick holes in 47/1

holler 97/14

hollow, beat hollow 16/3

home, home stretch/straight 21/23; home and dry 79/19; at home in 91/5; who is so. when he is at home? 170/13

homework, do one's homework 88/4

honest-to-goodness 61/14

honey (address) 102/4

honeymoon, the honeymoon is over 25/10

honky 169/19

hooch 152/10

hood (gangster) 35/9

hoodlum 35/8

hoodwink 59/1

hooey 96/9

265

hoof, on the hoof 143/4
hoof, hoof it 143/2
hoo-ha 31/5
hook, by hook or by crook 4/13; off the hook 48/3; swallow hook, line and sinker 85/19; get one's hooks into so. 186/2
hook, hook it 144/7; hook so. 186/2
hooked, hooked on 108/8
hooker 187/20
hookey, play hookey 92/11
hoot, not give a hoot 119/1; not give two hoots 119/2
hooter 176/6
hop, hop (dance) 139/18; catch on the hop 131/4
hop, hop (travel) 145/10; hop along (leave) 144/2; hop it (leave) 144/13
hopping, hopping mad 112/4
horny 187/2
horse, flog a dead horse 13/12; work like a horse 2/1; hold one's horses 23/11; horse sense 83/11; straight from the horse's mouth 87/18; wild horses wouldn't drag it from me 89/18; a dark horse 91/19; get on one's high horse 122/3; eat like a horse 150/10; I could eat a horse 151/5
horse, horse around 117/24
horseplay 117/25
hot, hot (stolen) 34/11; hot at 7/10; hot seat 33/3; hot stuff 7/11; hot stuff (sex) 187/11; make it/things hot for 43/2; hot favourite 76/19
hotbed 80/7
hotch-potch 135/12
hot-rod 132/8
house, like a house on fire 22/12; safe as houses 79/15; get on like a house on fire 164/12
house-warming 154/2
how, and how! 105/4
how-d'ye-do, a fine how-d'ye-do 30/6
howler 17/2
how's-your-father, a bit of how's-your-father 188/9
hubby 165/1
hue, hue and cry 31/8
huff, in a huff 112/27
huffy 112/27
hugger-mugger (chaos) 30/10; (secrecy) 123/2
hullabaloo, kick up a hullabaloo 174/2
hum, hum (smell) 183/23; make things hum 31/11

humble, eat humble pie 168/8
humbug 96/9
humdinger 67/2
hump, have the hump 112/1
hump, hump (carry) 146/1; hump so. 188/14
humpty 112/1
hunch 91/22
hunky-dory 25/5
hush-hush 123/1
husky 178/16
hussy 187/19
hustler 35/3
hype 12/8

ice, cut no ice 39/10; skate on thin ice 78/7; break the ice 116/18
idea, what's the big idea 80/3
iffy 79/24
ilk, of that ilk 73/15
in, be in (fashion) 173/12; be in for it 46/9
inkling 91/22
in-laws 165/11
innings, have had a good innings 161/10
ins and outs 87/7
inside, (in gaol) 37/16; an inside job 34/4
into, be into sth. 139/4
iron, iron out 27/16

jab 181/15
jabber 95/4
Jack, Jack of all trades 11/17; before you can say Jack Robinson 20/12; Jack tar 11/5; I'm all right Jack! 166/14
jack, jack in 19/2; jack up 62/10
jackpot, hit the jackpot 15/6
Jag 132/11
jailbird 37/20
jakes 184/8
jalopy 132/5
jam, in a jam 29/1; money for jam 26/5; jam packed 148/1
jam, jam on (brakes) 146/10
jammy 75/1
Jap 169/2
jar (glass) 152/5
jaw, (talk) 94/1
jay-walking 34/21
jazz, and all that jazz 135/10
jazz, jazz up 173/6
jelly, (gelignite) 35/19
jemmy 35/20
jerk (person) 171/4
jerk, jerk so. around 27/15; jerk off 189/7
Jerry 169/22
jerry-built 133/2

jet-lag 145/13
jet-set 167/8
Jew, Jew boy 169/21
jiffy 20/10
jiggered, I'll be jiggered! 104/2; jiggered (tired) 180/1
jiggery-pokery 59/20
jimmy 35/20
jingle 12/2
jingo, by jingo! 104/6
jinks, high jinks 117/26
jinx 75/17
jitterbug 113/22
jitters, have the jitters 113/21
jittery 113/21
job, a job (machine) 134/11; come with the job 1/19; do a job (crime) 34/1; have a job to 28/8; inside job 34/4; make a good job of sth. 1/16; make a bit of a job of sth. 4/30; just the job 74/1; a bad job 29/30; it's a good job ... 75/11
Jock 169/10
Joe, Joe Public 170/15; Joe Bloggs 170/15
jog, jog so.'s memory 84/4
john 184/9
johnnie 188/27
joint (drugs) 158/3
joke, the joke is on so. 46/16
Jones, keep up with the Joneses 167/12
josh 60/14
Jove, by Jove 104/6
joy, no joy 75/15; get no joy out of (information) 88/12; get no joy out of (satisfaction) 121/7
joy-ride, be no joy-ride 28/12; joy-riding 34/14
JP 11/26
judge, sober as a judge 156/2
jug (jail) 37/12
juggernaut 132/12
juggins 82/9
juice 134/16
jump, go and take a running jump! 110/28; be for the high jump 46/9
jump, jump to it 22/3, jump at a chance 76/12
jumper, stick it up your jumper! 110/29
jumping-off, jumping-off place 147/10
jumpy 113/21
jungle, jungle telegraph 87/16
jungle-juice 152/9
junk, junk mail 12/11; junk food 149/8
junkie 158/10

kangaroo court 37/8

keep, keep in with 164/8
keeps, for keeps 137/6
kerb-crawl 34/18
kerfuffle 31/5
kettle, a pretty kettle of fish 30/5; a different kettle of fish 72/7
keyed, keyed up 113/19
khazi 184/8
kick, kick (activity) 139/2; better than a kick up the arse 63/7; get a kick out of 117/27; for kicks 117/28
kick, kick (a habit) 19/6; kick off 1/1; I could kick myself 112/22
kid, kid (child) 160/4; kid's stuff 26/1; kid (address) 102/5; our kid (brother) 165/9
kid, (tease) 60/12
kiddie 160/4
kike 169/20
kill, kill (pain) 183/19; dressed to kill 173/5
killing, make a killing 50/1
kill-joy 118/17
kingdom, send to kingdom come 163/1
kinky 187/3
kip 179/3
kiss-and-tell-all 188/1
kisser 176/2
kit, kit out 173/1
kitchen, everything but the kitchen sink 64/19
kite, kite (plane) 132/2; fly a kite 88/5
kittens, have kittens 114/5
kitty 49/22
Kiwi 169/6
knack, the knack (skill) 7/1; a knack (habit) 80/18
knackered 71/3; knackered (tired) 180/2
knee-jerk, knee-jerk reaction 80/21
knees-up 154/7
knickers, get one's knickers in a twist 113/16
knick-knack 135/13
knife, before you can say 'knife' 20/12
knob (penis) 189/2
knobs, with knobs on 68/10
knock, take a knock 53/11
knock, knock (criticize) 47/2; knock around (go) 143/16; knock around (travel) 145/3; knock back (cost) 55/13; knock back (drink) 153/4; knock off (work) 1/2; knock sth. off (steal) 34/6; knock off (deduct) 54/4; knock it off 19/2; knock up (work)

1/14; knock so. up (sex) 188/21
knock-down, knock-down prices 54/3
knockers 189/9
knocking, be knocking (old) 161/2; knocking shop 188/20
knock-out, a knock-out 67/3
knot, tie the knot 186/5
knots, tie so. in knots 113/10
knotted, get knotted! 110/30
know, in the know 91/9
knuckle, knuckle down 4/2; knuckle under 168/9
kook 125/2
kosher 61/1
kowtow 120/3
Kraut 169/22

lab 133/12
la-di-da 122/7
lag, old lag 37/22
lager-lout 35/7
laid, laid back 5/1; laid up with 181/7; get laid (sex) 188/12
lam, lam into so. 40/15
lamppost 178/8
land, see how the land lies 88/7
land (a job) 1/4;
landslide, a landslide victory 16/12
language, mind one's language 127/2
lap, in the lap of luxury 51/10
lap, lap up (believe) 85/17
lark, lark around 117/24
Larry, happy as Larry 117/6
lash, lash out (spend) 55/3
lashings 64/10
latch, latch on to sth. 85/10
late, late in the day 21/24
lathering (beating) 42/1
laugh, laugh on the other side of one's face 46/17
laughing, laughing all the way to the bank 50/11
launder, launder money 34/12
laurels, rest on one's laurels 130/14
lav 184/8
law, the law (police) 36/1
lay, a lay (sex) 188/13
lay, lay into so. 40/15; lay off (dismiss) 6/2; lay off (stop) 19/1; lay on 10/3; lay it on thick (with a trowel) 66/9; lay it on the line 100/4
layabout 5/6
lazybones 5/5
leaf, turn over a new leaf 127/9; take a leaf out of so.'s book 129/1; shake like a leaf 181/9
league, not in the same league 68/5

leak, take a leak 184/5
lean, lean on so. 43/7
leap, a leap in the dark 77/6
leave, leave be 19/5; leave off 19/5
left, left right and centre 147/17
leg, pull so.'s leg 60/9; shake a leg 22/2; be on one's last legs 162/1; be on one's last legs (fail) 18/16; get one's leg over 188/12
leg, leg it 143/2
legless 155/14
lemon 71/12
lengths, go to great lengths 4/14
let, let so. have it 41/10; let off (pass wind) 184/14; let on (reveal) 89/6; let up (slow) 23/8
level, do one's level best 4/10; on the level 61/9; level pegging 73/11; keep a level head 116/5
liability, 27/9
licence, licence to print money 50/9
lick (inability) 8/1; (defeat so.) 16/1
lid, lid (hat) 172/19; blow the lid off 89/5; flip one's lid 112/15; put the lid on 19/11
lie, lie in 179/15
life, for the life of me 8/10: take one's life in one's hands 78/3; low life 39/9
lifer 37/21
lift, (steal) 34/9
lightning, like greased lightning 22/19
like, (meaningless expletive) 103/10; as like as not 79/10; that's more like it! 105/3; like it or lump it! 106/5; I like that! 11/8
likely, as likely as not 79/10; not likely! 110/3
likes, the likes of 73/14
lily-livered 115/7
limb, out on a limb 29/15
Limey 169/9
line, all along the line 20/15; draw the line at 128/6; lay it on the line 100/4; toe the line 168/10; the bottom line 80/20
lines, hard lines 75/16
lingo, 93/4
lip, lip (cheek) 124/1; my lips are sealed 89/17; keep a stiff upper lip 116/2
litterbug 175/8
litter-lout 175/8
live, a live wire 170/6
live, live sth. down 130/9; live up to 159/6; live it up 159/7

livid 112/4
load, get a load of 183/6; come one's load 189/5; a load of old nonsense 96/1
loaded, (rich) 51/1
loads (a lot) 64/1
loaf, use one's loaf 84/1
loaf, loaf around 5/8
local, the local 153/6
loco 81/9
log, easy as falling off a log 26/12; sleep like a log 179/4
loggerheads, at loggerheads 32/13
logo 12/1
lollipop, lollipop man/lady 11/8
lolly, (money) 49/2
loner 166/17
long, long johns 172/10
loo 184/8
look, never look back 15/12; look here! 101/13
looker 178/23
look-in, 76/4
look-out, so.'s look-out 33/1
loony 81/8; a loon(y) 81/17
loony-bin 81/18
loopy 81/8
loot, (money) 49/4
lord, drunk as a lord 155/18
lorry, fall off the back of a lorry 34/10
loss, a dead loss 18/21
lost, get lost! 144/12
louse, louse up 9/9
lousy, lousy (nasty) 70/4; lousy with money 51/1; lousy with sth. (a lot) 64/11
love, love 102/2; no love lost between 110/23
love, I must love you and leave you! 101/21
lover 102/2
low-down 87/1
luck, tough/hard luck 75/15
lucre, filthy lucre 49/5
lug, (carry) 146/1
lugs 176/9
lumbered, lumbered with 27/10
lump (tolerate) 106/4
lurch, leave in the lurch 19/16
lush (drunk) 155/7
lying, not take sth. lying down 106/2

ma 165/6
mac, (coat) 172/22; (address) 102/10
macho 126/5
mackerel, holy mackerel! 104/1
mad, like mad 21/16

made, have it made 15/13
madhouse 30/7
magic, work magic 14/12
make, on the make 50/6
make, make (a day) of it 20/6; make good 15/10; make it (success) 15/9; as they make them 66/20; make out (claim) 85/12; make out (pretend) 59/33; make out (progress) 14/10; make it with so. (sex) 188/11
malark(e)y, nonsense 96/11; misbehaviour 128/2
mam(my), mammy 165/6; the mammy of all 65/8
man, man in the street 170/15; man or beast 170/14; see a man about a dog 184/1
manhandle 40/16
map, put on the map 147/12
March, mad as a March hare 81/14
marching, marching orders 6/5
Maria, black Maria 36/6
marines, tell that to the marines 60/11
master, past master 7/7
mate, a mate 164/2
mate(y) (address) 102/8
matey, matey with 164/6
McCoy, the real McCoy 61/15
measly 63/3
measure, measure up to 74/5
meat, easy meat 26/9
medicine, a dose of one's own medicine 46/13; take one's medicine 46/14
memory, memory lane 84/8
mend, on the mend 182/3
mend, mend one's ways 127/10
mental (crazy) 81/8
Merc 132/11
merchant, (speed etc.)-merchant 33/16
mess, mess so. around 27/15; mess around 139/6
message, get the message 90/5
Mick (Irishman) 169/12
mickey, take the mickey 60/13
Mickey Mouse, 39/3
middle, knock into middle of next week 41/14; the middle of nowhere 147/23
middle-age, middle-age spread 178/6
middle-of-the-road 69/2
midnight, burn the midnight oil 2/9
miffed 111/27
mike, mike (microphone) 134/4; for the love of Mike 104/16
mile, stand/stick out a mile 183/10

mill, go through the mill 29/10; trouble at t'mill 31/14
mince, not mince matters/one's words 100/2
mincemeat, make mincemeat of 16/4
mind, a piece of one's mind 45/8; to my mind 85/2; have a good mind to 85/13; in two minds 85/14; drunk out of one's mind 155/15
mind, don't mind me! 110/9
mind-boggling 90/21
minder 36/15
mint, in mint condition 67/15
minute, one born every minute 82/2
mischief, do oneself a mischief 181/18
misery, long streak of misery 118/14
misery-guts 98/4
misfit 74/9
mishmash 135/12
miss, give it a miss 19/4
missus 165/5
mistake, make no mistake about it 79/6
mit (hand) 176/12
mix, mix it (fight) 40/13
mixed-up 113/13
mixer, a bad mixer 166/15
mo 20/10
Mob, the Mob 35/10
mod, mod cons 133/8
mog(gie) 140/6
mole (spy) 36/26
moll 187/15
mollycoddle 121/1
money, money to burn 51/5; in the money 51/3; not made of money 52/10; for my money 85/1
money-bags 51/7
money-spinner 50/8
monger (speed etc)-monger 33/16
monkey, a cheeky monkey 124/6; monkey business 59/20; get so.'s monkey up 112/20; not give a monkey's 119/1
monkey, monkey with 9/7
moo, silly moo 82/19
mooch 143/8
moo-cow 140/13
moon, once in a blue moon 20/17; over the moon 117/3
moon, to moon 110/26
moonlight (work) 1/29
moonshine 152/11
Mop, Mrs Mop 11/7
morning, the morning after (the night before) 156/5
moron 82/15

mortal, every mortal thing 64/20

mosey 143/9

mother, a mother 171/3; the mother of all 65/8

mountain, make a mountain out of a mole-hill 66/6

mouth, down in the mouth 118/12; shoot one's mouth off 97/13; make so.'s mouth water 151/4

mouth-watering 151/3

move, get a move on 22/4

muck, common as muck 64/13; Lord/Lady Muck 38/9

muck, muck so. around 27/15; muck in 1/8; muck up 9/9

muck-raking, 47/9

mucky 175/1

mud, so.'s name is mud 130/1

muddle, muddle along/on 13/11

muddle through 13/10

mud-slinging, 47/9

mug, mug (fool) 82/22; mug (face) 176/3; a mug's game 82/23

mug, mug up on 92/2

mugger 35/4

muggins 82/22

mug-shot 36/17

mullarkey 128/2

mum(my), mum's the word 89/20; mother 165/6

mumbo-jumbo 96/17

murder, blue murder 31/12; get away with murder 48/6

murder, murder a language 95/6; I could murder sth. (appetite) 151/6

Murphy, Murphy's Law 30/12

muscle, muscle into 33/21

mush, mush (sentiment) 118/6; mush (face) 176/3

music, face the music 46/3; music to so.'s ears 117/19

must, a must 38/14

mustard, keen as mustard 109/2

mutt, (fool) 82/9; (dog) 140/8

mutton, dead as mutton 162/16

nab, (arrest) 36/7

naff, naff 70/6; naff off! 110/30

nag, (horse) 140/12

nail, on the nail 55/1

nail, (arrest) 36/9

nails, hard as nails 178/15; right as nails 182/6

namby-pamby 122/10

name, the name of the game 38/18; drop names 130/13

nana 82/10

nancy-boy 187/27

nap, (sleep) 179/8

napping, catch napping 131/4

nark, (copper's) nark 36/24

nark, nark so. 112/3

nasty, a video nasty 136/8

natter 94/7

natty 173/7

necessary, the necessary 49/1

neck, stick one's neck out 77/5; get it in the neck 45/6; talk through the back of one's neck 96/14; so.'s neck of the woods 147/14

neck (kiss) 188/4

nelly, nelly (fool) 82/10; not on your nelly 110/1

nerve (cheek) 124/2

nest-egg 49/14

never, well I never! 104/2

never-never, on the never-never 57/4

new, a new one on me 91/17

newt, drunk as a newt 155/17

next, next-door to 73/16

nibs, his/her nibs 38/8

nick, old Nick 171/28; nick (jail) 37/12; in the nick of time 21/14; in good nick 67/16

nick, (steal) 34/6; (arrest) 36/7

nicker, (money) 49/7

niff 183/25

nifty, (clever) 83/8; (smart) 173/7

nigger, work like a nigger 2/1

niggly 111/25

nightcap 152/17

nightie 172/14

nincompoop 82/9

nine, nine days' wonder 20/8; dressed to the nines 173/4

nip, Nip (Japanese) 169/2; a nip in the air 141/2

nip (go) 143/1

nipper 160/3

nippy 141/3

nit-picking 47/14

nitty-gritty 87/5

nitwit 82/9

nob, big nob 38/3

nobble (cheat) 59/16

nod, the land of nod 179/11

nod, nod off 179/10

noddle 176/4

noggin 176/4

no-hoper 76/20

noise, big noise 38/3

nookie 188/9

nope 101/22

nose, pay through the nose 53/8; poke one's nose into 33/17; not see beyond the end of one's nose 82/3; turn one's nose up at 110/9; look down one's nose at 110/19;

get up so.'s nose 111/16; keep one's nose clean 127/6; follow one's nose 143/19; powder one's nose 184/2

nosh 149/1

nostrils, get up so.'s nostrils 111/16

nosy, nosy parker 33/18

notch, notch up 15/8

nothing, have nothing on 3/11

nowhere, get nowhere fast 14/14

nuke 134/15

number, cushy number 1/27; so.'s number is up 162/8; number one 170/4; so.'s opposite number 167/2

numbered, so.'s days are numbered 162/9

numskull, 82/9

nut, a tough nut 28/1; put the nut on so. 41/25; off one's nut 81/12; do one's nut 112/16

nut-case 81/17

nut house 81/18

nuts, nuts (testicles) 189/1; not do for nuts 8/11; nuts and bolts 87/6; nuts about sth. 108/7

nutshell, in a nutshell 63/14

nutter 81/17

nutty, nutty as a fruit-cake 81/15; nutty about sth. 108/7

oats, off one's oats 151/9; sow one's wild oats 159/9; get one's oats 188/12

object, be no object 27/1

oddball 125/3

odd-job man 11/18

odd-man-out 72/1

odds, make no odds 39/11; odds and ends 135/8

off-beat 80/17

off-chance, on the off-chance 77/8

off-colour 181/4

off-day 17/9

off-putting 113/7

oil, no oil painting 178/17

okey-doke 105/8

old, old (emphasis) 103/9; old wives' tale 96/16; the Old World 147/8; old man (father) 165/4; old man (penis) 189/2; any old thing 79/22

old-boy, old-boy network 164/20

olde-worlde 161/20

oldie 161/12

old-timer 7/5

on, be on at so. 47/13; you're

on! 105/9; not on (unacceptable) 110/17
once-over 183/8
one, you are a one! 101/17; a real one for 109/13
one-man, one-man band/show 166/18
one-off, one-off job 1/28
oneself, keep oneself to oneself 166/13
one-track, one-track mind 86/1
one-upmanship 68/15
onions, know one's onions 91/3
oodles 64/1
oomph 4/21
oops, oops-a-daisy! 104/10
open-and-shut 26/14
operator, smooth operator 7/9
opt, opt out of 166/12
or, or else! 101/18
ouch 104/20
out, be out (unfashionable) 173/13; out with it! 89/9
out-and-out 66/19
outfit 10/2
outside, at the outside 66/15
overboard, go overboard 109/6
overshoot, overshoot the mark 66/1
overstep, overstep the mark 66/1
owl, night owl 178/6
own, own up 89/11
Oz 147/5

P, mind one's Ps and Qs 127/3
pa 165/2
paces, put through paces 7/19,
pack, pack in/up (defective) 71/8; pack it in 19/2; pack clout 38/5; pack a punch 41/22
packet, 49/21
packing, send packing 166/9
pad 133/6
paddy, Paddy (Irishman) 169/12; in a paddy 112/11; paddy wagon 36/6
paid, put paid to 19/11
pain, a pain in the arse/neck 111/10
paint, paint the town red 154/11
pal, a pal 164/2
pal, pal up with 164/5
palaver, 31/4
pally 164/6
palm, in the palm of one's hand 168/4
palm, palm sth. off 58/9
pan, pan out 80/12
pander 187/24
panic, panic stations 30/8
pansy 187/27

panties 172/12
pants, smarty pants 83/7; bore the pants off so. 111/6; scare the pants off so. 114/4
papa 165/2
paradise, a fool's paradise 159/21
paralytic 155/14
paraphernalia 135/9
parched 153/14
park, park oneself 147/20
parky 141/3
parrot, learn parrot-fashion 92/4; a mouth like the bottom of a parrot's cage 156/6; sick as a parrot 181/19
party, the party is over 25/9
party-pooper 118/17
pass, a pretty pass 29/13; make a pass 185/10
pass, pass out 181/6; pass up (a chance) 76/13
past, past it 161/6
paste (beat) 42/2
patch, not a patch on 68/6
patch, patch up (quarrel) 32/18
patter, 94/4
paw (hand) 176/12
pay, pay off (succeed) 15/23
pea-brain 82/18
peach, a peach 67/1
peaches, not all peaches and cream 25/4
peanuts, 49/20
peas, like as two peas 73/2
pea-souper 141/15
pebbles, other pebbles on the beach 76/9
pecker, keep one's pecker up 116/1
pecking, the pecking order 167/1
peckish 151/7
pee 184/3
peeled, keep one's eyes peeled 183/4
peep, not a peep from 99/6
peepers 176/7
peeping, peeping tom 187/32
peer, peer pressure 167/13
peg, peg (leg) 176/13; take down a peg 44/6
peg, peg out 162/12
pelt (speed) 22/24
penny, cost a pretty penny 53/2; not have a penny to one's name 52/2; two a penny 39/4; a penny for your thoughts 84/7; the penny drops 90/9; spend a penny 184/1
pen-pusher 11/11
pep 4/21
pep-talk 93/6
perisher 171/9

perishing (cold) 141/4; (oath) 103/3
perk, a perk (profit) 50/13
perk, perk up 182/1
pernickety 125/7
pesky 111/26
Pete, for Pete's sake 104/16
peter, peter out 18/4
petting, petting 188/2
pew, take a pew 147/19
phew, phew! 104/19
phoney 59/30
pick, pick on so. 44/12; pick up (progress) 14/3; pick up (learn) 91/12; pick up the tab 55/12; pick up (health) 182/1; pick up so. 185/6
pickings, rich pickings 50/12
pickle, in a pickle 29/2
pickled 155/13
pick-me-up 182/2
picnic, a picnic (easy) 26/8
picture, a picture of health 182/5; get the picture 90/5; put so. in the picture 87/10
pictures (cinema) 133/11
piddle 184/3
piddling 63/3
pidgin, pidgin English 95/1
pie, easy as pie 26/12; pie in the sky 24/1
piece, in one piece 78/4
pieces, go to pieces 30/13
piffle 96/7
piffling 63/3
pig, (policeman) 36/3; pig's breakfast 30/4; a pig in a poke 56/5
pigeon, so.'s pigeon 33/1
piggyback 146/2
pig-ignorant 82/7
pigs, pigs might fly 24/12
pile, make a pile 50/4
pile, pile it on (exaggerate) 66/9
pill, on the pill 188/26
pillock 82/10
pimp 187/24
pin, pin (leg) 176/13; not a pin to choose between them 73/1; not give two pins 119/2; able to hear a pin drop 174/5
pin, pin sth. on so. 37/2
pinch, at a pinch 66/10; feel the pinch 53/12
pinch, (steal) 34/6; (arrest) 36/7
pink, in the pink 182/5
pinny 172/21
pint-sized 65/13
pip, pip at the post 16/13
pipe, put that in your pipe and smoke it! 103/7
pipe, pipe down 99/4
pipe-dream 24/1

pipeline, in the pipeline 24/5
piping, piping hot 149/10
pipsqueak 39/6
piss, take the piss out of 60/13; piss off! (refusal) 110/30; piss so. off (bore) 111/7; piss off (leave) 144/14
piss-artist 155/7
pissed 155/13
piss-up, piss-up 155/20; piss-up in a brewery 8/12
pit, a bottomless pit 150/12
pitch, pitch into 40/15
pits, the pits 147/16
pity, more's the pity! 105/6
place, all over the place (chaos) 30/11; all over the place 147/18
places, go places (succeed) 15/11; go places (travel) 145/1
plague, avoid like the plague 166/7
plant, plant evidence 37/7
plastered 155/13
plate, hand sth. to so. on a plate 26/17; have enough on one's plate 3/1
plateful 3/2
play, play down 39/16; play up 27/12; play safe 79/16
please, if you please! 110/10
plebs 167/10
plonk (drink) 152/6
plonk, plonk oneself 147/20; plonk on the piano 139/20
plonky 155/7
plough (fail) 92/16
plug, pull the plug on sth. 18/32
plug, plug (advertise) 12/6; plug (shoot) 41/27; plug away at 13/1
plug-ugly 178/18
plum job 1/26
plumb, plumb crazy 81/13
plumbing 184/10
plump, plump (fall) 146/14; plump for 85/9
plunge, take the plunge 186/4
po 184/11
pocket, out of pocket 53/10
podgy 178/1
point, not put too fine a point on it 100/5
poker, a poker face 116/12
poky 148/5
pole, up the pole 81/11; not touch with a ten-foot pole 166/5
poles, poles apart 72/3
polish, polish off (work) 1/13; polish off (defeat) 16/7; polish off (food) 150/6; polish off (kill) 163/2; polish up (improve) 92/3

Polack 169/23
pom(mie) 169/8
ponce 187/27
pond, the (herring-)pond 147/3
pong 183/24
pooch 140/7
poof 187/27
poop 184/11
pooped 180/2
poo-poo 39/15
poor, the poor man's ... 52/13
pop, pop (go) 143/1; pop (put) 146/9; pop up (occur) 80/13; pop off (die) 162/12
pop (address) 102/7; pop (lemonade) 152/4; pop (father) 165/3; on the pop 155/3
poppycock 96/4
pore, pore over (study) 92/5
porker 140/10
porridge, do porridge 37/17
posh, posh (rich) 53/7; posh (smart) 173/6
possum, play possum 59/13
posted, keep so. posted 87/11
pot, pot (drugs) 158/2; take pot luck 77/9; go to pot! 110/28; go to pot 18/9
potato, a couch potato 136/14; a hot potato 27/7; drop like a hot potato 19/14
pot-belly 178/3
pots (a lot) 64/1
potted, (shortened) 63/15
potter, potter around 139/6
potty, a potty 184/11
potty (crazy) 81/8; potty about sth. 108/7;
pour, pour down 141/10
power, a power of (a lot) 64/7
prat 82/10
precious 63/4
pressed, hard pressed 28/10; pressed for sth. 63/11
presto, hey presto 15/28
price, what price ...? 76/18
priceless, priceless (funny) 117/17; priceless idiot 82/8
pricey 53/5
prick, (fool) 82/10; (penis) 189/2
private eye 36/16
privy 184/8
prize, prize idiot 82/8
pronto 22/10
proper (total) 66/26
prowler 35/15
pudding, the proof of the pudding 15/24; join the pudding club 188/24
puff, puff (homosexual) 187/27; out of puff 180/4
puke 181/20
pull, pull in (earn) 1/20; pull in

(arrest) 36/7; pull sth. off (success) 15/17, pull the other one 60/10
punch, punch 4/21; not pull one's punches 44/16; pleased as Punch 117/5
punch-drunk 41/18
punch-up 40/4
punk, (criminal) 35/6; (worthless person) 171/6
punter, 55/11
pup, sell so. a pup 56/6
puppy, puppy love 108/15
push, the push 6/4
push, push one's luck 75/6; push off 144/3
pushed, hard pushed 28/10; pushed for sth. 63/11
pusher (drugs) 158/11
pushing, be pushing (old) 161/2
push-over (easy) 26/6; (person) 121/4
pushy 126/1
puss (face) 176/3
pussy (vagina) 189/8
pussyfoot 131/3
put, put away (jail) 37/14; put away (food) 150/8; put down (kill) 163/9; put in (work) 1/11; put it/one across so. 59/5; put it on 59/12; put it right there! 105/12; put so. out (trouble) 113/9; I wouldn't put it past so. 130/8
putty, like putty in so.'s hands 168/5
put-up, a put-up job 59/18

quantity, an unknown quantity 91/19
queen 187/28
queer, queer (homosexual) 187/27; in Queer Street 29/3
question, pop the question 186/3; sixty-four-thousand-dollar question 38/16
quickie 22/33
quid 49/7
quod (jail) 37/12

R, the three Rs 92/10
rabbit, pull/produce the rabbit out of the hat 15/18
rabbit, rabbit on 94/12
rack, rack one's brains 84/5
racket, kick up a racket 174/2
rag 136/11
rag-bag 135/12
rage, all the rage 173/11
ragged, ragged around the edges 181/1
rags, rags to riches 51/12

ragtag, ragtag and bobtail 39/7
railroad, railroad so. into 43/10
rails, go off the rails 30/14
rain, take a rain check 24/4; right as rain 182/6
rainy, a rainy day 49/13
rake, thin as a rake 178/9
rake, rake it in 50/2
rake-off (share) 50/3
ramble (talk) 94/13
randy 187/2
rank, pull rank 167/3
rank-and-file 167/9
rap, a rap (punishment) 46/1
rap, (talk) 93/1
rap-sheet 36/18
raring, raring to 109/4
raspberry 110/27
rat, smell a rat 91/24
rat on so. 36/22
rather, rather! 105/4
rat-race 167/11
rattle, rattle so. 113/2; rattle off 93/12; rattle away nineteen to the dozen 97/1
rattling, rattling (excellent) 67/8; at a rattling pace 22/17
ratty 112/5
rave-up 154/8
raw, a raw deal 61/7; in the raw 177/1
razzamatazz 12/10
razzle, on the razzle 154/12
razzle-dazzle 12/9
ready, the ready (money) 49/1
record, track record 130/11
red, not have a red cent 52/1; red tape 10/7; in the red 57/7; see red 112/14
red-handed, catch red-handed 36/12
red-letter, red-letter day 38/12
reefer (drugs) 158/3
reek 183/23
reel, reel off 93/12
ref 11/22
register, register with 90/8
regular (total) 66/26
Reilly, the life of Reilly 159/10
remember, remember oneself 127/4
rent, rent boy 187/23 rent-a-mob 31/17
rep 11/23
rest, give it a rest 19/3
rhino 140/14
rid, get rid of 19/18
riddance, good riddance 19/19
ride, give a rough ride 27/13; take so. for a ride 59/8
riff-raff 39/8
rig, rig sth. 59/17
right, right (immediately) 21/19; right (total) 66/26; right old (mess) 30/1; right

you are! 105/8; Mr Right 186/1
right-royal 67/12
rights, by rights 101/12
righty-oh 105/8
rig-out 172/8
rile, rile so. 112/3
ring, give so. a ring (phone) 93/9
rings, run rings around 16/5
riot, a riot (fun) 117/16; read the riot act 45/10
rip, rip off (steal) 34/8; rip so. off (defraud) 58/3; let rip 47/12
rise, rise and shine! 179/16
ritzy, 53/6
river, sell down the river 59/25
road, any road 101/10; hit the road 144/1; one for the road 152/18
road-hog 35/16
rock-bottom, rock-bottom price 54/2
rocker, off one's rocker 81/12
rocket, a rocket (reprimand) 45/5
rocks, rocks (precious stones) 172/26; on the rocks 152/14
roll, roll so. (rob) 34/5; roll on . . .! 24/10; roll up 142/2
roller 132/11
rollie, (cigarette) 157/6
rolling, rolling in (money) 51/2
roly-poly 178/2
romp, romp home/away 16/9
roof, hit the roof 112/17; raise the roof 174/3
rook, rook so. 58/4
rookie 8/17
roost, rule the roost 168/2
root, root for 106/11
rope, money for old rope 26/5
rope, rope in 1/7
ropes, the ropes 7/2
rop(e)y 70/8
roses, not all roses 25/4; a bed of roses 25/3; smelling of roses 130/19
rot 96/6
rot-gut 152/9
rotten 70/7
rotter 171/11
rough, rough it 159/18; rough up 42/4
rough, rough (unwell) 181/1; be rough on so. 29/17; take the rough with the smooth 18/30; a rough house 40/6; rough-and-ready 70/12; sleep rough 179/13
rough-and-tumble 40/7
roughshod, ride roughshod over 44/17
round, go round 62/7

rub, 27/3
rub, rub sth. in 46/20; not have two cents to rub together 52/3; rub so. up the wrong way 111/14; rub out (kill) 163/3; rub off on 164/23
rubber (condom) 188/27
rubberneck 170/12
rubbish, rubbish sth. 39/16
ructions 31/12
rug, pull the rug from under so.'s feet 18/33
rugger, 139/13
rule, rule of thumb 70/11
rum (strange) 125/6
rumble, rumble so. 88/9
rumpus, kick up a rumpus 31/2
run, give so. a run for his money 4/27
run, run away with (idea) 85/18; run along (leave) 144/2; run so. in (arrest) 36/7; run up (sew) 172/16
run-about (car) 132/7
run-around, give the run-around 27/14
run-down 181/3
run-of-the-mill 69/3
runs, the runs 184/13
Russky 169/5
rustle, rustle up (food) 149/17
rusty in 8/14
rut, in a rut 159/20

sack, the sack 6/4; to sack 6/3; hit the sack 179/1
saddled, saddled with 27/10
sailing, plain sailing 26/7
salt, salt of the earth 61/12; take with a pinch of salt 85/20
salt, salt away 123/9
sandwich, sandwiched between 148/3
sandwich, sandwich man 11/13
sardines, packed/crammed like sardines 148/2
sarky 124/4
sauce 124/3
sausage, not a sausage 63/9
savvy, 90/7
say, say to (opinion) 85/7; you don't say! 104/13; you can say that again! 105/5; I'll say 105/5
scallywag 128/4
scam 59/19
scamp 128/4
scapegoat 46/5
scarce, make os. scarce 144/11
scarecrow 173/22
scaredy-cat 115/8
scarper 144/6
scat, scat! 144/12

scatter-brained 82/31
scatty 82/31
scene, not so.'s scene 110/21
science, blind so. with science 87/19
scoff 150/7
scoot (speed) 22/23
scorch (speed) 22/26
scorcher 141/8
scorching 141/7
score, know the score 91/8
score, score with so. 188/11
scot-free, get off scot-free 48/5
Scott, great Scott! 104/5
scram 144/13
scrap (fight) 40/3
scrap, not do a scrap 3/14; scrap sth. (abandon) 19/10
scrape, get into a scrape 29/12
scrape, scrape through (pass) 92/13; scrape along 159/17; scrape a living 159/16
scratch, start from scratch 21/5; up to scratch 74/10
scratch, scratch a living 159/16
scream, a scream 117/16
screw, screw (gaoler) 37/19; have a screw loose 81/1
screw, screw so. (defraud) 58/5; screw so. (sex) 188/14; screw up 9/9
screwball 125/4
screws, put the screws on so. 43/1
screwy 81/8
scrimshank 5/3
scrounge, 57/3
scrub, scrub (abandon) 19/10; scrub it 19/9
scrubber 187/18
scruffy 173/19
scrumptious 151/2
scrumpy 152/12
sea, worse things happen at sea 39/14; all at sea 113/5
search, search me! 91/16
second, second thoughts 85/15
second-guess 47/7
see, see off (defeat) 16/6
seedy (dirty) 175/6; (unwell) 181/1
seize, seize up 84/15
sell, the hard sell 56/3; sell so. a pup 56/6
send-up 129/5
senses, drunk out of one's senses 155/15
serve, serve so. right 46/12
set, set about so. 40/14; set back (cost) 55/13; set so. up 37/6
set-to 40/2
set-up (organization) 10/1; (law) 37/5
sew, sew up (defeat) 16/8; sew

up (a deal) 79/20
sex-kitten 187/4
sex-pot 187/5
shack, shack up with 186/7
shaft, shaft so. 188/14
shag, shag so. 188/14
shagged 180/2
shake, shake down 179/12; shake so. up 113/14
shake-out 6/7
shakes, the shakes 181/8; no great shakes 69/7
sham, a sham 59/11
shambles 30/2
shambolic 30/3
Shanks, on Shanks's mare/ pony 143/3
shape, shape up 127/8
shark, loan-shark 57/6
sharp, sharp (time) 21/11; look sharp (speed) 22/5
sharper, 58/17
shattered 180/1
shave, close shave 48/2
shebang, the whole shebang 64/22
sheeny 169/20
sheep, separate sheep from goats 72/9; like sheep 129/4; make sheep's eyes at so. 185/9
shelf, on the shelf 186/13
shell, come out of one's shell 89/15
shell, shell out (pay) 55/2
shenanigans 128/2
shift, shift (speed) 22/22; shift for oneself 7/15
shilly-shally 23/2
shindig 32/6
shindy 32/6
shine, take a shine to 107/9
shiner 41/23
shipshape, (tidy) 175/12; (fit) 182/4
shirk 5/3
shirt, keep your shirt on! 112/19; a stuffed shirt 122/5
shirty 112/5
shit, shit 184/11; shit-scared 114/1; drop so. in the shit 29/9; knock the shit out of 42/11; scare the shit out of 114/4; not give a shit 119/3
shits 184/13
shoe-string, on a shoe-string 54/8
shoo 114/13
shoot, the whole shoot 64/22
shoot, (speak) shoot! 93/3; shoot off 97/13
shooter, (gun) 35/21
shooting-match, the whole shooting-match 64/22
shop, shut up shop 19/8; all

over the shop (chaos) 30/11; all over the shop (everywhere) 147/18; talk shop 93/2
shop, shop so. 36/21
short, have so. by the short and curlies 168/7; be taken/ caught short 184/6
shot, a shot (attempt) 77/1; big shot 38/3; get shot of (abandon) 19/18; get shot of (kill) 163/4; like a shot 22/18
shotgun, shotgun wedding 186/6
shots, call the shots 168/1
shoulder, rub shoulders with 164/8; give the cold shoulder 166/1
shout (drinks) 152/21
shouting, all over bar the shouting 79/17
shove, shove it! 110/29; shove off 144/3
shovel, shovel down 150/7
show, put up a good show 4/26; steal the show 68/16; give the show away 89/1; good show! 105/18; run the show 168/1
show, it just goes to show! 104/3
shower 171/18
shrimp 178/11
shrink (job) 11/10
shucks 104/17
shush 99/3
shut-eye, get some shut-eye 179/2
sick, sick and tired 111/3
side, get on the wrong side of 112/21; split one's sides laughing 117/11; the wrong side of forty 161/3; not let the side down 164/22; (earn) on the side 50/7; a bit on the side 188/17
side-kick 164/3
sieve, memory like a sieve 84/17
sight, a sight (lot) 64/9; a sight for sore eyes 117/18
sign, the finger/'V' sign 110/25
silver, born with a silver spoon in one's mouth 51/9
simmer, simmer down 116/16
sin, ugly as sin 178/18; live in sin 186/8
sing (reveal) 36/20
sink, sink or swim 29/14; sink a drink 153/3; sink in with 90/8
sins, for my sins 46/19
sis 165/10
sissy 171/22
sit, sit on sth. (slow) 23/17;

sitting pretty 25/7; sit tight 23/18; from where I'm sitting 85/3
sitcom 136/4
six, at sixes and sevens 30/9; hit for six 41/15; six and two threes 73/5; six of one and half a dozen of the other 73/5
size, the size of it 87/9
sizzling 141/7
skate, a cheap skate 58/19
skates, get one's skates on 22/1
skedaddle 144/6
skid, Skid Row 52/12
skin, by the skin of one's teeth 48/1; get under so.'s skin 111/13; no skin off so.'s back/nose 119/4
skin, skin alive 42/8
skinflint 52/9
skinful, a skinful 155/11
skinned, keep eyes skinned 183/4
skinny 178/10
skinny-dipping 177/4
skint 52/5
skip, skip (leave) 144/7; skip it 19/9
skirt, a bit of skirt 187/12
skive 5/3
skulduggery 59/20
sky, the sky's the limit 76/10
sky-high (prices) 53/4; blow sky-high 89/5
slack, to slack 5/4
slam (criticize) 47/3; slam on (brakes) 146/10
slammer (jail) 37/12
slanging-match 32/8
slap, better than a slap in the face/eye 63/7; slap and tickle 188/3
slap-bang (time) 21/12, (exactly) 66/24; (headlong) 146/11
slap-up, a slap-up meal 149/7
slash 184/5
slate, a clean slate 37/9
slating, a slating 45/4
slaughter (defeat) 16/2
sleazy 175/6
sleep, put to sleep 163/9
sleep, sleep around 188/15
sleeve, sth. up one's sleeve 138/7; laugh up one's sleeve 117/12
sliced, the best thing since sliced bread 108/10
slicker 173/18
sling (throw) 146/4
slip, slip (mistake) 17/7; give so. the slip 48/4
slip, slip (go) 143/1; slip one across so. 59/5; slip up (mistake) 17/7; slip one's

mind 84/16
slob 82/14
slog, slog away 2/4; hard slog 2/6
slosh (hit) 41/9
sloshed (drunk) 155/13
slowcoach 23/7
slowpoke 23/7
slug (hit) 41/11
sly-boots 59/27
smack, a smack in the chops 41/19
smacker, 49/8; smacker (kiss) 188/5
small-time 39/3
smarmy 120/7
smash, a smash hit 15/4
smashed (drunk) 155/14
smasher 67/1
smashing 67/8
smattering, a smattering of 91/11
smidgen, 63/1
smoke, a smoke (cigarette) 157/3; holy smoke 104/1
smooch 188/4
smoothie 116/14
snag, hit a snag 27/4
snail, a snail's pace 23/6
snakes, snakes and ladders 18/29
snap (photo) 139/10
snap, snap (photograph) 139/10; snap up 109/10; snap out of it 116/7
snappy, make it snappy 22/6
snapshot 139/10
snazzy 173/7
sneezed, not to be sneezed at 38/20
snifter 152/13
snip, a snip (easy) 26/3; snip (bargain) 54/6
snitch 36/20
snog 188/4
snooker 8/5
snoop 33/20
snoot 176/6
snooty 122/4
snooze 179/8
snot 184/15
snow, snowed under 3/4
snowball, not a snowball's chance in hell 76/23
snuff, snuff (kill) 163/3; snuff it 162/11
soaking, get a soaking 141/13
so-and-so 135/1; (negative) 171/2
soap, soap (opera) 136/3
sob-story 118/4
soccer 139/12
sock, sock (hit) 41/6; sock it to so. 44/1, 87/13; sock it to me 87/13

sock, pull one's socks up 4/18; put a sock in it 99/2
sod, sod (person) 171/14; sod all 63/9; Sod's law 30/12; sod off! 110/30
soft, soft in the head 81/2; soft on sth. 107/6; have a soft spot for 107/6; a soft touch 121/4
softie 170/23
soft-soap, soft-soap so. 120/6
sold, sold on sth. 109/7
soldier, soldier on 13/2
something, make something of it 32/14
song, make a song and dance 31/3; going for a song 55/5
sonny 102/5
son-of-a-bitch 171/1
son-of-a-gun 170/7
sopping, sopping wet 141/14
soppy 118/7
sort, sort so. out 44/5; sort itself out 15/26
sorts, out of sorts 181/1
so-so 69/1
sound, sound off 97/13
soup, in the soup 29/2
soup, soup up 132/9
sourpuss 118/8
soused 155/13
sozzled 155/13
spade, spade work 2/8; call a spade a spade 100/1
spanker 67/1
spanking, at a spanking pace 22/17
spanner, throw a spanner in the works 30/15
spark, a bright spark 83/6
spark(y) 11/2
sparklers 172/25
spec, on spec 77/7
specimen, specimen (person) 171/17; a bright specimen 82/24
specs 183/12
speed (drug) 158/7
spick, spick and span 175/11
spike, spike a drink 152/19
spin, spin a yarn 60/3; spin out 20/7
spin-off 80/22
spit, spit it out 89/10; spit (rain) 141/9
spitting, spitting image 73/3
spiv 35/14
splash, make a splash 31/20
splash, splash (money) 55/8
spliced, get spliced 186/5
split, (money) 49/3
split (reveal) 36/20; split (run away) 144/7
split-second 21/13
splosh 146/13

274

spoiling, spoiling for 40/1
spoil-sport 118/17
sponge, to sponge 57/3
spoof 129/5
spooky 114/12
sport, be a sport! 121/5
sporting, a sporting chance 76/3
spot, a spot of sth. 63/2; high spot 38/13; in a spot 29/1
spot-on 66/25
spots, knock the spots off 16/2
spout, up the spout (difficulty) 29/5; up the spout (broken) 71/2; up the spout (pregnant) 188/23
spout, (talk about) 97/13
spread, a spread 149/7
spree, spending/shopping spree 55/5; on the spree 154/12
spring, spring sth. on so. 131/5
spud 149/13
spud-bashing 149/14
spunk (courage) 115/1; spunk (sperm) 189/6
spunky 115/1
spur, on the spur of the moment 21/16
squaddy 11/6
square, back to square one 18/27
square, square (old-fashioned) 173/14; square peg in a round hole 74/8; a square deal 61/6; a square meal 149/5
squeaky, squeaky clean 175/10
squeal (reveal) 36/20
squeeze, squeeze time in 21/25
squire (address) 102/6
squirt 171/13
stab, a stab (attempt) 77/1
stack, blow one's stack 112/17
stacks (a lot) 64/1
stag-night 154/4
stake, stake so. 106/13
stamping, stamping-ground 147/13
stand, stand in for 1/6; stand to (lose etc.) 76/16; stand to reason 90/22; stand up (be valid) 90/23; stand for sth. 106/1; stand up for 106/10; stand a drink 152/20; stand so. up 185/5
standing, leave standing 68/4
stand-up, stand-up (row) 31/1
stark, stark raving mad 81/13; stark naked 177/2
starkers 177/2
stars, thank one's lucky stars 75/5
start, start on so. 47/11

starters, for starters 21/2
starving 151/8
stash (money) 49/12
stay, stay put 23/14
stead, stand in good stead 67/19
steady, steady on! 110/12; go steady 185/4
steam, run out of steam 18/3; under one's own steam 145/12
steamed, steamed up 112/6
steaming, steaming drunk 155/16
steamroller 43/12
steep, (expensive) 53/3, (excess) 66/7
step, step on it 22/8
stephen(s), even stephen(s) 73/10
stew, in a stew 113/18
stew, stew over 92/5
stewed (drunk) 155/13
stick, give so. some stick 47/4; get hold of the wrong end of the stick 90/17
stick, stick around 23/15; stick at it 13/6; stick it out 13/7; stick on 8/8; stick out for 13/4; stick to one's guns 13/3; stick with 13/5; make (charge) stick 37/3; stick sth. 106/4; stick up for 106/10; stick (put) 146/8
stick-in-the-mud 171/19
sticks, up sticks 144/10
stick-up 34/2
sticky, a sticky patch 29/8; sticky about sth. 110/11; come to a sticky end 162/13
stiff (corpse) 162/17
stiff, stiff (excessive) 66/7; bore stiff 111/5; scared stiff 114/1
sting, sting so. 58/5
stink, raise a (hell of a) stink 31/1
stinker, a stinker 28/3; a stinker of a cold 181/14
stinking, stinking rich 51/4; stinking drunk 155/16; a stinking cold 181/14
stint, do a stint 1/10,
stir, stir it up (fuss) 31/10
stitch, in stitches 117/10; not have a stitch on 177/3
stitch, stitch up (defeat) 16/8
stodgy 149/9
stomach (tolerate) 106/3
stone, leave no stone unturned 4/11; stone cold 149/11; a stone's throw 145/15; stone cold sober 156/2
stoned 155/13
stony, stony broke 52/4
stooge 168/13

stool-pigeon 36/23
stop (receive a blow) 41/29
stops, pull out all the stops 4/8
store, in store 24/6; set great store by 38/19
storm, storm in a teacup 31/18
straight, straight (immediately) 21/9; straight (sex) 187/25; the straight and narrow 35/17; go straight 35/18; straight as a die 61/13; set so. straight 87/14; give it to so. straight 100/4; be straight with so. 100/4
strapped, strapped for 63/11
straw, the last straw 66/5
streaker 187/31
street, in Easy Street 51/10; not in the same street as 68/5; streets ahead 68/4; up so.'s street 74/2
street-wise 91/10
stretch, a stretch (in jail) 37/18; at a stretch 20/14; at full stretch 3/8; fully stretched 3/8
strewth 104/19
stride, take in one's stride 7/16,
strike, strike so. (opinion) 84/14; strike it rich 51/6; strike a deal 79/20
string, string so. along (fool) 59/15; string along (accompany) 143/20
string, strings attached 27/8; another string to one's bow 138/8; pull strings 164/17
strip, tear so. off a strip 45/13
stroke, not do a stroke 3/14; on the stroke of 21/9; put so. off his stroke 113/6
stroppy 128/5
struck, struck on 108/3
stuck, stuck with (problem) 27/10; get stuck into (work) 4/3; get stuck into (food) 150/3
stuck-up 122/4
stuff, stuff (belongings) 135/5; and stuff 135/10; do one's stuff 33/11; know one's stuff 91/3; that's the stuff! 105/18
stuff, stuff it! 110/29; stuff so. 188/14
stuffed, get stuffed! 110/30
stuffing, knock the stuffing out of 42/11
stump, stump 8/6; stump up 55/2
stunner 67/1
stunning 178/21
stymie 8/4
suchlike, and suchlike 135/10
suck, up the suck 29/5

suck, (be nasty) 70/9; suck up to 120/1

sucker, sucker 82/21; a sucker for sth. 121/3

sugar, sugar daddy 187/6

suitcase, live out of a suitcase 145/4

sun, call so. everything under the sun 47/8; think that the sun shines out of someone's backside 108/9

Sunday, a month of Sundays 20/3; Sunday best 172/7

sunk (failed) 18/15

sunshine (address) 102/1

sunspot 147/9

super-duper 67/6

supergrass 36/25

sure (certainly) 79/13

sure-fire 79/2

surface (appear) 142/4

suss, suss out 88/1

swag, 49/4

swan (go) 143/13

Swanee, down the Swanee 18/10

swanky 173/8

swear, swear by 105/20

sweat, no sweat! 26/16

sweetie-pie 102/4

swell, a swell 38/6

swell (excellent) 67/10

sweltering 141/6

swig 153/5

swill, swill down 153/10

swilling, beer/wine-swilling 153/11

swing, swing (hang) 162/14; swing a deal 79/20

swings, swings and roundabouts 18/28

swipe 34/6

switched, switched on 183/2

swiz(z) (disappointment) 58/11

swizzle (fraud) 58/11

swot 92/1

systems, all systems go 3/6

ta 101/6

tab (cigarette) 157/4

table, drink so. under the table 153/9

tabloid 136/12

tabs, keep tabs on 91/13

tackle, tackle (effort) 4/4; tackle so. about 93/7; tackle a meal 150/4

Taff 169/11

tag (hit) 41/9; tag along 143/20

take, take so. on 40/12; take it out on 44/13; take so. in (defraud) 59/6; take so. for a ride 59/8; take it from me

79/5; take to sth. like a duck to water 107/7; take to sth. in a big way 107/7; take in (visit) 145/8; you can't take it with you 159/8; take so. back 161/21; take out (kill) 163/3

talent 187/10

talk, the talk of the town 130/12

talk, money talks 49/6; look who's talking 101/16; now you're talking 105/2

talking-to, give so. a talking-to 45/4

tall, a tall story 60/1; tall order 66/8

tan (beat) 42/3

tangle, tangle with 32/17

tank, tank up 153/12

tantrum, throw a tantrum 112/12

tap, tap so. for 57/1; on tap 138/1

taped, have so. taped 90/10

tart 187/19

tash 177/7

ta-ta 101/20

tatty, 70/1

tea, not for all the tea in China 110/2

tear, tear so. off a strip 45/13

tear-jerker 118/5

teaser 28/4

tee, tee up 87/4

teem, teem down 141/10

teeny 65/9

teeny-bopper 160/5

teeny-weeny 65/10

teeter, teeter on the brink 78/8

teeth, get one's teeth stuck into 4/3; kick so. in the teeth 44/15; lie through one's teeth 60/8; fed up to back teeth 111/2

teething, teething troubles 27/5

teetotaller 156/1

tell, I'm telling you 79/5; there's no telling 79/21; that would be telling 89/16; you're telling me! 105/5; tell so. off 45/2

telly 136/1

temp 11/21

ten, ten to one 79/12

tenterhooks, on tenterhooks 113/20

terrible, terrible 70/7; something terrible 66/18

tether, the end of one's tether 106/8

thick, thick (excessive) 66/7; thick and fast 64/16; thick ear 41/24; thick as two short planks 82/1; thick as thieves 164/14

thin, thin on the ground 63/12; have a thin time 118/11; thin on top 177/5

thing, first thing 21/3; have a good thing going 25/8; have a thing about 86/3; not know the first thing about 91/14; know a thing or two about 91/7; do one's own thing 139/7; have another thing coming 79/8

thingumabob 135/2

thingumajig 135/2

thingummy 135/2

thingy 135/2

think, not be able to hear oneself think 174/1

thinking, to my way of thinking 85/2

thinking-cap, put on one's thinking-cap 84/2

thousand, a thousand and one 64/5

thrash, thrash sth. out 97/9

thrilled, thrilled to bits 117/3

throat, jump down so.'s throat 45/14

through, through (dismissal) 6/6; through with (finished) 19/15; get through to 90/13

throw, throw so. (confuse) 113/8; throw a party 154/1; throw up 181/20

thumb, have so. under one's thumb 168/4; stand/stick out like a sore thumb 183/10; twiddle one's thumbs 3/13

thumb, thumb a lift 145/11

thumbs-down, give the thumbs-down 110/6

thumbs-up, give the thumbs-up 105/17

thumper (lie) 60/7

thumping (large) 65/3

thundering (large) 65/3

tick, (credit) 57/5; (time) 20/10

tick, tick so. off 45/2; what makes so. tick 80/5

ticker 176/10

ticket, just the ticket 74/1

tickled, tickled pink/to death 117/8

tiddler 140/2

tiddly (small) 63/3; (drunk) 155/8

tide, tide mark 175/9

tidy, tidy sum 49/19

tie, tie in with 90/25

tied, tied up 3/9

tiff 32/9

tight (money) 52/7; (drunk) 155/10

tight-arsed 52/8

tight-fisted 52/8

tiles, on the tiles 155/19

up-market 12/12
upstairs, kick upstairs 167/4
uptake, slow/quick on the uptake 90/12
uptight 111/24
U-turn, make a U-turn 72/10

vamoose 144/9
vanishing, do a vanishing-trick 144/11
varmint 140/4
versed, versed in 91/5
vibes 183/1
vim 4/21
visit, pay a visit 184/1
vital, vital statistics 178/13
vote, vote (suggest) 85/5; vote with one's feet 19/17
V-sign, 110/25

wacky 81/7
wade, wade into so. 40/15
waffle 94/14
wagon, on the (water-)wagon 156/3
walk, walk it 26/15; sth. has walked 144/16
walk-over 16/11
wall, go to the wall 18/11; drive up the wall 111/17
wallah 170/2
wallop 41/7
walloping (large) 65/3
wally (fool) 82/10
waltz (go) 143/12
wangle 15/21
wank 189/7
wanker 171/3
war, play war with 45/9; war paint 173/24
warpath, on the warpath 112/8
wars, have been in the wars 173/20
wash, come out in the wash 15/25
wash (be valid) 90/23
washed up 18/25
wash-out (failure) 18/26; (event) 141/12
waste (kill) 163/3
waster 171/5
water, in deep water 29/11; get into hot water 29/12; hold water 90/23
waterworks, turn on the waterworks 118/2
waves, make waves 31/20
way, go out of one's way 4/15; no two ways about it 76/8; take to sth. in a big way 107/7; no way! 110/3
way-out 125/1
wear (tolerate) 106/1
weather, make heavy weather

of 28/16; under the weather 181/1
weaving, get weaving 22/1
wedge, thin edge of the wedge 80/6
wee, (small) 65/9
wee(-wee) 184/4
weed (drug) 158/2
weekend, a dirty weekend 188/7
weigh, weigh into so. 40/15; weigh up 84/3
weight, pull one's weight 1/9; throw one's weight about 43/9
weirdo 125/3
weirdy 125/3
welch, welch on so. 59/24
well, well away 14/4; just as well 75/11
well-and-truly 66/22
well-heeled 51/8
well-off 51/8
well-oiled 155/12
well-stacked 178/7
well-to-do 51/8
welsh, welsh on so. 59/24
wenching, go wenching 185/3
West, go West 71/10
wet, behind the ears 8/15
wet-back 169/17
whack, a whack (attempt) 77/1
whack, 62/1
whacked 180/1
whacking (large) 65/3
whale, a whale of a 65/6; a whale of a time 117/20
whale, (hit) 41/7
wham, wham, bam, thank you ma'am 188/10
what, what it takes 7/12; what with . . . 80/8; know what's what 91/6
what-do-you-call-it 135/3
what-for, give so. what-for 44/4
whatnot, and whatnot 135/11
what's-his-name 135/4
wheels (car) 132/10
when, say when 152/22
where, tell where to get off 45/7; where it's at 80/11
wherewithal, the wherewithal 49/1
whiff 183/25
whinge 98/3
whip, (steal) 34/6; whip up 149/18
whipper-snapper 160/6
whipping-boy 46/5
whip-round 49/17
whirl, give it a whirl (try) 77/3
whirlybird 132/3
whisker, escape by a whisker 48/1; within a whisker of

63/6; the cat's whiskers 67/4; think one is the cat's whiskers 122/1
whistle, blow the whistle on 89/4; wet one's whistle 153/1
white, a white lie 60/6
whiz-kid 15/15
whodunit 136/9
whoop, whoop it up 154/9
whoopee 104/11
whoops, whoops! 104/10
whop (hit) 41/4
whopper (lie) 60/7; (sth. big) 65/2
whopping 65/3
wick, get on so.'s wick 111/15
wicket, bat on a sticky wicket 29/7
wide, a wide-boy 59/28
widget 134/12
wigging, a wigging 45/1
wildfire, spread like wildfire 22/28
wild goose, wild goose chase 18/31
willie (penis) 189/2
willies, give so. the willies 114/8
wimp, a spineless wimp 171/21
win, you can't win 121/6
wind, see which way the wind blows 88/6; get wind of 88/2; look what the wind's blown in! 101/2; put the wind up so. 114/3
wind, wind so. up 113/19; wind up 142/7
windbag 97/12
window-dressing 59/31
wing (shoot) 41/28
wingding 154/8
winge 98/3
wink, not sleep a wink 179/5
winks, snatch forty winks 179/7
winning 14/9
wino 155/7
wires, get one's wires crossed 113/11; pull wires 164/17
wise, get wise to 88/10
wise, wise up 87/12
wisecrack 94/17
wish, wish sth. on so. 27/11
wishy-washy 70/10
witch, old witch 178/19
with, with it 7/14; with so. (understand) 90/6
wits, keep one's wits about one 116/4
witter, witter on 94/12
wizard (excellent) 67/10
wobbly, wobbly in 8/13; throw a wobbly 112/13
wog 169/16
wolf, keep the wolf from the

278